Computer Vision: Advanced Techniques and Applications

Computer Vision: Advanced Techniques and Applications

Edited by Steve Holden

CLANRYE
INTERNATIONAL
www.clanryeinternational.com

Clanrye International,
750 Third Avenue, 9th Floor,
New York, NY 10017, USA

ISBN: 978-1-63240-814-3

Cataloging-in-Publication Data

Computer vision : advanced techniques and applications / edited by Steve Holden.
    p. cm.
Includes bibliographical references and index.
ISBN 978-1-63240-814-3
1. Computer vision. 2. Artificial intelligence. I. Holden, Steve.
TA1634 .C66 2019
006.37--dc23

For information on all Clanrye International publications
visit our website at www.clanryeinternational.com

Contents

Preface

Computer vision is the field of science that is concerned with the development of computers to achieve high-level understanding using digital images or videos. It includes the processes of acquiring, processing and understanding of digital images. It also involves the extraction of data from the real world for the purpose of producing numerical or symbolic information. Some of the areas of interest in computer vision include scene reconstruction, object recognition, 3D pose interpretation, motion estimation, image restoration, etc. The applications of computer vision are in the development of artificial intelligence, surveillance, medical imaging, topographical modeling and navigation, among many others. This book brings forth some of the most innovative concepts and elucidates the unexplored aspects of this discipline. From theories to research to practical applications, studies related to all contemporary topics of relevance to this field have also been included. This book attempts to assist those with a goal of delving into the field of computer vision.

This book has been the outcome of endless efforts put in by authors and researchers on various issues and topics within the field. The book is a comprehensive collection of significant researches that are addressed in a variety of chapters. It will surely enhance the knowledge of the field among readers across the globe.

It gives us an immense pleasure to thank our researchers and authors for their efforts to submit their piece of writing before the deadlines. Finally in the end, I would like to thank my family and colleagues who have been a great source of inspiration and support.

Editor

Multibody motion segmentation for an arbitrary number of independent motions

Yutaro Sako and Yasuyuki Sugaya* iD

Abstract

We propose a new method for segmenting feature point trajectories tracked through a video sequence without assuming a number of independent motions. Our method realizes motion segmentation of feature point trajectories by hierarchically separating the trajectories into two affine spaces in a situation that we do not know the number of independently moving objects. We judge that input trajectories should be separated by comparing the likelihoods computed from those trajectories before/after separation. We also consider integration of the resulting separated trajectories for avoiding too much segmentations. By using real video images, we confirmed the efficiency of our proposed method.

1 Introduction

Separating independently moving objects in a video sequence is one of the important tasks in computer vision applications. Costeira and Kanade [1] proposed a segmentation algorithm based on the shape interaction matrix. Sugaya and Kanatani [3] proposed a multi-stage learning strategy using multiple models. Yan and Pollefeys [8] proposed a new local subspace fitting scheme. Vidal et al. [7] proposed a segmentation algorithm based on generalized principal component analysis (GPCA) [6]. By introducing GPCA for computing an initial segmentation, Sugaya and Kanatani [4] improved the multi-stage learning.

However, all these methods assume the number of moving objects. Kanatani and Matsunaga [2] proposed a method for estimating the number of independently moving objects based on the rank estimation of the affine space using the geometric minimum description length (MDL). However, estimating the number of independently moving objects based on the rank of the affine space is very difficult for real image sequences. For example, if an object motion is planar, the dimension of an affine space which includes its trajectories degenerates from 3-D to 2-D. Moreover, if two objects merely translate without rotation, the two 2-D affine spaces are parallel to each

other. This means that a 3-D affine space which includes those 2-D affine spaces exists.

For this problem, we propose a new method for segmenting feature point trajectories without assuming the number of objects. Based on the fact that trajectories of a rigidly moving object is constrained to a 2-D or 3-D affine space, we hierarchically separate input trajectories into two affine spaces until all the trajectories are divided into 2-D or 3-D affine spaces. In order to judge whether input trajectories should be divided or not, we compare the likelihoods before/after separation. After the separation process, we also check whether the separated trajectories should be integrated by comparing the likelihoods to avoid that the trajectories which belong to the same object are separated into different groups.

2 Proposed method

From the fact that trajectories of a rigidly moving object is constrained to a 2-D or 3-D affine space, we can separate independently moving objects by hierarchically separating input trajectories into two affine spaces until all the trajectories are divided into 2-D or 3-D affine spaces. In order to realize the above separation, we need to overcome two problems. One problem is to properly estimate the dimension of the affine space which includes input trajectories. The other problem is that we need to judge whether input trajectories should be divided to stop hierarchical separation.

*Correspondence: sugaya@iim.cs.tut.ac.jp
Toyohashi University of Technology, 1-1-1, Tempakucho, Hibarigaoka,
Toyohashi, Aichi 441-8580, Japan

For the first problem, we can regard the rank of the moment matrix of the input trajectory vectors. The rank of the moment matrix can be obtained as the number of positive eigenvalues of the matrix. However, in the presence of noise, all eigenvalues are non-zero in general. Hence, we need to truncate small eigenvalues, but it is difficult to determine a proper threshold. We compute the rank of the moment matrix by using the geometric MDL [2].

For the second problem, we compare the average likelihoods of the trajectories for the affine spaces which are fitted to all the trajectories and the divided ones. We compute the average likelihoods before/after division and divide those trajectories if the likelihood after division is larger than that before division.

We summarize the algorithm of our proposed method as follows:

1. Fit an affine space to the input trajectories, and compute its dimension d by using the geometric MDL.
2. If $d \leq 2$, then we stop the division process for the target trajectories.
3. Divide the trajectories into two affine spaces.

   (a) Convert the trajectory vectors into 3-D vectors.
       Please refer to [4] for the detail computation.
   (b) Fit two planes to those 3-D vectors by the Taubin method.
   (c) Convert the trajectory vectors into d-D vectors.
   (d) Separate the d-D vectors into two affine spaces by the EM algorithm of Sugaya and Kanatani [3, 4].

4. Compute the average likelihoods P and P' of the trajectories before/after separation and accept the separation, and go to step 1 if the following inequality is satisfied.

$$\lfloor \log_{10} P' \rfloor - \lfloor \log_{10} P \rfloor > 0, \tag{1}$$

   where $\lfloor \cdot \rfloor$ is the floor function. In our experience, if we compared the average likelihoods directly, the separation judgement was not stable. Thus, we compare the exponent part of the average likelihood.
5. Else, reject the separation.

We hierarchically iterate the above procedures until all the input trajectories are not separated.

3 Rank estimation of the affine space

We compute the eigenvalues of the moment matrix of the $2M$-D trajectory vectors $\boldsymbol{p}_\alpha$ [4], $\alpha = 1, \ldots, N$ and estimate its rank by using the geometric MDL. M is the number of the image frame.

(1) Define the $2M \times 2M$ moment matrix $\boldsymbol{M}$ by

$$\boldsymbol{M} = \sum_{\alpha=1}^{N} (\boldsymbol{p}_\alpha - \boldsymbol{p}_C)(\boldsymbol{p}_\alpha - \boldsymbol{p}_C)^\top, \quad \boldsymbol{p}_C = \frac{1}{N} \sum_{\alpha=1}^{N} \boldsymbol{p}_\alpha. \tag{2}$$

(2) Compute the eigenvalues of $\boldsymbol{M}$, and let $\lambda_1 \geq \cdots \geq \lambda_{2M}$ be the sorted eigenvalues.
(3) Compute the residuals J_r, $r = 2, \ldots, 2M$, for the fitted r-D affine space by

$$J_r = \sum_{\beta=r+1}^{2M} \lambda_\beta. \tag{3}$$

(4) Compute the geometric MDLs [2] for each rank by

$$\text{G-MDL}(r) = J_r - \left(rN + (r+1)(2M-r) \right) \epsilon^2 \log\left(\frac{\epsilon}{L}\right)^2, \tag{4}$$

where ϵ is the standard deviation of feature point tracking accuracy, which we call this *noise level*, and L is a reference length, for which we can use an arbitrary value whose order is approximately the same as the data, say the image size.

(5) Estimate the rank $\hat{r}$ of the affine space which includes the input trajectories as

$$\hat{r} = \arg \min_r \text{G-MDL}(r) \tag{5}$$

4 Separation of the trajectories

We separate the input trajectories by using the EM algorithm of Sugaya and Kanatani [3, 4] and can compute the likelihood $P(\alpha|k)$ of the α-th point for the fitted affine space k in the separation process. The likelihood $P(\alpha|k)$ can be computed in the form

$$P(\alpha|k) = \frac{e^{-(\boldsymbol{p}_\alpha - \boldsymbol{p}_C^{(k)}, \boldsymbol{V}^{(k)-1}(\boldsymbol{p}_\alpha - \boldsymbol{p}_C^{(k)}))/2}}{\sqrt{\det \boldsymbol{V}^{(k)}}}, \tag{6}$$

where $\boldsymbol{p}_C^{(k)}$ and $\boldsymbol{V}^{(k)}$ are the centroid and the covariance matrix of class k, respectively.

We compute the likelihoods $P(\alpha)$ and $P'(\alpha)$ of $\boldsymbol{p}_\alpha$ for the affine spaces before/after separation and then compute the average likelihoods P and P' by

$$P = \frac{1}{N} \sum_{\alpha=1}^{N} P(\alpha), \quad P' = \frac{1}{N} \sum_{\alpha=1}^{N} P'(\alpha). \tag{7}$$

(a) The input video sequence of 30 frames, which are the first, 8th, 15th, 23th, and 30th frame respectivelly. Red points are the tracked feature points.

(b) Separation result of the first stage.   **(c)** Separation result of the second stage.   **(d)** Final result.

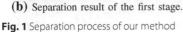

Fig. 1 Separation process of our method

5 Integration of the separated trajectories

After separation, we check whether the separated trajectories should be integrated by comparing the average likelihoods to avoid that the trajectories which belong to the same object are separated into different groups.

For all the separated trajectory groups, we integrate the two groups of the separated trajectories if the average likelihood Q before integration and Q' after integration satisfy the following inequality:

$$\lfloor \log_{10} Q' \rfloor - \lfloor \log_{10} Q \rfloor > 0, \qquad (8)$$

where Q and Q' are computed from Eqs. (6) and (7) for each affine space.

6 Real image experiments

By using real video images, we tested our method and computed the separation accuracy with RANSAC and LSA of Yan and Pollefeys [8] and GPCA of Vidal et al. [7].

6.1 Separation process

Figure 1 shows a separation process of our method. Figure 1a shows the five decimated images of the input video sequence. The red points are the tracked feature points by the KLT tracker. We explain this separation process by showing tree expression of our separation in Fig. 2.

First, we estimated the dimension of the affine space which includes all the input trajectories and obtained that its dimension was 4. Since the resulting dimension was

larger than 2, then we separated those input trajectories. We show the separation result in Fig. 1b. For this result, we computed the average likelihoods for the affine spaces before/after separation and obtained the results 5.63×10^{-7} and 8.11×10^{-5}, respectively. Since these values satisfied the inequality in Eq. (1), we accepted the separation.

In the second stage, we estimated the dimensions of the affine spaces for the separated trajectories shown in Fig. 1b of green and blue points. The resulting dimension of the blue points was 2 and stopped separation. Since the estimated dimension of the green points was 3, we separated those trajectories. The result is shown in Fig. 1c. For this separation, the computed average likelihoods satisfied Eq. (1), and then, we accepted the separation. In the third stage, we estimated the dimensions of the affine spaces for the separated trajectories shown in Fig. 1c of red and green points. The resulting dimension of the red points

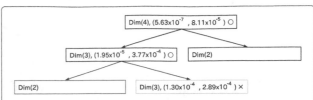

Fig. 2 Tree expression of the separation for Fig. 1. Dim (·) indicates the estimated dimension of the affine space which includes input trajectories. (·, ·) is paired likelihoods for the affine spaces before/after separation. The symbols *circle* and *multiplication* mean that the input trajectories should be separated or not. *Blue*, *red*, and *green rectangles* correspond to the *boxes* in Fig. 1d

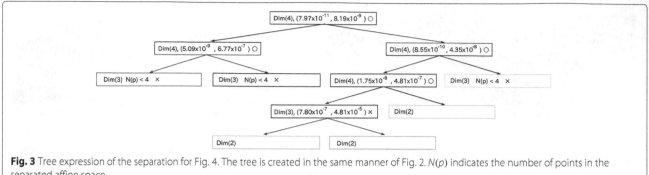

Fig. 3 Tree expression of the separation for Fig. 4. The tree is created in the same manner of Fig. 2. $N(p)$ indicates the number of points in the separated affine space

was 2 and stopped separation. The estimated dimension of the green points was 3, but the average likelihoods before/after separation did not satisfy Eq. (1). Hence, we stop separation. We show the final separation result in Fig. 1d. In this sequence, the number of independently moving objects, which includes background points, is 3 and our method correctly separates the input trajectories into three groups.

6.2 Integrating process

We show another result in Fig. 4. Figure 4a shows the five decimated images of the input video sequence. We

also show the separation process in Fig. 3 and show the results in each separation process in Fig. 4b–f. Figure 4g is the final separation result. From this result, we can see that miss-separation exists in Fig. 4e and the points which belong to the same object are separated into three groups, which are the blue, green, and orange points in Fig. 4g.

For all the pairs of the separated groups, we computed the average likelihoods before/after integration and check whether the separated groups should be integrated or not. Table 1 shows the computed average likelihoods. From this, the blue, green, and orange points are integrated. Figure 4g shows the integrated result.

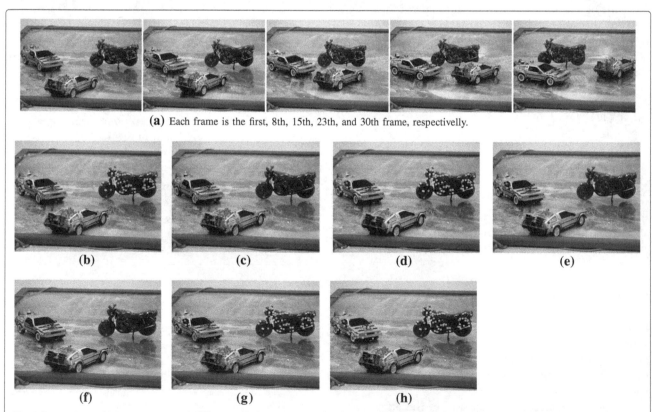

(a) Each frame is the first, 8th, 15th, 23th, and 30th frame, respectivelly.

(b)   **(c)**   **(d)**   **(e)**

(f)   **(g)**   **(h)**

Fig. 4 Separation and integration process. **a** The input video sequence of 30 frames. *Red points* are the tracked feature points. **b–f** Results of the hierarchical separation process. **g** Separation result. **h** Integration result

Table 1 Comparison of the likelihoods before/after integration of Fig. 4f. The top and middle rows in each cell show the average likelihoods before/after integration. The bottom row in each cell shows whether Eq. (8) is satisfied or not

	Cyan	Green	Orange	Magenta
Red	4.89×10^{-7}	8.76×10^{-7}	3.76×10^{-8}	8.81×10^{-7}
	8.40×10^{-10}	5.73×10^{-9}	4.65×10^{-9}	6.15×10^{-9}
	×	×	×	×
Blue	1.05×10^{-7}	1.03×10^{-10}	3.12×10^{-10}	2.93×10^{-7}
	1.73×10^{-9}	6.03×10^{-9}	5.52×10^{-9}	1.68×10^{-8}
	×	○	○	×
Cyan		1.63×10^{-6}	7.48×10^{-7}	7.07×10^{-8}
		2.24×10^{-9}	3.02×10^{-9}	3.57×10^{-9}
		×	×	×
Green			1.52×10^{-29}	4.26×10^{-8}
			6.58×10^{-9}	9.15×10^{-9}
			×	×

6.3 Accuracy comparison

We compared the accuracy of our method with RANSAC and LSA of Yan and Pollefeys [8] and GPCA of Vidal et al. [7]. We used the T-Hopkins database [5] and original data and computed the separation accuracy for each method. Table 2 shows the result. The accuracy is computed by (number of correctly separated points)/(number of input points). As we can see, our method is superior to the compared existing methods.

7 Conclusions

In this paper, we propose a new method for segmenting feature point trajectories without assuming the number of objects. Based on the fact that trajectories of a rigidly moving object is constrained to a 2-D or 3-D affine space, we hierarchically separate input trajectories into two affine spaces until all the trajectories are divided into 2-D or 3-D affine spaces. In order to judge whether input trajectories should be divided or not, we compare the likelihoods before/after separation. After the separation process, we also check whether the separated trajectories should be integrated by comparing the likelihoods to avoid that the trajectories which belong to the same object are separated into different groups.

By using real video sequences, we checked the separation and integration processes of our method and confirmed the accuracy of our method by comparing existing methods.

Competing interests
The authors declare that they have no competing interests.

Authors' contributions
YSa introduced the hierarchical separation of the feature point trajectories, carried out all the experiments, and wrote the manuscript. YSu introduced the rank estimation of the affine space using the geometric MDL and separation judgement using likelihoods of the fitted affine spaces and revised the manuscript written by YSa. Both authors read and approved the final manuscript.

References
1. Costeira JP, Kanade T (1998) A multibody factorization method for independently moving objects. Int J Comput Vision 29(3):159–179
2. Kanatani K, Matsunaga C (2002) Estimating the number of independent motions for multibody motion segmentation. In: Proc of the 5th Asian Conference on Computer Vision (ACCV2002), Melbourne, Australia. pp 7–12
3. Sugaya Y, Kanatani K (2004) Multi-stage unsupervised learning for multi-body motion segmentation. IEICE Trans Inform Syst E87-D(7):1935–1942
4. Sugaya Y, Kanatani K (2010) Improved multistage learning for multibody motion segmentation. In: Proc. of International Conference of Computer Vision Theory and Applications (VISAPP2010), Angers, France Vol. 1. pp 199–206
5. Sugaya Y KanataniK (2013) Removing mistracking of multibody motion video database Hopkins155. In: Proc. of the 24th British Machine Vision Conference (BMVC2013), Bristol, U.K.
6. Vidal R, Ma Y, Sastry S (2005) Generalized principal component analysis (GPCA). IEEE Trans Pattern Anal Mach Intell 27(12):1945–1959
7. Vidal R, Tron R, Hartley R (2008) Multiframe motion segmentation with missing data using PowerFactorization and GPCA. Int J Comput Vis 79(1):85–105
8. Yan J, Pollefeys M (2006) A general framework for motion segmentation: independent, articulated, rigid, non-rigid, degenerate and non-degenerate. In: Proc. of the 9th European Conference on Computer Vision (ECCV2006), Graz, Austria. pp 94–106

Table 2 Accuracy comparison

	Our method (%)	RANSAC (%)	LSA (%)	GPCA (%)
Data1	100	92.50	93.43	89.31
Data2	98.16	57.60	77.42	62.21
Data3	100	84.82	96.43	81.25
Data4	99.52	80.95	90.48	80.95
Data5	100	80.30	92.75	80.30
Data6	99.06	68.40	99.53	68.40
Data7	100	45.49	96.99	45.49
Data8	90.82	78.31	89.54	Not converge
Data9	100	72.22	96.43	90.87
Data10	100	91.03	93.40	92.08
Data11	99.61	92.87	76.11	85.55
Data12	99.63	85.56	94.44	80.00
Data13	100	90.26	56.06	77.67

2

Real-time rendering of aerial perspective effect based on turbidity estimation

Carlos Morales[1][*], Takeshi Oishi[1] and Katsushi Ikeuchi[2]

Abstract

In real outdoor scenes, objects distant from the observer suffer from a natural effect called aerial perspective that fades the colors of the objects and blends them to the environmental light color. The aerial perspective can be modeled using a physics-based approach; however, handling with the changing and unpredictable environmental illumination as well as the weather conditions of real scenes is challenging in terms of visual coherence and computational cost. In those cases, even state-of-the-art models fail to generate realistic synthesized aerial perspective effects. To overcome this limitation, we propose a real-time, turbidity-based, full-spectrum aerial perspective rendering approach. First, we estimate the atmospheric turbidity by matching luminance distributions of a captured sky image to sky models. The obtained turbidity is then employed for aerial perspective rendering using an improved scattering model. We performed a set of experiments to evaluate the scattering model and the aerial perspective model. We also provide a framework for real-time aerial perspective rendering. The results confirm that the proposed approach synthesizes realistic aerial perspective effects with low computational cost, outperforming state-of-the-art aerial perspective rendering methods for real scenes.

Keywords: Real-time rendering, Aerial perspective, Shader programming

1 Introduction

In real open-air scenes, when a target object viewed by an observer is far, the perceived object's appearance changes, being fainted and blended to the environmental light color. This natural effect is known as *aerial perspective* and is due to the light scattering by particles suspended in the atmosphere.

The importance of aerial perspective rendering is reflected in several applications, as illustrated in Fig. 1. It can be employed in image and video composition to generate artistic atmospheric effects over real scenes. It can also be used in computer vision (CV) and computer graphics (CG) for rendering virtual objects with an appearance according to the outdoor scene. Namely, fields such as mixed reality (MR), where CG models are merged into a real scene, can exploit aerial perspective rendering to output more realistic virtual objects.

In general, we have to render an artificial aerial perspective effect on a target object to emulate the natural

atmospheric effect. This goal is specially more difficult in real-time applications in outdoor scenes, which present a challenge due to the variant illumination and atmospheric conditions such as clear, hazy, or cloudy days.

A conventional approach for aerial perspective rendering is to find an outdoor light scattering model with parameters that lead to generate a realistic synthesized look according to the real scene. Such scattering models can be analyzed from captured skies using sky illumination models [1–7]. Due to its simplicity and accuracy for scattering modeling, a heuristic parameter called *turbidity* (T) has been used to categorize atmospheric conditions [8–12]. Following that approach, we propose a full-spectrum turbidity-based aerial perspective model that enables us to render realistic aerial perspective effects in real time. Our model heavily relies on estimating turbidity from clear-sky regions of a captured omnidirectional sky image. Thus, scenes where the sky is not visible are beyond the scope of this work.

Method overview: The overview of our aerial perspective rendering approach is illustrated in Fig. 2. Input data is a *real omnidirectional sky image* captured by fisheye lens camera and the *input scene*, which can be captured by

*Correspondence: carlos@cvl.iis.u-tokyo.ac.jp
[1]The University of Tokyo, Tokyo, Japan
Full list of author information is available at the end of the article

Fig. 1 Aerial perspective rendering with our method. *Top row*: An input image and the re-targeted synthesized aerial perspective effect (from left to right). *Bottom row*: A MR application before and after aerial perspective rendering

the same camera or a different perspective or panoramic camera. In image and video composition applications, the input scene is represented by its RGB intensity color, its depth map, and the spectral sensitivity of the camera used to capture the input scene. In MR applications, the input scene is composed of the RGB intensity color of the real scene, the color and depth of the virtual object, and the camera's spectral sensitivity. The problem addressed in this paper is to estimate the turbidity from the omnidirectional sky image and then use it to render an aerial perspective effect. While the aerial perspective is rendered over the de-hazed input scene in composition applications, it is rendered only on the virtual object in MR. For this purpose, our method consists of the following stages:

1) *Turbidity estimation*: The captured omnidirectional sky image is compared with turbidity-based sky models to find the turbidity value that provides the best matching (Section 3.4).
2) *Aerial perspective rendering*: An improved turbidity-based scattering model (Section 5) is used in a full-spectrum aerial perspective rendering equation (Section 4) to generate the final *synthesized scene*. This stage is performed in real time in a graphics processing unit (GPU) framework (Section 6).

Contributions: The main contributions of this work are threefold:

1) Improved turbidity-based scattering model for rendering that fit to real atmospheric effects more accurately than previous works [3, 13].
2) A novel full-spectrum, turbidity-based aerial perspective rendering model that synthesizes plausible aerial perspective effects in real scenes and improves over previous works [13–15] in terms of visual coherence.
3) A real-time framework for aerial perspective effect rendering. The implementation delivers more than two orders of magnitude speed-up compared to prior art [13], allowing real-time performance needed in applications such as MR.

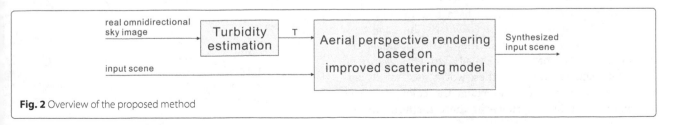

Fig. 2 Overview of the proposed method

2   Related work

Previous methods for aerial perspective modeling and rendering rely on understanding the scattering phenomena in the atmosphere. McCartney [16] presented an excellent review of former works on atmospheric optics. His work contains relevant data about the scattering phenomena under different weather conditions categorized by the heuristic parameter turbidity (T). T is used to model the scattering by molecules of air and larger particles, such as haze, and is employed for classifying various atmospheric conditions ranging from pure air to fog. Since the atmospheric phenomenon in [16] is modeled using real data, it has been used in both CV and CG fields. However, such models have been used differently, varying depending on whether the aim is oriented to CV or CG.

2.1   CG-oriented aerial perspective rendering

In this category, the atmospheric optics models are targeted for completely virtual scenes. Preetham et al. [3] presented a full-spectrum turbidity-based analytical sky model for various atmospheric conditions. Based on that model, they developed an approximated scattering model for aerial perspective rendering. Dobashi et al. [17] introduced a fast rendering method to generate various atmospheric scattering effects via graphics hardware. Nielsen [18] presented a real-time rendering system for simulating atmospheric effects. Riley et al. [19] presented a lighting model for rendering several optical phenomena. Schafhitzel et al. [20] rendered planets with atmospheric scattering effects in real time. Bruneton and Neyret [5] rendered both sky and aerial perspective from all viewpoints from the ground to outer space.

The synthesized atmospheric effects generated by the mentioned works are visually plausible in fully CG scenes where the illumination is controlled. However, their direct implementation in real scenes does not have a similar performance, since the scattering models need to be tuned to fit the variant, natural outdoor illumination. Moreover, such models are usually targeted as post processing effects where visual quality is more important than computational cost.

2.2   CV-oriented aerial perspective rendering

This group of methods model the atmospheric phenomenon in real outdoor scenes. Using scattering models, several works were able to restore captured images at different weather conditions. Gao et al. [21] presented an aerial perspective model for haze filtering based on a parameter called *maximum visibility*. Zhu et al. [15] developed a linear color attenuation prior for image dehazing based on a parameter called *scattering coefficient*. The synthesized results from these works successfully corrected and restored at some extent the color of images under hazy conditions. However, these methods are not automatic and the results depend on manual tuning of either the maximum visibility in [21] or the scattering coefficient in [15], which control the amount of de-hazing.

Automatic image restoration approaches have also been proposed in the literature. Narasimhan and Nayar [22] proposed a physics-based scattering model to describe the appearances of real scenes under uniform bad weather conditions. Using that scattering model, their method restored the contrast of one image; nonetheless, their method required a second image of the same scene under a different weather condition. This limitation was overcome by He et al. [14], who proposed an automatic haze-removal approach for single images using a dark channel as prior. Results in [14] showed consistent and fast image de-hazing. However, using their method for aerial perspective rendering leads to appearances that are inconsistent with natural aerial perspective, especially in cases with high haze densities.

To solve the previous drawbacks, Zhao [13] proposed an automatic turbidity-based aerial perspective model. In his approach, turbidity was estimated from captured omnidirectional sky images. The camera's spectral sensitivity was estimated for conversion from spectral radiance to RGB pixel values. Combining the estimated spectral sensitivity and a simple correction of Preetham's scattering model [3], his method was able to generate an aerial perspective effect over virtual objects for outdoor MR. However, his method makes the appearance of the synthesized virtual object suffer from a strong aerial perspective effect even for low turbidity values at short distances. Moreover, his approach has a high computational cost.

3   Preliminary

3.1   Aerial perspective modeling

Figure 3 illustrates a general model of aerial perspective. The total light perceived by the observer is a summation of two components: *direct transmission* and *airlight*. The direct transmission stands for the light that comes

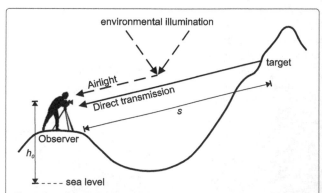

Fig. 3 General aerial perspective model. The total light perceived by the observer is a summation of the direct transmission and airlight

from the target following the optical path and is attenuated until it reaches the observer. The airlight is the environmental light that is scattered in the same direction as the direct transmission and then is attenuated in the way to the observer. The aerial perspective under various atmospheric conditions is broadly modeled as [22–24]:

$$\begin{aligned}L(s,\lambda) &= L(0,\lambda)e^{-\beta_{sc}(\lambda)s}\\ &+ L(\infty,\lambda)\left(1-e^{-\beta_{sc}(\lambda)s}\right),\end{aligned} \quad (1)$$

where $L(s,\lambda)$ is the total light perceived by the observer, $L(0,\lambda)$ is the light coming from the target without aerial perspective effect, and $L(\infty,\lambda)$ is the atmospheric light. s is the distance between the target and the observer, and λ is the light wavelength. β_{sc} is the total atmospheric scattering coefficient modeled as

$$\beta_{sc} = \beta_R + \beta_M, \quad (2)$$

where β_R is the Rayleigh scattering coefficient that analyzes particles much smaller than λ, such as molecules of air, and β_M is the Mie scattering coefficient that models particles whose size is nearly equal to λ, such as particles of haze.

The Rayleigh scattering coefficient is given by [25]

$$\beta_R = \frac{8\pi^3(n^2-1)^2}{3N\lambda^4}\left(\frac{6+3p_n}{6-7p_n}\right)e^{-\frac{h}{H_{R0}}}, \quad (3)$$

and the Mie scattering coefficient is expressed by [26]

$$\beta_M = 0.434c(T)\pi\left(\frac{2\pi}{\lambda}\right)^{\nu-2}K(\lambda)e^{-\frac{h}{H_{M0}}}, \quad (4)$$

where $n = 1.0003$ is the refractive index of air in the visible spectrum, $N = 2.545 \times 10^{25}$ m^{-3} is the molecular number density of the standard atmosphere, $p_n = 0.035$ is the depolarization factor for air, h is the altitude at the scattering point, $H_{R0} = 7994$ m is the scale height for the Rayleigh scattering, $c(T)$ is the concentration factor that depends on the atmospheric turbidity, $\nu = 4$ is the Junge's exponent, $K(\lambda)$ is the wavelength-dependent fudge factor, and $H_{M0} = 1200$ m is the scale height for Mie scattering.

3.2 Atmospheric condition via turbidity
Turbidity is defined as the ratio of the optical thickness of the atmosphere composed by molecules of air plus larger particles to the optical thickness of air molecules alone [16]:

$$T = \frac{\int_{h_i}^{h_f}\beta_R(h)\,\mathrm{d}h + \int_{h_i}^{h_f}\beta_M(h)\,\mathrm{d}h}{\int_{h_i}^{h_f}\beta_R(h)\,\mathrm{d}h}, \quad (5)$$

where h_i and h_f are the initial and final altitudes of the optical path, respectively.

Preetham et al. [3] presented an analytical sky model for various atmospheric conditions through turbidity. Their model relates the luminance Y(cd/m^2) of sky in any

viewing direction V with respect to the luminance at a reference point Y_z by

$$Y = \frac{F(\theta,\gamma,T)}{F(0,\theta_s,T)}Y_z, \quad (6)$$

where F is the sky luminance distribution model of Perez et al. [27], θ is the zenith angle of viewing direction, θ_s is the zenith angle of the sun, and γ is the angle of the sun direction with respect to the viewing direction (see coordinates in Fig. 4).

3.3 Rendering equation
In MR applications, we need an equation to convert radiometric formulas, such as the spectral radiance, to pixel color values, such as RGB. In general, when an object is illuminated by a source of light, the reflected light goes through the camera lens and is recorded by its charged couple device (CCD). Then the recorded image intensity for the channel $c\in\{r,g,b\}$ can be modeled as

$$I_c = \int_{380\text{ nm}}^{780\text{ nm}} L(\lambda)q_c(\lambda)\,\mathrm{d}\lambda, \quad (7)$$

where $L(\lambda)$ is the reflected spectral radiance at the object surface, the range 380 to 780 nm stands for the visible spectrum of light, and $q_c(\lambda)$ is the spectral sensitivity of the camera.

The camera's spectral sensitivity is important for color correction since it compensates the effects of the recording illumination. In this matter, we benefited from Kawakami et al. [28] and the public data of spectral sensitivity for various cameras [29]. They estimated $q_c(\lambda)$ from omnidirectional captured sky images and turbidity-based sky spectra.

3.4 Atmospheric turbidity estimation
The atmospheric turbidity can be estimated by matching the luminance distribution of turbidity-based Preetham sky models and an omnidirectional sky image captured by

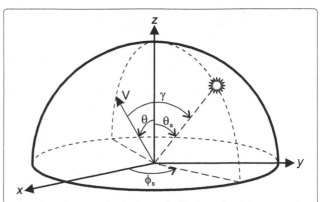

Fig. 4 Coordinates in the sky hemisphere where the observer is at the origin

a fisheye lens camera as in [13]. First, the sun position is estimated at the captured sky image by either finding the center of the saturated area of the sun or using the longitude, latitude, date, and time at the observer's position. Then the luminance ratio Y_i/Y_{ref} (Y from the XYZ color space) is calculated between a sampling point i and a reference point ref that can be the zenith or any other visible point in the captured sky image. The ratio $Y_i(T)/Y_{ref}(T)$ is computed at the corresponding points in the Preetham sky models with the same sun position using Eq. (6). The turbidity-based sky model that best matches the captured sky image is the one with the lowest difference between both ratios. Therefore, the targeted turbidity is the solution to the minimization problem:

$$\arg\min_{T\in[1,20]} \sum_{n=1}^{N} \left| \frac{Y_i(T)}{Y_{ref}(T)} - \frac{Y_i}{Y_{ref}} \right|, \tag{8}$$

where N is the number of sample points used in the calculation process. In this paper, we solve for the turbidity using the Levenberg-Marquardt algorithm (LMA), a simpler yet efficient approach compared to the particle swarm optimization used in [13].

Since the Preetham sky model does not provide equations for calculating the brightness of cloudy pixels, the Random Sample Consensus (RANSAC) approach is used to remove cloudy pixels (outliers) from the sampling and estimate turbidity only from clear-sky pixels (inliers).

4 Aerial perspective rendering equation

In order to render an aerial perspective effect in applications that contain only real scenes or both real and virtual objects, the RGB color system is more convenient to use than a spectral radiance system. Originally, the aerial perspective rendering equation for one viewing direction can be obtained by replacing the aerial perspective model of Eq. (1) in Eq. (7). From these equations, the observer perceives the intensity value I_c of a target object's pixel at distance s for the channel $c\in\{r,g,b\}$ as

$$I_c = \int L(0,\lambda)e^{-\beta_{sc}(\lambda,T,h_0)s}q_c(\lambda)\,d\lambda$$
$$+ \int L(\infty,\lambda)\left(1-e^{-\beta_{sc}(\lambda,T,h_0)s}\right)q_c(\lambda)\,d\lambda, \tag{9}$$

where $L(0,\lambda)$, $L(\infty,\lambda)$, $\beta_{sc}(\cdot)$, and s are same as in Eq. (1) and h_0 is the altitude at the observer position.

To simplify Eq. (9) into an RGB-based rendering equation, we can assume $q_c(\lambda)$ to be a narrow band. In this way, we approximated the spectral sensitivity in the direct transmission and airlight by Dirac's delta function. Generalizing this approximation for any observer's viewing direction $V(\theta,\phi)$, we obtain

$$I_c(s,V) = I_c^0(V)\Gamma_c(T,s) + I_c^\infty(T,V)\left(1-\Gamma_c(T,s)\right), \tag{10}$$

where I_c^0 is the intensity value of a pixel at the target object, at distance s, and viewing direction V, without any aerial perspective effect. I_c^∞ is the sky intensity value at an infinite distance in the same viewing direction V, and Γ_c is the attenuation factor approximated as

$$\Gamma_c(T,s) = \frac{\int_{380\,nm}^{780\,nm} e^{-\beta_{sc}(\lambda,T,h_0)s}q_c(\lambda)\,d\lambda}{\int_{380\,nm}^{780\,nm} q_c(\lambda)\,d\lambda}. \tag{11}$$

In real daylight scenes, we can calculate $I_c^\infty(T,V)$ from another viewing direction $V'(\theta',\phi)$, with the same azimuth ϕ but different zenith θ', of the captured sky. First, the visible sky is roughly segmented from the textureless area of the captured image using a watershed algorithm. Then, a *horizon region* within the visible sky pixels with the highest azimuth angles is estimated. Finally, $I_c^\infty(\cdot)$ is computed from pixels in the horizon region that have the highest intensity value $I_c^\infty(\theta')$ by

$$I_c^\infty(T,\theta) = I_c^\infty(\theta')\varsigma(T,\theta,\theta'), \tag{12}$$

where $\varsigma(\cdot)$ is an intensity ratio modeled according to Preetham sky models as

$$\varsigma(T,\theta,\theta') = \frac{1 + (0.178T - 1.463)e^{(-0.355T+0.427)/\cos\theta}}{1 + (0.178T - 1.463)e^{(-0.355T+0.427)/\cos\theta'}}. \tag{13}$$

5 Improved scattering model for rendering

Scattering models for real scenes require parameters that guarantee a realistic result when rendering the aerial perspective effect. For this purpose, we propose an improved scattering model based on real data of [16] about weather conditions via scattering coefficients, which is summarized in Table 2 of the Appendix. The data in [16] was measured under *standard conditions*, which is using a spectrally weighted average wavelength ($\lambda = 550$ nm) for daylight within the visual spectrum at sea level ($h = 0$ m).

5.1 Rayleigh scattering coefficient correction

We can obtain the value of the Rayleigh scattering coefficient of $\beta_R = 0.0141$ km^{-1} under standard conditions from Table 2 in the Appendix. However, using Eq. (3) for such conditions results in $\beta_R = 0.0135$ km^{-1}. This slight variation in β_R of 0.0006 km^{-1} is actually considerable in terms of the attenuation factor. According to the International Visibility Code summed up in [16], the visibility range in pure air is up to 277 km. This means that a variation of 0.0006 km^{-1} in the scattering coefficient in that visibility range affects the attenuation factor in 84.69%. To adjust this disparity, we propose a straightforward multiplicative correction factor K_R given by

$$K_R = 0.0141/0.0135 = 1.0396. \tag{14}$$

Then our modified Rayleigh scattering coefficient is given by

$$\hat{\beta}_R = \frac{8\pi^3(n^2-1)^2}{3N\lambda^4}\left(\frac{6+3p_n}{6-7p_n}\right)e^{-\frac{h_0}{H_{R0}}} \times K_R, \quad (15)$$

where n, N, p_n, and H_{R0} are the same as in Eq. (3), h_0 is the altitude at the observer, and K_R is given by Eq. (14).

5.2 Mie scattering coefficient correction

One issue in Preetham's scattering model [3] is related to the turbidity itself. From Eq. (5), $T = 1$ refers to the ideal case where the Mie scattering coefficient is zero. Thus, the concentration factor $c = (0.6544T - 0.6510) \times 10^{-16}$ of Preetham [3] and $c = (0.6544T - 0.6510) \times 10^{-18}$ of Zhao [13] should be zero for $T = 1$. We corrected this issue to ensure a more reliable fitting to the real data in [16] by

$$\hat{c}(T) = (0.65T - 0.65) \times 10^{-16}. \quad (16)$$

Another issue is the value of the fudge factor K in [3, 13]. The fudge factor affects exponentially to the part of the attenuation factor corresponding to the Mie scattering. Thus, adjusting K to the real data in [16] is essential to handle hazy atmospheric conditions accurately. Preetham et al. [3] and Zhao [13] used a wavelength-dependent $K \in [0.65, 0.69]$ for wavelengths $\lambda \in [380, 780]$ nm. However, such fudge factor values do not match the data in [16]. Therefore, we corrected K according to Table 2, calculating an average fudge factor solving Eq. (4) under standard conditions ($\lambda = 550$ nm and $h = 0$ m). The obtained fudge factor was

$$K_M = 0.0092. \quad (17)$$

Then our modified Mie scattering coefficient can be written as

$$\hat{\beta}_M = 0.434\hat{c}(T)\pi\left(\frac{2\pi}{\lambda}\right)^{\nu-2}e^{-\frac{h_0}{H_{M0}}} \times K_M, \quad (18)$$

where $\hat{c}$ is given by Eq. (16), ν and H_{M0} are the same as in Eq. (4), h_0 is the altitude at the observer, and K_M is given by Eq. (17).

6 GPU implementation of the aerial perspective rendering

Nowadays, GPU implementation is common in CV and CG. Given the proposed aerial perspective model, we now present how to implement it on a GPU. First, we show the GPU rendering pipeline that includes both a general rendering pipeline and our proposed fragment shader. Then we explain the fragment shader in more detail.

6.1 GPU rendering pipeline

A 3D graphics rendering pipeline employs 3D objects described by their vertices and primitives to generate color values of pixels to be shown on a display. Figure 5

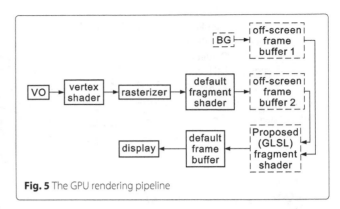

Fig. 5 The GPU rendering pipeline

illustrates a general GPU rendering pipeline in solid lines and the proposed GLSL (OpenGL Shader Language) fragment shader in dashed lines.

In MR applications, we denote VO for the virtual object and BG for the background to which the virtual object is merged. In case of composition applications, the input image is considered as VO, while there is no BG. Without lost of generality, we explain the rendering pipeline only for the MR case.

In general, raw vertices and primitives of a VO inputted to a vertex shader are processed and transformed for a rasterizer. The rasterizer scans and converts the transformed primitives into 3D fragments, which are then processed in the default fragment shader and merged to obtain textured and lighten 2D fragments. Normally, the resulting 2D fragments are stored in a default frame buffer and then go to the display. We propose to employ one off-screen frame buffer for storing the 2D fragments of the VO coming from the default fragment shader and another off-screen frame buffer for storing the captured real scene that we will call BG. Since the aerial perspective rendering of Eq. (10) is an RGB-based model, we implement it on a GPU at a fragment level. We insert the fragment shader between the two off-screen buffers and the default frame buffer in order to render a MR frame where the VO has a synthesized aerial perspective effect seamlessly to the natural atmospheric effect visualized on BG.

6.2 Proposed GLSL fragment shader

Figure 6 illustrates the required parameters for the GLSL fragment shader in order to render an aerial perspective effect. In MR, BG stands for one frame of the real scene with turbidity T captured by a camera with spectral sensitivity q_c. Since we estimate T off-line, the proposed fragment shader only needs the position and color of a BG pixel and a VO fragment, respectively, for the computation. The position of a point in world coordinates with respect to an observer located in the origin is given by the depth s, azimuth ϕ, and zenith θ. The BG's pixel color I_{BG} is given by its RGB values, and the VO's fragment color

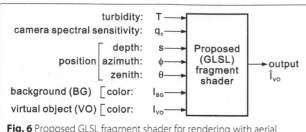

Fig. 6 Proposed GLSL fragment shader for rendering with aerial perspective effect

I_{VO} is given by the RGB values of the CG model textured and illuminated without aerial perspective effect.

Using the abovementioned parameters, the GLSL fragment shader consists of the following steps:

1) *Initialization*: The program calls the textures I_{VO} and I_{BG}, the target's relative depth $\bar{s} \in [0, 1]$ and position (l_x, l_y) in 2D screen coordinates, the turbidity T, and the spectral sensitivity q_c.

2) *Positioning*: The target's absolute position in world coordinates is estimated by

$$s = s_{near}/(1 - \bar{s}(1 - s_{near}/s_{far})), \quad (19)$$

$$\phi = \arctan(y/x), \quad (20)$$

$$\theta = \arccos(z/\sqrt{x^2 + y^2 + z^2}), \quad (21)$$

where the depth s is in meters; s_{near} and s_{far} are the distances of near and far planes, respectively; and (x, y, z) is the target's relative position in world coordinates computed from

$$\begin{bmatrix} x \\ y \\ z \\ w \end{bmatrix} = [M_{4\times4} \times P_{4\times4} \times R_{4\times4}]^{-1} \begin{bmatrix} l_x \\ l_y \\ \bar{s} \\ 1 \end{bmatrix}, \quad (22)$$

where M and P are the model view matrix and the projection matrix, respectively, and R is the remap matrix given by

$$R_{4\times4} = \begin{bmatrix} 2 & 0 & 0 & -1 \\ 0 & 2 & 0 & -1 \\ 0 & 0 & 2 & -1 \\ 0 & 0 & 0 & 1 \end{bmatrix}. \quad (23)$$

3) *Aerial perspective rendering*: The attenuation factor $\Gamma_c(T, s)$ is computed using Eq. (11). $I_c^\infty(T, \phi, \theta)$ is computed according to Eqs. (12) and (13). The target with aerial perspective effect $\hat{I}_{VO}$ is calculated using Eq. (10) and then blended with I_{BG} to produce the final result.

7 Experimental results

In this section, we evaluated the turbidity estimation approach and the aerial perspective rendering model. Composition application was used for qualitative and quantitative evaluation of the method. We also provide an application on mixed reality. All the following experiments were run on C++ on a PC with OS: Windows 7; CPU: Corei7 2.93 GHz; RAM: 16 GB; GPU: nVIDIA GTX 550 Ti 4049 MB.

7.1 Turbidity estimation test

We tested our approach for turbidity estimation using static omnidirectional images of both simulated skies and captured skies.

7.1.1 Evaluation with sky models

We estimated turbidity 100 times taking Preetham sky models as input images. For this purpose, we implemented the Preetham sky models, which are illustrated in Fig. 7. These models are sky images of 500 by 500 pixels with different values of turbidity ranging from 2.0 to 9.0 and sun position $\theta_s = 58.4°$ and $\phi_s = -179.4°$. The atmospheric turbidity was estimated for each input image using Eq. (8). $N = 100$ random sampling points were taken for each turbidity estimation. The results are shown in Table 1, where $\bar{T}$ stands for the mean value of turbidity and σ_T stands for the corresponding standard deviation. The speed of the turbidity estimation method was 200 sampling points/second.

7.1.2 Evaluation with captured sky images

We estimated turbidity for omnidirectional sky images captured by Canon EOS5D with a fisheye lens at 12 p.m. in different days. The sky images are illustrated in Fig. 8. $N = 100$ random sampling points were used for each turbidity estimation. Turbidity was estimated 50 times for each sky image.

Fig. 7 Implemented Preetham sky models. From left to right: $T = 2, T = 3, T = 4, T = 5, T = 7, T = 9$

Table 1 Estimated turbidity values using the Preetham sky models as an input image

$T_{\text{sky model}}$	$\bar{T}$	σ_T
2.0	2.011791	0.004660
3.0	2.851666	0.027230
4.0	4.241544	0.043840
5.0	4.992700	0.055292
6.0	5.836839	0.061853
7.0	7.138090	0.062630
8.0	8.010996	0.135764
9.0	9.099154	0.089461

7.2 Aerial perspective model evaluation

7.2.1 Evaluation of the scattering coefficients

From the proposed corrections, under standard conditions ($\lambda = 550$ nm and $h_0 = 0$ m), our $\hat{\beta}_M$ is approximately 70 times smaller than the β_M of [3] and roughly 1.43 times smaller than the corrected Mie scattering coefficient of [13]. We can compare the impact of the Mie scattering coefficient on the aerial perspective effect. To this end, we can employ the approximated values of the attenuation factor of [3, 13] and ours, given by $e^{-\beta_{\text{sc}}s}$, $e^{-0.01\beta_{\text{sc}}s}$, and $e^{-0.0137\beta_{\text{sc}}s}$, respectively. The results illustrated in Fig. 9 show that our attenuation is weaker than Preetham's attenuation but stronger than Zhao's attenuation.

We also provide a classification of scattering coefficients through turbidity, as illustrated in Fig. 10. From Eqs. (15) and (18), we have

$$\hat{\beta}_{M1}/\hat{\beta}_{M2} = (T_1 - 1)/(T_2 - 1), \qquad (24)$$

where $\hat{\beta}_{M1}$ and $\hat{\beta}_{M2}$ refer to our improved Mie scattering coefficient for turbidities T_1 and T_2, respectively. Considering a turbidity of 1.6 for an exceptionally clear atmospheric condition, we plotted Fig. 10 using Eq. (24).

7.2.2 Airlight evaluation

We performed a qualitative evaluation of the airlight constituent of real images using our rendering model of Eq. (10). Real scenes of Tokyo city were captured using Canon EOS5D. The experiments aim to show performance using a single image as input. Because of this, we used Google earth to manually estimate a rough depth map of the scenes. Nonetheless, depth maps can be estimated either from two images of the same scene at different weather conditions using the proposed aerial perspective model or from single images using approaches as in [14, 15]. For a fair evaluation and comparison with state-of-the-art approaches [13–15], the input images were manually segmented to only apply aerial perspective effect over the scene excluding the sky. In addition, the parameters used in the mentioned approaches were set to be optimal.

Figure 11 illustrates our results as well as the results obtained using methods of [13–15] for different atmospheric conditions. Theoretically, the airlight component should only contain information from the environmental light affected by the attenuation factor. While our airlight visibly proved to follow such theoretic consistency, the airlights from the other methods clearly retained color information from the target objects.

Moreover, due to the attenuation factor, the more distant the target object is, the more similar to the environmental illumination color the airlight should be. Certainly, observing the far way mountains in Fig. 11 we notice that our airlight also followed that theoretic definition, while [13–15] did not succeed to do so.

7.2.3 Evaluation of the aerial perspective effect

In this experiment, we rendered an aerial perspective effect using a given source image I_s and compared the synthesized output $\hat{I}_t$ with a ground truth target image I_t of the same scene. We use the subscripts s and t to refer to the source and target, respectively. We dropped the subscript channel $c \in \{r,g,b\}$ just for readability; however, the computation was carried out in the three channels. In general, based on Eq. (10), if we assume constant reflectance properties for objects in the scene, we can first estimate the normalized radiance $\rho(\mathbf{x})$ at pixel $\mathbf{x}$ in the source image. Since $\rho(\mathbf{x})$ does not depend on the atmospheric condition, that is

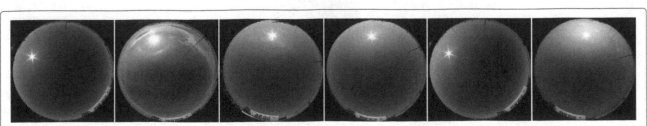

Fig. 8 Captured sky images by EOS5D with fisheye lens. From left to right: $T = 1.90$, $T = 2.52$, $T = 2.54$, $T = 2.94$, $T = 3.11$, $T = 4.36$

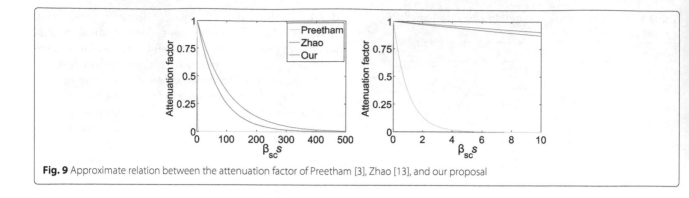

Fig. 9 Approximate relation between the attenuation factor of Preetham [3], Zhao [13], and our proposal

$$\rho(\mathbf{x}) = \frac{I_s^0(\mathbf{x})}{I_s^\infty(\mathbf{x})} = \frac{I_t^0(\mathbf{x})}{I_t^\infty(\mathbf{x})}, \tag{25}$$

the desired aerial perspective can be applied on the normalized radiance. We compute this two-step process directly by

$$\hat{I}_t(\mathbf{x}) = I_s(\mathbf{x}) \left(\frac{I_t^\infty(\mathbf{x})\Gamma_t(T_t, \mathbf{x})}{I_s^\infty(\mathbf{x})\Gamma_s(T_s, \mathbf{x})} \right)$$
$$+ I_t^\infty(\mathbf{x}) \left(1 - \frac{\Gamma_t(T_t, \mathbf{x})}{\Gamma_s(T_s, \mathbf{x})} \right), \tag{26}$$

In the evaluation, we used the input image with $T_s = 1.9$ of Fig. 11 as the source image since it provides more detailed color information than scenes with higher turbidities. We targeted to ground truth images with $T_t = \{2.11, 2.54, 2.94, 4.36\}$.

Figure 12 displays our qualitative results as well as a comparison with results from [13–15]. As can be appreciated from the results, our method generated more visually coherent appearances than the state-of-the-art techniques. Synthesized results of all methods were similar to the ground truth for close objects, such as the biggest building in the scenes. However, while our method prevailed effectively along the entire scene, [13–15] suffered from appearance inconsistencies in more distant regions.

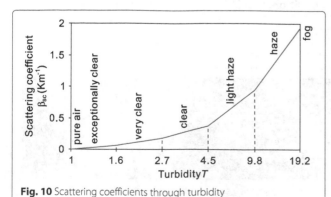

Fig. 10 Scattering coefficients through turbidity

We also performed a quantitative evaluation using two metrics: the hue saturation brightness (HSV) histogram correlation and the structural similarity (SSIM) image quality index [30] (see Fig. 13). The histogram correlation was calculated as

$$\text{Corr}_c(H_1, H_2) = \frac{\sum_c (H_1(c) - \bar{H}_1)(H_2(c) - \bar{H}_2)}{\sqrt{(H_1(c) - \bar{H}_1)^2 (H_2(c) - \bar{H}_2)^2}}, \tag{27}$$

where H is histogram, $\bar{H}$ stands for the histogram mean, $c \in \{$H-S,V$\}$, and lower indexes 1 and 2 correspond to $\hat{I}_t$ and I_t, respectively. In both the HSV correlation and the SSIM index metrics, a higher value represents a higher similarity between the synthesized aerial perspective and the ground truth.

The quantitative results showed that our approach outperformed the methods mentioned beforehand. It is worth noting that while [14] had a better SSIM index than ours only at the least hazy scene, our method provided the highest combined HSV histogram correlation for all scenes. In general, at lower turbidities, [14] rendered compelling results closer to ours than [13, 15]. However, contrary to our method, the quality of [13–15] drastically decreased as the haze became denser.

7.3 Application on MR

We applied the aerial perspective effect to a CG model rendered in a real scene. For convenience of the experiment, we employed a fixed view in order to avoid occlusion and tracking issues and focus on the appearance issue. However, this feature is not a limitation since the fixed view issue can be handled using conventional track-

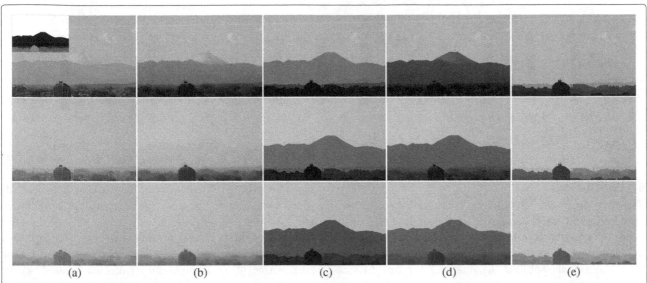

Fig. 11 Airlight evaluation with real scenes. From *top* to *bottom rows*: scenes with turbidities $T = 1.9$, $T = 2.94$, and $T = 4.36$. **a** Input images. Airlight results of **b** He et al. [14], **c** Zhao [13], **d** Zhu et al. [15], and **e** ours. Depth map in *top-left image* was used only by [13] and our method

ing systems. The altitude at the observer position was $h_0 = 40$ m above sea level. The distance from the CG model to the observer was around 3500 m. The real scenes of the experiments correspond to the scenes captured for the turbidity estimation test seen in Fig. 8. We use the real scenes with estimated atmospheric turbidities of 1.9, 2.10, 2.94, and 4.36.

The rendered results are shown in Fig. 14. We provide the MR results using Zhao's method [13] for the comparison. We found that the proposed method synthesized more plausible results in terms of visual coherence between the virtual object and the real scene. In terms of computational cost, our rendering speed (14 fps for a full HD frame size) was 225 times faster than Zhao's method.

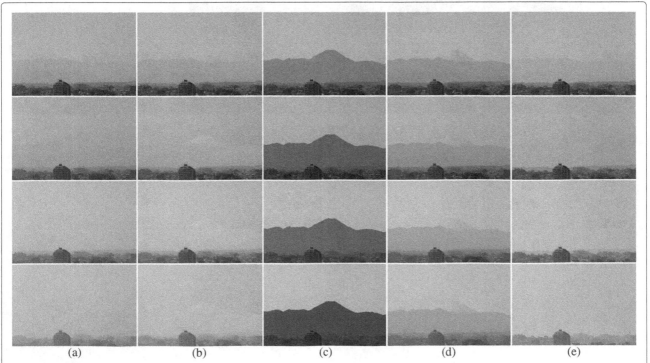

Fig. 12 Aerial perspective rendering evaluation on real-world images. From *top* to *bottom rows*: scenes with $T = 2.11$, $T = 2.54$, $T = 2.94$, and $T = 4.36$. **a** Ground truth target images. Synthesized results of **b** He et al. [14], **c** Zhao [13], **d** Zhu et al. [15], and **e** ours

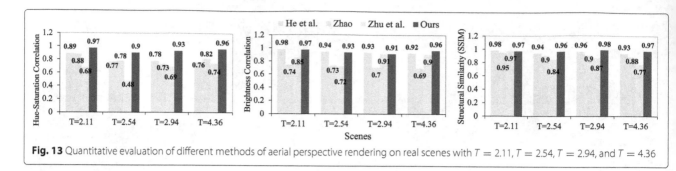

Fig. 13 Quantitative evaluation of different methods of aerial perspective rendering on real scenes with $T = 2.11$, $T = 2.54$, $T = 2.94$, and $T = 4.36$

8 Conclusions

We have proposed an efficient turbidity-based method for aerial perspective rendering in real scenes. The atmospheric turbidity is effectively estimated by matching the luminance distributions of a sky model and an omnidirectional captured sky image. An improved scattering model was deduced using real data to classify scattering coefficient values via turbidity. The enhanced scattering model was employed to provide a novel full-spectrum aerial perspective rendering model. Qualitative and quantitative evaluations on real and synthesized data show that the rendering method accomplishes realistic appearances seamlessly to the natural aerial perspective in real time, outperforming related works in terms of appearance quality and computational cost.

(a)   (b)   (c)   (d)

Fig. 14 MR application with aerial perspective effect. From *top* to *bottom rows*: scenes with turbidities $T = 1.9$, $T = 2.11$, $T = 2.94$, and $T = 4.36$. **a** Input real scenes. **b** Virtual object without aerial perspective. **c** Results of [13]. **d** Our results

Appendix

Table 2 corresponds to the classification of weather conditions based on scattering coefficients. The data was adapted from [16], where measurements were carried out under standard conditions. Standard conditions refer to a spectrally weighted average wavelength ($\lambda = 550$ nm) for daylight within the visual spectrum at sea level ($h = 0$ m).

Table 2 Weather conditions via scattering coefficients

Weather condition	β_R (km^{-1})	Min β_M (km^{-1})	Max β_M (km^{-1})
Pure air	0.0141	0	0
Exceptionally clear	0.0141	0	0.0639
Very clear	0.0141	0.0639	0.1819
Clear	0.0141	0.1819	0.3769
Light haze	0.0141	0.3769	0.9399
Haze	0.0141	0.9399	1.9459
Fog	0.0141	1.9459	More than 78

Acknowledgements
This work was, in part, supported by JSPS KAKENHI Grant Number 16H05864.

Authors' contributions
CM, TO, and KI designed the study, developed the methodology, and performed the analysis. CM collected the data. CM wrote the manuscript, and TO and KI helped to polish it. All authors read and approved the final manuscript.

Competing interests
The authors declare that they have no competing interests.

Author details
[1]The University of Tokyo, Tokyo, Japan. [2]Microsoft Research Asia, Beijing, China.

References
1. Nishita T, Sirai T, Tadamura K, Nakamae E (1993) Display of the earth taking into account atmospheric scattering. In: Proceedings of the 20th Annual Conference on Computer Graphics and Interactive Techniques, SIGGRAPH'93. ACM, New York. pp 175–182
2. Nishita T, Dobashi Y, Kaneda K, Yamashita H (1996) Display method of the sky color taking into account multiple scattering. In: Proceedings of the Fourth Pacific Conference on Computer Graphics and Applications (Pacific Graphics '96). pp 66–79
3. Preetham AJ, Shirley P, Smits B (1999) A practical analytic model for daylight. In: Proceedings of the 26th Annual Conference on Computer Graphics and Interactive Techniques, ser. SIGGRAPH '99. ACM Press/Addison-Wesley Publishing Co., New York. pp 91–100
4. Haber J, Magnor M, Seidel HP (2005) Physically-based simulation of twilight phenomena. ACM Trans Graphics (TOG) 24(4):1353–73
5. Bruneton E, Neyret F (2008) Precomputed atmospheric scattering. Comput Graphics Forum 27(4):1079–1086
6. Hosek L, Wilkie A (2012) An analytic model for full spectral sky-dome radiance. ACM Trans Graphics (TOG) 31(4):95
7. Hosek L, Wilkie A (2013) Adding a solar-radiance function to the Hosek-Wilkie skylight model. IEEE Comput Graphics Appl 33(3):44–52
8. Kerker M (1969) The scattering of light and other electromagnetic radiation. Academic press, New York
9. Kider Jr, Knowlton D, Newlin J, Li YK, Greenberg DP (2014) A framework for the experimental comparison of solar and skydome illumination. ACM Trans Graphics (TOG) 33(6):180
10. Jung J, Lee JY, Kweon IS (2015) One-day outdoor photometric stereo via skylight estimation. In: Proceedings of the IEEE Conference on Computer Vision and Pattern Recognition, Boston. pp 4521–4529
11. Satilmis P, Bashford-Rogers T, Debattista K, Chalmers A (2016) A machine learning driven sky model. In: IEEE Computer Graphics and Applications
12. Wang X, Gao J, Fan Z, Roberts NW (2016) An analytical model for the celestial distribution of polarized light, accounting for polarization singularities, wavelength and atmospheric turbidity. J Optics 18(6):065601
13. Zhao H (2012) Estimation of atmospheric turbidity from a sky image and its applications. Ph.D. dissertation, Graduate School of Information Science and Technology, The University of Tokyo
14. He K, Sun J, Tang X (2011) Single image haze removal using dark channel prior. IEEE Trans Pattern Anal Mach Intell 33(12):2341–2353
15. Zhu Q, Mai J, Shao L (2015) A fast single image haze removal algorithm using color attenuation prior. IEEE Trans Image Process 24(11):3522–3533
16. McCartney EJ (1976) Optics of the atmosphere: scattering by molecules and particles, vol. 1. John Wiley and Sons, Inc., New York, p. 421
17. Dobashi Y, Yamamoto T, Nishita T (2002) Interactive rendering of atmospheric scattering effects using graphics hardware. In: Proceedings of the ACM SIGGRAPH/EUROGRAPHICS Conference on Graphics Hardware, ser. HWWS '02. Eurographics Association, Aire-la-Ville, Switzerland. pp 99–107
18. Nielsen RS (2003) Real time rendering of atmospheric scattering effects for flight simulators. Master's thesis, Informatics and Mathematical Modelling, Technical University of Denmark, DTU, Richard Petersens Plads, Building 321, DK-2800 Kgs. Lyngby
19. Riley K, Ebert DS, Kraus M, Tessendorf J, Hansen C (2004) Efficient rendering of atmospheric phenomena. In: Proceedings of the Fifteenth Eurographics Conference on Rendering Techniques, ser. EGSR'04. Eurographics Association, Aire-la-Ville, Switzerland. pp 375–386
20. Schafhitzel T, Falk M, Ertl T (2007) Real-time rendering of planets with atmospheres. In: Journal of WSCG 15(1–3). pp 91–98
21. Gao R, Fan X, Zhang J, Luo Z (2012) Haze filtering with aerial perspective. In: 19th IEEE International Conference on Image Processing (ICIP). pp 989–992
22. Narasimhan SG, Nayar SK (2003) Contrast restoration of weather degraded images. Pattern Anal Mach Intell IEEE Trans 25(6):713–724
23. Nayar S, Narasimhan S (1999) Vision in bad weather. In: International Conference on Computer Vision. pp 820–827
24. Tan R (2008) Visibility in bad weather from a single image. In: Proceedings of IEEE International Conference on Computer Vision and Pattern Recognition. pp 1–8
25. Strutt JW (1871) Lviii. On the scattering of light by small particles. London, Edinburgh Dublin Philos Mag J Sci 41(275):447–454
26. Mie G (1908) Beitrage zur optik truber medien, speziell kolloidaler metallosungen. Annalen der Physik 330(3):377–445
27. Perez R, Seals R, Michalsky J (1993) All-weather model for sky luminance distribution-preliminary configuration and validation. Solar Energy 50(3):235–245
28. Kawakami R, Zhao H, Tan RT, Ikeuchi K (2013) Camera spectral sensitivity and white balance estimation from sky images. Int J Comput Vis 105(3):187–204
29. Zhao H (2013) Spectral sensitivity database. http://www.cvl.iis.u-tokyo.ac.jp/rei/research/cs/zhao/database.html. Accessed 31 May 2013
30. Wang Z, Bovik A, Sheikh H, Simoncelli E (2004) Image quality assessment: from error visibility to structural similarity. IEEE Trans Image Process 13(4):600–612

3

Combining deep features for object detection at various scales: finding small birds in landscape images

Akito Takeki* ⓘD, Tu Tuan Trinh, Ryota Yoshihashi, Rei Kawakami, Makoto Iida and Takeshi Naemura

Abstract

Demand for automatic bird ecology investigation rises rapidly along with the widespread installation of wind energy plants to estimate their adverse environmental effect. While significant advance in general image recognition has been made by deep convolutional neural networks (CNNs), automatically recognizing birds at small scale together with large background regions is still an open problem in computer vision. To tackle object detection at various scales, we combine a deep detector with semantic segmentation methods; namely, we train a deep CNN detector, fully convolutional networks (FCNs), and the variant of FCNs, and integrate their results by the support vector machines to achieve high detection performance. Through experimental results on a bird image dataset, we show the effectiveness of the method for scale-aware object detection.

1 Introduction

Wind turbines, one of the mainstream technologies for cultivating renewable energy sources, are yet at the same time considered serious threats to endangered bird species [1]. Assessments of bird habitats around planned sites are now required for the operators [2], whereas the surveys rely on experts who conduct manual observations. Automatic bird detection has hence drawn the attention of industry, as it can reduce the cost and increase the accuracy of investigations. It may also assist automatic systems that decelerate the blades or sound an alarm at the approach of birds.

When conducting bird surveillance with fixed-point cameras, however, three issues occur related to resolution and precision.

First, finding various scales of objects in large images has been addressed as a difficult problem because of the large differences in resolution. Second, images of surveillance cameras have different characteristic from those in general image recognition datasets, as objects captured by wide-field-of-view cameras are often ambiguous due to low resolution.

Finally, the number of flying birds is irregular and there are many scenes without any birds; thus, the detector is required to reduce false detections of backgrounds as few as possible for practical use.

To solve these problems, this paper presents a scale-aware bird detection method with practically high precision. Following the idea of scene parsing (e.g., [3]), we carefully select the combination of methods, each of which are suited for objects at different scales; specifically, a successor [4] of convolutional neural networks (CNNs) [5] for small birds and two kinds of fully convolutional networks (FCNs) for larger areas: the original FCNs [6] and DeepLab [7]. FCN-based methods can recognize both birds and backgrounds, while FCNs is more suited for middle-size birds, and DeepLab is good at backgrounds. Linear SVMs [8] are used to merge all the features for final results. This paper is based on our previous work [9] but improved so that features in the selected methods are all based on deep learning.

The proposed method was experimentally evaluated with a bird dataset especially constructed for ecological investigations around wind farms, showing that combining deep features from a detector and semantic segmentation is effective for scale-aware object detection. It achieved precision of 97 % in the bird detection task with 80 % recall rate.

*Correspondence: takeki@hc.ic.i.u-tokyo.ac.jp
The University of Tokyo, 7-3-1 Hongo, Bunkyo-ku, Tokyo 113-8656, Japan

1.1 Related work

The advances in CNNs and the growing availability of large-scale image datasets have brought outstanding improvements in image recognition. In particular, stronger learning models [10, 11] as well as effective techniques for suppressing overfitting [12] and avoiding the vanishing gradient problem [13] have significantly improved the performance of CNNs.

Many new detection methods have been proposed along with the advances in CNNs. In popular region-based CNN methods (R-CNN) [14], a selective search [15] is first used to identify potentially salient object regions (referred to as region proposal), from which image features are extracted by CNNs and classified by SVMs. We utilize ResNet [4], one of the most successful networks in detection, while we leave the region proposals as future work and use background subtraction for candidate region selection in this study.

Significant progress has also been made in semantic segmentation. There has been much debate about how to parse both object categories (*things*) and background categories (*stuff*), each of which account for smaller and larger parts of images. Various methods parse stuff and things separately with region-based and detector-based methods [3, 16].

Recently, a number of semantic segmentation methods have been proposed that are based on FCNs [6, 7].

FCNs can obtain a coarse object label map from the networks by combining the final prediction layer with lower layers (skip layer) [17], where the context and localization information are available for pixel-wise labeling.

DeepLab use the hole algorithm [18], which convolutes every other pixel. This approach can grasp the feature map more sparsely, which improves the ability to recognize background.

2 Method

An overview of the proposed method is illustrated in Fig. 1.

An input image is fed into three pipelines: (1) ResNet-based CNNs as a detector for small birds after a background subtraction pre-processing, (2) FCNs as a method that works as a detector but also as a semantic segmentation, and (3) DeepLab as a method that works as a semantic segmentation. SVMs combine the class likelihoods and scores derived from three pipelines. The outcomes of the method are regions estimated to be birds.

2.1 CNNs for bird detection

We designed the CNN network model using ResNet [4], which achieved the best results in the detection and classification of ILSVRC 2015. In ResNet, the input of a convolutional (conv) layer bypasses one or more layers and is added to the outputs of the stacked layers. Compared with previous net structures, ResNet learns so-called residual mappings, which make the learning easier even with deeper structures.

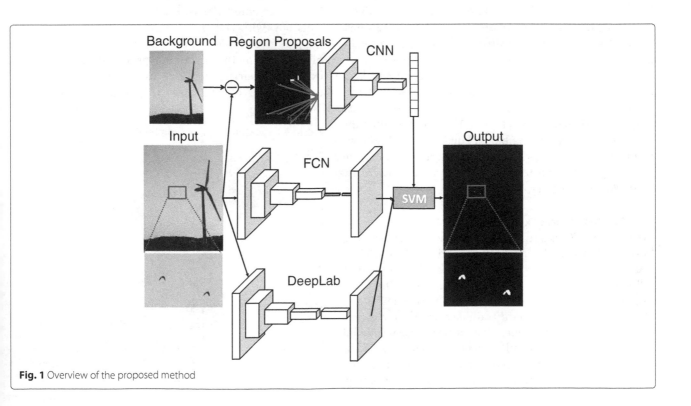

Fig. 1 Overview of the proposed method

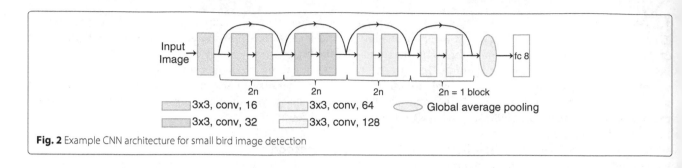

Fig. 2 Example CNN architecture for small bird image detection

Figure 2 shows our network architecture based on ResNet. We assume the sizes of the bird images ranges from 10 to 200 pixels square; thus, we design the networks to take 64×64 images as inputs, doubled the size of the original. Any size of detected bounding boxes will be fitted to 64×64 and fed into the networks. Because of this, one more block (the layers in yellow) is added before the global average pooling to capture features effectively with more hierarchies. Experimentally, the combination of four blocks with $n = 2$ produces the best results; four blocks with $n = 3$ produce similar results but require a longer training time, fewer blocks have less accuracy even with larger n, and more blocks cause overfitting even with fewer n.

The rest of the networks follows [4]; here, we briefly explain it for completeness. In every conv layer, the size of the kernels is 3×3. The very first conv layer has 16 kernels. Subsequently, there are four blocks, each of which includes four ($2n$ with $n = 2$) conv layers. The number of kernels is 16, 32, 64, and 128 in each block, respectively. When the dimensions increase by shortcut connections, we use 1×1 convolutions with a stride of 2 to equalize the input and output dimensions.

The first of four conv layers in the second and later blocks includes a stride of two subsamples, and this reduces the feature map size into half. Thus, the feature map size (64×64) becomes 64, 32, 16, and 8, after the process of each respective block. Finally, the ends of convolutions are connected using global average pooling, an eight-way fully connected layer (fc 8) and softmax. We use 18 stacked weighted layers in total.

2.2 Combining class likelihoods by SVM

We modified FCNs and DeepLab to have four classes (i.e., bird, sky, forest, and wind turbine), and CNNs have eight classes from its architecture, which we selected them as follows: bird, blade, tower, anemometer, nacelle, hub, forest, and other. The implementation details of FCNs and DeepLab are provided in the training section.

Each of the three pipelines yields a class-wise likelihood or score: FCNs and DeepLab generate pixel-wise likelihoods of classes, whereas CNNs generate a bounding box-wise score of the likelihoods of classes. For SVM training,

we use only the pixels at the center of the bounding boxes of candidate regions proposed by the inter-frame difference method in order to reduce calculation time, so that it finishes within a reasonable amount of time. After the first training, we use hard negative mining to reduce false positives and to improve the overall performance. Specifically, image regions of anemometers, night lights, the lower parts of nacelles, in which the FCNs often produce false detections, are added for SVM training. The pixels collected by the inter-frame difference have statistical difference from the true pixel distribution. Because of this, when CNNs are simply combined with semantic segmentation-based methods, the whole framework inclines to include many misdetections by CNNs; thus, we add the background regions (sky, cloud, forest, and wind turbine) inside the candidate bounding boxes in the training.

3   Experimental results

We implemented CNNs, FCNs, and DeepLab, as well as AdaBoost with Haar-like feature [19, 20] and SuperParsing [21] as baselines. Then, we also trained several combinations of methods with our proposed framework and evaluated their performance using a wide-area surveillance dataset of wild birds [22], which contains a set

Table 1 F-measure of various methods

Method	Precision	Recall	F-measure
HA	0.064	0.514	0.114
SP	*1.000*	0.366	0.536
FCN	0.684	0.519	0.590
FCN*	0.709	0.585	0.641
SP*	0.989	0.508	0.672
DL	*1.000*	0.557	0.716
CNN	0.598	*0.902*	*0.719*
FCN+DL	0.979	0.527	0.664
CNN+DL	0.799	0.628	0.703
CNN+FCN	0.924	0.798	0.856
CNN+FCN+DL	*0.974*	*0.803*	*0.880*

*represents the method combined with SVMs

of images with 2806×3744 pixels taken nearby a wind turbine.

3.1 Data

For training of SuperParsing, FCNs, and DeepLab, we picked out 82 images with different weather conditions from the dataset and manually annotated them into four classes: bird, wind turbine, sky, and forest, which are all classes included in [22]. Finally, 77 images out of 82 were used and 5 were omitted since they were too dark due to stormy weather. Except for SuperParsing, the images were cropped to 500×500 pixels because the original images were too large to process with FCNs and DeepLab on our GPU memory. Cropping the entire image randomly causes many frames only tagged with

the sky labels because more than a half of each image was occupied by sky. With this in mind, we performed cropping around the wind turbine area more intensively, and obtained 70 frames from each image by shifting a 500×500 pixel window through the area. Eventually, we had 77×70 = 5390 frames for training FCNs and DeepLab.

The training images for ResNet were acquired as candidate regions of moving objects with background subtraction from the entire dataset. The training images include bird and non-bird regions, and we prepared a class of bird and seven background classes.

These extra classes help training the networks because they are frequently included in the candidate regions and likely to cause misdetection. We categorized candidate

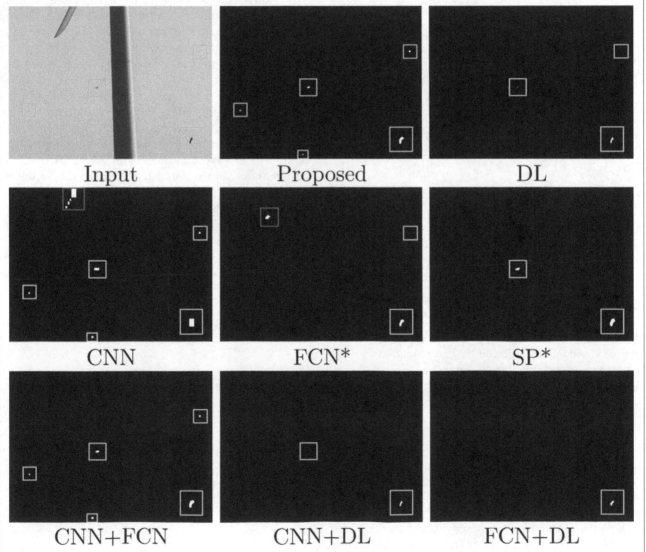

Fig. 3 Examples of detection results on the bird image dataset intended for ecological investigations. The *green squares* mean TP. The *red squares* mean FP

regions into those eight classes manually. To train the AdaBoost with Haar-like features, we used 15,705 bird images and 18,688 non-bird images similarly collected to train ResNet.

3.2 Training
3.2.1 FCNs
We used an FCN-8s model [6] pretrained on PASCAL-Context [23], which contains 59 category (+ background) segmentations. We then fine-tuned the model with the images we prepared for training by using twofold cross validation.

3.2.2 DeepLab
We used an DeepLab-MSc-LargeFOV model [7] pre-trained on PASCAL VOC 2012 [24], which contains 20 category (+ background) segmentations. We modified the layer "fc8" from 21 outputs to 4: bird, forest, sky, and wind turbine. As FCNs, we then fine-tuned the model with the prepared images by using twofold cross validation.

3.2.3 CNNs
We trained the ResNet-based model with eight-class training images from scratch. In the same way as [4], we used the method described in [25] for weight initialization. In addition, we used batch normalization [13] to reduce the internal covariate shift and accelerate learning.

3.2.4 Haar+AdaBoost
AdaBoost with Haar-like features was trained following [22]. Moving object regions were chosen by the inter-frame difference. Then, the proposed regions were marked with square bounding boxes and then trained the detector with the bird and non-bird labels.

3.2.5 SVMs
We combined the class likelihoods and scores by using pixel-wise SVM training and evaluated the performances of the individual methods and their combinations.

3.3 Evaluation
We used 44 of the 77 labeled images that included more birds (183 in total) than the others for the evaluation. The performance of the method is ranked by using the F-measure, i.e., the harmonic mean of precision and recall.

In the evaluation, we regarded detected bounding boxes that had any overlap with ground-truth boxes as correct detections and boxes with no overlap as misdetection.

Similarly, in segmentation-based methods, we regarded the outputs that had any region of overlap with the ground truth as correct detections and those without overlap as misdetections.

3.4 Results
We counted the true positives (TP) and false positives (FP) of birds and calculated the precision, recall, and F-measure. The results are summarized in Table 1.

AdaBoost with Haar-like features, SuperParsing, and DeepLab are denoted as HA, SP, and DL, respectively. In addition, SP* and FCN* represent the method combined with SVMs. Usually, SP or FCNs output class label with the highest likelihood, while SVMs consider all of the class likelihoods for the output through training.

The upper part of Table 1 shows the results of individual methods. SP and DL achieved the highest precision, while CNNs achieved the best recall rate. FCNs achieved the intermediate score between SP and CNNs. As expected, CNNs highly outperform HA. DL performed similarly to SP, but with much higher recall rate. SP* and FCN* performed better than the ones without SVMs.

The lower part of Table 1 shows the results of combination of methods, where most combinations exceed each single method in terms of F-measure. Particularly, combinations with DL have higher precision, suggesting that DL can suppress false positives because it can recognize backgrounds well. The CNN+FCN result shows FCNs also can recognize backgrounds. The CNN+DL did not achieve a good score in spite of the combination of the best detector and semantic segmentation, and it shows that FCN is also necessary for better performance. Figure 3 shows typical examples of detection results of each method. More results can be found in the Additional file 1.

To show the robustness of our method to the size of the bird images, Table 2 summarizes the results according to image size. The three image sizes, tiny ($\leq 15 \times 15$), small ($\leq 45 \times 45$), and normal ($> 45 \times 45$) are determined according to [26].

Table 2 F-measure of various methods by size

Size	Method	Precision	Recall	F-measure
Tiny	FCN+DL	0.333	0.149	0.029
	CNN+DL	0.432	0.239	0.308
	CNN+FCN	0.808	0.627	0.706
	CNN+FCN+DL	0.915	0.642	0.754
Small	FCN+DL	1.000	0.738	0.849
	CNN+DL	0.844	0.813	0.828
	CNN+FCN	0.972	0.863	0.914
	CNN+FCN+DL	1.000	0.863	0.926
Normal	FCN+DL	1.000	0.890	0.941
	CNN+DL	1.000	0.972	0.986
	CNN+FCN	1.000	0.972	0.986
	CNN+FCN+DL	1.000	0.972	0.986

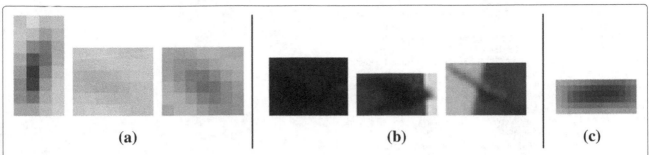

Fig. 4 Examples of bird images which could not be detected by the proposed method: **a** blurred shape, **b** overlap with the wind turbine, and **c** part occlusions

In all image sizes, the proposed method produces the best F-measure. DL is not suited for detecting tiny images of birds, but CNN+FCN detects tiny bird images more effectively. With DL, the performance is more improved particularly in precision. This shows that FCN detects more birds and DL is good at backgrounds.

Regarding the region proposals obtained by background subtraction, the number of them was about 1000 to 2000 per an input image. As shown in the Fig. 2, almost all the region proposals belong to the forest class. CNN succeeded to filter most of them and contributed to precision.

To clarify the limitation, we analyzed bird images which could not be detected by the proposed method, as shown in Fig. 4. Overlooked bird images were classified into three patterns: blurred shape due to extremely low resolution, overlap with other objects (e.g., wind turbine), and part occlusions (e.g., a bird is at the end of the image).

Almost all images with ambiguous shape were either only detected by CNN or not detected by any methods. In detail, FCN and DeepLab showed too weak reaction to very small birds to detect them. A few bird images over the wind turbine were detected by FCN and DeepLab, but when combined with CNN, they were missed because of low likelihood of birds. There was only one bird image whose parts were occluded; thus, it was hard to train such pattern of bird images.

4 Conclusion

We combined different types of deep features from a CNN-based detector and fully convolutional networks by using support vector machines to achieve high performance in detecting objects at various scale in large images.

Experiments on a bird image dataset intended for ecological investigations showed that our method detects birds with high precision.

We showed combination of multiple deep convolutional features are effective for scale-aware detection.

Competing interests
The authors declare that they have no competing interests.

Authors' contributions
AT designed and executed the experiments and wrote the manuscript. TT contributed to the concept and wrote the manuscript. RY collected the experimental data, helped the implementation, and wrote the manuscript. RK advised AT on the concept and experiments and wrote the manuscript. MI and TN supervised the work and edited the manuscript. All authors reviewed and approved the final manuscript.

Acknowledgements
This work is in part entrusted by the Ministry of the Environment, JAPAN (MOEJ), the project of which is to examine effective measures for preventing birds, especially sea eagles, from colliding with wind turbines, and by JSPS KAKENHI Grant Number JP16K16083.

References
1. Smallwood KS, Rugge L, Morrison ML (2009) Influence of behavior on bird mortality in wind energy developments. J Wildl Manage 73(7):1082–1098
2. Bassi S, Bowen A, Fankhauser S (2012) The case for and against onshore wind energy in the UK. Grantham Res. Inst. on Climate Change and Env. Policy Brief
3. Tighe J, Lazebnik S (2013) Finding things: image parsing with regions and per-exemplar detectors. In: CVPR. IEEE. pp 3001–3008
4. He K, Zhang X, Ren S, Sun J (2016) Deep residual learning for image recognition. In: Proc. of Computer Vision and Pattern Recognition. IEEE. pp 770–778
5. Krizhevsky A, Sutskever I, Hinton GE (2012) Imagenet classification with deep convolutional neural networks. In: NIPS. pp 1097–1105
6. Long J, Shelhamer E, Darrell T (2015) Fully convolutional networks for semantic segmentation. In: CVPR. IEEE
7. Chen LC, Papandreou G, Kokkinos I, Murphy K, Yuille AL (2015) Semantic image segmentation with deep convolutional nets and fully connected CRFs. In: ICLR. http://arxiv.org/abs/1412.7062
8. Cortes C, Vapnik V (1995) Support-vector networks. Mach Learn 20(3):421–436
9. Takeki A, Tuan Trinh T, Yoshihashi R, Kawakami R, Iida M, Naemura T (2016) Detection of small birds in large images by combining a deep detector with semantic segmentation. In: ICIP. IEEE
10. Simonyan K, Zisserman A (2015) Very deep convolutional networks for large-scale image recognition. In: ICLR. IEEE
11. Szegedy C, Liu W, Jia Y, Sermanet P, Reed S, Anguelov D, Erhan D, Vanhoucke V, Rabinovich A (2015) Going deeper with convolutions. In: CVPR. IEEE
12. Srivastava N, Hinton G, Krizhevsky A, Sutskever I, Salakhutdinov R (2014) Dropout: a simple way to prevent neural networks from overfitting. JMLR 15(1):1929–1958
13. Ioffe S, Szegedy C (2015) Batch normalization: accelerating deep network training by reducing internal covariate shift. In: ICML

14. Girshick R, Donahue J, Darrell T, Malik J (2014) Rich feature hierarchies for accurate object detection and semantic segmentation. In: CVPR
15. Uijlings JR, van de Sande KE, Gevers T, Smeulders AW (2013) Select search object recognition. IJCV 104(2):154–171
16. Dong J, Chen Q, Yan S, Yuille A (2014) Towards unified object detection and semantic segmentation. In: ECCV. Springer. pp 299–314
17. Hariharan B, Arbeláez P, Girshick R, Malik J (2015) Hypercolumns for object segmentation and fine-grained localization. In: CVPR
18. Mallat S (1999) A wavelet tour of signal processing. Academic press
19. Viola P, Jones M (2001) Rapid object detection using a boosted cascade of simple features. In: CVPR. IEEE Vol. 1. p 511
20. Freund Y, Schapire RE (1997) A decision-theoretic generalization of on-line learning and an application to boosting. J Comput Syst Sci 55(1):119–139
21. Tighe J, Lazebnik S (2013) Superparsing. IJCV 101(2):329–349
22. Yoshihashi R, Kawakami R, Iida M, Naemura T (2015) Construction of a bird image dataset for ecological investigations. In: ICIP. IEEE. pp 4248–4252
23. Mottaghi R, Chen X, Liu X, Cho NG, Lee SW, Fidler S, Urtasun R, Yuille A (2014) The role of context for object detection and semantic segmentation in the wild. In: CVPR. IEEE. pp 891–898
24. Everingham M, Van Gool L, Williams CK, Winn J, Zisserman A (2010) Pascal vis object class (VOC) challenge. IJCV 88(2):303–338
25. He K, Zhang X, Ren S, Sun J (2015) Delving deep into rectifiers: surpassing human-level performance on imagenet classification. In: ICCV. IEEE
26. Pepik B, Benenson R, Ritschel T, Schiele B (2015) What is holding back convnets for detection? In: Patt. Recog. Springer. pp 517–528

4-D light field reconstruction by irradiance decomposition

Takahito Aoto* (iD), Tomokazu Sato, Yasuhiro Mukaigawa and Naokazu Yokoya

Abstract

Common light sources such as an ordinary flashlight with lenses and/or reflectors make complex 4-D light field that cannot be represented by conventional isotropic distribution model nor point light source model. This paper describes a new approach to estimate 4-D light field using an illuminated diffuser. Unlike conventional works that capture a 4-D light field directly, our method decomposes observed intensities on the diffuser into intensities of 4-D light rays based on inverse rendering technique with prior knowledge. We formulate 4-D light field reconstruction problem as a non-smooth convex optimization problem for mathematically finding the global minimum.

Keywords: Light field reconstruction, Illumination, Inverse lighting, Convex optimization

1 Introduction

Estimation of lighting environment is important for many applications in photometric methods in computer vision, e.g., photorealistic image synthesis, photometric stereo, and BRDF estimation. For representing a radiant intensity distribution of light sources, various models have been proposed and they can be categorized into four groups as shown in Fig. 1.

As a simplest model of a radiant intensity distribution for a light source, an isotropic point light source has conventionally been used (Fig. 1a). This type of model has only one intensity parameter. Due to its simplicity, this model established a standard in the field of photometric computer vision [1, 2]. This simplest model is extended to two directions for representing the directivity and the spatial distribution of light sources. For the directivity, an angular radiance distribution is considered (Fig. 1b) by assigning different intensity parameters for different directions. This model can handle an anisotropic point light source, and is essential for modeling a light with hard directivity like an LED [3]. The other extension is for the spatial distribution for representing the volume of lighting environment (Fig. 1c). By simply arranging multiple isotropic point-light-sources in a space, the model can handle the spatial distribution of lights. Although these extensions increase the accuracy

of lighting environment modeling, they cannot be used to model an actual complex light field, e.g., generated by LEDs or bulbs with reflectors and/or lenses. Differences between illuminating effects of actual lights and modeled ones by (a), (b), (c), become bigger when lights are placed near from the objects, and it prevents photo realistic rendering and high accurate inverse rendering in this situation. 4-D light field (Fig. 1d), which presents light field by 2-D directivity × 2-D spatial distribution of light sources, is essential for modeling actual lighting environments.

In this study, we focus on reconstructing 4-D light field from images on an illuminated object. In order to estimate 4-D light field, most of conventional works directly capture a huge number of images for all the directions from all 3-D positions and resultantly, they suffer from the cost problem for measuring all rays. Instead of direct capturing, our method estimates unknown parameters of the 4-D light field so that the images rendered with reconstructed lighting would become as similar as possible with captured original images based on an inverse lighting techniques [4]. To achieve the goal of both accurate and robust estimation, we have developed a new inverse lighting method based on a convex optimization technique. Our method introduces the range of possible radiant intensities from a physical constraint and it actualizes the reconstruction of the 4-D light field from a few images.

*Correspondence: takahito-a@is.naist.jp
Nara Institute of Science and Technology, Takayamacho 8916-5, Ikoma, Japan

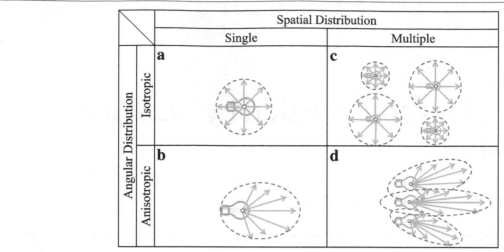

Fig. 1 Categorization of light field models. **a** Isotropic point light source. **b** Anisotropic point light source. **c** Set of point light sources. **d** 4-D light field

Remainder of this paper is organized as follows. Section 2 discusses related work and highlights our contributions. Section 3 expresses a basic idea for 4-D light field reconstruction. Section 4 describes an efficient solution for non-smooth convex optimization problem. Section 5 shows experimental results in real scenes. Finally, Section 6 concludes the present study.

2 Related work and contributions

2.1 Direct method for 4-D light field acquisition

Direct methods directly capture the 4-D light field by back-tracing the rays from the camera. Measured 4-D light field is represented by a form of 4-D light ray space based on a set of 2-D images of a scene captured from different view points.

As straight-forward methods for measuring the 4-D light field, some methods that capture 2-D images for all directions from all the 3-D positions using camera mounted on a robot arm have been used [5–8]. These methods are generally expensive in both measuring cost and time. In order to reduce them, Unger et al. [9, 10] used an array of mirrored spheres and a moving mirrored sphere that travels across the plane. Goesele et al. [11] and Nakamura et al. [12] used various kinds of optical filters that spatially limit the incident light rays to the camera. Cossairt et al. [13] used a lens array and created augmented scenes relighting synthetic objects using captured light field. Although these methods are related to our problem, the direct methods still require a comparatively large amount of images.

2.2 Indirect method for light field reconstruction

Indirect methods, also known as inverse lighting, reconstruct the lighting parameters in a scene by minimizing the difference of observed and computed intensities that can be simulated using CG rendering techniques with known scene geometry, surface property, and lighting environment.

Conventionally, many researches utilized a specular reflection or diffuse reflection components to estimate a lighting environment [14, 15]. These approaches solve a linear system. Ramamoorthi and Hanrahan [16] have shown the reason that inverse lighting problem for global illumination is ill-posed or numerically ill-conditioned, based on the theoretical analysis in the frequency domain using spherical harmonics. On the other hand, Park et al. [3] estimate the 2-D light field emitted from a point light source, which rigidly attached to a camera, using a illuminated plane.

Shadows are areas where direct lights from a light source cannot reach due to the occlusion by other object and thus can provide useful information for estimating the lighting environment. By using the cast shadow information, Sato et al. [17] proposed a method to recover positions of a set of point light sources. Okabe et al. [18] used a Haar wavelet basis to approximate the lighting effect by a small number of basis functions. Takai et al. [4] proposed a skeleton cube as a reference object that creates a self cast shadows from a point light source of arbitrary position.

2.3 Our contributions

As described above, the direct method suffers from the cost problem for data capturing and there is no method that can estimate 4-D light field with the indirect method, as far as we know. In this paper, we propose a method for estimating 4-D light field in an indirect manner that can estimate light field from a few images. In order to achieve this, the problem of estimating 4-D light field is formed as energy minimization problem with several constraints and the problem is solved by convex optimization. It should be noted that this paper is an extension of our conference paper [19]. In this paper, for stable and accurate estimation, we have newly introduced physical constraint with ℓ_1-norm regularization for energy function and we have also conducted completely new experiments with new solution.

3 Basic idea for 4-D light field reconstruction

In this section, we first formulate the problem of basic 4-D light field reconstruction as a linear system.

Figure 2 illustrates the conceptual setup for our approach. The light rays, which are emitted from light sources, are passing through the light field plane $\mathcal{L}$, on which the 4-D light field is defined. The emitted light rays are hitting to the diffuser $\mathcal{B}$. The camera observes the integral of light ray intensities on the illuminated diffuser. In this situation, our method reconstructs the 4-D light field by decomposing observed intensities into light ray intensities using multiple images in which the diffuser is illuminated from various directions, while camera position and diffuser position are fixed.

For reconstructing 4-D light field, we make the following assumptions:

- The relative positions and postures of a camera, a diffuser and light sources are known.
- The radiance distribution of light sources is static.
- The sensor response is linear.
- The light is not attenuated by scattering or absorption
- The diffuser's property (transmission model) is given.

In the followings, we first review the relationship between 4-D light field and observed intensities, and then discuss how to model the inverse problem of estimating 4-D light field from observed intensities.

3.1 Relationship between light field and observed intensities

In this work, we model a 4-D light field as the intensities of rays defined by the parameters of position (u, v) and direction (ϕ, θ) on the light field plane $\mathcal{L}$ as illustrated in Fig. 3. The center of hemispheres in this figure show sampled positions (u, v) on the light field plane $\mathcal{L}$ and the arrows inside the hemisphere indicate directions (ϕ, θ) of rays. The observed intensity o_i in the local region x_i on the diffuser $\mathcal{B}$ is proportional to the integral of all the intensities of rays that are hitting to x_i as follows [1]:

$$o_i = \alpha \int a_i(j)s(j)dj,$$
$$j = (u, v, \phi, \theta)^{\mathrm{T}}, \tag{1}$$

where

$$a_i(j) = \begin{cases} \rho, & \text{if ray } j \text{ hits } x_i, \\ 0, & \text{otherwise.} \end{cases} \tag{2}$$

α is a constant value that decides a relative scale of an observed intensity and a light ray intensity. $s(j)$ is an intensity of ray j and ρ is attenuation ratio on $\mathcal{B}$ [2]. Suppose that we observe N intensities $\boldsymbol{o} = \{o_1, \cdots, o_N\} \in \mathbb{R}^N$ at different regions $\{x_1, \cdots, x_N\}$ on the diffuser $\mathcal{B}$, and the ray j is discretized by $(u, v, \phi, \theta)^T$ into M of bundled rays whose intensities are redefined as $\boldsymbol{s} = \{s_1, \cdots, s_M\} \in \mathbb{R}^M$,

$$s_j = \int_{u,v \in l_i} \int_{\phi,\theta \in d_i} s(j)d\theta \, d\phi \, du \, dv, \tag{3}$$

where l_i is a local region on light field plane $\mathcal{L}$ and d_i is a set of directions that pass through the local region l_i on hemisphere. The relationship between the observed intensities $\boldsymbol{o}$ and the radiant intensities $\boldsymbol{s}$ can be formed as a linear system as

$$\boldsymbol{o} = \boldsymbol{As}, \tag{4}$$

where, $A : \mathbb{R}^M \mapsto \mathbb{R}^N$ is a matrix of known parameters that represents a rendering process. Equation (4) can be

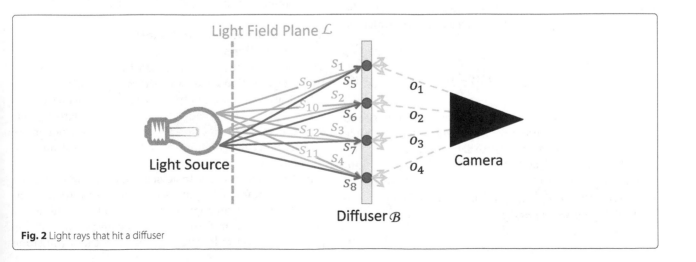

Fig. 2 Light rays that hit a diffuser

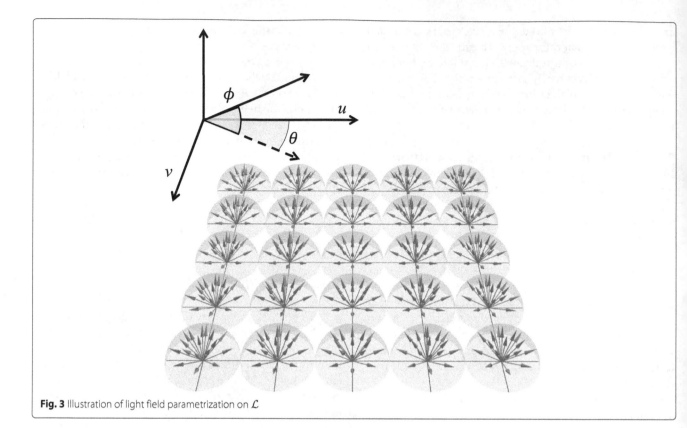

Fig. 3 Illustration of light field parametrization on $\mathcal{L}$

solved by linear least squares in principle if we have sufficient observations.

3.2 Size reduction using spherical harmonics function

In practice, the size of A in Eq. (4) is too large to be solved due to the large number of unknown parameters.

In order to reduce the number of unknown parameters, in this research, we approximate s by the real-spherical harmonics function that is often employed in photometric reconstruction. More specifically, the radiant intensity s_i in Eq. (3) of the ray passing through the local region l_i on light field plane $\mathcal{L}$ in the direction d_i, is approximated by an weighted sum of the bases of the real-spherical harmonics function, which is represented as

$$s_i = \sum_{f=0}^{F} \sum_{f=-g}^{+g} c_{i,f,g}(\phi,\theta)y_{f,g}, \tag{5}$$

where $y_{f,g}$ is the basis of real-spherical harmonics, and $c_{i,f,g}$ are $H = (F+1)^2$ unknown parameters. Representable distribution of radiant intensities depends on H.

In the case we discretize the light field plane $\mathcal{L}$ into L regions, we have $\hat{H} = H \times L$ unknown parameters: $c = \{c_1, \cdots, c_{\hat{H}}\} \in \mathbb{R}^{\hat{H}}$ for modeling 4-D light field. The relationship between s and c can be expressed as:

$$s = Yc, \tag{6}$$

where $Y : \mathbb{R}^{\hat{H}} \mapsto \mathbb{R}^{M}$ is the matrix that satisfies an orthonormal basis property. By substituting, Eq. (6) to Eq. (4), the following equations are derived.

$$
\begin{aligned}
o &= AYc, \\
&= Bc, \\
b_{i,j} &:= \frac{y_{i,j}(\phi,\theta)R(\omega)}{D(u,v,x_i)^2},
\end{aligned} \tag{7}
$$

where $b_{i,j}$ is an element of matrix $B \in \mathbb{R}^{\hat{H}} \mapsto \mathbb{R}^{N}$, $R(\omega)$ is a transmission distribution function that is determined by diffuser's property, ω is determined by the angle between a normal of the diffuser and the ray, and $D(\cdot)$ represents the distance between (u,v) and x_i on the diffuser $\mathcal{B}$.

4 Efficient solution under insufficient observations

The solution of the linear equation given in Eq. (7) is sensitive to observation noises and errors in pose estimation of the diffuser and often outputs negative intensities due to the lack of valid observations, as shown in the latter experiment. Possible approaches to overcome this problem are gaining more observations or introducing constraints on the parameters.

In this work, in order to achieve stable estimation from a limited number of inputs, we introduce a physical constraint and ℓ_1-norm regularization into a light field reconstruction algorithm formulated as a convex optimization problem. In the following, we first give the formulation of the problem, and then describe the details of each constraint.

4.1 Formulation of light field reconstruction problem

We formulate the problem of light field reconstruction as follows:

$$\arg\min_{c}\{||o - Bc||_2^2 + \lambda||c||_1 + \iota_{\mathcal{V}}(Yc)\}, \tag{8}$$

where the first term represents the squared error between observed intensities and rendered intensities, and the second term represents the ℓ_1-norm of spherical harmonics coefficients and the λ is a weight parameter for ℓ_1-norm. The third term represents the physical constraint that limits the numerical range of light ray intensities.

Since each term is convex in Eq. (8), whole function is also convex. Hence, this function has a unique solution.

The convex optimization problem of Eq. (8) can be solved by alternating direction method of multipliers [20], which effectively minimizes the function with iterative manner. By solving this problem, we can get the 4-D light field Yc.

4.2 ℓ_1-norm regularization

In general, regularization is introduced to prevent over fitting when the number of observations is not sufficiently larger than that of unknown parameters. In this research, we employ ℓ_1-norm of the unknown parameters c as a regularization term for preventing this problem. This term makes most elements in c become zero and it selects important bases on the matrix B. The weight parameter λ, which is empirically determined in the experiment, adjusts the number of selected bases.

4.3 Physical constraint based on non-negative constraint for light ray intensity

From physical limitation of radiant intensities, we can make some constraints for intensities s_j of rays j. Physically, all the light ray intensities must have non negative values. This property gives:

$$s_j \geq 0 \ \forall j \in j. \tag{9}$$

On the other hand, as illustrated in Figs. 2 and 4, each ray affects multiple regions x_i on the diffuser B in different positions and each region is also affected by multiple radiant intensities s_j. Here, if there is no ray except for rays j, observed intensity o_i illuminated by s_j is represented by $A_{j,i}s_j$ where $A_{j,i}$ is a corresponding element of A in Eq. (4). As a result, the intensity of o_i is represented:

$$o_i = A_{0,i}s_0 + A_{1,i}s_1 + \cdots + A_{j,i}s_j. \tag{10}$$

Each term has a non-negative value, and thus this leads the following constraint:

$$s_j \leq \frac{o_i}{A_{j,i}}. \tag{11}$$

From Eqs. (9) and (11), we can derive the following constraint:

$$0 \leq s_j \leq \min_{i \in \mathcal{X}_j}(\frac{o_i}{A_{j,i}}), \tag{12}$$

where $\mathcal{X}_j$ is a set of light rays j which hits to local region x_i on the diffuser B.

Above constraint can be formed as $s \in \mathcal{V}$, where $\mathcal{V}$ is a closed convex set. From Eq. (6), this formulation can be written as follows due to the orthogonality of the matrix Y:

$$Yc \in \mathcal{V}. \tag{13}$$

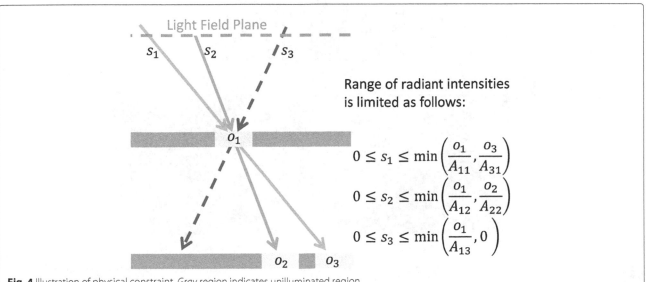

Fig. 4 Illustration of physical constraint. *Gray* region indicates unilluminated region

This constraint can be rewritten as a convex function using indicator function $\iota_{\mathcal{V}} : \mathbb{R}^M \to [0, \infty]$, which is defined by

$$\iota_{\mathcal{V}}(Yc) = \begin{cases} 0, & \text{if } Yc \in \mathcal{V}, \\ \infty, & \text{otherwise.} \end{cases} \quad (14)$$

5 Experiments

In this section, we verify the effectiveness of the proposed method using a real data set. We first compare our method with several kinds of approaches under different conditions. In these experiments, since the ground-truth light-field map is not available, we quantitatively verify the correctness of our algorithm by computing the photometric errors that is the difference between the captured image and the corresponding relit image using reconstructed light field in real scene. In the following, we call the least square as LS, ℓ_1-norm regularization as L1 and physical constraint as PC.

5.1 Setup

Figure 5a shows an overview of experimental setup in the dark room. An illumination source which is attached to the translation motorized stage is placed for illuminating the diffuser from variable distances. We have used

a polystyrene board as the diffuser, and we assumed the board has the Lambertian transmission property. A high dynamic range camera (ViewPLUS Xviii) with the resolution of 642×514 pixels is located at the opposite side of the diffuser from the light source and it captures images as shown in Fig. 5b. Upper 16-bit depth is used as intensity for each pixel. To reduce the noise effect of acquisition process for all the experiments, we used an average images of 256 images captured with fixed setup. To remove the perspective distortion effect in the captured images, we rectified the captured images so as to orthogonalize images whose each pixel size corresponds to $1 \times 1mm$ as shown in Fig. 5c. We have used these orthogonalized images as input images. The illumination distance d is defined as $0mm$ when the illumination source touches to the diffuser. In this experiment, a light field plane $\mathcal{L}$ is defined in the coordinate system of the light source at the position of the diffuser plane with $d = 0mm$, for efficiently representing all the 4-D rays emitted from the light source. With above setup, we have estimated light field maps using designated points which are extracted from the saturated areas on a close-up image. Unless otherwise stated, we have used four input images for estimating the light field, the parameter of $\lambda = 0.01$ in Eq. (8) and the dimension F of the real spherical harmonics function is set to 34.

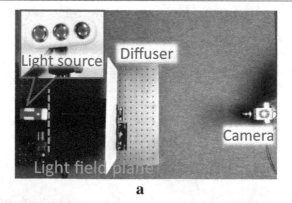

Fig. 5 Experimental setup. **a** Setup for measurement and flashlight with lens and reflector. **b** Captured image for distance $100mm$. **c** Rectified image for distance $100mm$

It should be noted that, some reconstructed light fields have negative radiant intensities. In this experiment, we permit a negative intensity for generating relit images.

5.2 Quantitative evaluation

In this section, we have employed a comparatively simple light source shown in Fig. 5a in which three LEDs are horizontally arranged. In this experiment, for making the discussion simple, we first gave three light source positions for 4-D light field on $\mathcal{L}$ by computing three center points of saturated regions on the image shown in Fig. 5c which is taken at the distance $d = 0mm$. We have estimated parameters of three anisotropic light sources for given three points as 4-D light field. We captured ten images of the lit diffuser, and in each image, the light source was at a different position. These zoomed images are shown in the top row of Fig. 6. Among these ten images, four images taken with the light source at distance $d = (60, 90, 120, 150mm)$ are used as input images and the rest are used for evaluation.

With this configuration, the relit images rendered by estimated 4-D/2-D light-fields from the following six methods are compared to show the effectiveness of the proposed method.

(I)   4-D light field reconstruction with L1 + PC,
(II) 4-D light field reconstruction with L1,
(III) 4-D light field reconstruction with PC,
(IV) 4-D light field reconstruction by LS without L1 and PC,
(V)   2-D light field reconstruction assuming an anisotropic point light source, and
(VI) 2-D light field reconstruction assuming a set of isotropic point light sources.

Here, (I)∼(III) are the variations of the proposed method and (IV) is the baseline method[3]. For the method (V), middle of given three light positions is used as a position of a point light source since (V) does not have the spatial dimension. For the method (VI), box-style region of the diffuser shown in Fig. 5c that contains 91×64 points is used as the spatial distribution of lights on $\mathcal{L}$.

Figure 7 shows light field maps estimated by the methods (I) to (VI). As we can see, each method gives different light fields. In the followings, we discuss the differences of above methods with further results.

5.2.1 Comparison of 4-D and 2-D light field reconstruction methods

Figure 6 shows relit images for various light positions rendered by estimated light fields shown in Fig. 7 for

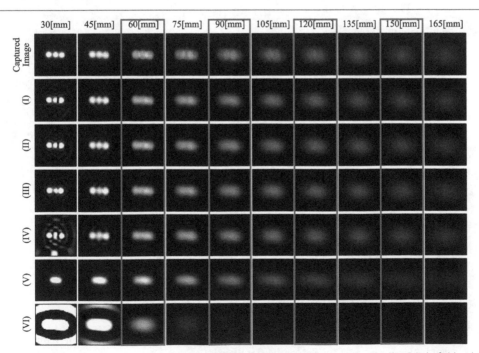

Fig. 6 Captured images and relit images by reconstructed light fields from compared methods with $F = 34$. (*I*) 4-D light field with L1 + PC, (*II*) 4-D light field with L1, (*III*) 4-D light field with PC, (*IV*) 4-D light field by LS without L1 and PC, (*V*) 2-D light field with an anisotropic point light source, (*VI*) 2-D light field with a set of isotropic point light sources. Dimension F of spherical harmonics function for (*I*)–(*V*) is set to 34. Surrounding *red boxes* indicate that these distances are included in a set of input images for light field estimation. Images are clipped for zooming-up

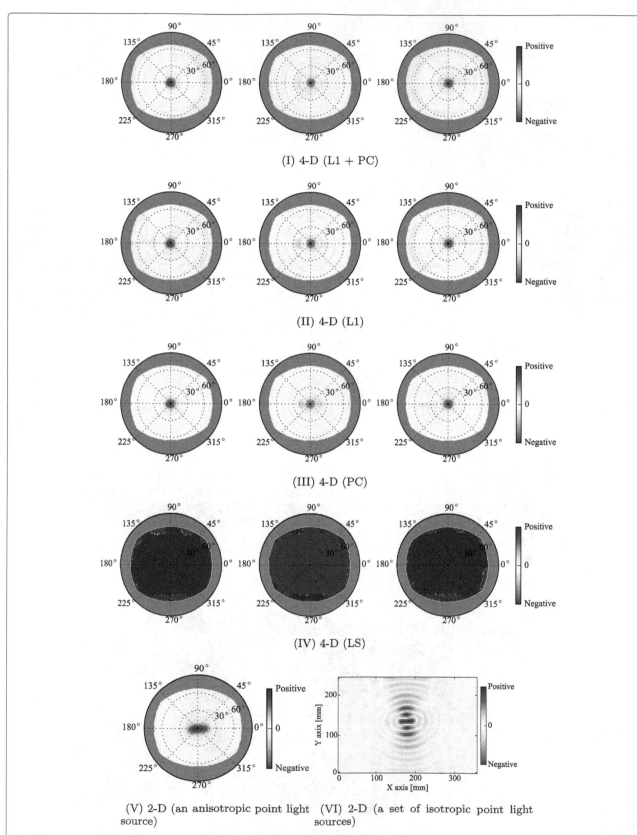

(I) 4-D (L1 + PC)

(II) 4-D (L1)

(III) 4-D (PC)

(IV) 4-D (LS)

(V) 2-D (an anisotropic point light source)   (VI) 2-D (a set of isotropic point light sources)

Fig. 7 Reconstructed light field maps for the light sources in Fig. 5a. *Gray color* indicates unobserved region

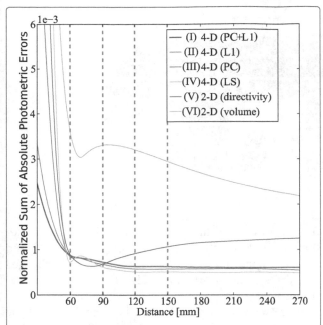

Fig. 8 Photometric errors between relit images and captured images. *Gray dashed lines* indicate positions of input images

all the compared methods. Figure 8 shows estimation errors which are defined as normalized sum of absolute intensity differences between a ground-truth image and a relit image. As we can see in Fig. 6, 4-D light field based methods (I)-(IV) could reproduce three separated lights on relit images for near range $d =[30, 45]$ despite

2-D based methods could not separate them. From Fig. 8, we can see that errors of both 2-D based methods are larger than that of 4-D based methods except for the range $d =[60, 90]$ of the method (V). It is considered that larger errors are due to over optimization of the method (V) for near range images. From the results of the methods (V) and (VI), it is obvious that the 2-D light field based methods do not have capability to reproduce good relit images for this light source. We can conclude that 4-D light field estimation is necessary even for a comparatively simple light source.

5.2.2 Effect of constraints
As shown in Figs. 6 and 8, there are very small quantitative and subjective differences in the results for middle to far range $d =[60, 165]$ among compared 4-D based methods. However, for near range $d = [30, 45]$, considerable differences are exposed. First, we can see unnatural ripples around the lights for the methods (I) to (IV). The ripples for (IV) are harder than others.

As shown in Fig. 7 (IV), LS gives large negative intensities in estimated light field and it has caused over parameter fitting problem. By comparing the pairs of {(I), (II)} and {(III), (IV)} in this figure, we can confirm that negative intensity on the estimated light field is successfully suppressed by using PC. Although we cannot see any subjective differences among relit images

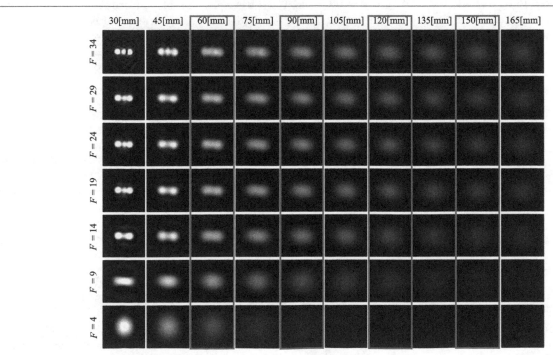

Fig. 9 Relit images by proposed method (I) with variable *F*. Surrounding *red boxes* indicate that these distances are included in a set of input images for light field estimation. Images are clipped for zooming-up

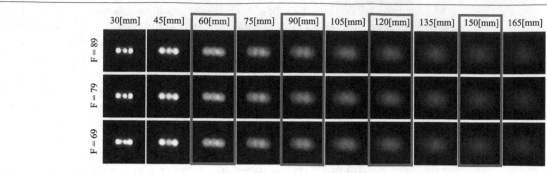

Fig. 10 Relit images by proposed method (I) with $F = 69, 79$, and 89

for (I), (II), and (III), quantitatively, the errors become smaller when we employed L1 and the method (I) which uses both PC and L1 gives the best scores for near range.

5.2.3 Effect of dimension

Here, we confirm the effect of dimensions for spherical-harmonics function on relit images. Figure 9 shows relit images for variable F for the proposed method (I). Because there are very small differences in far range images when F is 34 or larger, in Fig. 10, we have shown the images for near to middle range images for higher $F = 69, 79$ and 89.

Figure 11 shows estimation errors for them. As shown in these figures, the errors rapidly decrease as the dimension F is raised, slightly increasing then decreasing at around $F = 24$, but then eventually leveling out. This effect is considered to be caused by the difference of the definitions in photometric errors, as Fig. 11 shows the absolute photometric errors, but the proposed method's energy function, described in Eq. (8) minimizes the L2 norm of photometric errors. This effect is considered to

be caused by the difference of the definitions in photometric errors, although the errors in In Figs. 9 and 10, relit images for near range are continuously changed and the separation of three lights becomes clearer for higher F.

As shown in Figs. 9 and 10, We can confirm that the ripples artifacts appeared especially for the near rage of [30-45], become weaker when we can give more resolution for angle direction, i.e., F become higher. In the case, the model does not have enough resolution for angle direction, the model cannot represent both the details of shapes of lights and background region behind the lights. In this situation, from the characteristic of the spherical harmonic function, repetitive patterns easily appear in the image. On the other hand, the reason, why the ripples for (IV) become harder than others, is considered as an over-fitting problem of standard linear programming. Our method successfully reduced this error by convex optimization. Ripples around lights, mentioned in the previous section, are almost disappeared when $F = 89$. From these results, we can say that we need high dimensional parameters for spherical-harmonics function for accurate reconstruction of 4-D light field.

5.2.4 Effect of spacial resolution and arrangement of virtual light sources

Here, we confirm the effect of spacial resolution and arrangement of virtual light sources on relit images. Figure 12 shows the position of virtual light sources (a) to (e), and Fig. 13 shows relit images for them modeled by the proposed method (I). If some virtual light sources

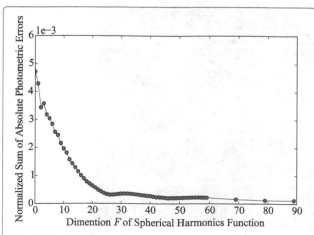

Fig. 11 Photometric errors between relit images and captured images for variable F

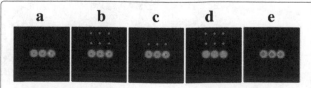

Fig. 12 Variational position of virtual light sources. A *red point* indicates a position of virtual light source

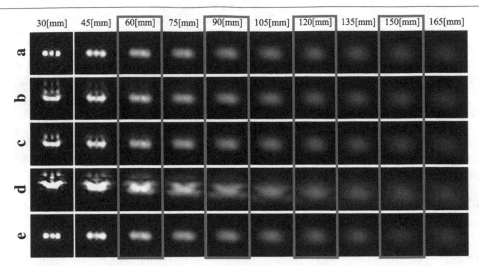

Fig. 13 Relit images by reconstructed light field from variable pattens of light source positions with $F = 34$. Each variable pattern of light source positions (**a**) - (**e**) corresponds to variational position of virtual light sources in Fig. 12. Surrounding *red boxes* indicate that these distances are included in a set of input images for light field estimation. Images are clipped for zooming-up

exist near the actual light sources positions (except (d) in Fig .12), they could reproduce a similar results with (a) for range $d = [60, 165]$.

However, in the range $d = [30, 45]$, different images are generated except for the images (a) and (e). For (a), we arranged virtual light sources at the center positions of highlights and for (e) number of point light sources are increased as shown in Fig. 12. From this comparison, we can say that as far as we can put virtual light sources in front of the true light positions (i.e., centers of highlights), good results will be given with minimum number of virtual light sources. By comparing (e) with $F = 69$ in Fig. 10, which have the same number of parameters with (e), we can see that latter result is better than (e)'s. It means the angle resolution is more important than the special resolution, as long as we can put virtual lights to appropriate positions. When we cannot arrange them for centers of highlights (case (d)), the relit image becomes different shapes from ideal ones. On the other hand, when we gave more virtual light sources to different positions from highlights, as shown in (b) and (c), undesired highlights appear on near range images. This is considered as the effect of an overfitting problem for these unnecessary positions. It should be noted that except for near range images, good results are obtained even for (b) and (c), and intensities of undesired highlights on near range images are also darker than those of true highlights. It is because the L1 norm suppress the value of coefficients by selecting an important basis of a spherical harmonic function.

5.2.5 *Computational cost*

In order to reconstruct 4-D light field with the method (I), it takes 31 h for $F = 34$ in this experiment using a PC (*intel⁶ core^{TM}* i7-3970 3.50GHz × 12, Memory 32 GB, C++ implementation). The core time for computation spent for solving a convex optimization problem in Eq. (8). In this experiment, 5.3 GB memory was required for our implementation. When we set $F = 89$, it takes more than 1 week for 4-D light field reconstruction. In order to reduce the cost, we should find more efficient bases for representing light field and efficient way for solving the problem.

5.3 Results for more complex lights

We have conducted further tests for the proposed method using more complex light sources shown in Fig. 14. In this experiment, we automatically set 35 light source positions for 4-D light field estimation by computing the center of saturated regions on the image with $d = 0mm$. Figures 15 and 16 show the captured images and relit images with

Fig. 14 Light sources used for further tests. **a** Triangularly-aligned shell type LED. **b** Flash light with lens and reflector

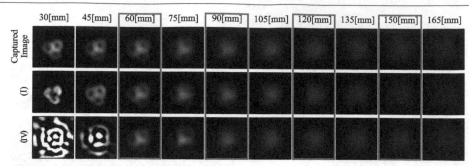

Fig. 15 Captured images of triangularly aligned shell type LED and relit images by reconstructed light field form two method: (*I*) 4-D light field with L1 + PC and (*IV*) 4-D light field by LS. Dimension *F* of spherical harmonics function of (*I*) and (*IV*) is 34, and 35 light source positions are used to reconstruct 4-D light field. Surrounding *red boxes* indicate that these distances are included in a set of input images for light field estimation

$F = 34$ in Fig. 14a, b, respectively. In these figures, the relit images by the proposed method with L1 and PC (I) and LS based method (IV) are compared.

The light source in Fig. 14a has three LEDs triangularly arranged. We can see that projected shape of each light looks like torus, and part of three shapes are overlapped as shown in Fig. 15. In the relit images, both the methods (I) and (IV) could reproduce good results for the position where input images were captured (red boxed images). However, the LS method (IV) gave completely different shapes for near range $d = [30, 45]$ due to the over fitting. In contrast, the proposed method (I) could reproduce much better relit images even for near range.

The light source in Fig. 14b is a flash light with lens and reflectors. For this light source, although the method (I) recovers higher frequency component in the relit images compared with the method (IV), relit results does not reach a satisfactory level as shown in Fig. 16. It is considered that the poor results are due to the lack of parameters to model the 4-D light field for this complex light, and more input images are also necessary to acquire stable results. At this moment, we need more computational resources to estimate this kind of complex 4-D light field in which virtual light source positions, arose by reflectors in the light, are spatially distributed.

6 Conclusion

In this paper, we have presented a novel 4-D light field reconstruction technique utilizing a physical constraint and a regularization. We have formulated the light field reconstruction problem as a convex optimization problem. This optimization problem was designed to decompose the observed intensities on the measurement plane into light ray intensities. Unlike conventional works, the proposed method can estimate the 4-D light field from a few images without special optics such as a mirror-array, a lens array, and filters. As shown in experiments, we could confirm the effectiveness of both the physical constraint and ℓ_1-norm regularization. A remaining weakness in the current implementation of the proposed method is the difficulty for increasing dimensions of parameters due to its high computational cost which prevents to handle more complex lighting environments. In order to relax this problem, we should find more efficient bases for representing the light model to reduce the computation cost, in future work.

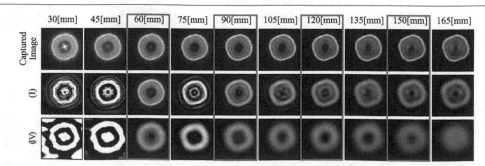

Fig. 16 Captured images of flash light and relit images by reconstructed light field form two method: (*I*) 4-D light field with L1 + PC and (*IV*) 4-D light field by LS. Dimension F of spherical harmonics function of (*I*) and (*IV*) is 34, and 35 light source positions are used to reconstruct 4-D light field. Surrounding *red boxes* indicate that these distances are included in a set of input images for light field estimation

Although we assumed the board has Lambertian-transmission property and scattering effect is ignored, which did not give obvious effects in the results in the experiment, for more precise reconstruction, calibration method for the diffuser board should be considered. In addition, we should confirm the sensitivity of the proposed method by using images with artificially added noises.

Endnotes

[1] In this equation, the intensity o_i is represented by a continuous system. The effect of the attenuation and incident angle are considered by the integral of ray j.

[2] In this paper, we regard ρ as constant by assuming the transmission property of the diffuser is Lambertian.

[3] For LS, we iteratively minimize the function from zero vector using conjugate gradient method, since B in Eq. (7) has small singular values due to the insufficient observations in this experiment. In this case, LS cannot give a unique solution or a stable solution by linear solvers.

Acknowledgements
This research was supported in part by JSPS KAKENHI Grant No. 23240024 and Grant-in-Aid for Exploratory Research Grant No. 25540086.

Authors' contributions
TA designed the study, performed the experiments, and drafted the manuscript. TS participated in the design of the study and helped to draft the manuscript. YM conceived of the study and participated in its design. NY gave technical support and conceptual advice. All authors discussed the results and implications and commented on the manuscript at all stages. All authors read and approved the final manuscript.

Competing interests
The authors declare that they have no competing interests.

References

1. Debevec P, Malik J (1997) Recoverring high dynamic range radiance maps from photo graphs. In: Proc. ACM SIGGRAPH. ACM, Los Angeles. pp 369–378
2. Hara K, Nishino K, Ikeuchi K (2003) Determining Reflectance and light position from a single image without distant illumination assumption. In: Proc. IEEE Conf. Computer Vision and Pattern Recognition. IEEE, Nice. pp 560–567
3. Park J, Sinha SN, Matsushita Y, Kweon I (2014) Calibrating a non-isotropic near point light source using a plane. In: Proc. IEEE Conf. Computer Vision and Pattern Recognition. IEEE, Ohio. pp 226–2274
4. Takai T, Nimura S, Maki A, Matsuyama T (2007) Self shadows and cast shadows in estimating illumination distribution. In: Proc. European Conf. on Visual Media Production. IEEE, England. pp 1–10
5. Ashdown I (1993) Near-field photometry : a new approach. J Illum Soc 27(4):1293–1301
6. Seigel MW, Stock RD (1996) A general near-zone light source model and its application to computer automated reflector design. SPIE Optical Eng 35(9):2661–2679
7. Rykowski RF, Wooley C (1997) Source modeling for illumination design. In: Lens Design, Illumination, and Optomechanical Modeling, SPIE Vol. 3130. pp 204–208
8. Jenkins DR, Monch H (2000) Source imaging goniometer method of light source characterization for accurate projection system design. In: Proc. of SID Conf. Blackwell Publishing Ltd. Vol. 31, No 1. pp 862–865
9. Unger J, Wenger A, Hawkins T, Gardner A, Debevec P (2003) Capturing and rendering with incident light fields. In: Proc. Eurographics symposium on rendering. ACM, Leuven. pp 141–149
10. Unger J, Gustavson S, Larsson P, Ynnerman A (2008) Free form incident light fields. Comput Graphics Forum 27(4):1293–1301
11. Goesele M, Granier X, Heidrich W, Seidel H-P (2003) Accurate lightsource acquisition and rendering. In: Proc SIGGRAPH. ACM, California. pp 621–630
12. Nakamura M, Oya S, Okabe T, Lensch H (2008) Acquiring 4D light fields of self-luminous extended light sources using programmable filter. ACM Trans Graphics 27(3):57:1–57:6
13. Cossairt O, Nayar S, Ramamoorthi R (2008) Light field transfer: global illumination between real and synthetic objects. Proc. ACM Graphics 27(3):57:1—57:6
14. Wang Y, Samaras D (2016) Estimation of multiple illuminants from a single image of arbitrary known geometry. IEICE Trans Inf Syst E99D(9):2360–2367
15. Frolova D, Simakov D, Basri R (2004) Accuracy of spherical harmonic approximations for images of Lambertian objects under far and near lighting. In: Proc. European Conf. on Computer Vision. Springer, Berlin. pp 574–587
16. Ramamoorthi R, Hanrahan P (2001) A signal-processing framework for inverse rendering. ACM Trans Graphics 12:117–128
17. Sato I, Sato Y, Ikeuchi K (2003) Illumination from shadows. IEEE Trans Pattern Anal Mach Intell 25(3):290–300
18. Okabe T, Sato I, Sato Y (2004) Spherical harmonics vs. Haar wavelets. In: Proc. IEEE Conf. Computer Vision and Pattern Recognition. IEEE, Washington. pp 50–57
19. Aoto T, Taketomi T, Sato T, Mukaigawa Y, Yokoya N (2013) Linear estimation of 4-D illumination light field from diffuse reflections. In: Proc. IAPR Asian Conference on Pattern Recognition. IAPR, Naha. pp 496–500
20. Gabay D, Mercier B (2004) A dual algorithm for the solution of nonlinear variational problems via finite element approximation. Comput Math Appl 23(9):1022–1027

5

A practical person authentication system using second minor finger knuckles for door security

Daichi Kusanagi, Shoichiro Aoyama, Koichi Ito[*] and Takafumi Aoki

Abstract

This paper proposes a person authentication system using second minor finger knuckles, i.e., metacarpophalangeal (MCP) joints, for door security. This system acquires finger knuckle patterns on MCP joints when a user takes hold of a door handle and recognizes a person using MCP joint patterns. The proposed system can be constructed by attaching a camera onto a door handle to capture MCP joints. Region of interest (ROI) images around each MCP joint can be extracted from only one still image, since all the MCP joints are located on the front face of the camera. Phase-based correspondence matching is used to calculate matching scores between ROIs to take into consideration deformation of ROIs caused by hand pose changes. Through a set of experiments, we demonstrate that the proposed system exhibits the efficient performance of MCP recognition and also show the potential possibilities of second minor finger knuckles for biometric recognition.

Keywords: Finger knuckle, Biometrics, Phase-only correlation, Door security, Metacarpophalangeal joint

1 Introduction

A hand has a lot of biometric traits such as fingerprint, palmprint, finger/palm vein, finger knuckle, and hand geometry. Among such traits, a finger knuckle is a relatively new biometric trait in contrast with famous biometric traits such as face, fingerprint, and iris [1]. An outer surface of a finger has three knuckles: a distal interphalangeal (DIP) joint, a proximal interphalangeal (PIP) joint, and a metacarpophalangeal (MCP) joint as shown in Fig. 1. Kumar et al. [2] categorized three finger joints into major and minor finger knuckles, where a DIP joint is a first minor finger knuckle, a PIP joint is a major finger knuckle, and an MCP joint is a second minor finger knuckle. It is easy to capture such patterns on a finger knuckle by a camera. This advantage allows us to develop a flexible and compact biometric authentication system. A finger knuckle is also expected to be distinctive as well as a fingerprint and a palmprint, although statistical analysis using a huge dataset has to be required to demonstrate the uniqueness of finger knuckle patterns [2]. This paper focuses on the use of finger knuckle patterns to develop a person authentication system for door security.

Table 1 shows a summary of researches on finger knuckle recognition. Most researches [3–17] focused on recognition algorithms for texture patterns of PIP joints and evaluated its performance using a public finger knuckle image database such as the PolyU FKP database [18]. The images in the PolyU FKP database are captured under the controlled conditions, since the subject puts his/her finger on fixed blocks in order to reduce the spatial variations and capture clear line features of a finger knuckle. Although it is suitable for researchers to develop a fundamental recognition algorithm using finger knuckle patterns, it may not be practical. Most researches [6, 7, 11–16, 19] employed coding approaches to extract features by applying spatial filters to images and binarizing their responses, where a variety of types of Gabor filter are usually used as a spatial filter. Effectiveness of such coding approaches have been demonstrated in iris recognition [20] and palmprint recognition [21]. Some researches [8–10] employed local feature descriptors such as SIFT and SURF, which are used in the field of computer vision. Another approach [5, 12, 15, 17] employed Band-Limited Phase-Only Correlation (BLPOC), which is an

*Correspondence: ito@aoki.ecei.tohoku.ac.jp
Graduate School of Information Sciences, Tohoku University, 6-6-05, Aramaki Aza Aoba, Sendai, Japan

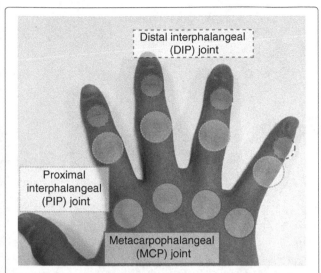

Fig. 1 A taxonomy of finger knuckle joints: *Blue-colored circles* indicate distal interphalangeal (DIP) joints, *green-colored circles* indicate proximal interphalangeal (PIP) joints, and *red-colored circles* indicate metacarpophalangeal (MCP) joints

image matching technique using the phase components in 2D Discrete Fourier Transforms (2D DFTs) of given images [22]. Among of them, some researches [15–17] exhibited efficient performance on person authentication using finger knuckle patterns.

There are also a few works on finger knuckle recognition under practical situations. Kumar et al. [4] have proposed a finger knuckle recognition algorithm using multiple patterns acquired from the index, middle, ring, and little fingers. They demonstrated that the matching score calculated by combining four PIP joints is effective for person authentication. Cheng et al. [19] have proposed a contactless PIP joint recognition system using a camera embedded on smartphones. This was the first attempt to develop a practical person authentication system using PIP joints for smartphones. Therefore, the recognition performance was not necessarily good. Aoyama et al. [23] have proposed a finger knuckle recognition system for a door handle. This system acquired PIP joint patterns when a user takes hold of a door handle and recognized a person using acquired patterns. Hence, the users do not pay attention to the authentication process. This system also used the combined information of the four knuckles to improve performance of finger knuckle recognition. Kusanagi et al. [24] have developed an improved version of Aoyama's system by using video sequences.

There are a few works on finger knuckle recognition using MCP and DIP joints compared with PIP joints. Kumar [25] has proposed a finger knuckle recognition algorithm using both major and first minor finger knuckle patterns, i.e., PIP and DIP joints. Combination of two

joint patterns improved performance of finger knuckle recognition. Kumar et al. [2] have also considered the use of texture patterns around MCP joints to identify persons. Both works gave us the fundamental investigation of biometric recognition using minor finger knuckle joints, since the performance has been evaluated using images of a hand with the fingers and thumb spread apart put on a flat plane.

This paper focuses on the use of second minor finger knuckles, i.e., MCP joints, for biometric recognition and develop a practical person authentication system using MCP joints. We consider person authentication using MCP joints for a door handle which is inspired by the concept of Aoyama's system [23]. Aoyama's system has to embed a camera into a door, since this system captures texture patterns on PIP joints when a user took hold of a door handle, resulting in increasing the cost. Local images around each PIP joint are not always extracted from only one still images suggested by Kusanagi et al. [24]. On the other hand, our proposed system uses MCP joints for person authentication. Texture patterns on MCP joints can be captured using a camera attached on a door handle. In this case, MCP joints are located on the front face of the camera. Therefore, a local image around each MCP joint can be extracted from only one still image. Phase-based correspondence matching [26] is used to calculate matching scores between MCP joint patterns as well as the conventional PIP joint recognition systems [23, 24]. Through a set of experiments, we demonstrate that the proposed system exhibits the efficient performance of MCP recognition and also shows the potential possibilities of minor finger knuckles for biometric recognition.

The main contributions of this work are summarized as follows:

1. This is the first attempt to use finger knuckle pattern on MCP joints for person authentication in a practical situation.
2. The prototype of a door security system using finger knuckle recognition is developed. The use of MCP joints makes it possible to develop a user-friendly person authentication system for door security.

2 Finger knuckle recognition system for door security

This section describes an overview of the proposed system. We develop the MCP joint recognition system inspired by the concept of finger knuckle recognition systems for door handles [23, 24].

Fingers have three joints, i.e., DIP, PIP, and MCP joints, as shown in Fig. 1. When a user takes hold of a door handle to open a door, it is easy to capture PIP and MCP joints by a camera. DIP joints are faced to the floor, and DIP joints of the index and middle fingers may be behind

Table 1 Summary of researches on finger knuckle recognition

Author	Joint	Finger	Feature	Similarity	Database
C. Ravikanth and A. Kumar [3]	PIP	I, M, R and L	Subspace (PCA, LDA and ICA)	Distance	Own (Flat plane)
A. Kumar and C. Ravikanth [4]	PIP	I, M, R and L	Subspace (PCA, LDA and ICA)	Distance	Own (Flat plane)
L. Zhang et al. [5]	PIP	I and M	BLPOC	Correlation	PolyU FKP DB
A. Kumar and Y. Zhou [6]	PIP	M	Modified Finite Radon Transform	Distance	Own (Flat plane)
L. Zhang et al. [7]	PIP	I and M	Improved Competitive Code and Magnitude Code	Distance	PolyU FKP DB
A. Morales et al. [8]	PIP	I and M	Orientation enhanced SIFT	Distance	PolyU FKP DB
Z. Le-qing [9]	PIP	M	SURF	Distance	PolyU FKP DB
G.S. Badrunath et al. [10]	PIP	I and M	SIFT and SURF	Distance	PolyU FKP DB
M. Xiong et al. [11]	PIP	I and M	Log Gabor Binary Patterns	Distance	PolyU FKP DB
L. Zhang et al. [12]	PIP	I and M	Competitive Code and BLPOC	Distance and correlation	PolyU FKP DB
L. Zhang et al. [13]	PIP	I and M	Riesz Competitive Code	Distance	PolyU FKP DB
Z.S. Shariatmadar and K. Faez [14]	PIP	I and M	Average Absolute Deviation and Gabor Filter	Distance	PolyU FKP DB
L. Zhang et al. [15]	PIP	I and M	Phase Congruency and BLPOC	Distance and correlation	PolyU FKP DB
G. Gao et al. [16]	PIP	I and M	Sparse Reconstruction and Adaptive Binary Fusion	Distance	PolyU FKP DB
S. Aoyama et al. [17]	PIP	I and M	Local Block Matching (BLPOC)	Correlation	PolyU FKP DB
K.Y. Chen and A. Kumar [19]	PIP	I	1D Log Gabor Filter	Distance	Own (Smartphone)
S. Aoyama et al. [23]	PIP	I, M and R	Correspondence Matching (BLPOC)	Correlation	Doorhandle
D. Kusanagi et al. [24]	PIP	I, M, R and L	Correspondence Matching (BLPOC)	Correlation	Own (Doorhandle)
A. Kumar [25]	DIP and PIP	M	Improved Local Binary Patterns and 1D Log Gabor Filter	Distance	Own (Flat plane)
A. Kumar and Z. Xu [2]	MCP	I, M, R and L	Local Radon Transform, Ordinal Code and BLPOC	Distance and correlation	Own (Flat plane)
Proposed	MCP	I, M, R and L	Correspondence Matching (BLPOC)	Correlation	Own (Doorhandle)

I index finger, M middle finger, R ring finger, and L little finger

the thumb. Therefore, DIP joints are not suitable to use person authentication for door security.

The conventional systems using PIP joints consist of a handle, a camera, and a light source, where the camera has to be located so as to face toward PIP joints. When a user takes hold of a door handle, the system captures an image or a video sequence and recognizes a user using PIP joint patterns. The advantage is that the image acquisition process is not intrusive, that is, the user only has to open the door by taking hold of the door handle. The disadvantage is that the shape of PIP joints may be varied in each image acquisition due to hand pose variations, resulting in decreasing the recognition performance. In addition, the camera and the light source have to be embedded into the door. Hence, the door has to be refined and it takes much cost.

According to the fundamental investigation by Kumar et al. [2], MCP joints have sufficient distinctiveness for person authentication as well as PIP joints. MCP joints can be captured by attaching a camera onto a door handle and using the ambient light. Therefore, only a little effort is required to make a system for MCP joint recognition compared with the case of PIP joint recognition. Moreover, the variation of MCP joints is smaller than that of PIP joints, when a user takes hold on a door handle.

To clarify the potential possibilities of MCP joint recognition based on the above consideration, we developed a prototype system for MCP joint recognition as shown in Fig. 2. Table 2 shows the specification of the developed system. The camera is located above the door handle, assuming that the camera is attached on the door. There is no light source, that is, the ambient light is used to take images, assuming the indoor use. Images captured by this system include illumination changes caused only by the ambient light. In practical situation, images include strong daylight, reflection, etc., resulting in images with halation and blur, which significantly decrease recognition performance. In order to take desired images for MCP joint recognition, an appropriate camera filter and an optional light source have to be used.

3 MCP joint recognition

This section describes the proposed MCP joint recognition algorithm, which consists of four steps: (i) image acquisition, (ii) region of interest (ROI) extraction, (iii) ROI matching, and (iv) score fusion. Figure 3 shows the flow diagram of the proposed algorithm. The detail of each step is described in the following.

3.1 Image acquisition

An image of back of a hand including the MCP joints of the index, middle, ring, and little fingers is captured under ambient light conditions using a camera located onto a

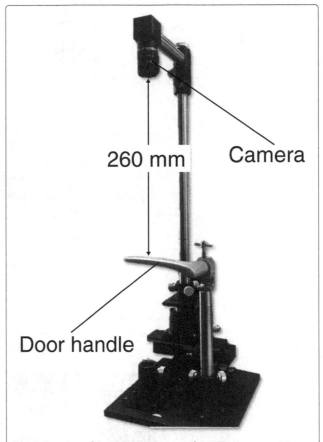

Fig. 2 Overview of the developed system for MCP joint recognition

door handle. Figure 4a shows an acquired input image by the developed system.

3.2 ROI extraction

This step extracts a ROI image from the captured hand image. The position of MCP joints is detected according to the valleys between fingers. The size of images is 1280 × 960 pixels as mentioned in Section 2. The captured image is resized into 640 × 480 pixels in order to reduce the amount of memory usage and the computation time, assuming that this algorithm is implemented on embedded systems. The input image is indicated by $f(n_1, n_2)$, where $1 \leq n_1 \leq 480$ and $1 \leq n_2 \leq 640$.

Table 2 Specification of the developed system

Camera	PointGrey FL3-U3-13E4C-C [31]
	Image size 1280 × 960 pixels
Lens	μ-tron 0420
	Focal length 15 mm
Light source	Ambient light

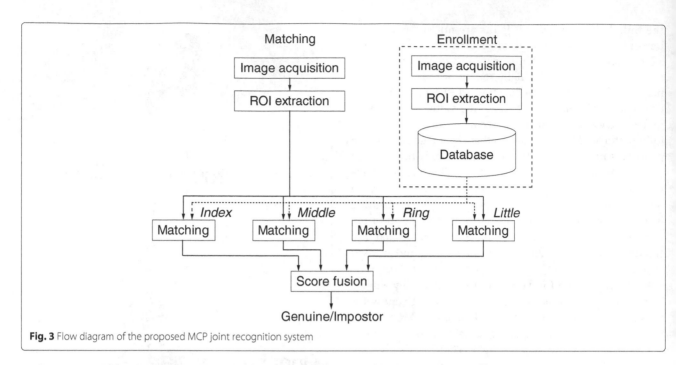

Fig. 3 Flow diagram of the proposed MCP joint recognition system

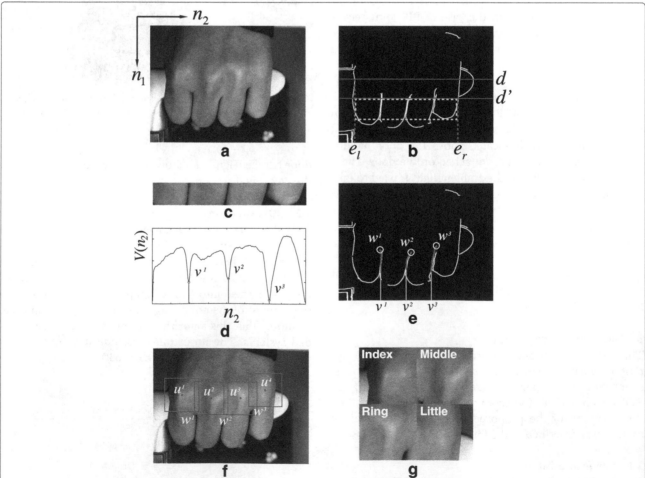

Fig. 4 MCP joint detection and ROI extraction. **a** Input image $f(n_1, n_2)$. **b** Edge image $f_e(n_1, n_2)$. **c** Region around fingers $f'(n_1, n_2)$. **d** Vertical projection $V(n_2)$. **e** Valley detection between fingers. **f** MCP joint detection. **g** Extracted ROI image for each finger

First, both ends of a hand are detected from the input image. The edge image $f_e(n_1, n_2)$ as shown in Fig. 4b is obtained by applying the Sobel filter to $f(n_1, n_2)$. The position between the camera and the door handle is fixed. Hence, the location of the door handle in the image is known in advance. Let d be the center of the handle in the vertical direction and d' be the coordinate of the end on the handle toward the door in the vertical direction as shown in Fig. 4b. In the case of the developed system, $d = 220$ and $d' = 300$. The horizontal coordinate of both ends of a hand is detected by

$$e_l = \min\{n_2|f_e(d, n_2) > 0\}, \tag{1}$$
$$e_r = \max\{n_2|f_e(d', n_2) > 0\}, \tag{2}$$

where e_l and e_r indicate the vertical coordinate of left and right ends of the hand, respectively. d' is used to detect e_r, since the right-sided end on the handle may be detected as the edge of the hand, if d is used.

Next, the vertical coordinate of each finger is obtained. To reduce the effect of background noise, the region $f'(n_1, n_2)$ located around the door handle is extracted from $f(n_1, n_2)$ as follows:

$$f'(n_1, n_2) = f(n_1, n_2)|_{320 \leq n_1 \leq 380, e_l \leq n_2 \leq e_r}. \tag{3}$$

As mentioned above, $f'(n_1, n_2)$ can be extracted from the fixed position of $f(n_1, n_2)$, since the relation between the camera and the handle is fixed in the developed system. The range $320 \leq n_1 \leq 380$ is empirically determined so as to extract the region between MCP and PIP joints in this paper. Figure 4c shows the extracted region $f'(n_1, n_2)$. The intensity value around the boundary between fingers is lower than others, and fingers are located in the vertical position. Hence, the boundary between fingers can be detected by projecting pixels of $f'(n_1, n_2)$ in the vertical direction. The vertical projection $V(n_2)$ of $f'(n_1, n_2)$ is calculated by

$$V(n_2) = \sum_{n_1} f'(n_1, n_2). \tag{4}$$

Figure 4d shows the result of vertical projection of $f'(n_1, n_2)$. The three local minima of $V(n_2)$ are detected as boundaries between fingers indicated by v^m ($m = 1, 2, 3$), where each index of m corresponds to the boundary between index and middle fingers, middle and ring fingers, and ring and little fingers, respectively.

Finally, the coordinates of each MCP joint are defined. The edge is tracked from each v_m to the valley between fingers using the boundary tracking algorithm [27] as shown in Fig. 4e. The coordinate of the end of each valley is indicated by $\mathbf{w}^m = (w_1^m, w_2^m)$. We can consider that the geometric relation among MCP joints and valleys is almost the same, since everyone has almost the same structure of a hand. Therefore, the rule-based approach

can be used to detect the coordinates of each MCP joint using valley location $\mathbf{w}^m$. The center coordinate of each MCP joint, $\mathbf{u}$, is defined by

$$\mathbf{u}^1 = (u_1^1, u_2^1) = \left(w_1^1 - 75, \frac{e^l + w_2^1}{2}\right), \tag{5}$$

$$\mathbf{u}^2 = (u_1^2, u_2^2) = \left(w_1^2 - 75, \frac{w_2^1 + w_2^2}{2}\right), \tag{6}$$

$$\mathbf{u}^3 = (u_1^3, u_2^3) = \left(w_1^2 - 75, \frac{w_2^2 + w_2^3}{2}\right), \tag{7}$$

$$\mathbf{u}^4 = (u_1^4, u_2^4) = \left(w_1^3 - 75, \frac{w_2^3 + e^r}{2}\right), \tag{8}$$

where $i = 1, 2, 3, 4$ and each index i corresponds to the index, middle, ring, and little fingers, respectively. The region with 150×150 pixels centered on $\mathbf{u}^i$ is extracted as the ROI image.

3.3 ROI matching

Phase-based correspondence matching [26] is used to calculate matching scores between ROI images, which employs (i) a coarse-to-fine strategy using image pyramids for robust correspondence search and (ii) a local block matching method using BLPOC. The image deformation is observed in ROI images captured in the different timing due to hand rotation, although ROI images extracted from MCP joints have smaller deformation than those from PIP joints. Such deformation can be approximated by small translations in a local area. Intensity variation can be observed in ROI images due to different illumination condition. BLPOC is one of the image matching methods robust against illumination changes. Therefore, we decide to employ phase-based correspondence matching as well as the conventional PIP joint recognition systems [23, 24].

Fundamentals of POC and BLPOC are briefly described in the following. Consider two $N_1 \times N_2$ images, $f(n_1, n_2)$ and $g(n_1, n_2)$, where the index ranges are $n_1 = -M_1, \cdots, M_1$ ($M_1 > 0$) and $n_2 = -M_2, \cdots, M_2$ ($M_2 > 0$) for mathematical simplicity, and hence $N_1 = 2M_1 + 1$ and $N_2 = 2M_2 + 1$. The discussion could be easily generalized to non-negative index ranges with power-of-two image size. Let $F(k_1, k_2)$ and $G(k_1, k_2)$ denote the 2D Discrete Fourier Transforms (DFTs) of $f(n_1, n_2)$ and $g(n_1, n_2)$, respectively. The normalized cross power spectrum $R_{FG}(k_1, k_2)$ is given by

$$R_{FG}(k_1, k_2) = \frac{F(k_1, k_2)\overline{G(k_1, k_2)}}{\left|F(k_1, k_2)\overline{G(k_1, k_2)}\right|}, \tag{9}$$

where $\overline{G(k_1, k_2)}$ is the complex conjugate of $G(k_1, k_2)$. The POC function $r_{fg}(n_1, n_2)$ is the 2D Inverse DFT (2D IDFT) of $R_{FG}(k_1, k_2)$ and is given by

$$r_{fg}(n_1, n_2) = \frac{1}{N_1 N_2} \sum_{k_1, k_2} R_{FG}(k_1, k_2) W_{N_1}^{-k_1 n_1} W_{N_2}^{-k_2 n_2}, \quad (10)$$

where $\sum_{k_1, k_2}$ denotes $\sum_{k_1=-M_1}^{M_1} \sum_{k_2=-M_2}^{M_2}$. When two images are similar, their POC function gives a distinct sharp peak. When two images are not similar, the peak drops significantly. The height of the peak gives a good similarity measure for image matching, and the location of the peak shows the translational displacement between the images. The idea of BLPOC is to eliminate meaningless high frequency components in the calculation of normalized cross power spectrum R_{FG} [22]. Assume that the ranges of the effective frequency band are given by $k_1 = -K_1, \cdots, K_1$ and $k_2 = -K_2, \cdots, K_2$, where $0 \leq K_1 \leq M_1$ and $0 \leq K_2 \leq M_2$. Thus, the effective size of frequency spectrum is given by $L_1 = 2K_1 + 1$ and $L_2 = 2K_2 + 1$. The BLPOC function is given by

$$r_{fg}^{K_1 K_2}(n_1, n_2) = \frac{1}{L_1 L_2} \sum_{k_1, k_2}' R_{FG}(k_1, k_2) W_{L_1}^{-k_1 n_1} W_{L_2}^{-k_2 n_2}, \quad (11)$$

where $n_1 = -K_1, \cdots, K_1$, $n_2 = -K_2, \cdots, K_2$, and $\sum_{k_1, k_2}'$ denotes $\sum_{k_1=-K_1}^{K_1} \sum_{k_2=-K_2}^{K_2}$. Note that the maximum value of the correlation peak of the BLPOC function is always normalized to 1 and does not depend on L_1 and L_2.

Phase-based correspondence matching consists of a coarse-to-fine strategy using image pyramids and a local block matching method using BLPOC. Let $\mathbf{p}$ be a coordinate vector of a reference point in the ROI image $I(n_1, n_2)$ registered in the database. In this paper, the number of reference points is 10×10. The problem of correspondence matching is to find a coordinate vector $\mathbf{q}$ in the input ROI image $J(n_1, n_2)$ that corresponds to the reference pixel $\mathbf{p}$ in the registered ROI image $I(n_1, n_2)$. The procedure of phase-based correspondence matching is briefly described in the following.

Step 1: For $l = 1, 2, \cdots, l_{\max} - 1$, create the l-th layer images $I^l(n_1, n_2)$ and $J^l(n_1, n_2)$, i.e., coarser versions of $I^0(n_1, n_2)$ and $J^0(n_1, n_2)$, recursively as follows:

$$I^l(n_1, n_2) = \frac{1}{4} \sum_{i_1=0}^{1} \sum_{i_2=0}^{1} I^{l-1}(2n_1 + i_1, 2n_2 + i_2),$$

$$J^l(n_1, n_2) = \frac{1}{4} \sum_{i_1=0}^{1} \sum_{i_2=0}^{1} J^{l-1}(2n_1 + i_1, 2n_2 + i_2).$$

Step 2: For every layer $l = 1, 2, \cdots, l_{\max}$, calculate the coordinate $\mathbf{p}_l = (p_1^l, p_2^l)$ corresponding to the original reference point $\mathbf{p}^0$ recursively as follows:

$$\mathbf{p}^l = \lfloor \tfrac{1}{2} \mathbf{p}^{l-1} \rfloor = \left(\lfloor \tfrac{1}{2} p_1^{l-1} \rfloor, \lfloor \tfrac{1}{2} p_2^{l-1} \rfloor \right), \quad (12)$$

where $\lfloor z \rfloor$ denotes the operation to round the element of z to the nearest integer toward minus infinity.

Step 3: We assume that $\mathbf{q}^{l_{\max}} = \mathbf{p}^{l_{\max}}$ in the coarsest layer. Let $l = l_{\max} - 1$.

Step 4: From the l-th layer images $I^l(n_1, n_2)$ and $J^l(n_1, n_2)$, extract two small images $f^l(n_1, n_2)$ and $g^l(n_1, n_2)$ with their centers on $\mathbf{p}^l$ and $2\mathbf{q}^{l+1}$, respectively. The size of image blocks is $W \times W$ pixels.

Step 5: Estimate the displacement between $f^l(n_1, n_2)$ and $g^l(n_1, n_2)$ using BLPOC. Let the estimated displacement vector be $\boldsymbol{\delta}^l$. The l-th layer correspondence $\mathbf{q}^l$ is determined as follows:

$$\mathbf{q}^l = 2\mathbf{q}^{l+1} + \boldsymbol{\delta}^l. \quad (13)$$

Step 6: Decrement the counter by 1 as $l \leftarrow l - 1$ and repeat from Step 4 to Step 6 while $l \geq 0$.

Step 7: From the original images $I^0(n_1, n_2)$ and $J^0(n_1, n_2)$, extract two image blocks with their centers on $\mathbf{p}^0$ and $\mathbf{q}^0$, respectively. Calculate the BLPOC function between the two blocks. The peak value of the BLPOC function is obtained as a measure of reliability in local block matching. Finally, we obtain the corresponding point pairs and their reliability.

In this paper, we employ parameters: $l_{\max} = 2$, $W = 48$, $K_1/M_1 = K_2/M_2 = 0.5$ for BLPOC.

The matching score is calculated according to the corresponding point pairs and their reliability. If the reliability, i.e., the peak value of BLPOC function, is below the threshold, the corresponding point pair is removed as outliers. We empirically confirmed that high recognition rate is obtained when the threshold is set from 0.2 to 0.5. The best result is obtained when the threshold is 0.3 in this paper. Figure 5 shows an example of correspondence matching. In the case of the genuine pair, the location of corresponding points on the registered image represents deformation between registered and input images. In addition, the reliability of almost all of corresponding point pairs exceeds the threshold. On the other hand, in the case of the impostor pair, the location of corresponding points on the registered image is random. This means that the translational displacement between the images cannot be estimated correctly. The reliability of almost all of corresponding point pairs is below the threshold. According to the above, the number of reliable corresponding points is used to evaluate the similarity between ROI images. The matching score S^i for each finger is defined by

$$S^i = \frac{\text{\# of corresponding point pairs}}{\text{\# of reference points}}, \quad (14)$$

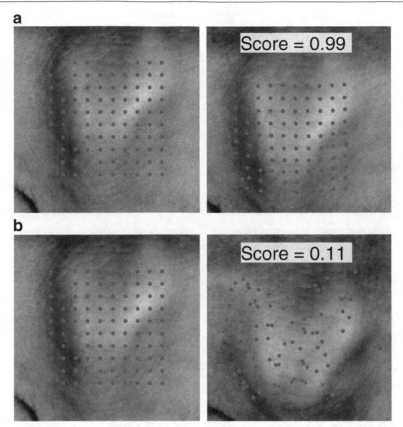

Fig. 5 Result of phase-based correspondence matching for middle fingers. **a** Genuine pair and **b** Impostor pair. The *left* is the input image and the *right* is the registered image, where *red dots* indicate corresponding point pairs and *blue dots* indicate outliers, i.e., their reliability is below threshold

where $i = 1, 2, 3, 4$ and each index i corresponds to the index, middle, ring, and little fingers, respectively.

3.4 Score fusion

The matching scores are calculated from four finger knuckles as mentioned above. To enhance the recognition performance, the final matching score S is calculated by combining all the matching scores. There are some approaches to combine matching scores [28]. We decide to use the simple sum rule, taking into consideration the performance and the computation time. The final matching score S is defined by

$$S = \sum_{i=1}^{4} S_i. \tag{15}$$

4 Experiments and discussion

This section describes experiments to evaluate performance of MCP joint recognition using the proposed system.

A hand image database is created using the proposed system as shown in Fig. 2. Images are collected from 28 subjects in two separate sessions, where the time interval between the first and second sessions is more than 1 week.

The size of images is 1280×960 pixels as mentioned in Section 2. In each session, five images are captured from the left and right hands. To increase the number of combinations, we assume that the left and right hand images taken from the same subject are different from each other. The mirror-reversed image of the left hand image is used in the experiments. As a result, the database contains 560 images with 56 subjects and 10 different images of each subject. The number of genuine pairs is 2520 ($= {}_{10}C_2 \times 56$), and the number of impostor pairs is 154,000 ($= {}_{56}C_2 \times 10 \times 10$).

Figure 6 shows examples of hand images and extracted ROI images. In the case of the developed system, all the ROIs can be extracted correctly. On the other hand, in the case of the finger knuckle recognition system using PIP joints, ROIs cannot be always extracted from captured hand images as described in [23, 24]. Therefore, the use of MCP joints makes it possible to achieve stable ROI extraction compared with that of PIP joints. There are two experiments: Experiment 1 uses each finger and Experiment 2 uses multiple fingers. The recognition performance is evaluated by a Receiver Operating Characteristic (ROC) curve and an Equal Error Rate (EER) [1].

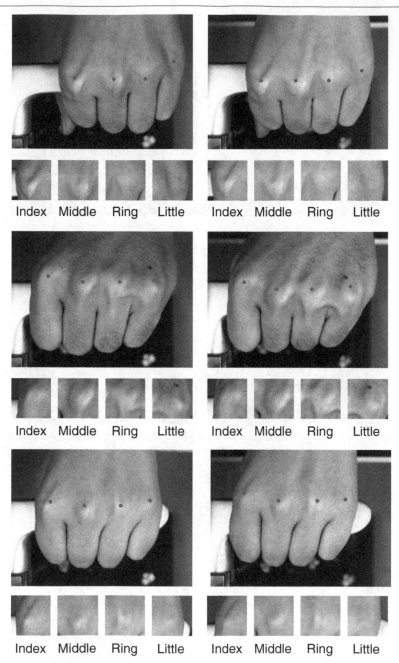

Fig. 6 Images in the database: Images in each row are captured from the same person, and *left* and *right columns* indicate 1st and 2nd sessions, respectively. Four small images below the acquired hand image are ROI images extracted from each MCP joint and *red points* indicate the detected MCP joints

The performance of the proposed method is compared with the conventional finger knuckle matching methods such as BLPOC [2, 5], CompCode [29], and LGIC [12]. BLPOC is used for PIP joints in [5] and MCP joints in [2]. The BLPOC function between two ROI images is calculated by Eq. (11), and its maximum peak value is obtained as a matching score. CompCode (competitive code) proposed by Kong et al. [30] is generated by applying a bank of Gabor filters with orientation parameters. ROI images are coded as orientations having the maximum response for each pixel. The matching score is calculated by the Hamming distance. LGIC, i.e., local-global information combination, is a combination of BLPOC and Comp-Code. BLPOC is used to extract global features, while CompCode is used to extract local features. A translational displacement between ROI images is estimated by

BLPOC, and the common areas are extracted according to the estimated displacement. A global matching score between common areas is calculated by BLPOC, while a local matching score is calculated by CompCode. The final matching score is obtained by a weighted sum of global and local matching scores. Kumar et al. [2] have suggested that BLPOC exhibited the best performance in finger knuckle recognition of MCP joints from their fundamental investigation. On the other hand, Zhang et al. [12] demonstrated that LGIC exhibited better performance than BLPOC in finger knuckle recognition of PIP joints. Hence, we decided to compare the performance of the proposed method with BLPOC, CompCode, and LGIC.

4.1 Experiment 1

Experiment 1 evaluates recognition performance for each finger such as the index, middle, ring, and little fingers. Figure 7 shows ROC curves for each finger, and Table 3 shows the summary of EERs for each finger and each matching method. BLPOC exhibits low performance for the index, ring, and little fingers, although BLPOC shows good performance on MCP joint pattern recognition in [2]. The global BLPOC-based methods [2, 5] can handle only the translational displacement between images. Therefore, the recognition performance is decreased,

since there is nonlinear deformation between ROI images due to hand pose changes. CompCode [29] exhibits the worst performance for the index, middle, and ring fingers, since CompCode can handle small translational displacement between images. LGIC [12] show better performance than BLPOC and CompCode, since LGIC is a combination of BLPOC and CompCode. On the other hand, the proposed method using phase-based correspondence matching exhibits the best performance for all the fingers compared with other methods, since phase-based correspondence matching can take into account nonlinear image deformation. The EER of the little finger is the highest for all the methods. The ROI image of the little finger includes large perspective deformation compared with those of other fingers. The position of the little finger is unstable compared with other fingers. As a result, the large deformation is caused even for a small hand pose change. In the case of using PIP joints, EERs of the index and little fingers are higher than those of other fingers, since image deformation of PIP joints on the index and little fingers is larger than that of MCP joints.

4.2 Experiment 2

Experiment 2 evaluates recognition performance for the combination of adjacent 2~4 fingers such as the (i) index

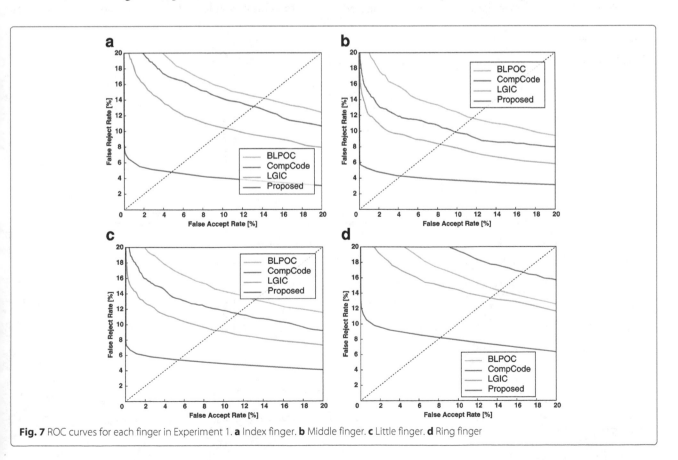

Fig. 7 ROC curves for each finger in Experiment 1. **a** Index finger. **b** Middle finger. **c** Little finger. **d** Ring finger

Table 3 EERs [%] for each finger knuckle recognition algorithm in Experiment 1

Algorithm	Index	Middle	Ring	Little
BLPOC	13.00	9.83	11.38	16.64
CompCode	13.74	11.45	13.11	14.03
LGIC	10.20	8.23	9.13	13.07
Proposed	3.99	4.07	4.22	7.36
PIP joint [23]	14.46	3.69	4.82	11.81
PIP joint [24]	9.96	4.83	6.09	17.52

EERs of PIP joint [23] and [24] are presented as a reference for discussion

and middle fingers, (ii) middle and ring fingers, (iii) ring and little fingers, (iv) index, middle, and ring fingers, (v) middle, ring, and little fingers, and (vi) all the four fingers. Figure 8 shows ROC curves for each combination, and Table 4 shows the summary of EERs for each combination and each matching method. Note that recognition performance when combining little fingers and other fingers was not evaluated in [23]. The extraction rate of ROIs in [23] was 46% for index fingers, 86% for middle fingers, 84.2% for ring fingers, and 27.8% for little fingers. The number of genuine pairs is not enough to evaluate performance when combining little fingers and other fingers, since the number of ROIs of little fingers is significantly small compared

with other fingers. The fused matching score is calculated by the sum rule as mentioned in Section 3.4. Combining multiple fingers improves recognition performance compared with the single finger use. When combining more than three finger knuckles, recognition performance of the methods is significantly improved. In all the cases, the recognition performance of the proposed method is the highest compared with other methods. The EER when combining four MCP joints for the proposed method is 2.36% as shown in Table 4. In the case of using PIP joints, EER was 1.54% combining middle and ring fingers [23] and 2.08% combining four fingers [24], although all the ROIs cannot be extracted from hand images. The advantage of the proposed method compared with [23] and [24] is that ROIs can be extracted from all the fingers and the matching score can be calculated from the combination of all the fingers. This advantage is important to develop a user-friendly person authentication system, since the conventional methods [23] and [24] may need multiple image acquisition even for the authenticated user to extract ROIs. The number of genuine pairs combining middle and ring fingers of [23] is 1166, which is 64.78% of all the possible combination of genuines and the number of genuine pairs combining four fingers of [24] is 1901, which is 84.49% of all the possible combination of genuines. Therefore, the use of MCP joints makes it possible to achieve stable and reliable person authentication

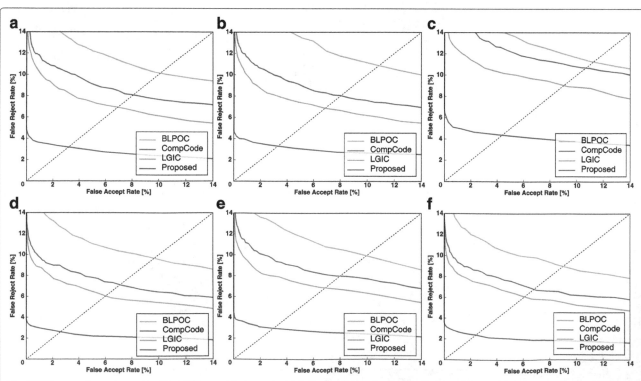

Fig. 8 ROC curves for each combination of fingers. **a** Index and middle fingers. **b** Middle and ring fingers. **c** Ring and little fingers. **d** Index, middle, and ring fingers. **e** Middle, ring, and little fingers. **f** all the fingers

Table 4 EERs [%] for each matching algorithm in Experiment 2

Algorithm	I+M	M+R	R+L	I+M+R	M+R+L	I+M+R+L
BLPOC	8.04	8.03	10.51	6.94	7.88	6.68
CompCode	9.97	10.80	11.13	9.62	9.41	8.82
LGIC	6.61	6.85	8.63	5.86	6.70	5.88
Proposed	2.84	3.02	4.19	2.50	2.50	2.36
PIP joint [23]	1.82	1.54	—	—	—	—
PIP joint [24]	2.72	2.98	4.89	2.19	2.94	2.08

EERs of PIP joint [23] and [24] are presented as a reference for discussion
I index finger, M middle finger, R ring finger, and L little finger

compared with that of PIP joints because of performance on ROI extraction and matching.

We also consider the other experiment which evaluates the recognition performance when the database is separately used as 1st and 2nd sessions. Table 5 shows the summary of EERs in this experiment. EERs are lower than those when images in both sessions are used. This result indicates that hand pose is significantly different between 1st and 2nd sessions even for the same person. To improve recognition performance for hand pose variation, we have to introduce geometric correction in preprocessing and employ the matching algorithm robust against large image deformation.

4.3 Computation time

The computation time of the proposed algorithm is evaluated using MATLAB R2013a on Intel Core i5-4250U (1.3 GHz). The computation time for ROI extraction and ROI matching is 141 and 91 ms, respectively.

5 Conclusion

This paper proposed a person authentication system using MCP joints for door security. The proposed system can be constructed by attaching a camera onto a door handle. This system can be applied to the existing doors with simple construction compared with the conventional systems

Table 5 EERs [%] for each matching algorithm in 1st session (upper) and 2nd session (lower)

Algorithm	I	M	R	L	I+M+R+L
BLPOC	6.93	4.10	7.32	8.67	3.31
	7.61	4.09	4.97	10.47	2.98
CompCode	7.29	5.26	6.76	8.59	4.06
	6.39	6.84	7.24	8.17	3.36
LGIC	5.13	3.46	6.48	6.78	3.09
	4.73	3.09	4.08	7.81	2.43
Proposed	1.61	2.01	2.85	3.03	0.77
	2.22	1.24	1.40	4.02	0.78

I index finger, M middle finger, R ring finger, and L little finger

using PIP joints for a door handle which need to embed a camera into a door. ROI images around each MCP joint can be extracted from only one still image, since MCP joints are located on the front face of the camera. ROI images captured in the different timing include deformation due to hand pose changes. The use of phase-based correspondence matching makes it possible to calculate reliable matching scores when ROI images have deformation compared with conventional methods. Through a set of experiments, we demonstrated that the proposed system exhibits the efficient performance of MCP recognition. Person authentication using finger knuckles may be difficult to introduce high security access applications such as border controls, since further investigation is required to demonstrate the uniqueness and the distinctiveness of finger knuckle patterns. On the other hand, this paper presented the potential possibilities of minor finger knuckles for biometric recognition. The proposed system will be acceptable for commercial applications such as building access control due to its convenience. In future, we will develop a multiple finger knuckle recognition system which employs major and minor finger knuckles.

A preliminary version of this paper is presented in ACPR 2015 [32].

Acknowledgements
This work was supported, in part, by JSPS KAKENHI Grant Numbers 15H02721.

Authors' contributions
DK carried out this study, made a database, performed the experiments, and drafted the manuscript. SA carried out this study, performed the experiments and their analysis, and helped to draft the manuscript. KI conceived of the study, performed the analysis of the experimental results, and drafted the manuscript. TA participated in the design and coordination of this study and helped to draft the manuscript. All authors read and approved the final manuscript.

Competing interests
The authors declare that they have no competing interests.

References
1. Jain AK, Flynn P, Ross AA (2008) Handbook of biometrics. Springer, US
2. Kumar A, Xu Z (2014) Can we use second minor finger knuckle patterns to identify humans? Proc IEEE Comput Soc Conf Conf Comput Vis Pattern Recognit Workshop:106–112
3. Ravikanth C, Kumar A (2007) Biometric authentication using finger-back surface. Proc IEEE Comput Soc Conf Conf Comput Vis Pattern Recognit:1–6
4. Kumar A, Ravikanth C (2009) Personal authentication using finger knuckle surface. IEEE Trans Inf Forensic Secur 4(1):98–110
5. Zhang L, Zhang L, Zhang D (2009) Finger-knuckle-print verification based on band-limited phase-only correlation. Lect Notes Comput Sci (CAIP2009) 5702:141–148
6. Kumar A, Zhou Y (2009) Personal identification using finger knuckle orientation features. Electron Lett 45(20):1023–1025
7. Zhang L, Zhang L, Zhang D, Zhu H (2010) Online finger-knuckle-print verification for personal authentication. Pattern Recog 43:2560–2571
8. Morales A, Travieso CM, Ferrer MA, Alonso JB (2011) Improved finger-knuckle-print authentication based on orientation enhancement. Electron Lett 47(6):380–381
9. Le-qing Z (2011) Finger knuckle print recognition based on SURF algorithm. Proc Int'l Conf Fuzzy Syst Knowl Discov:1879–1883

10. Badrinath GS, Nigam A, Gupta P (2011) An efficient finger-knuckle-print based recognition system fusing SIFT and SURF matching scores. Proc Intl' Conf Inf Commun Secur:374–387

11. Xiong M, Yang W, Sun C (2011) Finger-knuckle-print recognition using LGBP. Proc Int'l Conf Adv Neural Netw Part II:270–277

12. Zhang L, Zhang L, Zhang D, Zhu H (2011) Ensemble of local and global information for finger-knuckle-print recognition. Pattern Recognit 44:1990–1998

13. Zhang L, Li H, Shen Y (2011) A novel Riesz transforms based coding scheme for finger-knuckle-print recognition. Proc Int'l Conf Hand-Based Biom:1–6

14. Shariatmadar ZS, Faez K (2011) An efficient method for finger-knuckle-print recognition based on information fusion. Proc Int'l Conf Signal Image Process Appl:210–215

15. Zhang L, Zhang L, Zhang D, Guo Z (2012) Phase congruency induced local features for finger-knuckle-print recognition. Pattern Recog 45:2522–2531

16. Gao G, Zhang L, Yang Y, Zhang L, Zhang D (2013) Reconstruction based finger-knuckle-print verification with score level adaptive binary fusion. IEEE Trans Image Process 22(12):5050–5062

17. Aoyama S, Ito K, Aoki T (2014) A finger-knuckle-print recognition algorithm using phase-based local block matching. Inform Sci 268:53–64

18. PolyU FKP Database. http://www4.comp.polyu.edu.hk/~biometrics/. Accessed 8 Apr 2016

19. Cheng KY, Kumar A (2012) Contactless finger knuckle identification using smartphones. Proc Int'l Conf Biom Spec Interest Group:1–6

20. Burge MJ, Bowyer K (2013) Handbook of iris recognition. Springer-Verlag, London

21. Kong A, Zhang D, Kamel M (2009) A survey of palmprint recognition. Pattern Recog 42(7):1408–1418

22. Ito K, Nakajima H, Kobayashi K, Aoki T, Higuchi T (2004) A fingerprint matching algorithm using phase-only correlation. IEICE Trans Fundam E87-A(3):682–691

23. Aoyama S, Ito K, Aoki T (2013) A multi-finger knuckle recognition system for door handle. Proc Int'l Conf Biom Theory Appl Syst O-18:1–7

24. Kusanagi D, Aoyama S, Ito K, Aoki T (2014) Multi-finger knuckle recognition from video sequence: extracting accurate multiple finger knuckle regions. Proc Int'l Joint Conf Biom 1–8

25. Kumar A (2012) Can we use minor finger knuckle images to identify humans? Proc Int'l Conf Biom Theory Appl Syst 55–60

26. Ito K, Iitsuka S, Aoki T (2009) A palmprint recognition algorithm using phase-based correspondence matching. Proc Int'l Conf Image Process 1977–1980

27. Gonzalez RC, Woods RE (1992) Digital image processing. Pearson Education, New Jersey

28. Ross AA, Nandakumar K, Jain AK (2006) Handbook of multibiometrics. Springer, US

29. Zhang L, Zhang L, Zhang D (2009) Finger-knuckle-print: a new biometric identifier. Proc Int'l Conf Image Process 1981–1984

30. Kong AW-K, Zhang D (2004) Competitive coding scheme for palmprint verification. Proc Int'l Conf Pattern Recog 1:520–523

31. Flea3 1.3 MP Color USB3 Vision, Point Grey Research Inc. https://www.ptgrey.com/flea3-13-mp-color-usb3-vision-e2v-ev76c560-camera. Accessed 8 Apr 2016

32. Kusanagi D, Aoyama S, Ito K, Aoki T (2015) A person authentication system using second minor finger knuckles for door handle. Proc Asian Conf Pattern Recog OS9-01:1–5

6

Co-occurrence context of the data-driven quantized local ternary patterns for visual recognition

Xian-Hua Han[1*], Yen-Wei Chen[2] and Gang Xu[2]

Abstract

In this paper, we describe a novel local descriptor of image texture representation for visual recognition. The image features based on micro-descriptors such as local binary patterns (LBP) and local ternary patterns (LTP) have been very successful in a number of applications including face recognition, object detection, and texture analysis. Instead of binary quantization in LBP, LTP thresholds the differential values between a focused pixel and its neighborhood pixels into three gray levels, which can be explained as the active status (i.e., positively activated, negatively activated, and not activated) of the neighborhood pixels compared to the focused pixel. However, regardless of the magnitude of the focused pixel, the thresholding strategy remains fixed, which would violate the principle of human perception. Therefore, in this study, we design LTP with a data-driven threshold according to Weber's law, a human perception principle; further, our approach incorporates the contexts of spatial and orientation co-occurrences (i.e., co-occurrence context) among adjacent Weber-based local ternary patterns (WLTPs, i.e., data-driven quantized LTPs) for texture representation. The explored WLTP is formulated by adaptively quantizing differential values between neighborhood pixels and the focused pixel as negative or positive stimuli if the normalized differential values are large; otherwise, the stimulus is set to 0. Our approach here is based on the fact that human perception of a distinguished pattern depends not only on the absolute intensity of the stimulus but also on the relative variance of the stimulus. By integrating co-occurrence context information, we further propose a rotation invariant co-occurrence WLTP (RICWLTP) approach to be more discriminant for image representation. In order to validate the efficiency of our proposed strategy, we apply this to three different visual recognition applications including two texture datasets and one food image dataset and prove the promising performance that can be achieved compared with the state-of-the-art approaches.

Keywords: Local ternary pattern, Data-driven quantization, Weber's Law, Co-occurrence statistic, Visual recognition

1 Introduction

Visual recognition has posed a significant challenge to the research community of computer vision due to interclass variability, e.g., illumination, pose, and inclusion. The rich context of an image makes the semantic understanding (object, pattern recognition) very difficult. Although the community has spent a lot of effort on image-categorization classification [1–4], which leads to very powerful intermediate representation of images such as the bag-of-feature (BoF) model [5, 6], it still has some

space to improve the recognition performance in some specific recognition applications such as texture, food image, and biomedical data. The main idea of the popular BoF model is to quantize local invariant descriptors, for example, obtained by some interest point detector techniques [7, 8] and a description with SIFT [9], into a set of visual words [6]. The frequency vector of the visual words then represents the image, and an inverted file system is used for efficient comparison of such BOFs. Therein, the local descriptors for microstructure representation are often untouched, using standard, expert-provided ones such as the SIFT [9], PCA-Sift [10], and HOG [11], which result in a similar performance for image recognition. Further, since the learned codebook in BOF model has

*Correspondence: hanxh1216@gmail.com
[1]Graduate School of Science and Technology for Innovation, Yamaguchi University, Yamaguchi 753-8511, Japan
Full list of author information is available at the end of the article

of high diversity and irregularity, it is difficult to integrate the context information of co-occurrence for image representation.

On the other hand, microstructure simply using pixel neighborhoods as small as 3×3 pixels for local pattern representation has been proven to be possibly powerful for discriminating texture information, where the most popular one is a local binary pattern (LBP). LBP [12–14] characterizes each 3×3 local patch (microstructure) into a binary series by comparing the surrounding pixel intensity with the center one, which sets the bit of the surrounding pixel as 1 if its intensity is lager than the center one, otherwise 0. LBP is robust against uniform changes, and also easy for extension owing to the regularly decimated levels for all neighborhood pixels. However, due to the lack of spatial relationships among local textures, there have still serious disadvantages in the original LBP representation. Therein, an extension of the LBP called CoLBP [15, 16], has been proposed by considering the co-occurrence (spatial context) among adjacent LBPs, which proved promising performances on several classification applications [6]. In addition, by integrating orientation context, Nosaka et al. [17, 18] explored a rotation invariant co-occurrence among LBP, which is shown to be more discriminant on image classification compared to CoLBP. Qi et al. [19] proposed a pairwise rotation invariant CoLBP for texture representation and achieved the promising recognition performances in several visual recognitions.

Although LBP-based descriptors showed promising performances compared to other feature representations, it is obvious that LBP only thresholds the differential values between neighborhood pixels and the focused one to 0 or 1, which is very sensitive to noise existing in the processed image. Tan et al. extended LBP to local ternary pattern (LTP) [20], which considers the differential values between neighborhood pixels and the focused one as no or negative/positive stimulus, and successfully applied for face recognition under difficult lighting conditions. Given a pre-set positive threshold η, LTP [20] can obtain a series of ternary values for local pattern representation. However, regardless of the magnitude of the focused pixel, the pre-set threshold η remains fixed, which would violate the principle of human perception. Therefore, following the fact that human perception of a pattern depends not only on the absolute intensity of the stimulus but also on the relative variance of the stimuli, we propose to quantize the ratio between the neighborhood and the center pixels, which is equivalent to adaptively (data-driven) decide the quantization point according to the magnitude of the focus pixel. This proposed quantization strategy is inspired by Weber's law, a psychological law [21], which states that the noticeable change of a stimulus such as sound or lighting by a human being is a constant ratio of the original stimulus. When the stimulus has small magnitude, small change can be noticeable. Thus, we propose a data-driven quantized local ternary pattern (WLTP) based on Weber's law, which gives the activation status of the neighborhood pixels by data-driven thresholding the noticeable change according to the stimulus of the focus pixel: positively activated (magnitude: 1) if the ratio between the stimulus change and the focused one is larger than a constant η, negatively activated (magnitude: -1) if the change ratio is smaller than $-\eta$, not activated (magnitude: 0) otherwise. By incorporating a co-occurrence (here, i.e., spatial and orientation) context, we extend the proposed WLTP to a rotation invariant co-occurrence WLTP (RICWLTP), which is robust to image rotation and has the high descriptive ability among WLTP co-occurrences. Compared with the-state-of-the-art methods, our proposed strategy can achieve much better performance results for several visual recognitions including two texture datasets and one food image dataset.

2   Related work

In computer vision, local descriptors (i.e., features computed over limited spatial support) have been proved well adapted for matching and recognition tasks, as they are robust to partial visibility and clutter. The current popular one for local descriptors is SIFT feature, which is proposed in [9]. With the local SIFT descriptor, usually there are two types of algorithms for object recognition. One is to match the local points with SIFT features in two images, and the other one is to use the popular bag-of-feature model (BOF), which forms a frequency histogram of a predefined visual words for all sampled region features [6]. However, the extraction of SIFT descriptor itself is time-consuming, and then matching a large amount of them or quantizing them into a histogram in a large number of visual words, which are generally needed in BOF model for acceptable recognition of images, also exhausts a lot of time. On the other hand, some research works [22, 23] also have shown that it is possible to discriminate between texture patterns using pixel neighborhoods as small as 3×3 pixel region, which demonstrated that despite the global structure of the images, very good discrimination could be achieved by exploiting the distributions of such pixel neighborhoods. Therefore, exploiting such microstructures for representing images in the distributions of local descriptors has gained much attention and has led to state-of-the-art performances [24–28] for different classification problems in computer vision. The basic one of these approaches is local binary patterns (LBPs) introduce by Ojala et al. [22] as a means of summarizing local gray-level structures. As noted above, LBP is a simple yet efficient texture operator that labels pixels of an image by establishing thresholds for the neighborhood of each pixel based on the value of the central pixel; the result is a binary number associated with each neighborhood pixel. For image representation, LBP index histogram is generally calculated as feature. Unfortunately, because of the packed single histogram, spatial relations among the LBPs are mostly discarded; thus, it results in the loss of global image information. Motivated by the co-occurrence concept such as in Co-HOG [29–31] and joint haar-like features [30], Nosaka et al. [17, 18] proposed to integrate context information (i.e., spatial and orientation) into the conventional LBP for achieving high descriptive capacity in image representation; the similar extension of LBP for integrating context information also can be seen in the recent work [19].

However, the LBP-based descriptors only set differential values between neighborhood pixels and the focused pixel to zero or one, and then it has high sensitivity to noise in the processed image that in turn degrades discriminant of image representation. Thus, as noted above, Tan et al. extended LBP to a local ternary pattern (LTP) approach [20], which considers differential values between neighborhood pixels and the focused pixel as either a negative/positive stimulus or no stimulus whatsoever. Next, the series of ternary values are combined into an LTP index. Given intensities $[I(\mathbf{x}), I(\mathbf{x} + \triangle\mathbf{x}_1), \cdots, I(\mathbf{x} + \triangle\mathbf{x}_l), \cdots, I(\mathbf{x} + \triangle\mathbf{x}_{L-1})]$ of focused pixel $\mathbf{x}$ and its L neighbors $\mathbf{x} + \triangle\mathbf{x}_l$ (displacement vector), LTP thresholds differential values $[I(\mathbf{x}+\triangle\mathbf{x})_0 - I(\mathbf{x}), \cdots, I(\mathbf{x}+\triangle\mathbf{x}_l) - I(\mathbf{x}), \cdots, I(\mathbf{x}+\triangle\mathbf{x}_{L-1}) - I(\mathbf{x})]$ as

$$G(I(\mathbf{x}+\triangle\mathbf{x}_l)-I(\mathbf{x})) = \begin{cases} 1 & I(\mathbf{x}+\triangle\mathbf{x}_l) - I(\mathbf{x}) > \eta \\ -1 & I(\mathbf{x}+\triangle\mathbf{x}_l) - I(\mathbf{x}) < -\eta \\ 0 & \text{otherwise} \end{cases}$$

(1)

where η is the pre-set constant for thresholding the differential values. Then, the LTP index at $\mathbf{x}$ is defined as

$$LTP(\mathbf{x}) = \sum_{l=0}^{L-1} [G(I(\mathbf{x} + \triangle\mathbf{x}_l) - I(\mathbf{x})) + 1] \, 3^l$$

(2)

In the above equation, regardless of the magnitude of the focused pixel, the pre-set threshold η in LTP remains fixed, which violates the principle of human perception.

3 Data-driven quantized LTP and co-occurrence context

3.1 Weber's law

Ernst Heinrich Weber, an experimental psychologist in the nineteenth century, approached the study of the human response to a physical stimulus in a quantitative fashion and observed that the ratio of the increment threshold to the background intensity is a constant [32]. This observation shows that the just noticeable difference

(JND) between two stimuli is proportional to the magnitude of the stimuli, which is well known as Weber's law and can be formulated as:

$$\frac{\triangle I}{I} = a$$

(3)

where $\triangle I$ denotes the increment threshold (just noticeable difference for discrimination) and I denotes the initial stimulus intensity; a is known as the *weber fraction*, which indicates that the proportion on the left hand of the equation remains constant in spite of the variance in I. Simply speaking, Weber's Law states that the size of the just noticeable difference is a constant proportion (a times) of the original stimulus value, which is the minimum amount that stimulus intensity must be changed in order to produce a noticeable variation in sensory experience.

3.2 Weber-based LTP: WLTP

According to Weber's law, the JND of a focused pixel in relation to its neighboring pixels is proportional to the intensity $I(\mathbf{x})$ of the focused pixel. Thus, we quantize different values $[I(\mathbf{x} + \triangle\mathbf{x}_0) - I(\mathbf{x}), \cdots, I(\mathbf{x} + \triangle\mathbf{x}_l) - I(\mathbf{x}), \cdots, I(\mathbf{x} + \triangle\mathbf{x}_{L-1}) - I(\mathbf{x})]$ between a focused pixel $\mathbf{x}$ and its $L - 1$ neighbors $\{\mathbf{x} + \triangle\mathbf{x}_l\}(l = 0, 1, \cdots, L - 1)$ to form a ternary series as follows:

$$G\left(\frac{I(\mathbf{x} + \triangle\mathbf{x}_l) - I(\mathbf{x})}{I(\mathbf{x}) + \alpha}\right) = \begin{cases} 1 & \frac{I(\mathbf{x}+\triangle\mathbf{x}_l)-I(\mathbf{x})}{I(\mathbf{x})+\alpha} > \eta \\ -1 & \frac{I(\mathbf{x}+\triangle\mathbf{x}_l)-I(\mathbf{x})}{I(\mathbf{x})+\alpha} < -\eta \\ 0 & \text{otherwise} \end{cases}$$

(4)

where η is a predefined constant and α is a constant that avoids the case in which there is zero intensity (i.e., no stimulus); we always set α to one in our experimentation. Equation (3) adaptively quantizes differential values between the focus pixel and its neighboring pixels into a series of ternary codes; the WLTP index at $\mathbf{x}$ is defined as

$$\text{WLTP}(\mathbf{x}) = \sum_{l=0}^{L-1} \left[G\left(\frac{I(\mathbf{x} + \triangle\mathbf{x}_l) - I(\mathbf{x})}{I(\mathbf{x}) + \alpha}\right) + 1 \right] 3^l \quad (5)$$

In general LBP, neighborhood pixel number L is usually set to 8. Due to the detailed quantization (i.e., the ternary representation instead of binary), L is set to 4 to reduce computational cost. The lth displacement vector $\triangle\mathbf{x}_l$ is formulated as $\triangle\mathbf{x}_l = (\mathbf{r}\cos(\theta_l), \mathbf{r}\sin(\theta_l))$, where $\theta_l = \frac{360°}{L}l$ and r is the scale parameter (i.e., the distance from the neighboring pixels to the focused pixel) of WLTP. As a result, as shown in Fig. 1, WLTPs have $N_P = 81 (=3^L)$ possible patterns.

3.3 Integration of spatial and orientation contexts

LTP and WLTP discard information regarding spatial relationships between adjacent patterns; such information

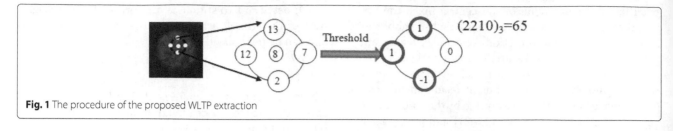

Fig. 1 The procedure of the proposed WLTP extraction

would be crucial to describing texture information for images. In this study, we first integrate the spatial context between the adjacent LTPs and WLTPs via co-occurrence information (called as CoLTP and CoWLTP, respectively). Without losing generalization, we describe the strategy of context integration for the proposed WLTP, while the same procedure can also be feasible by replacing WLTP with LTP. To obtain statistics of the co-occurrence (i.e., the spatial context) between two adjacent WLTPs, we consider the $N_P \times N_P$ auto-correlation matrix defined as:

$$H_{p,q}^\varphi = \sum_{x \subset I} \delta_{p,q} \left(\text{WLTP}(x), \text{WLTP}(x + \triangle x_\varphi) \right) \quad (6)$$

$$\delta_{p,q}(z_1, z_2) = \begin{cases} 1 & \text{if } z_1 = p \text{ and } z_2 = q \\ 0 & \text{otherwise} \end{cases}$$

where $p, q(=[0, 1, \cdots, N_P - 1])$ are possible pattern indexes for the two adjacent WLTPs and φ is the angle that determines the positional relations between the two WLTPs, which formulates displacement vector $\triangle x_\varphi = (d \cos \varphi, d \sin \varphi)$ with interval d. Then, co-occurrence matrix dimension is 6561 $(= N_P \times N_P)$.

Further, because of the possible different imaging viewpoints, rotation invariant (i.e., orientation context) is generally an indispensable characteristic for texture image representation. Thus, we also integrate orientation context among adjacent WLTPs and propose a rotation invariant co-occurrence WLTPs that would contribute much higher descriptive capability for image representation. We first denote two pairs of WLTP patterns, $P_{\varphi=0}^{\text{WLTP}} = [\text{WLTP}(x), \text{WLTP}(x + \triangle x_{\varphi=0})]$ and $P_\varphi^{\text{WLTP}} = [\text{WLTP}^\varphi(x), \text{WLTP}^\varphi(x + \triangle x_\varphi)]$, where $\text{WLTP}(x)$ gives the 4-b clockwise ternary digits with the first digit in

the right-horizontal direction ($\varphi = 0$), and $\text{WLTP}(x + \triangle x_{\varphi=0})$ is the co-occurrence WLTP in the $\varphi = 0$ direction; $\text{WLTP}^\varphi(x)$ and $\text{WLTP}^\varphi(x + \triangle x_\varphi)$ indicate the rotated entire WLTP pair with rotation angle φ. Thus, the rotation invariant statistics can be formulated if we assign the same index to P_φ^{WLTP} regardless of the different rotations designated by φ. Because we only used four neighbors of the focused pixel, only four rotation angles (i.e., $\varphi = 0°, 90°, 180°, 270°$) are available for computing rotation invariant statistics as shown in Fig. 2 (i.e., four equivalent WLTP pairs). According to the assigned labels for rotation invariant WLTP, the valid co-occurrence patterns can be reduced from 6561 to 2222. To efficiently calculate the rotation invariant co-occurrence of WLTP, we use mapping table $\mathbf{M}$ according to the algorithm shown in Table 1; the algorithm is to generate mapping table that converts a WLTP pair to an equivalent rotation index. In Table 1, $\text{shift}((p)_3, l)$ means circle-shift l bits of the transformed ternary digits of p. With the calculated mapping table, statistics of the rotation invariant co-occurrence WLTP can be formulated as

$$H_{M(\text{Index})}^{RI} = \sum_{x \subset I} \bigcup_\varphi \delta^{\text{index}} \left[M(\text{WLTP}^\varphi(x), \text{WLTP}^\varphi(x + \triangle x_\varphi)) \right] \quad (7)$$

$$\delta^{\text{index}}(z) = \begin{cases} 1 & \text{if } z = \text{index} \\ 0 & \text{otherwise} \end{cases}$$

where $M(\text{WLTP}^\varphi(x), \text{WLTP}^\varphi(x + \triangle x_\varphi))$ is the index of the rotation invariant co-occurrence between two WLTP pairs (RICWLTP). Finally, the statistics (i.e., histogram) of

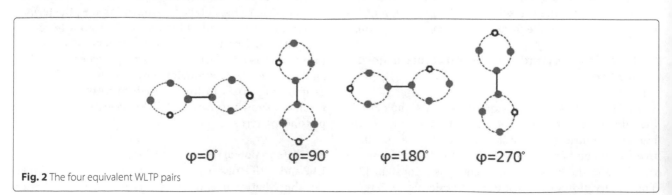

Fig. 2 The four equivalent WLTP pairs

Table 1 Calculation of mapping table between the WLTP pair and the rotation equivalent index

---

Mapping table generation algorithm

Input: Number of neighbor pixel L

Output: Mapping table **M** ($N_P \times N_P$ matrix)

Initialization: $Index=1, N_P = 3^L$, **M** $\Leftarrow \{null\}^{N_P \times N_P}$

for: $p = 0, \cdots, N_P - 1$ and $q = 0, \cdots, N_P - 1$

if $M(p, q) = null$, **then**

$M(p, q) \Leftarrow Index, p' \Leftarrow shift((p)_3, 2),$

$q' \Leftarrow shift((q)_3, 2), M(q', p') \Leftarrow Index$

$p' \Leftarrow shift((p)_3, 1),$

$q' \Leftarrow shift((q)_3, 1), M(p', q') \Leftarrow Index$

$p' \Leftarrow shift((p)_3, 3),$

$q' \Leftarrow shift((q)_3, 3), M(q', p') \Leftarrow Index$

$Index \Leftarrow Index + 1$

end if

end for

---

the RICWLTP can be used for discriminated representations of images. Similarly, if we formulate the Eq. (6) based on LTP instead of WLTP, the index of the rotation invariant co-occurrence between two LTP pairs (RICLTP) can be formed and then the statistics (i.e., histogram) of the RICLTP can be used for image representations.

3.4 Dimension analysis of LBP/LTP-based statistics

In general LBP, the used neighborhood pixel number L is usually set to 8, which results in 256 (2^8: 8 binary series) LBP indexes and the possible pattern value for any 3×3 local patch is ranged in $[0, 255]$. Thus, the LBP histogram for image representation has the dimension 256. The direct context integration considering the index combination of the adjacent LBP pairs would intuitively lead to a 256×256 co-occurrence matrix, where each element denotes the number of the LBP pairs with the same index combination in the image, and the reformed vector of the co-occurrence matrix is used as image representation with 65,536 (256^2) dimension. The high dimension of image representation results in high computational cost for the following classification procedure. Therefore, Nasaka et al. [17, 18] only adopted 4 ($L = 4$) neighborhood pixel number for producing 16 (2^4) LBP indexes, and then explored the co-occurrence statistics of LBP pairs (Co-LBP) and rotation invariant co-occurrence (RICLBP), which generated very compact LBP-based descriptors 256 $((2^4)^2)$ and 136 dimensional features, respectively. On the other hand, although Qi et al. [19] set the neighborhood pixel number L as 8, not all 256 LBP indexes are used for exploring co-occurrence of LBP pairs to avoid high-dimensional feature. In [19], the authors integrated the

low-frequency appeared LBP indexes into one group for retaining a small number of LBP indexes (uniform LBP: ULBP, 59 patterns), and then further produced the rotation invariant uniform LBP (RIU-LBP, only 10 patterns) as the basic pair patterns. The co-occurrence matrix is formed by counting the number of the adjacent ULBP and RIU-LBP pairs with the combination indexes, which produces the matrix with a size of 59×10. The reformed vector as image representation is 590 in dimension and in [19], further integrating two different configurations of pair combination that generated 1180-dimensional features.

In (W)LTP-based descriptors, if the neighborhood pixel number L is set as 8, the number of LTP indexes is 6561 (3^8: 8 ternary series). In addition, the context integration considering the index combination of the adjacent (W)LTP pairs would generate an extremely large size of co-occurrence matrix (656×6561), which results in a 43,046,721-dimensional feature and is infeasible for post-processing. Thus, this study explores four neighborhood pixels for (W)LTP-based descriptors. For the simple histogram of the LTP and WLTP indexes (3^4: 4 ternary series), 81-dimensional image feature can be obtained, and the co-occurrence statistics (called CoLTP and CoWLTP) have the dimension 6561 (81^2). After considering the orientation-invariant property, our proposed RICLTP and RICWLTP produce a 2222-dimensional feature for image representation. Basically, the computational cost for extracting the LBP- and LTP/WLTP-based descriptors mainly depends on the pattern and pair-pattern index numbers, and thus, high-dimensional (W)LTP-based descriptors would lead to high computational cost. This is also a reason that this study applies only four neighborhood pixels, and it is also possible to explore different neighborhood structures for integrating more context information and multiscale patterns in our proposed RICWLTP, which is left to the future work.

4 Experiments
4.1 Data sets and methodology

We evaluated our proposed framework on two texture datasets and one food image dataset.

(i) Two texture datasets: the first one is Brodatz32 [33] that is a standard dataset for texture recognition, and the second one is KTH-TIPS 2a [34], a dataset for material categorization [35]. In Brodatz32 dataset, three additional images are generated by (i) rotating, (ii) scaling, and (iii) both rotating and scaling an original sample. We use the standard protocol [36], of randomly splitting the dataset into two halves for training and testing and report average performance over 10 random splits. KTH-TIPS 2a dataset contains 11 materials, e.g., cork, wool, linen, with images of four physical, planar samples for each material. The samples were photographed at nine scales, three poses, and four different illumination conditions. It consists of 4395 images, most of which have the size of 200 × 200. All these variations on scale pose and illumination make it an extremely challenging dataset. For KTH-TIPS 2a texture dataset, we use the same evaluation protocol [36, 37] and report the average performance over four runs, where every time all images of one sample are taken for a test while the images of the remaining three samples are used for training.

(ii) Food dataset: Pittsburgh fast-food image dataset (PFID) [38], which is a collection of fast food images and videos from 13 chain restaurants, are acquired under lab and realistic settings. In our experiments, we focus on the set of 61 categories of specific food items (e.g., McDonald's Big Mac) with masked background. Each food category contains three different instances of the food (bought on different days from different branches of the restaurant chain) and six-viewpoint images (60° apart) of each food instance. We follow the experimental protocol in the published work [39] and perform threefold cross-validation for our experiments, using the 12 images from two instances for training and the 6 images from the third for testing. This procedure is repeated three times by using a different instance serving as the test set, and average performance is calculated as the results. The protocol ensures that no image of any given food item ever appears in both the training and test sets and guarantees that food items were acquired from different restaurants on different days. Two standard baseline algorithms, color histogram + SVM and bag of features with SIFT as the local descriptors + SVM, are shown for compared evaluation. In the baseline algorithm, the standard RGB color histogram with four quantization levels per color component is extracted to generate a $4^3 = 64$-dimensional representation for a food image, and a multi-class SVM is applied for classification. On the other hand, the BOF strategy combining a SVM classifier uses the histogram (low-order statistics) of visual words (representative words) with SIFT local descriptors. Recently, Yang et al. proposed Statistics of Pairwise Local Features (SPLF) [39] for food image representation, and the evaluation on PFID dataset showed the best performance on the state-

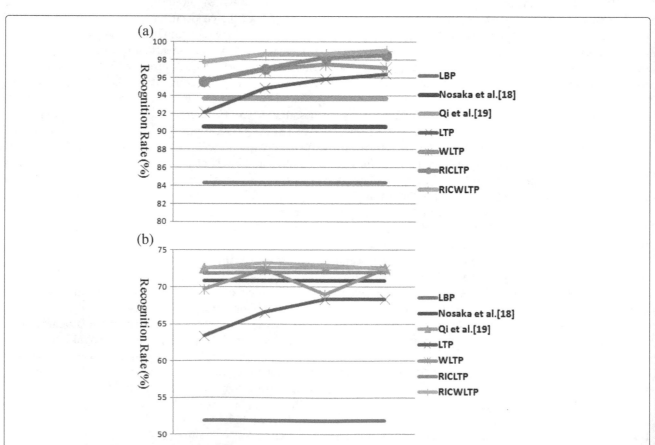

Fig. 3 Comparative results using our proposed framework and the conventional LBP-based descriptors by Nosaka et al. [17, 18] and Qi et al. [19]; *Horizontal axes* denotes the changed parameter with η introduced in Sections 2 and 3 for LTP, WLTP, RICLTP, and RICWLTP. Since there are no parameters in LBP-based descriptors, the recognition accuracies for LBP, the works by Nosaka et al. and Qi et al. remain the same in these graphs. **a** Bradatz dataset. **b** KTH-TIP 2a dataset

of-art methods, which are also as the compared results to our strategy.

4.2 Experimental results

We investigate the recognition performances using the statistics of our proposed WLTP, co-occurrence (i.e., spatial and orientation) context integration in WLTP, the corresponding versions without the using of Weber's law (not data-driven quantization, denote as LTP and RICLTP) and the conventional LBP and its extensions by Nosaka et al. [17, 18] and Qi et al. [19], which also incorporate the co-occurrence context into LBP. After obtaining the LBP/LTP-based features for image representation, we simply use linear support vector machine (SVM) due to its efficiency compared to the nonlinear one, for classification. In addition, we also pre-process the LBP/LTP-based histogram with the square root operation as the following:

$$\mathbf{P}'(\mathbf{I}) = \left[p_1'(\mathbf{I}), p_2'(\mathbf{I}), \cdots, p_L'(\mathbf{I}) \right]$$
$$= \left[\sqrt{p_1(\mathbf{I})}, \sqrt{p_2(\mathbf{I})}, \cdots, \sqrt{p_L(\mathbf{I})} \right] \quad (8)$$

where $\left[p_1(\mathbf{I}), p_2(\mathbf{I}), \cdots, p_L(\mathbf{I}) \right] = \mathbf{P}(\mathbf{I})$ is the raw LBP/LTP/WLTP, context-integrated co-occurrence of LBP as the works by Nosaka et al. and Qi et al., and our proposed features, and L is the dimension of the focused features. $\mathbf{P}'(\mathbf{I})$ is the pre-processed or normalized histogram, which is used as the input of SVM for classification. With the above normalization, we can enhance some local patterns with low absolute frequency (values in histogram) in an image but large relative difference when comparing two images. Furthermore, a linear SVM with the processed features can also be explained as a nonlinear classification strategy using the raw LBP/LTP histogram, which is equivalent to using Hellinger Kernel in the raw feature space.

As introduced in Section 3, the (W)LTP and their context integration versions, RIC(W)LTP in the proposed framework is formulated by quantization procedure with a predefined (data-driven) threshold η. Figure 3 shows the comparative recognition performances using the features in works by Nosaka et al. and Qi et al., LBP, and the conventional LTP, the proposed WLTP, RICLTP, and

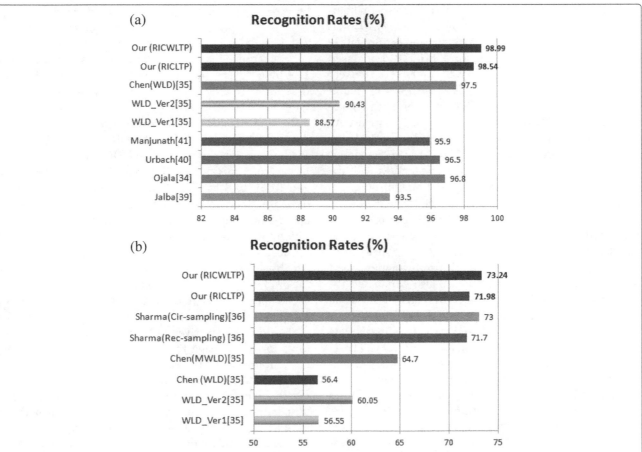

Fig. 4 Comparative results using our proposed framework and the state-of-the-art methods on both Brodatz32 [35, 36, 40–42] and KTH-TIP 2a datasets [36, 37]. "WLD_Ver1[35]" and "WLD_Ver2[35]" denote our re-implementations of the WLD features in [36] under different parameters ($M = 6, T = 4, S = 3$ and $M = 8, T = 8, S = 4$. "Chen(WLD)" denotes the recognition accuracy directly taken from [36]. **a** Bradatz dataset. **b** KTH-TIP 2a dataset

RICWLTP with different η on Brodatz32 and KTH-TIP 2a datasets; the LBP-based features (i.e., the works by Nosaka et al. and Qi et al., LBP) have no parameters. The parameters η in the LTP and RICLTP in our experiments are set as 1, 3, 5, and 7, and the ones (η) in the are set as 0.03, 0.05, 0.07, and 0.09. From Fig. 3, we observe that our proposed data-driven quantized versions (i.e., WLTP and RICWLTP) results in much better performance than that (i.e., LTP and RICLTP) with an absolute threshold, regardless of the magnitude of the focused pixel; the best recognition result was achieved by the proposed framework with data-driven quantization and co-occurrence context. Figure 4 gives the comparative recognition accuracies with our proposed frameworks and other state-of-the-art approaches [35–37, 40–42] on both Brodatz32 and KTH-TIP 2a datasets; the best results were achieved using our proposed approach with data-driven quantization and co-occurrence context. We also implemented the texture feature in [36] called the Weber local descriptor (WLD) for image representation and used the linear SVM with the normalized WLD histograms as Eq. (7) for classification. On both Brodatz32 and KTH-TIP 2a datasets, we extracted the histograms of WLD under different parameters ($M = 6, T = 4, S = 3$ and $M = 8, T = 8, S = 4$ as in [36], respectively, without block division for Brodatz32 but with nine block division for KTH-TIP 2a dataset) denoted as "WLD_Ver1" and "WLD_Ver2," respectively. Figure 4 shows that our proposed RIC(W)LTP methods can give much better performances on both texture datasets than WLDs implemented by [36] and us. All the above experiments were implemented using the linear SVM with the pre-processed LBP/LTP-based histograms by Eq. (8). As analyzed in [43], the linear SVM with the pre-processed image feature using root operator (Eq. (8)) is equivalent to the nonlinear SVM with Helinger kernel [43] on the raw image feature. This simple pre-processing combined with the linear SVM can achieve comparable classification performance with the nonlinear SVM and the raw image feature especially for histogram-based representation. For comparison, we also conducted the experiments using the nonlinear SVM with RBF kernel on both texture datasets. The compared recognition accuracies with RICLTP/RICWLTP and linear/nonlinear SVM are shown in Fig. 5a, b for Brodatz32 and KTH-TIP 2a datasets, respectively, which manifests that the comparable or a little better performances can be achieved by the nonlinear SVM than the linear one with the pre-processed RICLTP and RICWLTP descriptors. In the RBF kernel nonlinear SVM, there is a parameter γ, which is related to RBF kernel width and may greatly affect the classification performance. According to our experience [44, 45], we set $\frac{1}{\gamma}$ as the mean value of the pairwise Euclidean distances of all training samples' features in the nonlinear SVM experiments.

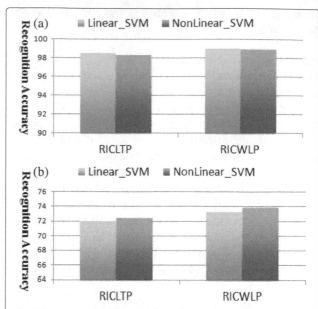

Fig. 5 Comparative results using linear SVM with pre-processed RICLTP and RICWLTP descriptors and the nonlinear SVM with RBF kernel on both texture datasets. **a** Bradatz dataset. **b** KTH-TIP 2a dataset

Next, we give the comparative results using our propose LTP-based descriptors and the conventional LBP-based descriptors (the features in the work by Nosaka et al. and Qi et al.) on PFID dataset in Fig. 6a that also shows the promising recognition performances by our strategy. Similar to the experiments for texture datasets, we also set the used parameter η in the LTP and RICLTP for food recognition experiments as 1, 3, 5, and 7 and η in the WLTP and RICWLTP as 0.03, 0.05, 0.07, and 0.09. For PFID database, the baseline evaluations by the color histogram and the BOF model using SIFT descriptor give the recognition rates 11.2 and 9.3%, respectively. In [39], the more promising performances on PFID database are achieved, which use statistics of pairwise local features. However, the proposed features need to firstly segment the different ingredients from the food image, which would cost more computational time. In our work, we apply the statistics of the simple data-driven quantization of the microstructures for food image representation and apply the very efficient linear SVM as classifier. The comparative results with the state-of-the-art methods are shown in Fig. 6b, where the best performance can be obtained by our proposed strategy. The more complex statistics of pairwise local features (denoted as SPLF) [39] can greatly improve the baseline evaluation (11.2, 9.3%) by conventional color histogram (denoted as CH) and the BOF model (denoted as BOF) to nearly three times (28.2%), which was the best performance on PFID in 2010. Our implementations of WLD histograms with different parameters [36] can also

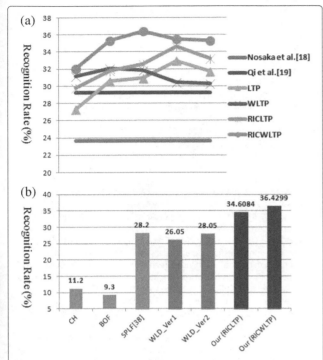

Fig. 6 Comparative results on PFID dataset **a** with the LBP based descriptors by Nosaka et al. [17, 18] and Qi et al. [19] and **b** with the state-of-the-art method [39]

give comparable performances with that by SPLF on PFID dataset, and our proposed strategy with data-driven quantization and co-occurrence context then can increase the recognition rate 28.2% with SPLF [39] to more than 36% about 8% improvement.

5 Conclusions

In this paper, we explored a robust representation strategy of texture images for visual recognition. The widely used local descriptor for texture analysis is local binary pattern, which characterizes each 3×3 local patch (microstructure) into a binary series by comparing the surrounding pixel intensity with the center one, and further has been extended to local ternary patterns via quantizing the difference values between the surrounding pixels and the center one into -1, 0, and 1, which can be explained as the active status (i.e., positively activated, negatively activated, and not activated). However, regardless of the magnitude of the focused pixel, the pre-set threshold η for quantization in the conventional LTP remains fixed, which would violate the principle of human perception. Motivated by the fact that human perception of a pattern depends not only on the absolute intensity of the stimulus but also on the relative variance of the stimuli, we proposed a novel local ternary pattern (LTP) with data-driven quantization according to Weber's law (called WLTP), which is equivalent to adaptively (data-driven)

decide the quantization point according to the magnitude of the focus pixel. This proposed quantization strategy is inspired by Weber's law, a psychological law, which states that the noticeable change of a stimulus such as sound or lighting by a human being is a constant ratio of the original stimulus. Further, we incorporated the spatial and orientation context into WLTP and explored the rotation invariant co-occurrence among WLTP that has much higher descriptive capability than that of conventional LBP-based descriptors for image representation. Our experiments on two texture datasets and one food dataset confirmed that our proposed strategy greatly improved recognition performance as compared to the LBP-based descriptors and other state-of-the-art approaches.

Acknowledgements
This work was supported in part by the Grand-in Aid for Scientific Research from the Japanese Ministry for Education, Science, Culture and Sports under Grant Nos. 15K00253, 15H01130, and 26330213; the Research Matching Fund for Private Universities from MEXT; and the Research Fund from Ritsumeikan University.

Authors' contributions
HXH carried out the method development, conducted experiments, participated in the sequence alignment, and drafted the manuscript. CYW and XG have revised the draft critically for important intellectual content and given the final approval of the version to be published. All authors read and approved the final manuscript.

Competing interests
The authors declare that they have no competing interests.

About the authors
Xian-Hua Han received a B.E. degree from ChongQing University, ChongQing, China, a M.E. degree from ShanDONG University, JiNan, China, a D.E. degree in 2005, from the University of Ryukyus, Okinawa, Japan. From Apr. 2007 to Mar. 2013, she was a post-doctoral fellow and an associate professor with the College of Information Science and Engineering, Ritsumeikan University, Japan. She is now a senior researcher at the Artificial Intelligence Researcher Center, National Institute of Advanced Industrial Science and Technology, Tokyo, Japan. Her current research interests include image processing and analysis, feature extraction, machine learning, computer vision, and pattern recognition. She is a member of the IEEE, IEICE.
Yen-Wei Chen received a B.E.degree in 1985 from Kobe University, Kobe, Japan, a M.E. degree in 1987 and a D.E. degree in 1990 both from Osaka University, Osaka, Japan. From 1991 to 1994, he was a research fellow with the Institute of Laser Technology, Osaka. From Oct. 1994 to Mar. 2004, he was an associate professor and a professor with the Department of Electrical and Electronics Engineering, University of the Ryukyus, Okinawa, Japan. He is currently a professor with the College of Information Science and Engineering, Ritsumeikan University, Japan, and a professor with the Institute for Computational Science and Engineering, Ocean University of China, China. He is an Overseas Assessor of the Chinese Academy of Science and Technology, an associate Editor of the International Journal of Image and Graphics(IJIG), an Editorial Board member of the International Journal of Knowledge-Based Intelligent Engineering Systems and an Editorial Board member of the International Journal of Information. His research interests include intelligent signal and image processing, radiological imaging, and soft computing. He has published more than 100 research papers in these fields. Dr. Chen is a member of the IEEE, IEICE Japan and IEE(Japan).
Gang Xu received his Ph.D from Osaka University, in 1989. He was then a visiting researcher at ATR till 1990, when he returned to Osaka University as an assistant professor. In 1996, he became a tenured associate professor in Department of Computer Science, Ritsumeikan University. He was a visiting researcher at Robotics Lab, Harvard University in 1994, at Microsoft Research China in 1999, and at Motorola Australian Research Centre in 2000. Since 2001, he has been a full professor in Ritsumeikan University. In 2000, he founded 3D MEDiA Company Ltd. and served as CEO since then. His research interests

include image-based 3D metrology, 3D object recognition for industrial robots, and underlying techniques for pattern recognition in general. He authored and coauthored "Epipolar Geometry in Stereo, Motion and Object Recognition: A Unified Approach" (Kluwer Academic Publishers, 1996), "3D Vision" (Kyoritsu Shuppan in Japanese, 1999) and "3D CG from Photographs" (Kindai Kagakusha in Japanese, 2001).

Author details

[1] Graduate School of Science and Technology for Innovation, Yamaguchi University, Yamaguchi 753-8511, Japan. [2] Ritsumeikan University, Kusatsu, Shiga 525-8577, Japan.

References

1. Nister D, Stewenius H (2006) Scalable recognition with a vocabulary tree. CVPR. IEEE, New York. pp. 2161–2168
2. Jegou H, Douze M, Schmid C (2008) Hamming embedding and weak geometric consistency for large scale image search. ECCV. Springer, Berlin
3. Philbin J, Chum O, Isard M, Sivic J, Zisserman A (2008) Lost in quantization: improving particular object retrieval in large scale image databases. CVPR. IEEE, New York
4. Han X-H, Chen Y-W, Ruan X (2012) Multilinear supervised neighborhood embedding of local descriptor tensor for scene/object recognition. IEEE Trans Image Process 21(3):1314–1326
5. Sivic J, Zisserman A (2003) Video Google: a text retrieval approach to object matching in videos. ICCV. IEEE, New York. pp. 1470–1477
6. Lazebnik S, Schmid C, Ponce J (2006) Beyond bags of features: spatial pyramid matching for recognizing natural scene categories. CVPR. IEEE, New York. pp. 2169–2178
7. Harris C, Stephens M (1988) A combined corner and edge detector. In: Proc. Alvey Vision Conference
8. Lowe D (1999) Object recognition from local scale-invariant features. Proc Int Conf Comput Vision. IEEE, New York. Vol. 2, pp. 1150–1157
9. Lowe D (2004) Distinctive image features from scale-invariant keypoints. Int J Comput Vis 60(2):91–110
10. Ke Y, Sukthankar R (2004) PCA-SIFT: A More Distinctive Representation for Local Image Descriptors. Proc. IEEE Int Conf Comput Vision Pattern Recognit. IEEE, New York. pp. 506–513
11. Dalal N, Triggs B (2005) Histograms of Oriented Gradients for Human Detection. Proc. IEEE Int Conf Comput Vision Pattern Recognit. IEEE, New York. pp. 886-893
12. Wang XY, Han TX, Yan SC (2009) An HOG-LBP human detector with partial occlusion handling. ICCV. Springer, Berlin
13. Heikkila M, Pietikainen M (2006) A texture-based method for modeling the background and detecting moving objects. IEEE Trans Pattern Anal Mach Intell 28(4):657–662
14. Kertesz C (2011) Texture-based foreground detection. Int J Signal Process Image Process Pattern Recognit (IJSIP) 4(4):51–62
15. Louis W, Plataniotis KN (2011) Co-occurrence of local binary patterns features for frontal face detection in surveillance applications. EURASIP J Image Video Process
16. Nosaka R, Ohkawa Y, Fukui K (2011) Feature extraction based on co-occurrence of adjacent local binary patterns. In: The 5th Pacific-Rim Symposium on Image and Video Technology (PSIVT2011), LNCS. IEEE, New York Vol. 7088. pp 82–91
17. Nosaka R, Fukui K (2013) HEp-2 cell classification using rotation invariant co-occurrence among local binary patterns. Pattern Recogn 47:2428–2436
18. Nosaka R, Suryanto CH, Fukui K (2013) Rotation invariant co-occurrence among adjacent LBPs. Computer Vision: ACCV 2012, Workshops, Lecture Notes in Computer Science, Vol. 7728. Springer, Berlin. pp. 15–25
19. Qi XB, Xiao R, Zhang L, Guo J (2012) Pairwise rotation invariant co-occurrence local binary pattern. In: 12th European Conference on Computer Vision (ECCV2012). Springer, Berlin
20. Tan XY, Triggs B (2010) Enhanced local texture feature sets for face recognition under difficult lighting conditions. IEEE Trans Image Process 19(6):1635–1650
21. Shen JJ (2003) On the foundations of vision modeling I. Weber's law and Weberized TV (total variation) restoration. Physica D: Nonlinear Phenom 175(3/4):241–251
22. Ojala T, Pietikainen M, Maenpaa T (2002) Multiresolution gray-scale and rotation invariant texture classification with local binary patterns. PAMI 25:971–987
23. Varma M, Zissermann A (2003) Texture classification: are filter banks necessary? CVPR. IEEE, New York. pp. 691–698
24. Xu Y, Yang X, Ling H, Ji H (2010) A new texture descriptor using multifractal analysis in multi-orientation wavelet pyramid. CVPR. IEEE, New York. pp. 161–168
25. Lazebnik S, Schmid C, Ponce J (2005) A sparse texture representation using local affine regions. PAMI 27:1265–1278
26. Zhang J, Marszalek M, Lazebnik S, Schmid C (2007) Local features and kernels for classification of texture and object categories: A comprehensive study. IJCV 73:213–238
27. Varma M, Zisserman A (2005) A statistical approach to texture classification from single images. IJCV 62:61–81
28. Crosier M, Griffin LD (2010) Using basic image features for texture classification. IJCV 88:447–460
29. Watanabe T, Ito S, Yokoi K (2009) Co-occurrence histograms of oriented gradients for pedestrian detection. In: The 3rd IEEE Pacific-Rim Symposium on Image and Video Technology. IEEE, New York. pp 37–447
30. Kobayashi T, Otsu N (2008) Image feature extraction using gradient local auto-correlations. ECCV2008 5302:346–358
31. Mita T, Kaneko T, Stenger B, Hori O (2008) Discriminative feature co-occurrence selection for object detection. IEEE Trans Pattern Anal Mach Intell 30:1257–1268
32. Shen JJ, Jung Y-M (2006) Weberized Mumford–Shah model with Bose-Einstein photon noise. IJCV 53(3):331–358
33. Brodatz P (1966) Textures: a photographic album for artists and designers. Dover Publications, New York
34. Caputo B, Hayman E, Mallikarjuna P (2005) Class-specific material categorisation. In: the Proceedings of the 10th International Conference on Computer Vision. IEEE, New York
35. Ojala T, Valkealahti K, Oja E, Pietikainen M (2001) Texture discrimination with multidimensional distributions of signed gray level differences. Pattern Recogn 34(3):727–739
36. Chen J, Shan S, He C, Zhao G, Pietikainen M, Chen X, Gao W (2010) WLD: a robust local image descriptor. PAMI 32:1705–1720
37. Sharma G, Hussain S, Jurie F (2012) Local higher-order statistics (LHS) for texture categorization and facial analysis. ECCV. Springer, Berlin. Lecture Notes in Computer Science, vol 7578. pp.1–12
38. Chen M, Dhingra K, Wu W, Yang L, Sukthankar R, Yang J (2009) PFID: Pittsburgh Fast-Food Image Dataset. In: The 16th IEEE international conference on Image processing. IEEE, New York. pp 289–292
39. Yang SL, Chen M, Pomerleau D, Sukthankar R (2010) Food recognition using statistics of pairwise local features. Proc. IEEE Int Conf Comput Vision. IEEE, New York. pp. 2246–2256
40. Jalba AC, Wilkinson MHF, Roerdink JBTM (2004) Morphological hat-transform scale spaces and their use in pattern classification. Pattern Recogn 37(5):901–905
41. Urbach ER, Roerdink JBTM, Wilkinson MHF (2007) Connected shape-size pattern spectra for rotation and scale-invariant classification of gray-scale images. IEEE Trans Pattern Anal Mach Intell 29(2):272–285
42. Manjunath B, Ma W (1996) Texture features for browsing and retrieval of image data. IEEE Trans Pattern Anal Mach Intell 18(8):837–842
43. Leung T, Malik J (2013) Effects of image retrieval from image database using linear Kernel and Hellinger Kernel mapping of SVM. Int J Sci Eng Res 4(5):1184–1190
44. Han X-H, Chen Y-W (2011) Biomedical imaging modality classification using combined visual features and textual terms. Int J Biomed Imaging 2011
45. Han X-H, Chen Y-W, Ruan X (2012) Multilinear supervised neighborhood embedding of local descriptor tensor for scene/object recognition. IEEE Trans Image Process 21(3):1314–1326

7

Selecting image pairs for SfM by introducing Jaccard Similarity

Takaharu Kato[1][*][†], Ikuko Shimizu[1][†] and Tomas Pajdla[2]

Abstract

We present a new approach for selecting image pairs that are more likely to match in Structure from Motion (SfM). We propose to use Jaccard Similarity (JacS) which shows how many different visual words is shared by an image pair. In our method, the similarity between images is evaluated using JacS of bag-of-visual-words in addition to tf-idf (term frequency-inverse document frequency), which is popular for this purpose. To evaluate the efficiency of our method, we carry out experiments on our original datasets as well as on "Pantheon" dataset, which is derived from Flickr. The result of our method using both JacS and tf-idf is better than the results of a standard method using tf-idf only.

Keywords: Structure from motion, tf-idf weighting, Jaccard Similarity

1 Introduction

Image matching, i.e., finding coincident points in several images, is one of the most important topics in computer vision. It is used in the field like object recognition, image stitching, and 3D reconstruction. In all of these fields, detecting features in each image and matching those features to find coincident image points are needed.

The Structure from Motion (SfM), which is one of the 3D reconstruction techniques, is an important application of image matching. SfM reconstructs 3D structure and camera positions from 2D image sequences (Fig. 1).

Recently, many applications in computer vision have been utilizing large datasets of photos on the Internet [1]. With the development of social networking service (SNS), such as Flickr and Facebook, every day, every minute, thousands of photos are uploaded to online databases. And those photos would cover large parts of the Earth. Several techniques utilizing photos on the Web for SfM have appeared [2–7].

Photo Tourism [8] was the first system which worked on the large photo collections on the Web for SfM. In the Photo Tourism system, large image collections from either personal photo collections or the photo collections on the Web are used as an input. First, camera positions are computed and a sparse 3D model of the scene is reconstructed. Then, features detected by using SIFT keypoint detector [9] are then matched exhaustively between all image pairs to accomplish reconstruction. However, a typical image has several thousand keypoints, so exhaustive matching of all image pairs in image collections requires too much computational time and resources to be practical.

To make matching feasible, it is required to find out which images may see the same scene without doing full expensive matching. Often, expensive image matching is replaced by much more efficient search based on meta-information, e.g., keywords or GPS location, or by visual search [10].

Most of the images in the image collections on the Web do not have the information of the locations of the cameras, although some of the images are available with GPS orientation information stored in Exif tags. Even when the GPS positions of images are available, it is not sure that nearby images see the same scene. The same holds true for matching images by keywords attached. Hence, an efficient image-based similarity hinting on seeing common scene is always useful.

Figure 2 shows an example of Flicker images tagged by "Notre Dame" keyword. No two images among the five images have a significant overlap to be worth matching. For example, the bottom right image shows the interior of Notre Dame while others show it from outside.

*Correspondence: kato@m2.tuat.ac.jp
†Equal contributors
[1]Tokyo University of Agriculture and Technology, Tokyo, Japan
Full list of author information is available at the end of the article

Fig. 1 Structure from Motion [19]

Speeding up the matching can be cast as image search where efficient form of image similarity is constructed. A classical example is the tf-idf (term frequency - inverse document frequency) document similarity used in document search. MatchMiner [11] selects image pairs for matching using bag-of-visual-words and tf-idf weighting to assess image pair similarity. Some other researches use bag-of-visual-words and tf-idf weighting as well [12–14].

We propose using Jaccard Similarity (JacS), which is also known as Jaccard Similarity Coefficient, for calculating image pair similarity in addition to using tf-idf. JacS is originally used for information retrieval [15], and when it is employed for estimating image pair similarity, it shows how many different visual words do image pairs have in common. The min-Hash, which is a locality-sensitive hashing of JacS, is used for image retrieval [16]. In our experiment with an image collection with ground truth, we show that the accuracy of JacS alone is sometimes better than the accuracy when using tf-idf alone and that the accuracy of JacS used together with tf-idf is always much better than using JacS or tf-idf alone.

Fig. 2 Photos of "Notre Dame" from Flickr. *Top left* photo shows Notre Dame from a distance. *Top middle* and *right* show typical outside appearances of Notre Dame. *Bottom left* shows an example of a photo full with people. *Bottom right* shows the inside of Notre Dame

2 Related work

For exploring image connectivity in large image collections, several techniques have been proposed. In this section, we will explain previous techniques for discovering image pairs for matching.

As we mentioned briefly in Chapter 1, Photo Tourism [8] proposed utilizing large photo collections on the Web. With using exhaustive pairwise image matching, this approach obtains image connectivity graph. However, it takes too much time and computational effort to match every pair of images.

Some SfM methods detect candidate image pairs beforehand in order to avoid exhaustive matching. MatchMiner [11] is one of the methods used for selecting image pairs. It adopts the bag-of-visual-words and tf-idf weighting to estimate image pair similarity. For constructing bag-of-visual-words, MatchMiner trains a vocabulary tree on 50,000 images of a single city, which are not used in experiments for selecting image pairs, to yield one million visual words. This bag-of-visual-words is used for all experiments. Those visual features are extracted by SIFT descriptor, and approximately the closest visual word is assigned to every keypoint of each image. Images are represented by histograms of visual words, with the standard normalized tf-idf weighting applied to each histogram. Image pair similarity is evaluated by the dot product of their normalized tf-idf weighted histograms. In MatchMiner, a modified version of Rocchio's relevance feedback [17] is applied on the Top k most similar images for each query images.

Using the bag-of-visual-words and standard tf-idf weighting is a common method for estimating image similarity. Near Duplicate Image Detection [16] uses a bag-of-visual-words with tf-idf weighting method into image similarity measures as well. Originally, bag-of-visual-words and tf-idf weighting method is used in text retrieval. Before MatchMiner or Near Duplicate Image Detection, Video Google [18] applied bag-of-visual-words and tf-idf weighting method to image retrieval . In Video Google, visual vocabulary is constructed by using Mahalanobis distance and K-means clustering on SIFT descriptors extracted from a video.

A bag-of-visual-words with tf-idf weighting is known as a successful approach for image and particular object retrieval. The tf index indicates that the visual words which appear frequent in an image are important, while the idf index indicates that the visual words which appear among several images are less important. However, SfM system requires an image pair which shares same points, and thus the concept of the idf does not seem to be suitable for the purpose.

In this paper, we propose to exploit Jaccard Similarity, which shows how many visual vocabularies do image pairs have in common, for calculating image pair similarity in addition to tf-idf method. We demonstrate the superiority of our method on our original datasets, as well as on the dataset which was used for testing in MatchMiner.

3 Proposed method overview

We propose to introduce Jaccard Similarity in addition to the similarity based on tf-idf weighting. The outline of our method is as follows: (1) constructing a bag-of-visual-words from image collections, (2) estimating similarities using dot product of tf-idf, (3) estimating similarities using JacS, and (4) selecting the image pairs which are selected in both tf-idf and JacS. In this section, the algorithm for each step is explained.

3.1 Constructing a bag-of-visual-words

We build a bag-of-visual-words by random sampling from each image collection for each experiment. For each image, we pick 10% of features, which are extracted by SIFT descriptor, randomly for building visual vocabularies. Every descriptor is then represented as the most appropriate visual word by the nearest neighbor clustering. In this paper, we assume 10% of the features from one image are enough to express images approximately.

3.2 Similarity using tf-idf weighting

In text as well as in image retrieval [18], tf-idf weighting is commonly used to weight histograms of word frequencies bag-of-words. The weighting by tf-idf is computed by the following formula,

$$t_i = \frac{n_{id}}{n_d} \log \frac{N}{n_i} \tag{1}$$

where n_{id} represents the number of occurrences of the visual word i in the image d, n_d represents the total number of visual words which appear in the image d, N represents the number of images in the image collection, and n_i represents the number of images which include the visual word i in the image collection. Figure 3 illustrates an example of tf-idf weighting.

After every image is expressed as a vector of weighted visual words, the vectors are normalized and all pairwise image similarities are obtained by the dot product of the vectors. In Fig. 3, the similarity between Img-A and Img-B equals 0.20 while the similarity between Img-B and Img-C equals 0.27. Although Img-B has two features in common with both Img-A and Img-C, tf-idf-based similarity shows Img-B is similar to Img-C more than Img-A.

3.3 Jaccard similarity

We introduce Jaccard Similarity of images. JacS calculates the similarity of an image pair as the fraction of distinct visual words, which are common to an image pair.

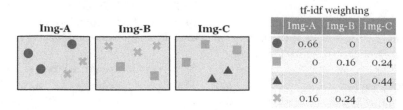

Fig. 3 An example of tf-idf weighting. Each visual word is weighted by their occurrences. The tf-idf weighting indicates *red circles* in *Img-A* and *purple triangles* in *Img-C* are important, while *blue crosses* and *green squares* which appear among the two images are less important

The image pair similarity by JacS is computed by the following formula,

$$s_{ij} = \frac{n_{ij}}{n_i + n_j - n_{ij}} \qquad (2)$$

where n_i is the number of visual words, which appear in image i; n_j is the number of visual words, which appear in image j; and n_{ij} is the number of visual words, which appear in both image i and j. Figure 4 illustrates an example of JacS-based similarity. In this figure, visual words occurrences are the same as in Fig. 3. By using JacS-based similarity, the image pair A and B gets the same similarity as the image pair B and C.

3.4 Top *k* most similar images

With the similarity matrix obtained by the tf-idf-based similarity and JacS, we select image pairs and evaluate those methods. For each image as a query image, top *k* most relevant images are selected according to the similarity matrix and are assumed as the true image pairs for matching. Then, the accuracy of selecting image pairs is obtained by comparing the selected image pairs to the ground truth image graph. We show in the next section that false image pairs obtained by the tf-idf-based similarity differ from the false image pairs obtained by the JacS. Therefore, we propose to use the intersection of two image pair sets obtained by both similarity methods: tf-idf and JacS.

4 Experimental evaluation

4.1 Our original datasets

We first demonstrate tf-idf-based method and JacS on our original datasets: "Bear" and "Dolls," to show the difference of behaviors between the two methods.

4.1.1 Dataset "Bear"

To compare the behaviors of tf-idf-based similarity and JacS, we first prepared photos of a figure taken from eight directions (Fig. 5).

The connected graph of dataset "Bear" is shown in Fig. 6. Each number on the vertex in the graph is corresponding to the number above the photos in Fig. 5. In this figure, tf-idf-based similarity shows better precision. The bear figure has similar texture on almost the entire surface. It appears that idf performs better here, while JacS tends to make more mistakes.

4.1.2 Dataset "Dolls"

Secondly, unlike the dataset "Bear," we prepared several images with different types of texture (Fig. 7).

Figure 8 shows the connected graph of dataset "Dolls." Black lines show false image pairs, while the other colors are corresponding to the frame colors in Fig. 7. In the figure, green vertexes have many connections with other colored vertexes in the tf-idf connected graph, while they does not have any connections with other colors in the JacS connected graph. The figure of green vertex has many similar feature descriptors, and thus JacS which simply

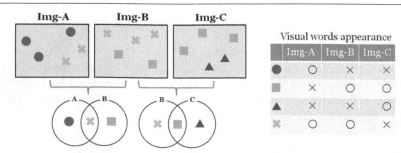

Fig. 4 An example of JacS. For the image pair A and B, *blue crosses* exist in common, while Img-A has *red circles* of it's own and Img-B has *green squares*. Totally, Img-A and Img-B has three visual vocabularies, and one of them appears in common. In this case, the similarity between Img-A and Img-B is 0.33

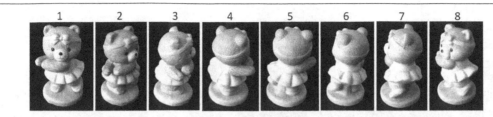

Fig. 5 Dataset "Bear". This dataset totally has eight images

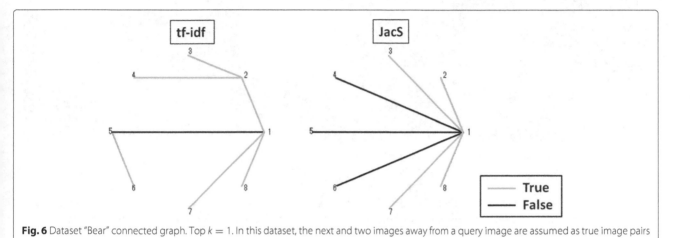

Fig. 6 Dataset "Bear" connected graph. Top $k = 1$. In this dataset, the next and two images away from a query image are assumed as true image pairs

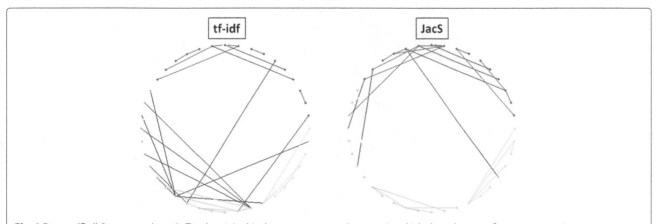

Fig. 7 Dataset "Dolls." Each figure is taken photos from eight directions. This dataset totally has 40 images

Fig. 8 Dataset "Dolls" connected graph. Top $k = 1$. In this dataset, we assume image pairs which show the same figure as true pairs

Fig. 9 Dataset "Pantheon". The images from Flickr tagged by "Pantheon" keyword. This dataset totally has 1123 images

estimate the number of shared visual words works better. It appears that the two methods obtain different false image pairs.

4.2 Dataset "Pantheon"

We finally evaluated the three methods: tf-idf-based method, JacS-based method, and our proposed method, with a dataset from MatchMiner [11]. In MatchMiner, the ground truth image graphs are computed by exhaustive geometric verification on all image pairs. We use this ground truth for evaluating our method. Figure 9 shows an example of the images in dataset "Pantheon".

With changing k value from 1 to 30, we select image pairs by each method. Then, selected image pairs are compared with the ground truth, and the average precision

is computed for each k value (Fig. 10). The method tf-idf with JacS showed the best precision in every k value.

5 Conclusion

We have introduced Jaccard Similarity (JacS) for selecting image pairs for matching in the Structure from Motion (SfM). JacS considers occurrences of visual words in two images for selecting image pairs while the previous method based on tf-idf considers occurrences of visual words in the whole database. To confirm the differences of behaviors between the JacS and the method based on tf-idf, we have tested with two datasets: "Bear" and "Dolls." As a result of the two experiments, it appears that JacS and tf-idf-based method obtain different false image pairs.

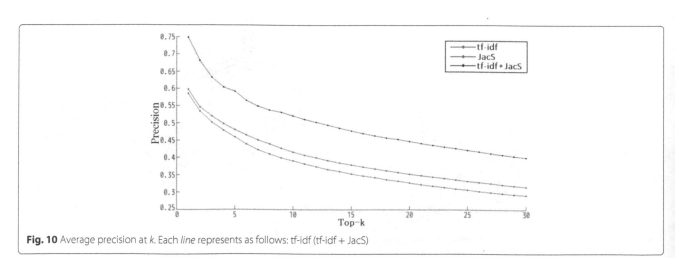

Fig. 10 Average precision at k. Each *line* represents as follows: tf-idf (tf-idf + JacS)

We have estimated image pair similarities by JacS and tf-idf-based method and have selected image pairs which are selected in both methods to make the accuracy higher. With the dataset "Pantheon," which is tested in Match-Miner [11] as well, our method has improved precision by 15%. We are now trying to extract connected components of high image similarities.

Acknowledgements
This work was partly supported by JSPS KAKENHI Grant Number 15X00445 and EU H2020-ICT-2016-2017 LADIO - Live Action Data Input and Output.

Authors' contributions
TK designed and carried out the experiments and wrote the manuscript. IS supervised the work and edited the manuscript. TP helped in the implementation and advised TK on the concept and experiments and edited the manuscript. All authors reviewed and approved the final manuscript.

Competing interests
The authors declare that they have no competing interests.

Author details
[1]Tokyo University of Agriculture and Technology, Tokyo, Japan. [2]CTU in Prague, FEE, Prague, Czech Republic.

References
1. Schaffalitzky F, Zisserman A (2002) Multi-view matching for unordered image sets, or "How do I organize my holiday snaps?". In: European conference on computer vision. Springer Berlin Heidelberg. pp 414–431. http://link.springer.com/chapter/10.1007/3-540-47969-4_28
2. Havlena M, Torii A, Pajdla T (2010) Efficient structure from motion by graph optimization. In: European Conference on Computer Vision. Springer Berlin Heidelberg. pp 100–113. http://link.springer.com/chapter/10.1007%2F978-3-642-15552-9_8
3. Havlena M, Torii A, Knopp J, Pajdla T (2009) Randomized structure from motion based on atomic 3d models from camera triplets. In: Computer Vision and Pattern Recognition, 2009. CVPR 2009. IEEE Conference on. IEEE. pp 2874–2881. http://ieeexplore.ieee.org/document/5206677/
4. Frahm JM, Fite-Georgel P, Gallup D, Johnson T, Raguram R, Wu C, Pollefeys M (2010) Building rome on a cloudless day. In: European Conference on Computer Vision. Springer Berlin Heidelberg. pp 368–381. http://link.springer.com/chapter/10.1007/978-3-642-15561-1_27
5. Wilson K, Snavely N (2014) Robust global translations with 1dsfm. In: European Conference on Computer Vision. Springer International Publishing. pp 61–75. http://link.springer.com/chapter/10.1007/978-3-319-10578-9_5
6. Cui Z, Tan P (2015) Global structure-from-motion by similarity averaging. In: Proceedings of the IEEE International Conference on Computer Vision. IEEE. pp 864–872. http://ieeexplore.ieee.org/document/7410462/
7. Schonberger JL, Radenovic F, Chum O, Frahm JM (2015) From single image query to detailed 3D reconstruction. In: Proceedings of the IEEE Conference on Computer Vision and Pattern Recognition. IEEE. pp 5126–5134. http://ieeexplore.ieee.org/document/7299148/
8. Snavely N, Seitz SM, Szeliski R (2006) Photo tourism: exploring photo collections in 3D. ACM Trans Graph (TOG) 25(3):835–846. ACM
9. Lowe DG (2004) Distinctive image features from scale-invariant keypoints. Int J Comput Vis 60(2):91–110
10. Heath K, Gelfand N, Ovsjanikov M, Aanjaneya M, Guibas LJ (2010) Image webs: Computing and exploiting connectivity in image collections. In: Computer Vision and Pattern Recognition (CVPR), 2010 IEEE Conference on. IEEE. pp 3432–3439. http://ieeexplore.ieee.org/abstract/document/5539991/
11. Lou Y, Snavely N, Gehrke J (2012) Matchminer: Efficient spanning structure mining in large image collections. In: Computer Vision–ECCV 2012. Springer Berlin Heidelberg. pp 45–58. http://link.springer.com/chapter/10.1007/978-3-642-33709-3_4
12. Agarwal S, Furukawa Y, Snavely N, Simon I, Curless B, Seitz SM, Szeliski R (2011) Building Rome in a day. Commun ACM 54(10):105–112
13. Chum O, Philbin J, Sivic J, Isard M, Zisserman A (2007) Total recall: automatic query expansion with a generative feature model for object retrieval. In: Computer Vision, 2007. ICCV 2007. IEEE 11th International Conference on. IEEE. pp 1–8. http://ieeexplore.ieee.org/document/4408891/
14. Chum O, Mikulik A, Perdoch M, Matas J (2011) Total recall II: query expansion revisited. In: Computer Vision and Pattern Recognition (CVPR), 2011 IEEE Conference on. IEEE. pp 889–896. http://ieeexplore.ieee.org/document/5995601/
15. Chahal M (2016) Information retrieval using Jaccard Similarity Coefficient. In: International Journal of Computer Trends and Technology (IJCTT)—Volume 36 Number 3. Seventh Sense Research Group. http://www.ijcttjournal.org/archives/ijctt-v36p124
16. Chum O, Philbin J, Zisserman A (2008) Near duplicate image detection: min-Hash and tf-idf weighting. In: BMVC. BMVA Press Vol. 810. pp 812–815. http://www.bmva.org/bmvc/2008/papers/119.html
17. Rocchio JJ (1971) Relevance feedback in information retrieval. In: The SMART Retrieval System: Experiments in Automatic Document Processing. Prentice-Hall Inc. pp 313–323
18. Sivic J, Zisserman A (2003) Video google: a text retrieval approach to object matching in videos. ICCV 2(1470):1470–1477
19. Heller J, Havlena M, Jancosek M, Torii A, Pajdla T (2015) 3D reconstruction from photographs by CMP SfM web service. In: Machine Vision Applications (MVA), 2015 14th IAPR International Conference on. IEEE. pp 30–34. http://ieeexplore.ieee.org/document/7153126/

8

Mobile hologram verification with deep learning

Daniel Soukup[*] and Reinhold Huber-Mörk

Abstract
Holograms are security features applied to security documents like banknotes, passports, and ID cards in order to protect them from counterfeiting. Checking the authenticity of holograms is an important but difficult task, as holograms comprise different appearances for varying observation and/or illumination directions. Multi-view and photometric image acquisition and analysis procedures have been proposed to capture that variable appearance. We have developed a portable ring-light illumination module used to acquire photometric image stacks of holograms with mobile devices. By the application of Convolutional Neural Networks (CNN), we developed a vector representation that captures the essential appearance properties of hologram types in only a few values extracted from the photometric hologram stack. We present results based on Euro banknote holograms of genuine and counterfeited Euro banknotes. When compared to a model-based hologram descriptor, we show that our new learned CNN representation enables hologram authentication on the basis of our mobile acquisition method more reliably.

Keywords: Mobile security inspection, Photometric hologram verification, Deep learning

1 Introduction

Holograms or Diffractive Optically Variable Image Devices (DOVID) change their appearances when viewed and/or illuminated under different angles (Fig. 1) and are a means to protect security documents (e.g., banknotes, passports) from counterfeiting. Checking their authenticity is an important, but still, challenging task. In practice, the holograms' grating structures are analyzed with microscopes or sparse point-wise projection and recording of the diffraction patterns [1]. For example, the *Universal Hologram Scanner* (UHS) [2] is a well known tool for hologram verification actually used in forensic analyses, where the holograms' diffraction patterns are analyzed at discrete steps over the hologram area.

A guided multi-view approach for hologram acquisition for mobile devices in order to capture hologram appearance variations was proposed recently [3], which further allowed for hologram detection and tracking [4]. A machine vision system combining multi-view and photometric approaches by acquiring holograms for different illumination angles with a light-field camera was proposed [5] in a recent publication. As illumination unit, a

photometric light-dome of 30 cm in diameter comprising 32 LEDs was presented. Despite the availability of multi-view information, the authors could only make use of the photometric variation in the data. By modeling the photometric reflectance properties, they developed a low-dimensional hologram representation, in which the essentials of holograms' appearances are compressed into only a few hundred vector entries. The properties of that so called *DOVID descriptor* were reported recently [6, 7].

We developed a portable ring-light module that can be mounted to a mobile device to make photometric acquisitions (Fig. 2), similar to the aforementioned illumination dome. Moreover, we additionally developed a new vector representation for holograms by means of deep learning a CNN from the holograms' photometric image stacks. While for our data, the modeled DOVID descriptor was tedious to parameterize and parameterization could only be accomplished with the aid of counterfeited holograms at hand, our new learned hologram representation is solely learned from genuine holograms. Nonetheless, the description is robust enough, to be able to reliably distinguish fake holograms from genuine holograms of the intended type.

The rest of the paper is structured as follows. In Section 2, we describe the acquisition system comprising

---
*Correspondence: daniel.soukup@ait.ac.at
AIT Austrian Institute of Technology GmbH, Donau-City-Straße 1, 1220 Vienna, Austria

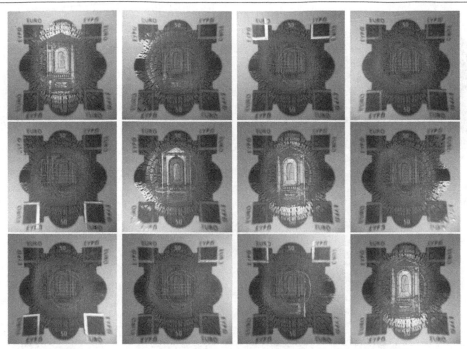

Fig. 1 Appearances of a Euro 50 hologram illuminated from 12 different directions

the portable ring-light module mounted to a Nexus P6 mobile device. The generation of the new hologram vector representation is outlined in Section 3. An experimental evaluation and comparison with a model-based representation based on the data sample described in Section 4 is given in Section 5, followed by the summary and conclusions in Section 6.

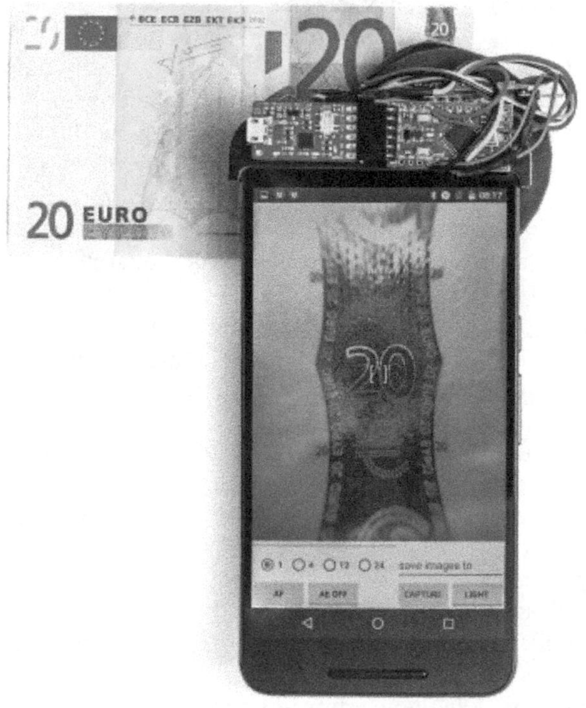

2 Mobile photometric hologram acquisition

The appearances of holograms shall be captured in a photometric image stack, which is a set of images taken from an object, e.g., a hologram, under different illumination directions. While similar work [6] used a rigid, rather bulky setup of a camera and a large illumination device, we intend to do acquisitions with a mobile device. In particular, for this study, we used a Nexus 6P from Google comprising a 12.3 MP camera. For that device, we developed an illumination module (Fig. 3) comprising a 3D printed retainer, a LED strip of 24 individually operable LEDs (WS2812b) mounted to the inner walls of the cylindrical dome (Fig. 4), and corresponding controls so that the LED module was controllable via the mobile device.

Due to the small diameter of the LED ring, acquisitions had to be done in very close range in order to achieve sufficiently large illumination angles to make the variability of the holograms visible. Thus, it was necessary to additionally mount a macro and wide-angle lens (Mantona 18672 objective set) to the NEXUS P6 to make the field of view wide enough.

The coordination of acquisition and illumination was controlled by a software, i.e., control of focus, exposure time, switching of illuminating LEDs, and actual acquisition. A single hologram is acquired 24 times, once for each illuminating LED, whereby the observation position is held constant. We call the resulting photometric set of

Fig. 2 Mobile photometric hologram acquisition setup

Fig. 3 LED ring-light module to be mounted to a mobile device

24 RGB images the *Photometric Hologram Stack* (PHS). When stacked along the color channel dimension, the PHS is a 3D array with $3 \times 24 = 72$ color channels.

3 Compressed hologram representation by deep learning

Given a PHS of a hologram, the goal is to generate a compressed representation of the variations that allows for easily comparing different holograms. We will compare our approach to the so called DOVID descriptor [6] which extracts properties of the Bidirectional Reflectance Distribution Function (BRDF) for each hologram position out of (in their case) the 32 available color values for each position. The final descriptor was constructed as a histogram vector of these properties over all hologram positions. The optimal parameterization of property thresholds, masking, and histogram bins has to be assessed by trial and error with the objective that fake holograms distinctly differ from the corresponding intended genuine hologram types. That means that a sufficient sample of fakes must be at hand during training, which is often difficult to achieve.

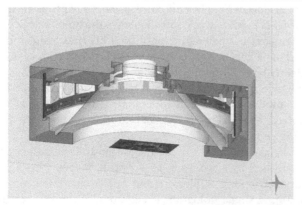

Fig. 4 Illustration of a cross-section of the cylindrical LED ring light-dome

Thus, an alternative method of generating reliable hologram representations is required, which

(1) learns hologram types' target appearances only from genuine samples,
(2) learns from the PHS directly without much image pre-processing, and
(3) reflects measurable deviations from genuine references for newly presented fakes.

Motivated by the great success of deep learning in various computer vision tasks over the last years, we employed deep learning a Convolutional Neural Net (CNN) for this task. The training objective is to *classify PHS stacks of genuine hologram types* (in our case Euro banknote holograms, i.e., EU5, EU20, EU50, EU100, and EU500). We use the vector output of a high-level layer of the trained CNN as the new hologram representation vector. Thereby, on the basis of a vector metric, the representation of a new hologram is compared with hologram representations of reference holograms which are known to be genuine.

Due to our very small sample of holograms, we were forced to make use of transfer learning. Yosinski et al. [8] showed that CNN features learned in one task can be transferred to another task. Azizpour et al. [9] presented a detailed study on relevant factors for transfer learning. Especially, when there is only a small sample set available in the second task, a CNN pre-trained on the first task as initial setting for training the second task showed to be preferable to random initializing the CNN. This is called *fine-tuning* the CNN on the second task. Fine-tuning meanwhile is commonly used, often by means of CNNs trained on ImageNet, as these nets have been trained extensively on very large data sets. Similarly to Wang et al. [10], we initialized our CNNs with the fully pre-trained CNN *ImageNetVgg-verydeep-16-4096* [11] trained by the Visual Geometry Group Oxford on the ILSVRC-2012 data set [12]. This architecture receives $224 \times 224 \times 3$ color images as input. In the convolutional part, those are processed through five convolutional blocks C1, C2, C3, C4, and C5 with 2, 2, 3, 3, and 3 convolutional layers, respectively, followed by 3 fully connected layers FC6, FC7, and FC8. Each convolutional block is completed by a max-pooling layer (Fig. 5).

To allow for the input of PHS, which in our case are image arrays with 72 "color channels," we copied the first convolutional layer weights 24 times. In the original setup, FC8 provides a 1000-vector representing probability scores of the 1000 object classes in the ImageNet2012 challenge. According to merely 5 hologram types to be classified in our task, we reduced FC8's output to a 5-vector.

As the new hologram representation, the highest-level CNN representation is used, which is the output

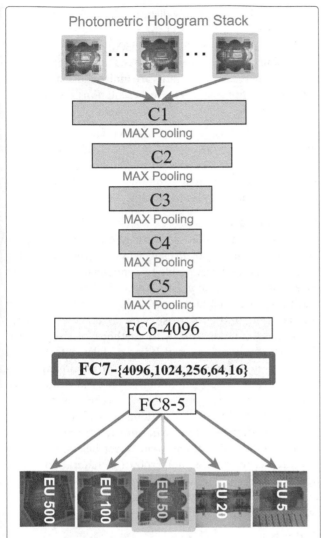

Fig. 5 Adjusted ImageNetVgg-verydeep-16 CNN architecture. Receives PHS instead of only RGB images and outputs scores for 5 classes instead of 1000. The new hologram representation is taken from the output of FC7. In 5 alternative architectures, FC7 is adjusted to 4096, 1024, 256, 64, and 16 dimensions

of FC7. Originally, FC7 is 4096-dimensional, which is far higher dimensional than the aforementioned model-based DOVID descriptor which is 150-dimensional in our experiments. Thus, we conducted experiments with alternative architectures, where FC7 outputs 4096-, 1024-, 256-, 64-, and 16-dimensional representations. Those five different architectures shall be referred to as *FC7-4096*, *FC7-1024*, *FC7-256*, *FC7-64*, and *FC7-16*.

4 Sample holograms

By courtesy of the OeNB[1], we had an access to samples of genuine Euro banknotes of the five denominations EU5, EU20, EU50, EU100, and EU500. Each genuine denomination contains a different type of hologram. For each of the five types, we acquired ten examples of genuine holograms. Additionally, ten examples of genuine but severely creased EU5 banknotes were available, which can be used to determine if the developed CNN hologram representation shows a similar structure for creased and uncreased holograms. This would be an important evidence of robustness to crease, as crease is a very natural source of variation of banknotes. While the EU5 sample only contains genuine holograms, for the other types, a number of counterfeited holograms were acquired, i.e., 16 examples for EU20, 23 examples for EU50, 14 examples for EU100, and 9 examples for EU500.

By means of our acquisition setup from Section 2, for each hologram, 24 RGB images were acquired, one for each of the ring-light device's LEDs. Hologram areas were cutout from the images and sampled so that each image is filled predominantly by the hologram and that it comprises a 224×224 pixel raster, which is the spatial input size for the CNN. Those 24 $224 \times 224 \times 3$ images were stacked along the color channel into the $224 \times 224 \times 72$ dimensional PHS.

5 Experimental results

The five CNN architectures *FC7-4096*, *FC7-1024*, *FC7-256*, *FC7-64*, and *FC7-16* were setup on a pre-trained ImageNetVgg-verydeep-16 CNN provided by the Visual Geometry Group Oxford as described in Section 3 . Each CNN was fine-tuned for further 30 epochs with the fixed learning rate $\alpha = 1e - 5$ and the objective to classify genuine Euro holograms of the types EU5, EU20, EU50, EU100, and EU500 (see Section 4). For each hologram type, seven genuine samples were used for training and three for validation. Additionally, data augmentation was applied, where each training sample was augmented by two randomly shifted ($\leq$ 15 pxl) and two randomly rotated ($\leq$ 8°) versions in each epoch. Well before epoch 30, each of the CNNs could classify genuine holograms perfectly.

After fine-tuning, each hologram PHS was processed through each of the CNNs and the corresponding hologram representation vectors received from the FC7 layers. In parallel, for each hologram, the histogram-based, modeled DOVID descriptor was generated. Required parameters were set by trial and error search using also the fakes with the objective that fake representations should distinctly differ from genuine ones. The final solution led to a 150-dimensional histogram representation to which we refer as *Hist-150*.

Thus, for a fixed representation type $R \in \{$FC7-4096, $\ldots$, FC7-16, Hist-150$\}$ of dimension $m \in \{4096, 1024, 256, 64, 16, 150\}$ and a hologram type $H \in \{$EU5, EU20, EU50, EU100, EU500$\}$, let

$$G_H^R = \{g_i \in \mathbb{R}^m\}, \quad F_H^R = \{f_i \in \mathbb{R}^m\} \qquad (1)$$

be the sets of representations of the genuine holograms G_H^R and faked holograms F_H^R. Note, F_{EU5}^R contains the set of indeed genuine, but severely creased, EU5 banknotes and no fakes.

In order to mutually compare hologram representations, we use the *cosine distance* as measure of dissimilarity of any two hologram representation vectors $p \in \mathbb{R}^m$ and $q \in \mathbb{R}^m$:

$$d_{cos}(p,q) = 1 - \frac{\langle p, q \rangle}{\|p\|_2 \cdot \|q\|_2}. \qquad (2)$$

For a hologram fake to be detectable as counterfeit, its nearest neighbor distance to the cluster of genuine hologram representations of the corresponding hologram type must be significantly larger than the maximal intra-cluster distance of mutual distances between the genuine holograms, i.e.,

$$\forall f \in F_H^R : min \left\{ d_{cos}(f, g_i) | g_i \in G_H^R \right\} \gg$$
$$max \left\{ d_{cos}(g_i, g_j) | g_i, g_j \in G_H^R, i \neq j \right\}. \qquad (3)$$

In this manner, we define a *fake separation factor* s_H^R, which indicates how well all available fake holograms are distinguishable from the genuine holograms of the hologram type intended to be faked, i.e.,

$$s_H^R := \frac{max \left\{ d_{cos}(g_i, g_j) | g_i, g_j \in G_H^R, i \neq j \right\}}{min \left\{ d_{cos}(f_i, g_j) | f_i \in F_H^R, g_j \in G_H^R \right\}}. \qquad (4)$$

In s_H^R, the maximum intra-genuine-cluster distance is set in relation to the minimum fake-to-genuine-cluster distance. If all the fakes $f \in F_H^R$ are well distinguishable from the corresponding genuine holograms in G_H^R, then $s_H^R \ll 1$. If $s_H^R \geq 1$, then at least one $f \in F_H^R$ at least touches the genuine hologram cluster G_H^R indicating that F_H^R cannot reliably be distinguished from the genuine holograms.

In Table 1, the fake separation factors s_H^R are listed for all hologram types and representation types. For *CNN representations*, results show the following:

- That fakes are reliably distinguishable from genuine holograms ($s_H^{FC7-*} \ll 1$ for $H \in \{EU20, EU50, EU100, EU500\}$),
- Robustness to crease ($s_{EU5}^{FC7-*} > 1$ shows that creased and uncreased holograms are indistinguishable)[2], and
- High compression rate (representations are robust even for $m = 16$).

The *DOVID descriptor* on the other hand does not have that robustness to crease as $s_{EU5}^{Hist-150} = 0.84 < 1$ indicates a gap between creased and uncreased hologram clusters. $s_{EU50}^{Hist-150} = 1.04 > 1$ further shows, that also fake detection could not be accomplished reliably.

6 Conclusion

We presented a mobile setup for photometric hologram acquisition by means of an especially constructed portable ring-light module mountable to a mobile device. In order to evaluate the obtained photometric hologram image stacks, we developed a new hologram representation for capturing and compressing the essential appearance properties of holograms with methods of deep learning. We compared its capability of fake detection on Euro banknote holograms with that of an already existing histogram-based photometric hologram descriptor. While our new learned representation can be easily computed only by the use of a genuine hologram sample, the already existing descriptor can only be parameterized by using a sample of fakes as well. Nevertheless, our hologram representation is more robust to natural hologram appearance variations and could more reliably detect fake holograms, despite those which have never been used in the training stage.

Endnotes

[1] National Bank of Austria (OeNB), Test Center, Vienna

[2] In a more detailed cluster analysis, we also verified that the CNN representations of the creased EU5 holograms are actually embedded in the cluster of genuine uncreased EU5 representations.

Acknowledgements
We acknowledge the National Bank of Austria (OeNB), Test Center Vienna, for providing us with genuine and faked hologram samples.

Funding
Not applicable.

Authors' contributions
In all the stages of the work, both authors have similar contributions. Both authors read and approved the final manuscript.

Competing interests
The authors declare that they have no competing interests.

Table 1 Fake separation factor s_H^R for all hologram types and all types of hologram representation vectors

Type	EU5	EU20	EU50	EU100	EU500
FC7-4096	1.33	0.3	0.24	0.29	0.11
FC7-1024	1.38	0.22	0.2	0.23	0.1
FC7-256	1.01	0.22	0.16	0.13	0.07
FC7-64	2.01	0.33	0.08	0.06	0.06
FC7-16	3.2	0.18	0.03	0.06	0.06
Hist-150	0.84	0.09	1.04	0.18	0.24

Note for EU5 no fakes are available, here we measured the separation between flat and creased genuine holograms

References

1. van Renesse RL (2005) Optical document security. 3rd edn. Artech House, Boston London
2. van Renesse RL (2005) Testing the universal hologram scanner: a picture can speak a thousand words. Keesing J Doc Identity 12:7–10
3. Hartl A, Grubert J, Schmalstieg D, Reitmayr G (2013) Mobile interactive hologram verification. In: Proc. Intl. Symp. on Mixed and Augmented Reality (ISMAR). IEEE, Adelaide. pp 75–82
4. Hartl A, Arth C, Schmalstieg D (2014) AR-based hologram detection on security documents using a mobile phone. In: Proc. Intl. Symp. on Visual Computing (ISVC). Springer, Las Vegas. pp 335–346
5. Štolc S, Soukup D, Huber-Mörk R (2015) Invariant characterization of DOVID security features using a photometric descriptor. In: Proc. IEEE Intl. Conf. on Image Processing (ICIP). IEEE, Quebec City
6. Soukup D, Štolc S, Huber-Mörk R (2015) Analysis of optically variable devices using a photometric light-field approach. In: Proc. SPIE-IS&T Electronic Imaging – Media Watermarking, Security and Forensics. SPIE-IS&T, San Francisco
7. Soukup D, Štolc S, Huber-Mörk R (2015) On optimal illumination for DOVID description using photometric stereo. In: Proc. Advanced Concepts for Intelligent Vision Systems (ACIVS). Springer, Catania. pp 553–565
8. Yosinski J, Clune J, Bengio Y, Lipson H (2014) How transferable are features in deep neural networks?. CoRR abs/1411.1792:14
9. Azizpour H, Razavian AS, Sullivan J, Maki A, Carlsson S (2016) Factors of transferability for a generic convnet representation. IEEE Trans Pattern Anal Mach Intell 38(9):1790–1802
10. Wang T, Zhu J, Ebi H, Chandraker M, Efros AA, Ramamoorthi R (2016) A 4D light-field dataset and CNN architectures for material recognition. CoRR abs/1608.06985:16
11. Simonyan K, Zisserman A (2014) Very deep convolutional networks for large-scale image recognition. CoRR abs/1409.1556:14
12. Russakovsky O, Deng J, Su H, Krause J, Satheesh S, Ma S, Huang Z, Karpathy A, Khosla A, Bernstein M, Berg AC, Fei-Fei L (2015) ImageNet Large Scale Visual Recognition Challenge. Intl J Comput Vision (IJCV) 115(3):211–252

9

Global ray-casting range image registration

Linh Tao[1*], Tam Bui[2] and Hiroshi Hasegawa[3]

Abstract

This paper presents a novel method for pair-wise range image registration, a backbone task in world modeling, parts inspection and manufacture, object recognition, pose estimation, robotic navigation, and reverse engineering. The method finds the most suitable homogeneous transformation matrix between two constructed range images to create a more complete 3D view of a scene. The proposed solution integrates a ray casting-based fitness estimation with a global optimization method called improved self-adaptive differential evolution. This method eliminates the fine registration steps of the well-known iterative closest point (ICP) algorithm used in previously proposed methods, and thus, is the first direct global registration algorithm. With its parallel implementation potential, the ray casting-based algorithm speeds up the fitness calculation for the global optimization method, which effectively exploits the search space to find the best transformation solution. The integration was successfully implemented in a parallel paradigm on a multi-core computer processor to solve a simultaneous 3D localization problem. The fast, accurate, and robust results show that the proposed algorithm significantly improves on the registration problem over state-of-the-art algorithms.

Keywords: Range image registration, Direct global registration, Adaptive differential evolution, Global optimization, Ray-casting, 3D localization

1 Introduction

The introduction of commercial depth sensing devices, such as the Microsoft Kinect and Asus Xtion, has shifted the research areas of robotics and computer vision from 2D-based imaging and laser scanning toward 3D-based depth scenes for environment processing. As physical objects or scenarios are built using more than a single image, images from different times and positions need to be aligned with each other to provide a more complete view. We call the alignment process registration, and it plays a key role in object reconstruction, scene mapping, and robot localization applications. Depending on the number of views that are processed simultaneously, registration is divided into multi-view [1] and pair-wise cases [2]. Our paper focuses on the latter case for constructed range images captured by 3D cameras. From two images, called the model and the data, the registration algorithm finds the best homogeneous transformation that aligns

the data and the model image in a common coordinate system.

The iterative closest point (ICP) algorithm [3] and its variants, such as EM-ICP [4] and generalized ICP [5], have been indispensable tools in registration algorithms. ICP's concept and implementation are easy to understand. It derives a transformation that draws images closer to each other using their L_2 error iteratively. ICP-class algorithms have a drawback for general registration in that they require a further assumption of near-optimal initial pose transformation; otherwise, the registration process is likely to converge to local instead of global or near global optima. Some mesh and point cloud editor software programs, such as Meshlab [6], include an ICP built-in registration tool; however, they require that users perform manual pre-alignment before ICP can be applied.

To overcome the shortage of ICP-class methods, automatic registration algorithms in general perform two steps: coarse initialization and fine transformation. If two point clouds are sufficiently close, the first step can be omitted. Otherwise, researchers are faced with

*Correspondence: nb14505@shibaura-it.ac.jp
[1]Department of Functional Control System, Shibaura Institute of Technology, 307 Fukasaku, Minuma-ku, Saitama City, Saitama, 337-8570, Japan
Full list of author information is available at the end of the article

a big challenge. Two approaches for coarse transformation, pre-alignment estimation, or initialization exist: local and global. The former uses local descriptors (or signatures), such as PFH [7] and SIFT [8], which encode local shape variation in neighborhood points. If the key points of these descriptors appear in both registered point clouds, the initialization movement can be estimated by using sample consensus algorithms, such as RANSAC [9]. Unfortunately, it is not always guaranteed that these signatures will appear in both registered point clouds. On the other hand, global approaches, such as Go-ICP [10] and SAICP [11], take all the points into account. The computation cost is the biggest problem in this approach. In big number data cases, the computation cost becomes large. By virtue of new search algorithms, in particular heuristic optimal methods, and the increase in computer speed achieved by using multi-core computer processor units (CPUs) and graphic computation units (GPUs) [12], it is possible to find reasonable solutions using global approaches for the registration problem. When the coarse transformation has been estimated, the ICP algorithm is an efficient tool for finding the fine transformation.

By integrating optimal search tools with an ICP algorithm, researchers have created hybrid algorithms that integrate global optimizers with ICP. However, this approach has its limitations. SAICP, a parameter-based algorithm, uses simulated annealing (SA) [13] as a search engine to find the best movement combination of rotation angles and translation. However, SA is not sufficiently effective to allow its application to a complicated fitness function, where the potential of a failed convergence is high. Go-ICP converges slowly, since it uses the branch-and-bound (BnB) method, a time consuming and non-heuristic method, as a search algorithm to ensure a 100% convergence rate. In addition, ICP algorithms frequently include a kd-tree structure for searching corresponding points. Using the kd-tree nearest neighbor search method also leads to a high computation cost and a long runtime.

In this paper, a new global direct registration method for 3D constructed surfaces captured by range cameras in cases where the initialization is not good is proposed.

- It eliminates the ICP algorithm from the registration process and thus becomes a direct method.
- As other global registration methods, the new method requires no local descriptors and operates directly on raw scanning data.
- The method uses the improved self-adaptive differential evolution (ISADE) algorithm [14] as a search engine to find the global minima as a direct method that does not use a fine registration procedure such as ICP.
- Furthermore, ray casting-based error calculation reduces the computation cost and runtime because

of the potential for using parallelized computation. CPU-based parallel computing procedures allow the algorithm to find the solution at a rate equivalent to the online rate.

The structure of this paper is as follows.

- Section 1 comprises the introduction.
- In Section 2, the classic and up-to-date methods of range image registration are presented.
- In Section 3, the methodology and the new approach of the proposed method are provided.
- In Section 4, the experiments and results are described.
- In Section 5, the discussion and conclusions are presented.

2 Range image registration

This part summarises some approaches for global range image registration problem up to date.

2.1 Registration error function and ICP approach

SVD and PCA [15] are integrated with ICP in classical methods and global search algorithms are integrated with ICP in most current hybrid methods. In this integration, SVD and PCA find the coarse transformation while ICP is the fine transformation estimation tool. The original version of the ICP algorithm relies on the L_2 error to derive the transformation (rotation $\mathbf{R} \in SO^3$ and translation $\mathbf{t} \in R^3$), which minimizes the L_2 type error:

$$E(\mathbf{R}, \mathbf{t}) = \sum_{i=1}^{n} e_i(\mathbf{R}, \mathbf{t}) = \sum_{i=1}^{n} |\mathbf{R}\mathbf{x_i} + \mathbf{t} - \mathbf{y_{j*}}| \tag{1}$$

where $X = \{x_i\}, \{i = 1, 2, 3, \ldots, m\}$ is the model point cloud and $Y = \{y_j\}, \{j = 1, 2, 3, \ldots, n\}$ is the data point cloud, x_i and $y_j \in R^3$ are the coordinates of the points in the point clouds, $\mathbf{R}$ and $\mathbf{t}$ are the rotation and translation matrix, respectively, $\mathbf{y_{j*}}$ is the corresponding point of $\mathbf{x_i}$ denoting the closest point in data point cloud Y. $\mathbf{R}$ and $\mathbf{t}$ are determined by Roll-Pitch-Yaw movement of three rotation angles (α, β, γ) and translation values (x, y, z).

Variants of the ICP algorithm rely on different distance categories to define the closest points. Point-to-point distance and point-to-plane distance are two popular examples. Equation 2 presents the former case.

$$j^* = \underset{j \in \{1, \ldots, n\}}{\operatorname{argmin}} ||\mathbf{R}\mathbf{x_i} + \mathbf{t} - \mathbf{y_j}|| \tag{2}$$

The following iterative process is designed to achieve the final transformation.

1. Compute the closest model points for each data point as in Eq. 2.
2. Compute the transformation $\mathbf{R}$ and $\mathbf{t}$ based on the error obtained using Eq. 1.

3. Apply **R** and **t** to the data point clouds.
4. Repeat steps 1, 2, and 3 until the error obtained using (1) is smaller than a set tolerance level or the procedure reaches its maximum iteration.

Step by step, the data point cloud becomes closer to the model point cloud and the process stops at local minima. ICP's variants, such as LMICP [16] and SICP [17], use different methods to calculate the transformation from error $E(\mathbf{R}, \mathbf{t})$. A well-known accumulation registration method in the KinectFusion algorithm [18] uses ICP to register two consecutive frames. The transformation matrix for the current frame is estimated by multiplying the matrices from the previous registration steps.

2.2 Global hybrid registration algorithm
ICP algorithms constitute the most suitable method for registering close or pre-aligned point cloud data. In other cases, the algorithm frequently converges incorrectly. Global search algorithms are suitable for solving this problem, since they can find the global instead of the local minima. To reduce the burden of the global search algorithm, researchers frequently flatten the search space by using ICP. Figures 1 and 2 show an example of ICP's operation as a flattening tool. In Fig. 1, from any beginning point, after many iterations, ICP finds the nearest local optima point. Figure 2 shows that a complex fitness function (colored black) becomes a simpler one (colored red). As a result, global search methods are able to find the global minima more effectively.

The integration is effective in the case of point cloud data where the point number is small. For cases where

the point number is large, the hybrid approach with ICP becomes slow. This method cannot therefore be implemented in real-time applications.

3 The new direct global approach
With the newly developed global search algorithms, flattening using ICP inner loops in registration becomes redundant. Our method integrates a new global search algorithm, ISADE, which is suitable for complicated fitness functions when the flattening process is not performed, and a ray casting-based corresponding search method to accelerate the objective function calculation in the registration procedure.

3.1 Ray-casting for fast corresponding point determination on constructed range image
The KinectFusion algorithm, a real-time scene reconstructing pipeline, uses ICP as the only method for registering two continuous frames. The procedure requires a powerful GPU to speed up calculations and reduce runtime. However, global registration algorithms calculate a thousand times more error functions than ICP and thus, so that these algorithms can be applied online or using less powerful processors, faster error calculation methods must be included.

ICP algorithms use the kd-tree [19] structure to speed up the process of determining j^* in Eq. 2. The complexity of the kd-tree nearest neighbor search algorithms is $O(log(n))$, where n is the set number of the search points. Figure 3 shows an example of the true closest corresponding points of the model and data point clouds.

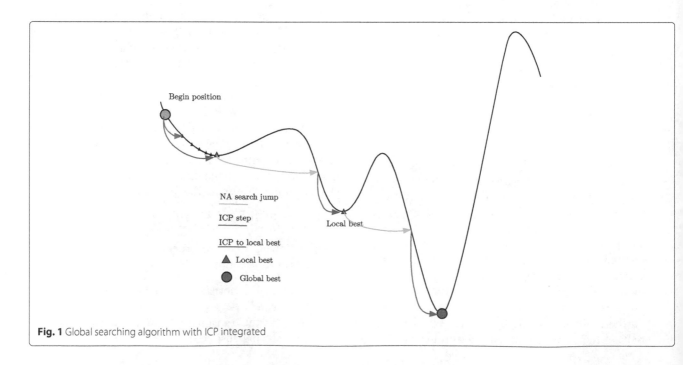

Fig. 1 Global searching algorithm with ICP integrated

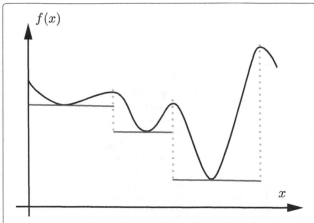

Fig. 2 Example of flatten objective function after ICP in *red* color where original function is in *black*

Ray casting [20] is one of the most basic of the many computer graphics rendering methods. The idea behind the ray-casting method is to direct a ray from the eye through each pixel and find the closest object blocking the path of the ray. Using the material properties and light effect in the scene, rendering methods can determine the shading of the object. Some hidden surface removal algorithms use ray casting to find the closest surfaces to the eye and eliminate all others that are at a greater distance along the same ray. The Point Cloud Library [21] uses ray casting as a filtering method; it removes all points that are obscured by other points.

We apply ray casting to find the approximated closest point using a range camera model. Constructed range images or point cloud data are frequently captured by a 3D range camera, where a range image can be considered a 2D gray image, G; the value of each pixel shows the depth of a point. To simplify the problem, we do not take distortion into consideration.

$$z_{i,j} = G_{i,j} \tag{3}$$

where $z_{i,j}$ is the depth of the image at pixel column i and row j.

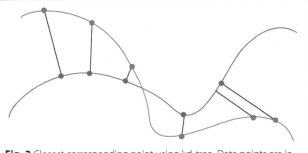

Fig. 3 Closest corresponding point using kd-tree. Data points are in *blue* and model points are in *red*

Equation 4 converts range image data points to real 3D depth data $\{x, y, z\}$ in R^3.

$$x_{i,j} = (i - cx)G_{i,j}/fx \tag{4a}$$

$$y_{i,j} = (j - cy)G_{i,j}/fy \tag{4b}$$

$$z_{i,j} = G_{i,j} \tag{4c}$$

where fx, fy, cx, and cy are the intrinsic parameters of the depth camera.

Inversely, pixel position i, j is to be calculated. Figure 4 shows the method's idea.

Using the corresponding points obtained in the ray-casting step, we determine the depth difference $\Delta z_{i,j}$ for the next step of calculating the objective function for the global search method, as

$$\Delta z_{i,j}(R, t) = \left\{ \begin{array}{cc} z_{i,j}^X - z_{i,j}^{Y^{R,t}} & \text{if} \quad |\Delta z_{i,j}(R, t)| < \text{threshold} \\ 0 & \text{otherwise} \end{array} \right\} \tag{5}$$

where R and t are the rotation and translation matrix, respectively, $z_{i,j}^X$ is the depth of the model point cloud, and $z_{i,j}^{Y(R,t)}$ is the depth of the data point cloud after applying the rotation and translation matrix with i, j from the ray casting process.

The ray-casting method is simple and fast (with a complexity of $O(1)$) and, more importantly, potentially parallel computing can be applied.

3.2 Objective function
Global optimization methods use fitness or objective functions to find the transformation that drives the fitness function to the smallest value. We propose a fitness function $F(R, t)$:

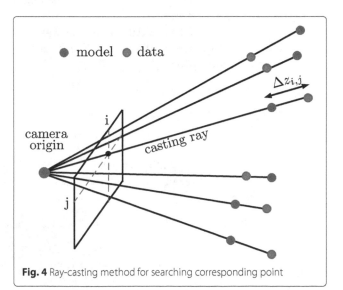

Fig. 4 Ray-casting method for searching corresponding point

$$F(R, t) = f(k)\frac{1}{k^2}\sum_{i=1}^{n}\sum_{j=1}^{m}(\Delta z_{i,j}(R, t))^2 \qquad (6)$$

where R and t are the rotation and translation matrix, respectively, m and n are the height and width of the image frame, and k is the inlier point number.

To gain a smaller error in a larger number of inlier points, we used an additional function $f(k)$:

$$f(k) = \left\{ \begin{array}{ll} \infty & \text{if } k < N/10 \\ 1 - k/N & \text{if } k \geqslant N/10 \end{array} \right\} \qquad (7)$$

where N is the number of points in the data point cloud.

The ray-casting-based method makes the algorithm run significantly faster than the kd-tree-based approach. However, since a global search algorithm handles a large number of points at a huge computation cost, we take parallel implementation into consideration. Since in most computers a multi-core processor is available, using the CPU for parallel computing is convenient in most applications. In addition, CPU multi-core parallel implementation is even easier with OpenMP library [22]. Furthermore, the ray-casting process adapts well to parallel computing, and the corresponding points can be calculated in different processes or threads.

3.3 ISADE, an efficient improved version of differential evolution algorithm

3.3.1 Differential evolution

Differential evolution (DE) is an evolutionary optimization technique originally proposed by Storn and Price [23], characterized by operators of mutation and crossover. In DE, the scaling factor F and crossover rate C_r determine the correction and speed of convergence, while another important parameter, NP, the population size, remains a user-assigned parameter to handle problem complexity. Figure 5 shows pseudo-code or implementation flowchart of DE algorithms.

a) Initialization in DE The initial population was generated uniformly at random in the range lower boundary (lb) and upper boundary (ub).

$$X_i^G = lb_j + \text{rand}_j(0, 1)(ub_j - lb_j) \qquad (8)$$

where $\text{rand}_j(0, 1)$ a random number $\in [0, 1]$.

b) Mutation operation In DE, there are various mutation schemes to create mutant vectors $V_i^G = (V_{i,1}^G, \ldots, V_{i,D}^G)$ for each individual of population at each generation G. X_i^G is target vector in the current population, D is vector dimension number.

$$\text{DE/rand/1}: V_{i,j}^G = X_{r_1,j}^G + F\left(X_{r_2,j}^G - X_{r_3,j}^G\right) \qquad (9a)$$

$$\text{DE/best/1}: V_{i,j}^G = X_{\text{best},j}^G + F\left(X_{r_1,j}^G - X_{r_2,j}^G\right) \qquad (9b)$$

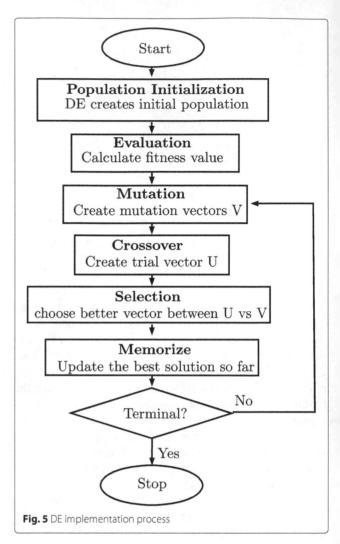

Fig. 5 DE implementation process

$$\text{DE/currenttobest/1}: V_{i,j}^G = X_{i,j}^G + F\left(X_{\text{best},j}^G - X_{i,j}^G\right) + F\left(X_{r_1,j}^G - X_{r_2,j}^G\right) \qquad (9c)$$

$$\text{DE/rand/2}: V_{i,j}^G = X_{i,j}^G + F\left(X_{r_2,j}^G - X_{r_3,j}^G\right) + F\left(X_{r_4,j}^G - X_{r_5,j}^G\right) \qquad (9d)$$

$$\text{DE/best/2}: V_{i,j}^G = X_{\text{best},j}^G + F\left(X_{r_1,j}^G - X_{r_2,j}^G\right) + F\left(X_{r_3,j}^G - X_{r_4,j}^G\right) \qquad (9e)$$

$$\text{DE/randtobest/1}: V_{i,j}^G = X_{\text{best},j}^G + F\left(X_{\text{best},j}^G - X_{r_2,j}^G\right) + F\left(X_{r_2,j}^G - X_{r_3,j}^G\right) \qquad (9f)$$

where $r_1, r_2, r_3, r_4,$ and r_5 are randomly selected integers in the range $[1, NP]$.

c) Crossover operation After mutation process, DE performs a binomial crossover operator on X_i^G and V_i^G to generate a trial vector $U_i^G = (U_{i,1}^G, \ldots, U_{i,D}^G)$ for each individual population i as shown in Eq. 10.

$$U_{i,j}^G = \begin{cases} V_{i,j}^G & \text{if } \text{rand}_j \leqslant C_r \quad \text{or} \quad j = j_{\text{rand}} \\ X_{i,j}^G & \text{otherwise} \end{cases} \quad (10)$$

where $i = 1, \ldots, NP$, $j = 1, \ldots, D$, j_{rand} is a randomly chosen integer in $[1, D]$, $\text{rand}_j(0, 1)$ is a uniformly distributed random number between 0 and 1 generated for each j and $C_r \in [0, 1]$ is called the crossover control parameter. Using j_{rand} ensures the difference between the trial vector U_i^G and target vector X_i^G.

c) Selection operation The selection operator is performed to select the better solution between the target vector X_i^G and the trial vector U_i^G entering to the next generation.

$$X_i^{G+1} = \begin{cases} U_i^G & \text{if } f(U_i^G) \leqslant f(X_i^G) \\ X_i^G & \text{otherwise} \end{cases} \quad (11)$$

where $i = 1, \ldots, NP$, X_i^{G+1} is a target vector in the next generation's population.

3.3.2 Improvement of self-adapting control parameters in differential evolution

a) Adaptive selection learning strategy in mutation operator In our study of ISADE, we randomly chose three mutation schemes: DE/best/1/bin, DE/best/2/bin, and DE/rand to best/1/bin. DE/best/1/bin and DE/best/2/bin have a good convergence property, and DE/rand to best/1/bin has a good population diverse property. The probability of applying these strategies is equal at values of $p_1 = p_2 = p_3 = 1/3$.

$$\text{DE/best/1}: V_{i,j}^G = X_{\text{best},j}^G + F\left(X_{r_1,j}^G - X_{r_2,j}^G\right) \quad (12a)$$

$$\text{DE/best/2}: V_{i,j}^G = X_{\text{best},j}^G + F\left(X_{r_1,j}^G - X_{r_2,j}^G\right) + F\left(X_{r_3,j}^G - X_{r_4,j}^G\right) \quad (12b)$$

$$\text{DE/randtobest/1}: V_{i,j}^G = X_{\text{best},j}^G + F\left(X_{\text{best},j}^G - X_{r_2,j}^G\right) + F\left(X_{r_2,j}^G - X_{r_3,j}^G\right) \quad (12c)$$

where r_1, r_2, r_3, r_4, and r_5 are randomly selected integers in the range $[1, NP]$, where NP is the population size.

b) Adaptive scaling factor To achieve a better performance, ISADE gives the scale factor F a large value initially to allow better exploration and a small value after the generations to allow appropriate exploitation. Instead of using sigmoid scaling in Eq. 13 taken from Tooyama and Hasegawa's study on APGA/VNC [24], ISADE adds a new factor to calculate F as shown in Eq. 14.

$$F_i = \frac{1}{1 + \exp\left(\alpha * \frac{i - NP/2}{NP}\right)} \quad (13)$$

$$F_i = \frac{F_i + F_i^{\text{mean}}}{2} \quad (14)$$

in which F_i^{mean} is calculated as Eq. 15.

$$F_i^{\text{mean}} = F_{\min} + (F_{\max} - F_{\min})\left(\frac{i_{\max} - i}{i_{\max}}\right)^{n_{\text{iter}}} \quad (15)$$

where $F_{\max}$ and $F_{\min}$ denote the lower and upper boundary condition of F with recommended values of 0.8 and 0.15, respectively. i, $i_{\max}$, and n_{iter} denote the current, max generation, and nonlinear modulation index as in Eq. 15.

$$n_{\text{iter}} = n_{\min} + (n_{\max} - n_{\min})\left(\frac{i}{i_{\max}}\right) \quad (16)$$

where $n_{\max}$ and $n_{\min}$ are typically chosen in the range $[0, 15]$. Recommended values for $n_{\min}$ and $n_{\max}$ are 0.2 and 6.0 respectively.

c) Crossver control parameter ISADE is able to detect whether the height of C_r values are useful. The control parameter C_r is assigned as

$$C_r^{i+1} = \begin{cases} \text{rand}_2 & \text{if } \text{rand}_1 \leqslant \tau \\ C_r^i & \text{otherwise} \end{cases} \quad (17)$$

where rand_1 and rand_2 are random values $\in [0, 1]$, τ represents the probability to adjust C_r, which is also updated using

$$C_r^{i+1} = \begin{cases} C_{r_{\min}} & C_{r_{\min}} \leqslant C_r^{i+1} \leqslant C_{r_{\text{medium}}} \\ C_{r_{\max}} & C_{r_{\text{medium}}} \leqslant C_r^{i+1} \leqslant C_{r_{\max}} \end{cases} \quad (18)$$

where $C_{r_{\min}}$, $C_{r_{\text{medium}}}$, and $C_{r_{\max}}$ denote a low value, median value, and high value of the crossover parameter, respectively. We use recommended values of $\tau = 0.1$, $C_{r_{\min}} = 0.05$, $C_{r_{\text{medium}}} = 0.50$, and $C_{r_{\max}} = 0.95$.

d) Combination of ISADE and ray-casting ISADE eliminates tuning tasks for the problem-dependent parameters F and C_r. With simple adaptive rules, the computation complexity of this new version of the DE algorithm remains the same as that of the original version. All the above ideas and theories of ISADE algorithm and ray-casting method are implemented as in the flowchart shown in Fig. 6.

4 Experiment and results

This section describes experiments that were conducted using the proposed method in real range image data registration and presents the results. We integrated different global search methods with the ray casting-based algorithm in order to obtain a comparison between ISADE and the state-of-the-art methods as follows.

1) SA proposed in Luck et al.'s paper, *Registration of range data using a hybrid simulated annealing and iterative closest point algorithm.*

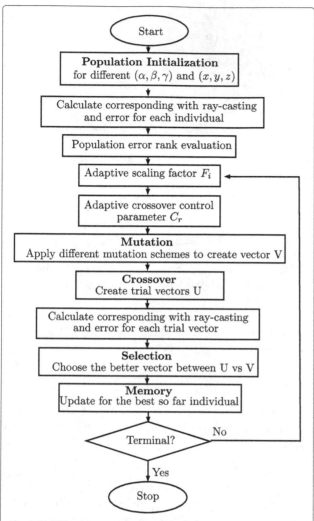

Fig. 6 ISADE implementation process with ray-casting corresponding method

2) Particle swarm optimization (PSO) proposed in Talbi et al.'s paper, Particle swarm optimization for image processing [25].
3) Genetic algorithm (GA) proposed in Valsecchi et al.'s paper, An image registration approach using genetic algorithms [26].
4) DE proposed in Falco et al.'s paper, Differential evolution as a viable tool for satellite image registration [27].

We also calculated the ray casting-based error of the KinectFusion and Go-ICP algorithms for further comparison. All algorithms were implemented in C++ and compiled with GNU/g++ tool.

4.1 Range image dataset
In our experiments, a number of pair-wise registrations was conducted using well-known depth data,

"RGB-D Dataset 7-Scenes," taken from the Kinect Microsoft Camera downloaded from the Microsoft Research Website, http://research.microsoft.com/en-us/projects/7-scenes/. Specifically, Figs. 7 and 8 show all the scenes: Chess, Fire, Heads, Office, Pumpkin, RedKitchen, and Stairs. The details of the data used in the registration experiments are as follows.

Chess dataset: image sequence 2, frame 960 vs frame 980.

Other datasets: image sequence 1, frame 000 vs frame 020.

These "PNG" format depth images are sub-sampled into a smaller resolution of 128×96, which is five times smaller than the original resolution of 640×480 in each dimension. The purpose of using a dataset with a smaller number of points is to achieve a suitable runtime while preserving robustness and accuracy.

4.2 Parameter settings
For each method, 30 runs were performed. The search space had rotation angles and translation limited at $[-\pi/5, \pi/5]$ and $[-1, 1]$ separately. This means that the limitation of the rotation angles was 36° and of the translation was 1 m.

The algorithm parameters shown in Table 1 constitute the configuration for all the algorithms. All methods were run on a desktop PC powered with an Intel core I7-4790 CPU 3.60 GHz × 8 processor, 8 GB RAM memory and Linux Ubuntu 14.04 64-bit Operation System. The new algorithm C++ code was written based on reference from Andreas Geiger's LIBICP code [28].

4.3 Comparison with KinectFusion algorithm
Accompanied by depth ranger images, "RGB-D Dataset 7-Scenes" provides homogeneous camera to world transposes at each frame calculated using the KinectFusion algorithm. We converted those camera transposes into transformation matrix between two frames as

$$T_i^j = T_i^{-1} * T_j \tag{19a}$$

$$T_i^j = \begin{bmatrix} R_i^j & t_i^j \\ 0\ 0\ 0 & 1 \end{bmatrix} \tag{19b}$$

where T_i^j is the transformation matrix to move frame j to align with frame i, T_i and T_j are the homogeneous transpose matrix for the camera at frame i and j, respectively, and R_i^j and t_i^j are the rotation and translation matrix of T_i^j, respectively.

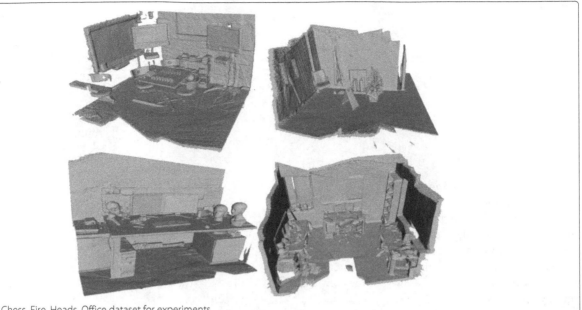

Fig. 7 RGB-D Chess, Fire, Heads, Office dataset for experiments

R_i^j and t_i^j are applied to ray-casting error calculation methods for two frames, as in Eq. 6, to describe the errors of the KinectFusion algorithm. Table 2 presents the mean errors of the proposed method in comparison with the error of the KinectFusion algorithm. The significantly smaller mean errors of the proposed method prove its superiority to the KinectFusion algorithm registration pipeline.

Figures 9 and 10 visually show the registration results of the proposed algorithm for the seven scenes in center and those of KinectFusion on the left hand side, to provide a visual comparison. The seven scenes included are Chess, Fire, Heads, Office, Pumpkin, Red-Kitchen, and Stairs. The model point clouds are colored red, and the data point clouds are colored green.

In these figures, the proposed algorithm outperforms KinectFusion is clearly seen. Even in the best case of KinectFusion, such as Stairs or RedKitchen, the overlapping regions, where the two colors are mixed together, are not as clearly seen as in the results of the proposed algorithm.

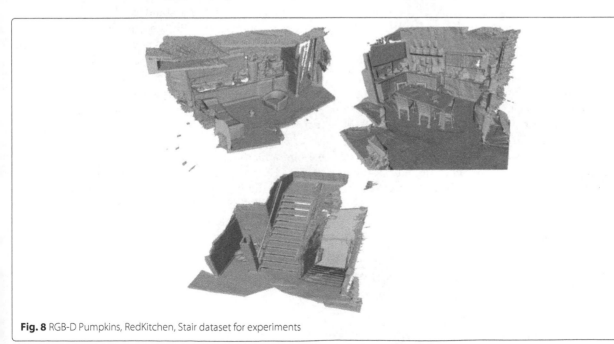

Fig. 8 RGB-D Pumpkins, RedKitchen, Stair dataset for experiments

Table 1 Algorithm configuration

Algorithm	DE	GA	SA	PSO	Go-ICP
Parameters	$F_0 = 0.8$	$Pc = 0.95$;	$\alpha = 0.995$	elites $= 4$	trimFraction $= 0.0$
	$C_r = 0.9$	$Pm = 0.1$;		neighbors $= 5$	
	DE/rand/1/bin	elites $= 5$		$c1 = c2 = c3 = 2.1$	distTransSize $= 50$
Maxgen	100	100	3000	100;	
Population	30	30		30	data subsample $= 1000$ points

An example of applying the new method to consecutive localizations can be seen in Fig. 11. The pumpkin 3D scene, which is built from seven different range images (frame 000, 020, ..., 120), visually shows the accuracy of the proposed method at various percentages of overlapping regions. The different frames are in different colors. A video at https://www.youtube.com/watch?v= sgaUry5qsxU gives a clearer view.

4.4 Comparison with Go-ICP algorithm

From authors contributed code [29], we performed experiments to compare our method with Go-ICP on accuracy, runtime, and robustness. Go-ICP configuration parameters were set as in Table 1 with the identical searching boundary with other methods. distTransSize is the number of nodes in translation searching boundary. It was set to 50 or translation resolution is at 40 mm. Raising accuracy by increasing distTransSize to 500 or 4 mm resolution effort failed due to infinite runtime. Go-ICP were able to register Heads and Office datasets at distTransSize of 100 with runtime presented in Table 5.

The disadvantage of big resolution could be compensated by inner ICP loops; however, the smaller the resolution, the more accurate the algorithm is. We set the data subsample to 1000; Go-ICP reaches infinitive runtime at the original 128×96 resolution.

Together with KinectFusion and our method errors, Table 2 presents the mean errors of Go-ICP algorithm where "nan" stands for undefined result in the case of infinitive runtime and "inf" stands for wrong convergence with few overlapse points. Over all, only heads and office showed good convergence with small error and run time. However, those small errors are still bigger than the new method.

Figures 9 and 10 also show the registration results of Go-ICP algorithm on the right side together with new method results in the center and KinectFusion algorithm result on the left side. From those figures, the new method better performance is clearly seen. In the case of RedKitchen dataset, the wrong convergence results of Go-ICP were observed, the error was small because of small over-lapsed percentage.

Average runtime for Go-ICP on different datasets are presented in Table 5 where average run times of the new algorithm at different generation numbers are presented. In the table, "inf" values stand for infinitive runtime. Go-ICP was fast in case of heads dataset or extreme slow for the case of Chess dataset.

Over all, the new methods outperformed Go-ICP on experiment datasets in accuracy, runtime, and robustness.

4.5 Comparison between different optimization algorithms

Tables 3 and 4 show the experimental results of all the integrations and methods in four categories: min, max, mean, and standard deviation.

The smaller means and standard deviations for every dataset in comparison with the other methods show the accuracy and robustness of the new search engine as compared to the state-of-the-art search algorithms. In some cases, the experimental results show that the other integrations performed better than KinectFusion. The ICP accumulating error is the reason for this poor performance.

4.6 Iterations vs convergence

In Fig. 12, we compare the robust results of convergence of the registration of the seven scenes for a small number of iterations between using ISADE and

Table 2 Error comparison between new method, KinectFusion, and Go-ICP algorithms

	Chess	Fire	Heads	Office	Pumpkin	RedKitchen	Stairs
Our method	**0.10230**	**0.03179**	**0.01000**	**0.03096**	**0.05563**	**0.03481**	**0.00883**
KinectFusion	22.37200	0.24311	2.99067	3.85941	0.11136	0.09836	0.01561
Go-ICP	nan	0.825212	0.01832	0.358507	inf	1.5387	2.28615

The boldface entries are for emphasis for better result in comparison between the new method with other methods

Table 3 Results of Chess, Fire, Heads, and Office datasets

Scene name	Algorithm	Min	Max	Mean	St. dev.
Chess	**ISADE**	**0.10047**	**0.11187**	**0.10230**	**0.002821482**
KinectFusion	DE	0.17453	3.92808	0.29860	0.112087291
ref: 22.372	GA	1.44923	1.80180	2.53723	0.691936150
	SA	1.11736	2.55157	1.65871	0.400817542
	PSO	1.19899	2.58186	1.72316	0.459892382
Fire	**ISADE**	**0.03169**	**0.03196**	**0.03179**	**8.70855E−005**
KinectFusion	DE	0.03873	0.26059	0.10263	0.066038287
ref: 0.243112	GA	0.22177	3.93133	1.58268	0.913837133
	SA	0.15060	0.88670	0.45855	0.249700426
	PSO	0.11158	0.63419	0.34592	0.151824890
Heads	**ISADE**	**0.00994**	**0.01016**	**0.01000**	**7.01799E−005**
KinectFusion	DE	0.01276	0.06570	0.02205	0.012768061
ref: 2.99067	GA	0.47056	1.70316	0.97758	0.358190303
	SA	0.30740	1.01428	0.65404	0.264058658
	PSO	0.20801	1.88772	0.54401	0.463097716
Office	**ISADE**	**0.03084**	**0.03115**	**0.03096**	**8.39925E−005**
KinectFusion	DE	0.03195	0.06436	0.04373	0.009462166
ref: 3.85941	GA	0.24518	4.05346	1.88819	0.928751342
	SA	0.10385	2.67972	0.84426	0.720046753
	PSO	0.07169	2.08078	0.58507	0.686244921

The boldface entries are for emphasis for better result in comparison between the new method with other methods

DE, where the horizontal axis represents the iteration, and the vertical axis represents the error. In comparison with ISADE, DE required significant larger iteration number to achieve convergence. With ISADE, from 70 iterations, all the results show a flat trend and no new optimal solutions with a significant difference are found. This iteration number for DE is 120.

These results show that, if we reduce the maximum number of iterations to 70, the results remain the same.

Table 4 Results of Pumpkin, RedKitchen and Stairs datasets

Scene name	Algorithm	Min	Max	Mean	St. dev.
Pumpkin	**ISADE**	**0.05541**	**0.05603**	**0.05563**	**0.000175987**
KinectFusion	DE	0.06555	0.16927	0.11105	0.111050113
ref: 0.111361	GA	0.45803	3.15529	1.42922	0.775060060
	SA	0.07468	0.90335	0.49504	0.248322702
	PSO	0.11181	1.43345	0.36443	0.334116975
RedKitchen	**ISADE**	**0.03423**	**0.03759**	**0.03481**	**0.000915588**
KinectFusion	DE	0.05879	0.60304	0.17479	0.149183155
ref: 0.0983645	SA	0.52141	5.48133	2.07233	1.339500137
	GA	0.12508	1.58015	0.62601	0.441544434
	PSO	0.05515	2.48188	0.54354	0.671268667
Stairs	**ISADE**	**0.00875**	**0.00898**	**0.00883**	**0.000079463**
KinectFusion	DE	0.00975	0.04665	0.01767	0.009514675
ref: 0.0156084	SA	0.21207	2.24988	1.19252	0.627554990
	GA	0.01405	1.08881	0.29528	0.304574563
	PSO	0.04632	0.96723	0.25021	0.239971819

The boldface entries are for emphasis for better result in comparison between the new method with other methods

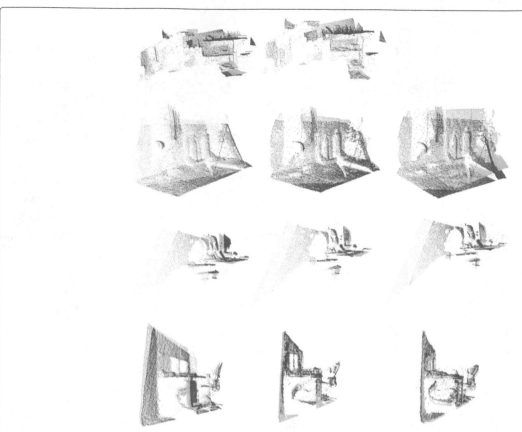

Fig. 9 First four scenes (Chess, Fire, Heads, Office) registration output example. KinectFusion results are in the *left* hand side, the new algorithm's results are in the *center*, and Go-ICP algorithm's results are on the *right* hand side

Fig. 10 Last three scenes (Pumpkin, RedKitchen, Stairs) registration output example. KinectFusion results are in the *left* hand side, the new algorithm's results are in the *center*, and Go-ICP algorithm's results are on the *right* hand side

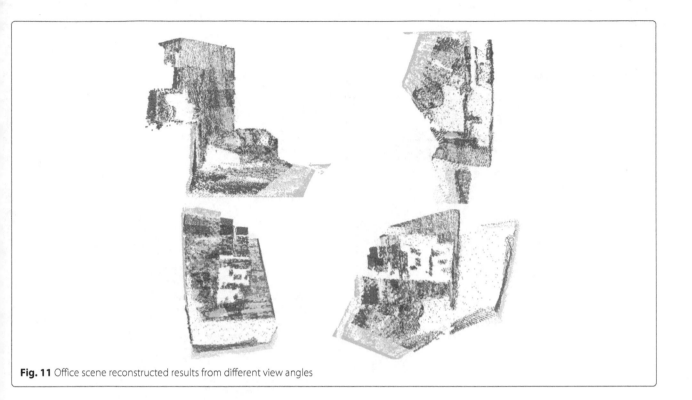

Fig. 11 Office scene reconstructed results from different view angles

Clearly, the smaller the iteration number, the shorter is the runtime.

4.7 Results from registering in different movement patterns and frame distances

Figure 13 shows the values of rotation angles (α, β, γ) in radian and translation distances (x, y, z) in meter of 3D camera movement. Those values were obtained by using new algorithm to register range images from frame 001 to 060 respectively into the frame 000 of seq-01 in different datasets. The process stops if the movement values get over searching boundaries. From all datasets, we choose three typical movement of Chess, Fire, and Heads

datasets for rotating, sliding, and forwarding with rotating movements respectively.

The results with no sudden value changing between two consecutive frames verify the feasibility of applying the new algorithm in registering range images of different movement patterns and frame distances.

4.8 Runtime

For the data of 128×96 resolution, average runtime for the proposed method are shown in Table 5. In the results, the average runtime for registration is around 0.6 s for 150 iterations of all scenes. Since the distance between two frames is 20, the registering equivalence rate is 33 frames

Table 5 Average running time (in second) on different scenes of new methods and Go-ICP

	New methods 100 generations	New method 150 generations	Go-ICP distTransSize = 50	Go-ICP distTransSize = 100
Chess	0.388414	0.516832	inf	inf
Fire	0.385928	0.625765	14.2786	inf
Heads	0.335828	0.562451	0.102944	0.104659
Office	0.378768	0.560734	0.030326	34.411
Pumpkin	0.410615	0.621756	104.468	inf
RedKitchen	0.415258	0.588466	30.3815	inf
Stairs	0.409834	0.597050	188.205	inf

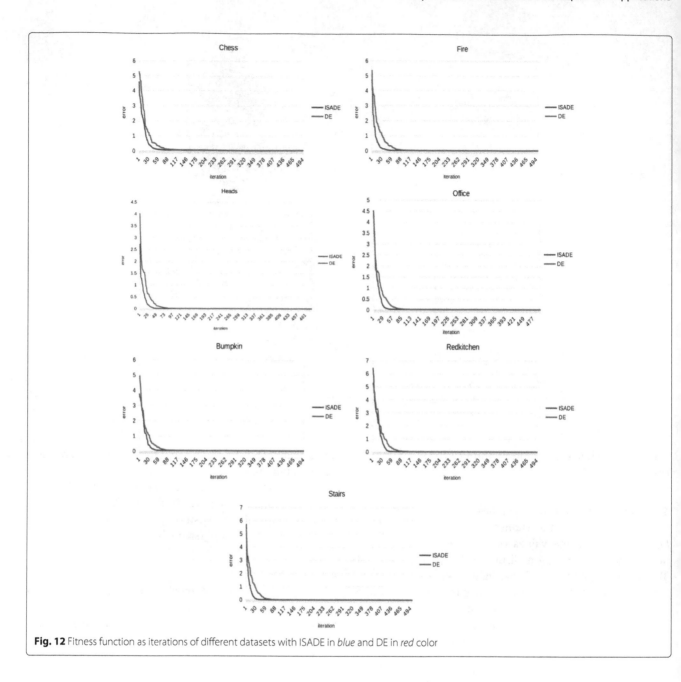

Fig. 12 Fitness function as iterations of different datasets with ISADE in *blue* and DE in *red* color

per second (fps). At this rate, when we move the camera, the algorithm are able to update the scenarios.

By subsampling the data range image and remaining the model range image, the new algorithm gain smaller runtime while error level stays unchanged. Figure 14 shows the runtime at different level of subsample on the right hand and the errors in the left hand for the RedKitchen scenario.

5   Discussion

Image registration has become a very active research area. Recently, the approach of using EAs, in particular in new methods, proved their potential for tackling the image registration problem based on their robustness and accuracy for searching for global optimal solutions. When EAs are used as search tools, good initial conditions are not necessary for avoiding local minima while converging to near-global minima solutions.

We proposed a novel registration method in which a fast ray-casting-based error calculation is integrated with a powerful self-adaptive optimization algorithm. The experimental results showed that ISADE is able to find a robust and accurate transformation matrix, while the ray-casting method is fast and efficient in calculating error for global registration problems.

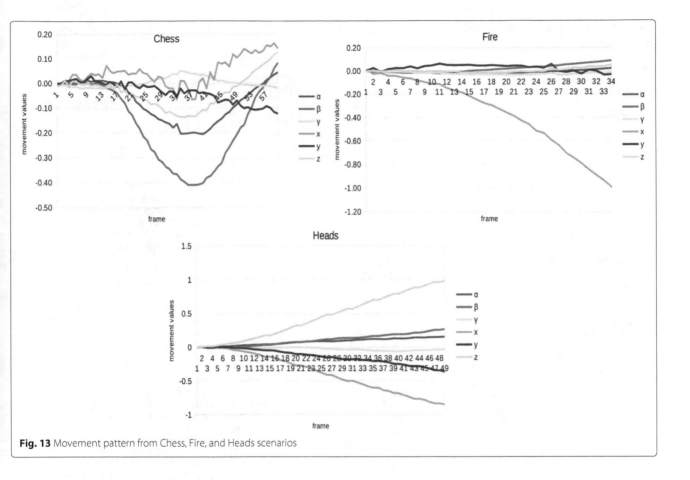

Fig. 13 Movement pattern from Chess, Fire, and Heads scenarios

A more important point is that, by eliminating inner ICP loops in hybrid integrations and fine-tuning procedures applied in previously proposed methods, the newly proposed method becomes the first direct, as well as the first online potential, global registration algorithm. Its robustness and accuracy were tested and verified in real 3D scenes captured by a Microsoft Kinect camera.

Currently, the algorithm is implemented using a CPU parallel procedure. In future work, the new algorithm can be implemented on a GPU to reduce its runtime and error while retaining its accuracy and robustness. Furthermore, the method can be extended for general point clouds from different sources by using a virtual camera surface and presenting it as a constructed surface. The proposed

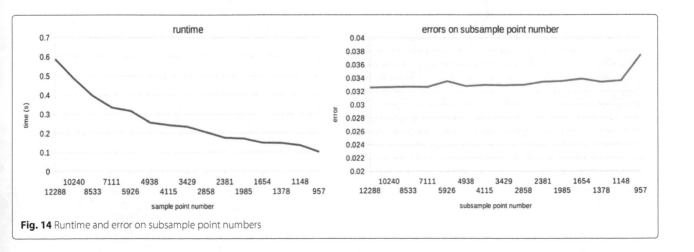

Fig. 14 Runtime and error on subsample point numbers

method is also potentially suitable for super resolution range images.

Authors' contributions

LT took charge of the system coding, doing experiments, data analysis and writing the whole paper excluding ISADE algorithm part at Subsection 3.3. TB took charge of coding and writing for ISADE algorithm part at Subsection 3.3. HH took charge of advisor position for paper presentation, experiment design, data analysis presentation as well English revising. All authors read and approved the final manuscript.

Competing interests

The authors declare that they have no competing interests.

Author details

[1]Department of Functional Control System, Shibaura Institute of Technology, 307 Fukasaku, Minuma-ku, Saitama City, Saitama, 337-8570, Japan. [2]School of Mechanical Engineering, Hanoi University of Science and Technology, 1 Dai Co Viet Road, Ha Noi, Viet Nam. [3]Department of Machinery and Control System, Shibaura Institute of Technology, 307 Fukasaku, Minuma-ku, Saitama City, Saitama, 337-8570, Japan.

References

1. Sharp GC, Lee SW, Wehe DK (2004) Multiview registration of 3D scenes by minimizing error between coordinate frames. IEEE Trans Pattern Anal Mach Intell 26(8):1037–1050. doi:10.1109/TPAMI.2004.49
2. Holz D, Ichim AE, Tombari F, Rusu RB, Behnke S (2015) Registration with the Point Cloud Library: a modular framework for aligning in 3-D. IEEE Robot Autom Mag 22(4):110–124. doi:10.1109/MRA.2015.2432331
3. Besl P, McKay ND (1992) A method for registration of 3-d shapes. IEEE Trans Pattern Anal Mach Intell 14(2):239–256. doi:10.1109/34.121791
4. Granger S, Pennec X (2002) Multi-scale EM-ICP: a fast and robust approach for surface registration. In: European Conference on Computer Vision, vol. 2353. pp 418–432
5. Segal A, Haehnel D, Thrun S (2009) Generalized-ICP. In: Proceedings of Robotics: Science and Systems, Seattle, USA. doi:10.15607/RSS.2009.V.021
6. Meshlab. http://meshlab.sourceforge.net/. Accessed 15 Jan 2017
7. Rusu RB, Marton ZC, Blodow N, Beetz M (2008) Persistent point feature histograms for 3D point clouds. In: Proceedings of the 10th International Conference on Intelligent Autonomous Systems (IAS-10), Baden-Baden. pp 119–128
8. Sehgal A, Cernea D, Makaveeva M (2010) Real-time scale invariant 3D range point cloud registration. In: Campilho A, Kamel M (eds). Image Analysis and Recognition. ICIAR 2010. Lecture Notes in Computer Science. Springer, Berlin Heidelberg Vol. 6111. doi:10.1007/978-3-642-13772-3_23
9. Wu F, Fang X (2007) An improved RANSAC homography algorithm for feature based image mosaic. In: Proceedings of the 7th WSEAS International Conference on Signal Processing, Computational Geometry & Artificial Vision, ISCGAV'07, World Scientific and Engineering Academy and Society (WSEAS), Stevens Point, Wisconsin. pp 202–207. http://dl.acm.org/citation.cfm?id=1364592.1364627
10. Yang J, Li H, Jia Y (2013) Go-icp: Solving 3D registration efficiently and globally optimally. In: 2013 IEEE International Conference on Computer Vision, Sydney. pp 1457–1464. doi:10.1109/ICCV.2013.184
11. Luck J, Little C, Hoff W (2000) Registration of range data using a hybrid simulated annealing and iterative closest point algorithm. In: Proceedings 2000 ICRA. Millennium Conference. IEEE International Conference on Robotics and Automation. Symposia Proceedings (Cat. No.00CH37065), San Francisco Vol. 4. pp 3739–3744. doi:10.1109/ROBOT.2000.845314
12. Neumann D, Lugauer F, Bauer S, Wasza J, Hornegger J (2011) Real-time RGB-d mapping and 3-D modeling on the GPU using the random ball cover data structure. In: 2011 IEEE International Conference on Computer Vision Workshops (ICCV Workshops), Barcelona. pp 1161–1167. doi:10.1109/ICCVW.2011.6130381
13. Ingber L (1993) Simulated annealing: practice versus theory. Math Comput Model 18(11):29–57. http://dx.doi.org/10.1016/0895-7177(93)90204-C
14. Bui T, Pham H, Hasegawa H (2013) Improve self-adaptive control parameters in differential evolution for solving constrained engineering optimization problems. J Comput Sci Technol 7(1):59–74. doi:10.1299/jcst.7.59
15. Marden S, Guivant J (2012) Improving the performance of ICP for real-time applications using an approximate nearest neighbour search. In: Proceedings of Australasian Conference on Robotics and Automation, New Zealand. pp 3–5
16. Lim Low K (2004) Linear least-squares optimization for point-toplane ICP surface registration. Tech Rep TR04-004, Department of Computer Science, University of North Carolina at Chapel Hill
17. Bouaziz S, Tagliasacchi A, Pauly M (2013) Sparse iterative closest point. In: Proceedings of the Eleventh Eurographics/ACMSIGGRAPH Symposium on Geometry Processing, SGP '13, Eurographics Association. Aire-la-Ville, Switzerland. pp 113–123. doi:10.1111/cgf.12178
18. Izadi S, Kim D, Hilliges O, Molyneaux D, Newcombe R, Kohli P, Shotton J, Hodges S, Freeman D, Davison A, Fitzgibbon A (2011) Kinect-Fusion: real-time 3d reconstruction and interaction using a moving depth camera. In: Proceedings of the 24th Annual ACM Symposium on User Interface Software and Technology, UIST '11. ACM, New York. pp 559–568. doi:10.1145/2047196.2047270
19. Chandran S (2012) Introduction to kd-trees. University of Maryland Department of Computer Science. https://www.cs.umd.edu/class/spring2002/cmsc420-0401/pbasic.pdf
20. Roth SD (1982) Ray casting for modeling solids. Comput Graph Image Process 18(2):109–144. doi:http://dx.doi.org/10.1016/0146-664X(82)90169-1
21. Point cloud library. http://pointclouds.org/. Accessed 15 Jan 2017
22. Openmp. http://openmp.org/wp/. Accessed: 15 Jan 2017
23. Storn R, Price K (1997) Differential evolution a simple and efficient heuristic for global optimization over continuous spaces. J Glob Optim 11(4):341–359. doi:10.1023/A:1008202821328
24. Tooyama S, Hasegawa H (2009) Adaptive plan system with genetic algorithm using the variable neighborhood range control. In: Evolutionary Computation, 2009. CEC '09. IEEE Congress on Evolutionary Computation, CEC '09. pp 846–853. doi:10.1109/CEC.2009.4983033
25. Chen YW, Mimori A, Lin C-L (2009) Hybrid particle swarm optimization for 3-d image registration. In: 16th IEEE International Conference on Image Processing (ICIP), Cairo. pp 1753–1756. doi:10.1109/ICIP.2009.5414613
26. Seixas FL, Ochi LS, Conci A, Saade DM (2008) Image registration using genetic algorithms. In: Proceedings of the 10th Annual Conference on Genetic and Evolutionary Computation, GECCO '08. ACM, New York. pp 1145–1146. doi:10.1145/1389095.1389320
27. Falco ID, Cioppa AD, Maisto D, Tarantino E (2008) Differential evolution as a viable tool for satellite image registration. Appl Soft Comput 8(4):1453–1462. Soft Computing for Dynamic Data Mining. doi:http://dx.doi.org/10.1016/j.asoc.2007.10.013
28. Iterative closest point implementation C++ code. http://www.cvlibs.net/software/libicp/. Accessed 15 Jan 2017
29. Go-ICP implementation C++ code. http://iitlab.bit.edu.cn/mcislab/~yangjiaolong/go-icp/. Accessed 15 Jan 2017

10

Visual SLAM algorithms: a survey from 2010 to 2016

Takafumi Taketomi[1]*, Hideaki Uchiyama[2] and Sei Ikeda[3]

Abstract

SLAM is an abbreviation for simultaneous localization and mapping, which is a technique for estimating sensor motion and reconstructing structure in an unknown environment. Especially, Simultaneous Localization and Mapping (SLAM) using cameras is referred to as visual SLAM (vSLAM) because it is based on visual information only. vSLAM can be used as a fundamental technology for various types of applications and has been discussed in the field of computer vision, augmented reality, and robotics in the literature. This paper aims to categorize and summarize recent vSLAM algorithms proposed in different research communities from both technical and historical points of views. Especially, we focus on vSLAM algorithms proposed mainly from 2010 to 2016 because major advance occurred in that period. The technical categories are summarized as follows: feature-based, direct, and RGB-D camera-based approaches.

Keywords: Survey, Visual SLAM, Computer vision, Augmented reality, Robotics

1 Introduction

Simultaneous Localization and Mapping (SLAM) is a technique for obtaining the 3D structure of an unknown environment and sensor motion in the environment. This technique was originally proposed to achieve autonomous control of robots in robotics [1]. Then, SLAM-based applications have widely become broadened such as computer vision-based online 3D modeling, augmented reality (AR)-based visualization, and self-driving cars. In early SLAM algorithms, many different types of sensors were integrated such as laser range sensors, rotary encoders, inertial sensors, GPS, and cameras. Such algorithms are well summarized in the following papers [2–5].

In recent years, SLAM using cameras only has been actively discussed because the sensor configuration is simple and the technical difficulties are higher than others. Since the input of such SLAM is visual information only, the technique is specifically referred to as visual SLAM (vSLAM). vSLAM algorithms have widely proposed in the field of computer vision, robotics, and AR [6]. Especially, they are suitable for camera pose estimation in AR systems because the configuration of the systems

can be simple such as camera-mounted tablets or smartphones. One of the important requirements in AR systems is real-time response to seamlessly and interactively merge real and virtual objects. To achieve the response with a limited computational resource on a light-weighted hand-held device, various low computational-cost vSLAM algorithms have been proposed in the literature. The application of such vSLAM algorithms is not limited to AR systems. For example, it is also useful for unmanned autonomous vehicles (UAV) in robotics [7]. Even though vSLAM algorithms have been proposed for different purposes in different research communities, they basically share overall parts of technical core ideas and can be used to achieve different purposes each other. Therefore, we categorize and summarize such algorithms as a survey paper.

In this paper, we review real-time vSLAM algorithms, which remarkably evolve forward in the 2010s. In general, the technical difficulty of vSLAM is higher than that of other sensor-based SLAMs because cameras can acquire less visual input from a limited field of views compared to 360° laser sensing which is typically used in robotics. From such input, camera poses need to be continuously estimated and the 3D structure of an unknown environment is simultaneously reconstructed. The early work of vSLAM using a monocular camera was based on tracking and mapping feature points in 2000s. This is called

---

*Correspondence: takafumi-t@is.naist.jp
[1]Nara Institute of Science and Technology, 8916-5 Takayama, Ikoma, 630-0192 Nara, Japan
Full list of author information is available at the end of the article

"feature-based approach." To cope with texture-less or feature-less environments, vSLAM without detecting feature points and directly with a whole image for tracking and mapping has been proposed. This is called "direct approach." With the advent of low-cost RGB-D sensors such as Microsoft Kinect, vSLAM algorithms with both a monocular image and its depth have been proposed. Therefore, the existing vSLAM algorithms introduced in this paper are categorized according to feature-based, direct, and RGB-D camera-based approaches. This paper will be helpful for readers who want to start to learn the basic framework of vSLAM, the difference among the algorithms, and the progress from 2010 to 2016. Also, remaining technical problems are discussed for further research topics and several benchmarking methodologies for comparing different algorithms are provided so that readers can have some perspectives for next research direction.

The remainder of the paper is organized as follows. In Sections 2 and 3, the elements of vSLAM and related techniques of vSLAM including visual odometry are introduced. In Sections 4, 5, and 6 where existing vSLAM algorithms are summarized, feature-based, direct, and RGB-D-based vSLAM algorithms are, respectively, introduced. In Section 7, remaining technical problems in vSLAM algorithms are discussed. In Section 8, datasets for evaluating a performance of vSLAM algorithms are introduced. Finally, we present the conclusion in Section 9. Note that there exist survey papers on vSLAM algorithms proposed till 2011 [8, 9]. These papers are also useful for understanding our survey on newer algorithms.

2   Elements of vSLAM

In this section, we first introduce the basic framework followed by most of vSLAM algorithms since late 2000s.

2.1   Basic modules

The framework is mainly composed of three modules as follows.

1. Initialization
2. Tracking
3. Mapping

To start vSLAM, it is necessary to define a certain coordinate system for camera pose estimation and 3D reconstruction in an unknown environment. Therefore, in the initialization, the global coordinate system should first be defined, and a part of the environment is reconstructed as an initial map in the global coordinate system. After the initialization, tracking and mapping are performed to continuously estimate camera poses. In the tracking, the reconstructed map is tracked in the image to estimate the camera pose of the image with respect to the map.

In order to do this, 2D–3D correspondences between the image and the map are first obtained from feature matching or feature tracking in the image. Then, the camera pose is computed from the correspondences by solving the Perspective-n-Point (PnP) problem [10, 11]. It should be noted that most of vSLAM algorithms assumes that intrinsic camera parameters are calibrated beforehand so that they are known. Therefore, a camera pose is normally equivalent to extrinsic camera parameters with translation and rotation of the camera in the global coordinate system. In the mapping, the map is expanded by computing the 3D structure of an environment when the camera observes unknown regions where the mapping is not performed before.

2.2   Additional modules for stable and accurate vSLAM

The following two additional modules are also included in vSLAM algorithms according to the purposes of applications.

- Relocalization
- Global map optimization

The relocalization is required when the tracking is failed due to fast camera motion or some disturbances. In this case, it is necessary to compute the camera pose with respect to the map again. Therefore, this process is called "relocalization." If the relocalization is not incorporated into vSLAM systems, the systems do not work anymore after the tracking is lost and such systems are not practically useful. Therefore, a fast and efficient method for the relocalization has been discussed in the literature. Note that this is also referred to as kidnapped robot problems in robotics.

The other module is global map optimization. The map generally includes accumulative estimation error according to the distance of camera movement. In order to suppress the error, the global map optimization is normally performed. In this process, the map is refined by considering the consistency of whole map information. When a map is revisited such that a starting region is captured again after some camera movement, reference information that represents the accumulative error from the beginning to the present can be computed. Then, a loop constraint from the reference information is used as a constraint to suppress the error in the global optimization.

Loop closing is a technique to acquire the reference information. In the loop closing, a closed loop is first searched by matching a current image with previously acquired images. If the loop is detected, it means that the camera captures one of previously observed views. In this case, the accumulative error occurred during camera movement can be estimated. Note that the closed-loop detection procedure can be done by using the same techniques as relocalization. Basically, relocalization is done for recovering a camera pose and loop detection is done for obtaining geometrically consistent map.

Pose-graph optimization has widely been used to suppress the accumulated error by optimizing camera poses [12, 13]. In this method, the relationship between camera poses is represented as a graph and the consistent graph is built to suppress the error in the optimization. Bundle adjustment (BA) is also used to minimize the reprojection error of the map by optimizing both the map and the camera poses [14]. In large environments, this optimization procedure is employed to minimize estimation errors efficiently. In small environments, BA may be performed without loop closing because the accumulated error is small.

2.3 Summary

As listed above, the framework of vSLAM algorithms is composed of five modules: initialization, tracking, mapping, relocalization, and global map optimization. Since each vSLAM algorithm employs different methodologies for each module, features of a vSLAM algorithm highly depend on the methodologies employed. Therefore, it is important to understand each module of a vSLAM algorithm to know its performance, advantages, and limitations.

It should be noted that tracking and mapping (TAM) is used instead of using localization and mapping. TAM was first used in Parallel Tracking and Mapping (PTAM) [15] because localization and mapping are not simultaneously performed in a traditional way. Tracking is performed in every frame with one thread whereas mapping is performed at a certain timing with another thread. After PTAM was proposed, most of vSLAM algorithms follows the framework of TAM. Therefore, TAM is used in this paper.

3 Related technologies

vSLAM, visual odometry, and online structure from motion are designed for estimating camera motion and 3D structure in an unknown environment. In this section, we explain the relationship among them.

3.1 Visual odometry

Odometry is to estimate the sequential changes of sensor positions over time using sensors such as wheel encoder to acquire relative sensor movement. Camera-based odometry called visual odometry (VO) is also one of the active research fields in the literature [16, 17]. From the technical point of views, vSLAM and VO are highly relevant techniques because both techniques basically estimate sensor positions. According to the survey papers in robotics [18, 19], the relationship between vSLAM and VO can be represented as follows.

$$\text{vSLAM} = \text{VO} + \text{global map optimization}$$

The main difference between these two techniques is global map optimization in the mapping. In other words, VO is equivalent to the modules in Section 2.1. In the VO, the geometric consistency of a map is considered only in a small portion of a map or only relative camera motion is computed without mapping. On the other hand, in the vSLAM, the global geometric consistency of a map is normally considered. Therefore, to build a geometrically consistent map, the global optimization is performed in the recent vSLAM algorithms.

The relationship between vSLAM and VO can also be found from the papers [20, 21] and the papers [22, 23]. In the paper [20, 22], a technique on VO was first proposed. Then, a technique on vSLAM was proposed by adding the global optimization in VO [21, 23].

3.2 Structure from motion

Structure from motion (SfM) is a technique to estimate camera motion and 3D structure of the environment in a batch manner [24]. In the paper [25], a SfM method that runs online was proposed. The authors named it as real-time SfM. From the technical point of views, there is no definitive difference between vSLAM and real-time SfM. This may be why the word "real-time SfM" is not found in recent papers.

As explained in this section, vSLAM, VO, and real-time SfM share many common components. Therefore, we introduce all of them and do not distinguish these technologies in this paper.

4 Feature-based methods

There exist two types of feature-based methods in the literature: filter-based and BA-based methods. In this section, we explain both methods and provide the comparison. Even though some of the methods were proposed before 2010, we explained them here because they can be considered as fundamental frameworks for other methods.

4.1 MonoSLAM

First monocular vSLAM was developed in 2003 by Davison et al. [26, 27]. They named it MonoSLAM. MonoSLAM is considered as a representative method in filter-based vSLAM algorithms. In MonoSLAM, camera motion and 3D structure of an unknown environment are simultaneously estimated using an extended Kalman filter (EKF). 6 Degree of freedom (DoF) camera motion and 3D positions of feature points are represented as a state vector in EKF. Uniform motion is assumed in a prediction model, and a result of feature point tracking is used as observation. Depending on camera movement, new feature points are added to the state vector. Note that the initial map is created by observing a known object where a global coordinate system is defined. In summary, MonoSLAM is composed of the following components.

- Map initialization is done by using a known object.
- Camera motion and 3D positions of feature points are estimated using EKF.

The problem of this method is a computational cost that increases in proportion to the size of an environment. In large environments, the size of a state vector becomes large because the number of feature points is large. In this case, it is difficult to achieve real-time computation.

4.2 PTAM

To solve the problem of a computational cost in MonoSLAM, PTAM [15] split the tracking and the mapping into different threads on CPU. These two threads are executed in parallel so that the computational cost of the mapping does not affect the tracking. As a result, BA that needs a computational cost in the optimization can be used in the mapping. This means that the tracking estimates camera motion in real-time, and the mapping estimates accurate 3D positions of feature points with a computational cost. PTAM is the first method which incorporates BA into the real-time vSLAM algorithms. After publishing PTAM, most vSLAM algorithms follow this type of multi-threading approaches.

In PTAM, the initial map is reconstructed using the five-point algorithm [28]. In the tracking, mapped points are projected onto an image to make 2D–3D correspondences using texture matching. From the correspondences, camera poses can be computed. In the mapping, 3D positions of new feature points are computed using triangulation at certain frames called keyframes. One of the significant contributions of PTAM is to introduce this keyframe-based mapping in vSLAM. An input frame is selected as a keyframe when a large disparity between an input frame and one of the keyframes is measured. A large disparity is basically required for accurate triangulation. In contrast to MonoSLAM, 3D points of feature points are optimized using lobal BA with some keyframes and global BA with all keyframes with the map. Also, in the tracking process, the newer vision of PTAM employ a relocalization algorithm [29]. It uses a randomized tree-based feature classifier for searching the nearest keyframe of an input frame. In summary, PTAM is composed of the following four components.

- Map initialization is done by the five-point algorithm [28].
- Camera poses are estimated from matched feature points between map points and the input image.
- 3D positions of feature points are estimated by triangulation, and estimated 3D positions are optimized by BA.

- The tracking process is recovered by a randomized tree-based searching [29].

Compared to MonoSLAM, in PTAM, the system can handle thousands of feature points by splitting the tracking and the mapping into different threads on CPU.

There have been proposed many extended PTAM algorithms. Castle et al. developed a multiple map version of PTAM [30]. Klein et al. developed a mobile phone version of PTAM [31]. In order to run PTAM on mobile phones, input image resolution, map points, and number of keyframes are reduced. In addition, they consider rolling shutter distortion in BA to get an accurate estimation result because a rolling shutter is normally installed in most mobile phone cameras due to its cheap cost. Since PTAM can reconstruct a sparse 3D structure of the environment only, the third thread can be used to reconstruct a dense 3D structure of the environment [32, 33].

4.3 Comparison between MonoSLAM and PTAM

The difference between the EKF-based mapping in MonoSLAM and the BA-based mapping with the keyframes in PTAM was discussed in the literature [34]. According to the literature, to improve an accuracy of vSLAM, it is important to increase the number of feature points in a map. From this point of view, the BA-based approach is better than the EKF-based approach because it can handle large number of points.

4.4 Techniques on global map optimization

Geometric consistency of the whole map is maintained by using BA for the keyframes as explained above. However, in general, BA suffers from a local minimum problem due to the numerous number of parameters including camera poses of the keyframes and points in the map. Pose-graph optimization is a solution to avoid this problem in the loop closing as described in Section 2. In the loop closing, camera poses are first optimized using the loop constraint. After optimizing the camera poses, BA is performed to optimize both 3D positions of feature points and the camera poses. For the loop closing, a visual information-based approach is employed [35]. They used a bag-of-words-based image retrieval technique to detect one of the keyframes which view is similar with the current view [36].

In a vSLAM system [35], a stereo camera is selected as a vision sensor. In this case, the scale of the coordinate system is fixed and known. However, in monocular vSLAM cases, there is a scale ambiguity and a scale may change during camera movement if global BA is not performed. In this case, a scale drift problem occurs and the scale of the coordinate system at each frame may not be consistent. In order to correct the scale drift, camera poses should be optimized in 7 DoF. Strasdat et al. [37] proposed a method for optimizing 7 DoF camera poses based on similarity transformation.

As an extension of PTAM, ORB-SLAM [38] includes BA, vision-based closed-loop detection, and 7 DoF pose-graph optimization. As far as we know, ORB-SLAM is the most complete feature-based monocular vSLAM system. ORB-SLAM is extended to the stereo vSLAM and the RGB-D vSLAM [39].

4.5 Summary

Figure 1 shows the summary of feature-based methods. MonoSLAM was developed in 2003 [26]. Both the tracking and the mapping are sequentially and simultaneously using EKF. PTAM was developed in 2007 [15]. They proposed to separate the tracking and the mapping into different threads on CPU. This multi-threading approach enables to handle thousands of feature points in the map. In large environments, it is difficult to get global optimal of the map and the camera poses due to the local minimum problem in BA. To avoid this problem, closed-loop detection and pose-graph optimization can be used before BA. ORB-SLAM [38] includes multi-threaded tracking, mapping, and closed-loop detection, and the map is optimized using pose-graph optimization and BA, and this can be considered as all-in-one package of monocular vSLAM. Since ORB-SLAM is an open source project[1], we can easily use this whole vSLAM system in our local environment.

In this section, we introduced feature point-based vSLAM algorithms. Feature point-based vSLAM algorithms normally employ handcrafted feature detectors and descriptors and can provide stable estimation results in rich textured environments. However, it is difficult to handle curved edges and other complex cues by using such handcrafted features. In some special cases such as poor textured environments, line features have been used as image features [40, 41]. Moreover, feature points and edgelets are combined to achieve robust estimation against to motion-blurred input images [42].

5 Direct methods

In contrast to feature-based methods in the previous section, direct methods directly use an input image without any abstraction using handcrafted feature detectors and descriptors. They are also called feature-less approaches. In general, photometric consistency is used as an error measurement in direct methods whereas geometric consistency such as positions of feature points in an image is used in feature-based methods. In this section, we introduce some leading direct methods.

5.1 DTAM

Newcombe et al. proposed a fully direct method [43] called DTAM. In DTAM, the tracking is done by comparing the input image with synthetic view images generated from the reconstructed map. This is simply equivalent to registration between an image and the 3D model of a map and is efficiently implemented on GPU in DTAM. The mapping is done by using multi-baseline stereo [44], and then, the map is optimized by considering space continuity [45] so that 3D coordinates of all pixels can be computed. The initial depth map is created using a stereo measurement like PTAM. In summary, DTAM is composed of the following three components.

- Map initialization is done by the stereo measurement.
- Camera motion is estimated by synthetic view generation from the reconstructed map.
- Depth information is estimated for every pixels by using multi-baseline stereo, and then, it is optimized by considering space continuity.

The DTAM algorithm is optimized for achieving real-time processing on mobile phones [46]. Basically, these methods [43, 46, 47] are designed for fast and online 3D modeling.

It should be noted that Stühmer et al. previously proposed a variational approach for estimating depth information for every pixels [47]. They use similar cost function for the mapping as DTAM. However, in this method, PTAM [15] was used for the tracking. Therefore, the tracking is the feature-based method and is not a fully direct method.

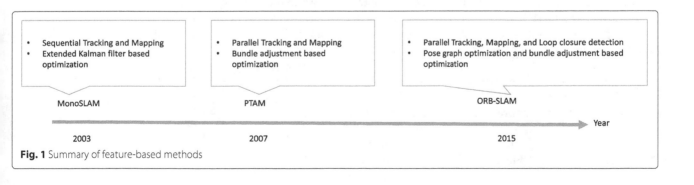

Fig. 1 Summary of feature-based methods

5.2 LSD-SLAM

LSD-SLAM is another leading method in direct methods. The core idea of LSD-SLAM follows the idea from semi-dense VO [20]. In this method, reconstruction targets are limited to areas which have intensity gradient compared to DTAM which reconstructs full areas. This means that it ignores textureless areas because it is difficult to estimate accurate depth information from images. In the mapping, random values are first set as initial depth values for each pixels, and then, these values are optimized based on photometric consistency. Since this method does not consider the geometric consistency of the whole map, this method is called visual odometry.

In 2014, semi-dense VO was extended to LSD-SLAM [21]. In LSD-SLAM, loop-closure detection and 7 DoF pose-graph optimization as described in the previous sections are added to the semi-dense visual odometry algorithm [20]. In summary, LSD-SLAM is composed of the following four components.

- Random values are set as an initial depth value for each pixel.
- Camera motion is estimated by synthetic view generation from the reconstructed map.
- Reconstructed areas are limited to high-intensity gradient areas.
- 7 DoF pose-graph optimization is employed to obtain geometrically consistent map.

Basically, these semi-dense approaches [20, 21] can achieve real-time processing with CPU. In addition, they optimized the LSD-SLAM algorithm for mobile phones by considering the CPU architecture for them [48]. In the literature [48], they also evaluated the accuracy of the LSD-SLAM algorithm for low-resolution input images. LSD-SLAM is extended to stereo cameras and omni-directional cameras [49, 50].

5.3 SVO and DSO

Forster et al. proposed semi-direct VO (SVO) [51]. Although the tracking is done by feature point matching, the mapping is done by the direct method. In feature-based methods, feature descriptors and the Lucas-Kanade tracker [52] are used to find correspondences. In contrast to feature-based methods, camera motion is estimated by minimizing photometric errors surrounding feature points. This method can be regarded as sparse version of DTAM and LSD-SLAM.

Recently, Engel et al. propose the direct sparse odometry (DSO) [53]. In contrast to SVO, DSO is a fully direct method. In order to suppress accumulative error, DSO removes error factors as much as possible from geometric and photometric perspectives. In DSO, the input image is divided into several blocks, and then, high intensity points are selected as reconstruction candidates. By using this strategy, points are spread within the whole image. In addition, to achieve highly accurate estimation, DSO uses both geometric and photometric camera calibration results. It should be noted that DSO considers local geometric consistency only. Therefore, DSO is classified into VO, not vSLAM.

5.4 Summary

Figure 2 shows the summary of direct methods. Direct methods can be categorized according to map density. Dense methods [43, 47] generate a dense map computed such that depth values are estimated for every pixels in each keyframe. These methods can be useful for realtime 3D modeling with GPU. In contrast to dense methods, semi-dense [21] and sparse [51, 53] methods focus on the applications based on the tracking of sensor poses. These methods can run in real-time on CPUs.

6 RGB-D vSLAM

Recently, structured light-based RGB-D cameras [54] such as Microsoft Kinect [55] become cheap and small. Since such cameras provide 3D information in real-time, these cameras are also used in vSLAM algorithms.

6.1 Difference with monocular vSLAM

By using RGB-D cameras, 3D structure of the environment with its texture information can be obtained directly. In addition, in contrast to monocular vSLAM algorithms, the scale of the coordinate system is known because 3D structure can be acquired in the metric space.

The basic framework of depth (D)-based vSLAM is as follows. An iterative closest point (ICP) algorithm [56] have widely been used to estimate camera motion. Then, the 3D structure of the environment is reconstructed by combining multiple depth maps. In order to incorporate RGB into depth-based vSLAM, many approaches had been proposed as explained below.

It should be noted that most of consumer depth cameras are developed for indoor usages. They project IR patterns into an environment to measure the depth information. It is difficult to detect emitted IR patterns in outdoor environments. In addition, there is a limitation of a range of depth measurement such that the RGB-D sensors can capture the environment from 1 to 4 m.

Fig. 2 Comparison of direct methods based on map density

6.2 KinectFusion

Newcombe et al. proposed KinectFution in 2011 [57]. In KinectFusion, a voxel space is used for representing the 3D structure of the environment. The 3D structure of the environment is reconstructed by combining obtained depth maps in the voxel space, and camera motion is estimated by the ICP algorithm using an estimated 3D structure and the input depth map, which is depth-based vSLAM. KinectFusion is implemented on GPU to achieve real-time processing.

Kahler et al. achieve realtime processing of KinectFusion on mobile devices [58]. To reduce a computational cost, they use a voxel block hashing in the mapping process. RGB-D vSLAM suffer from amount of data. In the literature [59], they reduce amount of data by unifying co-planar points.

6.3 SLAM++

Salas-Moreno et al. proposed an object level RGB-D vSLAM algorithm [60]. In this method, several 3D objects are registered into the database in advance, and these objects are recognized in an online process. By recognizing 3D objects, the estimated map is refined, and 3D points are replaced by 3D objects to reduce the amount of data.

As a similar algorithm, Tateno et al. proposed a real-time segmentation method for RGB-D SLAM [61]. Segmented objects are labeled, and then, these objects can be used as recognition targets.

6.4 Techniques on RGB-D VO and global map optimization

For the tracking, RGB images are also used in RGB-D vSLAM algorithms. In the literature [62, 63], relative camera motion is estimated by tracking feature points between successive frames. A translation matrix is then estimated using tracked feature points, and this translation matrix is refined by the ICP algorithm using depth maps. On the other hand, photometric consistency-based camera motion tracking methods have been proposed [22, 23, 64]. This photometric consistency-based camera motion tracking is also employed monocular camera-based dense vSLAM methods [20, 21, 43].

In order to obtain a geometrically consistent map, pose-graph optimization and deformation graph optimization are used in RGB-D vSLAM algorithms. Kerl et al. used pose-graph optimization to reduce the accumulative error [23]. This pose-graph optimization is almost the same as loop closure in monocular vSLAM algorithms. Whelan et al. used pose-graph optimization for camera motion refinement and deformation graph optimization for map refinement, respectively, [65]. In contrast to other works [23], the estimated map is also refined. In [66], deformation graph optimization is frequently used for certain frames, and camera motion is estimated by matching between a RGB-D image and a reconstructed model. They showed geometrically consistent model that can be acquired using deformation graph optimization as often as possible.

Note that RGB-D SLAM APIs are provided in consumer devices such as Google Tango[2] and Structure Sensor[3]. Especially, Google Tango provides a stable estimation result by combining internal sensor information.

7 Open problems

In practical situations, vSLAM faces some problems. In this section, we list the following problems: purely rotational motion, map initialization, estimating intrinsic camera parameters, rolling shutter distortion, and scale ambiguity.

7.1 Pure rotation

When users move a device in handheld augmented reality applications, purely rotational motion sometimes occurs. This is a problem because disparities cannot be observed during purely rotational motion with monocular vSLAM. To solve this problem, in the literature [67, 68], different projection models are used to handle general camera motion and purely rotational motion. For example, homography-based tracking is used for purely rotational motion and 6 DoF camera tracking is used for other camera motion. As another approach, two types of 3D point representation is used dependent on camera motion [69]. Points which can be observed with large disparities are represented as 3D points, and points which cannot be observed with large disparities are represented as 3D rays. In the tracking process, 3D ray information is also used to estimate camera motion. They use distances between 3D rays and feature points in the input image as reprojection errors.

Note that purely rotational motion is not a problem in RGB-D vSLAM. This is because tracking and mapping processes can be done by using obtained depth maps. On the other hand, monocular camera-based vSLAM cannot continue mapping during pure rotation movement.

7.2 Map initialization

Map initialization is important to achieve accurate estimation in vSLAM. Basically, in order to obtain an accurate initial map, baseline should be wide. However, in practical scenarios, it may be difficult to do ideal camera motion by novice people. To solve this problem, Mulloni et al. proposed an user-friendly initialization [70]. They used 2D/3D guides for instructing ideal camera motion for map initialization. Arth et al. proposed 2.5D map-based initialization for outdoor environments [71]. By using this method, vSLAM can be initialized in a global coordinate system on the earth.

Reference objects such as fiducial markers and known 3D objects have also been used to get a global coordinate system, and initial camera poses are estimated by tracking reference objects. In order to extend a trackable area, vSLAM is incorporated with it. Vuforia[4] provides marker-based SLAM initialization. In literature [72, 73], they use a known 3D object as a reference, and the known object shape is used to refine the map.

7.3 Estimating intrinsic camera parameters

Most vSLAM algorithms assume known intrinsic camera parameters. This means that camera calibration should be done before using vSLAM applications, and intrinsic camera parameters should be fixed during vSLAM estimation process. However, it is annoying for novice people. In the literature, they achieve intrinsic camera parameter estimation during vSLAM [74]. Intrinsic camera parameters are gradually converged during vSLAM estimation process. On the other hand, intrinsic camera parameter change can be handled [75]. They remove camera zooming effect by estimating focal length change based on an offline self-calibration technique [76].

7.4 Rolling shutter distortion

To achieve accurate camera pose estimation, it is important to consider a shutter type. Most vSLAM algorithms assume a global shutter, and these algorithms estimate one camera pose for each frame. However, most consumer cameras including RGB-D cameras employ rolling shutter due to its cost. In rolling shutter cameras, each row of a captured image is taken by different camera poses. It is obviously difficult to estimate camera poses of each row directly. In general, an interpolation-based approach is used to estimate rolling shutter camera pose estimation. In the literature [77–79], they use a spline function to interpolate a camera trajectory.

7.5 Scale ambiguity

Absolute scale information is needed in some vSLAM applications with monocular vSLAM. In order to obtain absolute scale information, user's body is used in the literature [80, 81]. Lee et al. used user's hand to determine an absolute scale and a global coordinate system [80]. Knorr et al. used user's face information to determine the absolute scale [81]. There is an assumption such that the size difference of these body parts is small within people. Therefore, these vSLAM systems can estimate scale information accurately.

As another approach, several sensors such as accelerometer, gyro, and magnetic sensor on mobile phones can also be used. In the literature [82], scale information is estimated by using accelerometer. They use frequency-domain filtering technique to remove sensor noise.

8 Benchmarking

To achieve fair comparison between vSLAM algorithms, benchmarking is obviously important and its methodologies have been discussed in recent years. Here, we introduce some benchmarking dataset as follows.

TrakMark provides image sequences with 6 DoF camera motion and intrinsic camera parameters [83]. In TrakMark, image sequences are divided into three scenarios: virtualized environments, indoor environments, and outdoor environments[5]. TrakMark assumes to be used for evaluating a performance of vSLAM algorithms in AR/MR research community. They also proposed an evaluation criteria from AR/MR research perspective. In AR/MR applications, image space errors are the most important because it is OK if the overlay of virtual objects onto an image is natural. In TrakMark, they employed the projection error of virtual object (PEVO) as a criteria for evaluating vSLAM algorithms [84]. In this criteria, virtual points are projected onto the input images using estimated and ideal camera poses, and then, distances are measured in the image space.

Martull et al. newly provided a stereo dataset which follows Tsukuba dataset [85]. Tukuba stereo dataset has been used for evaluating stereo algorithms. They created new Tukuba stereo dataset using computer graphics. Image sequences, camera poses, and depth maps for each frame are provided in the dataset. Image sequences are created using different camera trajectories and lighting conditions.

TUM RGB-D benchmarking dataset provides RGB-D image sequences with 6 DoF camera poses [86]. Camera poses are obtained using a motion capture system, which can be considered more accurate than vSLAM. They propose relative pose error (PRE) and absolute trajectory error (ATE) for evaluating local and global errors, respectively.

KITTI dataset is designed for evaluating vision systems in a driving scenario and includes many types of data [87]. In the dataset, visual odometry dataset is provided. Ground truth camera poses are obtained using RTK-GPS. In KITTI dataset webpage[6], evaluation results are listed. The results of LSD-SLAM and ORB-SLAM algorithms can be found in the Web page.

In contrast to other dataset, SLAMBench provides a framework for evaluating vSLAM algorithms from accuracy and energy consumption [88]. In addition, Kinect-Fusion implementation is included in SLAMBench in different options (C++, OpenMP, OpenCL, and CUDA).

On-site benchmarking have been organized in International Symposium on Mixed and Augmented Reality (ISMAR) since 2008, which is called "tracking competition." In the tracking competition, participants need to do specific tasks given by organizers using own vSLAM systems. Unlike dataset-based evaluation, participants can control

Table 1 Comparison of representative algorithms

	Method	Map density	Global optimization	Loop closure
Mono-SLAM [26]	Feature	Sparse	No	No
PTAM [15]	Feature	Sparse	Yes	No
ORB-SLAM [38]	Feature	Sparse	Yes	Yes
DTAM [43]	Direct	Dense	No	No
LSD-SLAM [21]	Direct	Semi-dense	Yes	Yes
SVO [51]	Semi-direct	Sparse	No	No
DSO [53]	Direct	Sparse	No	No
KinectFusion [57]	RGB-D	Dense	No	No
Dense visual SLAM [23]	RGB-D	Dense	Yes	Yes
ElasticFusion [66]	RGB-D	Dense	Yes	Yes
SLAM++ [60]	RGB-D	Dense	Yes	Yes

camera movement based on current tracking results. Therefore, the tracking competition can evaluate vSLAM algorithms as an interactive system.

9 Conclusions

In this paper, we introduced recent vSLAM algorithms mainly from 2010 to 2016. Basically, vSLAM algorithms are composed of initialization, camera motion estimation, 3D structure estimation, global optimization, and relocalization. Recently, direct methods are active research field in monocular vSLAM. RGB-D vSLAM has also been developed in recent years because many consumer RGB-D cameras can be obtained with a cheap price. In AR/MR research community, practical problems have been solved. Even though vSLAM algorithms have been developed since 2003, vSLAM is still an active research field.

To understand the difference between different methods, those modules should be compared. Table 1 shows the summary of representative methods. Each algorithm has different characteristics. We need to choose an appropriate algorithm by considering a purpose of an application.

This paper focused on recent vSLAM algorithms using cameras only. As another approach, SLAM algorithms which are using visual and inertial data are called visual-inertial SLAM. By combining visual and inertial data, we can get more stable estimation results. Also, in the literature [77, 82], they are using sensor information to solve scale estimation and rolling shutter distortion compensation. Currently, smartphone and tablet devices have cameras, GPS, gyroscope, and accelerometer. In the future, we believe sensor fusion is one direction to realize robust and practical vSLAM systems.

To learn the elements of vSLAM algorithms, we provide ATAM[7] which is a vSLAM toolkit for beginners [89]. It includes monocular vSLAM algorithm including real scale estimation from a chessboard. Users can easily install and

modify ATAM because the source code was designed to be well structured and only dependent on OpenCV [90] and cvsba [91].

Endnotes

[1] https://github.com/raulmur/ORB_SLAM2.

[2] https://get.google.com/tango/.

[3] https://structure.io/.

[4] https://developer.vuforia.com/.

[5] http://trakmark.net.

[6] http://www.cvlibs.net/datasets/kitti/.

[7] https://github.com/CVfAR/ATAM.

Authors' contributions
TT and HU collected and summarized visual SLAM papers. SI is an adviser and helped to draft the manuscript. All authors read and approved the final manuscript.

Competing interests
The authors declare that they have no competing interests.

Author details
[1] Nara Institute of Science and Technology, 8916-5 Takayama, Ikoma, 630-0192 Nara, Japan. [2] Kyushu University, 744 Motooka, Nishi-ku, 819-0395 Fukuoka, Japan. [3] Ritsumeikan University, 1-1-1 Nojihigashi, Kusatsu, 525-8577 Shiga, Japan.

References
1. Chatila R, Laumond JP (1985) Position referencing and consistent world modeling for mobile robots. In: Proceedings of International Conference on Robotics and Automation Vol. 2. pp 138–145
2. Durrant-Whyte H, Bailey T (2006) Simultaneous localization and mapping: part i. Robot Autom Mag IEEE 13(2):99–110
3. Bailey T, Durrant-Whyte H (2006) Simultaneous localization and mapping (slam): Part ii. IEEE Robot Autom Mag 13(3):108–117
4. Thrun S, Leonard JJ (2008) Handbook of robotics. Chap. Simultaneous localization and mapping

5. Aulinas J, Petillot YR, Salvi J, Lladó X (2008) The slam problem: a survey. In: Proceedings of Conference on Artificial Intelligence Research and Development: Proceedings of International Conference of the Catalan Association for Artificial Intelligence. pp 363–371

6. Billinghurst M, Clark A, Lee G (2015) A survey of augmented reality. Found Trends Human-Computer Interact 8(2-3):73–272

7. Engel J, Sturm J, Cremers D (2012) Camera-based navigation of a low-cost quadrocopter. In: Proceedings of International Conference on Intelligent Robots and Systems. pp 2815–2821

8. Ros G, Sappa A, Ponsa D, Lopez AM (2012) Visual slam for driverless cars: a brief survey. In: Intelligent Vehicles Symposium (IV) Workshops

9. Fuentes-Pacheco J, Ruiz-Ascencio J, Rendón-Mancha JM (2015) Visual simultaneous localization and mapping: a survey. Artif Intell Rev 43(1):55–81

10. Klette R, Koschan A, Schluns K (1998) Computer vision: three-dimensional data from images. 1st edn

11. Nister D (2004) A minimal solution to the generalised 3-point pose problem. In: Proceedings of IEEE Conference on Computer Vision and Pattern Recognition Vol. 1. pp 560–5671

12. Grisetti G, Kümmerle R, Stachniss C, Burgard W (2010) A tutorial on graph-based slam. Intell Transp Syst Mag IEEE 2(4):31–43

13. Kümmerle R, Grisetti G, Strasdat H, Konolige K, Burgard W (2011) g2o: A general framework for graph optimization. In: Proceedings of International Conference on Robotics and Automation. pp 3607–3613

14. Bundle adjustment a modern synthesis. In: Triggs B, McLauchlan PF, Hartley RI, Fitzgibbon AW (eds) (2000) Vision algorithms: theory and practice. pp 298–372

15. Klein G, Murray DW (2007) Parallel tracking and mapping for small AR workspaces. In: Proceedngs of International Symposium on Mixed and Augmented Reality. pp 225–234

16. Nistér D, Naroditsky O, Bergen J (2004) Visual odometry. In: Proceedings of IEEE Conference on Computer Vision and Pattern Recognition Vol. 1. p 652

17. Yousif K, Bab-Hadiashar A, Hoseinnezhad R (2015) An overview to visual odometry and visual slam: applications to mobile robotics. Intell Ind Syst 1(4):289–311

18. Scaramuzza D, Fraundorfer F (2011) Visual odometry [tutorial]. Robot Autom Mag IEEE 18(4):80–92

19. Fraundorfer F, Scaramuzza D (2012) Visual odometry: Part ii: matching, robustness, optimization, and applications. Robot Autom Mag IEEE 19(2):78–90

20. Engel J, Sturm J, Cremers D (2013) Semi-dense visual odometry for a monocular camera. In: Proceedings of International Conference on Computer Vision. pp 1449–1456

21. Engel J, Schöps T, Cremers D (2014) LSD-SLAM: large-scale direct monocular SLAM. In: Proceedings of European Conference on Computer Vision. pp 834–849

22. Kerl C, Sturm J, Cremers D (2013) Robust odometry estimation for RGB-D cameras. In: Proceedings of International Conference on Robotics and Automation. pp 3748–3754

23. Kerl C, Sturm J, Cremers D (2013) Dense visual SLAM for RGB-D cameras. In: Proceedings of International Conference on Intelligent Robots and Systems. pp 2100–2106

24. Agarwal S, Furukawa Y, Snavely N, Simon I, Curless B, Seitz SM, Szeliski R (2011) Building rome in a day. Commun ACM 54(10):105–112

25. Civera J, Grasa OG, Davison AJ, Montiel J (2010) 1-point ransac for extended kalman filtering: application to real-time structure from motion and visual odometry. J Field Robot 27(5):609–631

26. Davison AJ (2003) Real-time simultaneous localisation and mapping with a single camera. In: Proceedings of International Conference on Computer Vision. pp 1403–1410

27. Davison AJ, Reid ID, Molton ND, Stasse O (2007) Monoslam: real-time single camera SLAM. Pattern Anal Mach Intell IEEE Trans 29(6):1052–1067

28. Nistér D (2004) An efficient solution to the five-point relative pose problem. Pattern Anal Mach Intell IEEE Trans 26(6):756–770

29. Williams B, Klein G, Reid I (2007) Real-time SLAM relocalisation. In: Proceedings of International Conference on Computer Vision. pp 1–8

30. Castle R, Klein G, Murray DW (2008) Video-rate localization in multiple maps for wearable augmented reality. In: 2008 12th IEEE International Symposium on Wearable Computers. pp 15–22. doi:10.1109/ISWC.2008.4911577

31. Klein G, Murray DW (2009) Parallel tracking and mapping on a camera phone. In: Proceedngs of International Symposium on Mixed and Augmented Reality. pp 83–86

32. Newcombe RA, Davison AJ (2010) Live dense reconstruction with a single moving camera. In: Proceedings of IEEE Conference on Computer Vision and Pattern Recognition. pp 1498–1505

33. Pradeep V, Rhemann C, Izadi S, Zach C, Bleyer M, Bathiche S (2013) MonoFusion: real-time 3D reconstruction of small scenes with a single web camera. In: Proceedngs of International Symposium on Mixed and Augmented Reality. pp 83–88

34. Strasdat H, Montiel JM, Davison AJ (2012) Visual SLAM: why filter? Image Vision Comput 30(2):65–77

35. Mei C, Sibley G, Cummins M, Newman P, Reid I (2009) A constant-time efficient stereo slam system. In: Proceedings of British Machine Vision Conference. pp 54–15411

36. Cummins M, Newman P (2008) FAB-MAP: probabilistic localization and mapping in the space of appearance. Int J Robot Res 27(6):647–665

37. Strasdat H, Montiel J, Davison AJ (2010) Scale drift-aware large scale monocular slam. In: Proceedings of Robotics: Science and Systems. p 5

38. Mur-Artal R, Montiel JMM, Tardós JD (2015) ORB-SLAM: a versatile and accurate monocular SLAM system. IEEE Trans Robot 31(5):1147–1163. doi:10.1109/TRO.2015.2463671

39. Mur-Artal R, Tardós JD (2016) ORB-SLAM2: an open-source SLAM system for monocular, stereo and RGB-D cameras. CoRR. abs/1610.06475

40. Eade E, Drummond T (2009) Edge landmarks in monocular slam. Image Vis Comput 27(5):588–596

41. Hirose K, Saito H (2012) Fast line description for line-based SLAM. In: Proceedings of the British Machine Vision Conference

42. Klein G, Murray D (2008) Improving the agility of keyframe-based SLAM. In: Proceedings of European Conference on Computer Vision. pp 802–815

43. Newcombe RA, Lovegrove SJ, Davison AJ (2011) DTAM: dense tracking and mapping in real-time. In: Proceedings of International Conference on Computer Vision. pp 2320–2327

44. Okutomi M, Kanade T (1993) A multiple-baseline stereo. Pattern Anal Mach Intell IEEE Trans 15(4):353–363

45. Rudin LI, Osher S, Fatemi E (1992) Nonlinear total variation based noise removal algorithms. Phys D Nonlinear Phenom 60(1):259–268

46. Ondruska P, Kohli P, Izadi S (2015) MobileFusion: real-time volumetric surface reconstruction and dense tracking on mobile phones. IEEE Trans Vis Comput Graph 21(11):1251–1258

47. Stühmer J, Gumhold S, Cremers D (2010) Real-time dense geometry from a handheld camera. In: Goesele M, Roth S, Kuijper A, Schiele B, Schindler K (eds). Springer, Berlin, Heidelberg, pp 11–20

48. Schöps T, Engel J, Cremers D (2014) Semi-dense visual odometry for AR on a smartphone. In: Proceedngs of International Symposium on Mixed and Augmented Reality. pp 145–150

49. Caruso D, Engel J, Cremers D (2015) Large-scale direct SLAM for omnidirectional cameras. In: Proceedings of International Conference on Intelligent Robots and Systems

50. Engel J, Stueckler J, Cremers D (2015) Large-scale direct SLAM with stereo cameras. In: Proceedings of International Conference on Intelligent Robots and Systems

51. Forster C, Pizzoli M, Scaramuzza D (2014) SVO: fast semi-direct monocular visual odometry. In: Proceedings of International Conference on Robotics and Automation. pp 15–22

52. Baker S, Matthews I (2004) Lucas-kanade 20 years on: a unifying framework. Int J Comput Vis 56(3):221–255

53. Engel J, Koltun V, Cremers D (2016) Direct sparse odometry. CoRR. abs/1607.02565

54. Geng J (2011) Structured-light 3d surface imaging: a tutorial. Adv Opt Photon 3(2):128–160

55. Zhang Z (2012) Microsoft kinect sensor and its effect. MultiMedia IEEE 19(2):4–10

56. Besl PJ, McKay ND (1992) A method for registration of 3-d shapes. IEEE Trans Pattern Anal Mach Intell 14(2):239–256

57. Newcombe RA, Izadi S, Hilliges O, Molyneaux D, Kim D, Davison AJ, Kohi P, Shotton J, Hodges S, Fitzgibbon A (2011) KinectFusion: real-time dense surface mapping and tracking. In: Proceedngs of International Symposium on Mixed and Augmented Reality. pp 127–136

58. Kahler O, Prisacariu V, Ren C, Sun X, Torr P, Murray D (2015) Very high frame rate volumetric integration of depth images on mobile devices. IEEE Trans Vis Comput Graph 21(11):1241–1250

59. Salas-Moreno RF, Glocker B, Kelly PHJ, Davison AJ (2014) Dense planar SLAM. In: Proceedngs of International Symposium on Mixed and Augmented Reality. pp 157–164
60. Salas-Moreno RF, Newcombe RA, Strasdat H, Kelly PHJ, Davison AJ (2013) SLAM++: simultaneous localisation and mapping at the level of objects. In: Proceedings of IEEE Conference on Computer Vision and Pattern Recognition. pp 1352–1359
61. Tateno K, Tombari F, Navab N (2016) When 2.5D is not enough: Simultaneous reconstruction, segmentation and recognition on dense SLAM, IEEE International Conference on Robotics and Automation (ICRA). pp 2295–2302
62. Henry P, Krainin M, Herbst E, Ren X, Fox D (2012) RGB-D mapping: using Kinect-style depth cameras for dense 3D modeling of indoor environments. Int J Robot Res 31(5):647–663
63. Endres F, Hess J, Engelhard N, Sturm J, Cremers D, Burgard W (2012) An evaluation of the RGB-D SLAM system. In: Proceedings of International Conference on Robotics and Automation. pp 1691–1696
64. Steinbrücker F, Sturm J, Cremers D (2011) Real-time visual odometry from dense RGB-D images. In: Proceedings of IEEE International Conference on Computer Vision Workshops. pp 719–722
65. Whelan T, Kaess M, Leonard JJ, McDonald J (2013) Deformation-based loop closure for large scale dense RGB-D SLAM. In: Proceedings of International Conference on Intelligent Robots and Systems. pp 548–555
66. Whelan T, Leutenegger S, Moreno RS, Glocker B, Davison A (2015) ElasticFusion: dense slam without a pose graph. In: Proceedings of Robotics: Science and Systems. doi:10.15607/RSS.2015.XI.001
67. Gauglitz S, Sweeney C, Ventura J, Turk M, Höllerer T (2012) Live tracking and mapping from both general and rotation-only camera motion. In: Proceedngs of International Symposium on Mixed and Augmented Reality. pp 13–22
68. Pirchheim C, Schmalstieg D, Reitmayr G (2013) Handling pure camera rotation in keyframe-based SLAM. In: Proceedngs of International Symposium on Mixed and Augmented Reality. pp 229–238
69. Herrera C, Kim K, Kannala J, Pulli K, Heikkilä J, et al (2014) Dt-slam: deferred triangulation for robust SLAM. In: Proceedings of 3D Vision Vol. 1. pp 609–616
70. Mulloni A, Ramachandran M, Reitmayr G, Wagner D, Grasset R, Diaz S (2013) User friendly SLAM initialization. In: Proceedngs of International Symposium on Mixed and Augmented Reality. pp 153–162
71. Arth C, Pirchheim C, Ventura J, Schmalstieg D, Lepetit V (2015) Instant outdoor localization and SLAM initialization from 2.5 d maps. IEEE Trans Vis Comput Graph 21(11):1309–1318
72. Bleser G, Wuest H, Stricker D (2006) Online camera pose estimation in partially known and dynamic scenes. In: Proceedings of International Symposium on Mixed and Augmented Reality. pp 56–65
73. Tamaazousti M, Gay-Bellile V, Collette SN, Bourgeois S, Dhome M (2011) Nonlinear refinement of structure from motion reconstruction by taking advantage of a partial knowledge of the environment. In: Proceedings of IEEE Conference on Computer Vision and Pattern Recognition. pp 3073–3080
74. Civera J, Bueno DR, Davison A, Montiel JMM (2009) Camera self-calibration for sequential bayesian structure from motion. In: Proceedings of International Conference on Robotics and Automation. pp 403–408
75. Taketomi T, Heikkilä J (2015) Focal length change compensation for monocular slam. In: Proceedings of International Conference on Image Processing. pp 1–5
76. Pollefeys M, Koch R, Gool LV (1999) Self-calibration and metric reconstruction in spite of varying and unknown internal camera parameters. Int J Comput Vis 32(1):7–25
77. Lovegrove S, Patron-Perez A, Sibley G (2013) Spline Fusion: a continuous-time representation for visual-inertial fusion with application to rolling shutter cameras. In: Proceedings British Machine Vision Conference. pp 93.1–93.12
78. Kerl C, Stueckler J, Cremers D (2015) Dense continuous-time tracking and mapping with rolling shutter RGB-D cameras. In: Proceedings of International Conference on Computer Vision. pp 2264–2272
79. Kim JH, Cadena C, Reid I (2016) Direct semi-dense SLAM for rolling shutter cameras. In: Proceedings of International Conference on Robotics and Automation. pp 1308–1315
80. Lee T, Höllerer T (2008) Multithreaded hybrid feature tracking for markerless augmented reality. IEEE Trans Vis Comput Graph 15(undefined):355–368
81. Knorr SB, Kurz D (2016) Leveraging the user's face for absolute scale estimation in handheld monocular SLAM. In: Proceedngs of International Symposium on Mixed and Augmented Reality. pp 11–17
82. Mustaniemi J, Kannala J, Särkkä S, Matas J, Heikkilä J (2016) Inertial-based scale estimation for structure from motion on mobile devices. CoRR. abs/1611.09498
83. Tamura H, Kato H (2009) Proposal of international voluntary activities on establishing benchmark test schemes for ar/mr geometric registration and tracking methods. In: International Symposium on Mixed and Augmented Reality. pp 233–236
84. Makita K, Okuma T, Ishikawa T, Nigay L, Kurata T (2012) Virtualized reality model-based benchmarking of AR/MR camera tracking methods in TrakMark. In: IEEE ISMAR 2012 Workshop on Tracking Methods and Applications. pp 1–4
85. Martull S, Martorell MP, Fukui K (2012) Realistic CG stereo image dataset with ground truth disparity maps. In: ICPR2012 Workshop TrakMark2012. pp 40–42
86. Sturm J, Engelhard N, Endres F, Burgard W, Cremers D (2012) A benchmark for the evaluation of RGB-D SLAM systems. In: Proceedings of International Conference on Intelligent Robots and Systems
87. Geiger A, Lenz P, Urtasun R (2012) Are we ready for autonomous driving? The kitti vision benchmark suite. In: Proceedings of IEEE Conference on Computer Vision and Pattern Recognition
88. Nardi L, Bodin B, Zia MZ, Mawer J, Nisbet A, Kelly PHJ, Davison AJ, Luján M, O'Boyle MFP, Riley GD, Topham N, Furber SB (2015) Introducing SLAMBench, a performance and accuracy benchmarking methodology for SLAM. In: IEEE International Conference on Robotics and Automation. pp 5783–5790
89. Uchiyama H, Taketomi T, Ikeda S, do Monte Lima JPS (2015) [POSTER] Abecedary tracking and mapping: a toolkit for tracking competitions. In: IEEE International Symposium on Mixed and Augmented Reality. pp 198–199
90. Open Source Computer Vision. http://opencv.org/. Accessed 24 May 2017
91. cvsba: an OpenCV wrapper for sba library. http://www.uco.es/investiga/grupos/ava/node/39. Accessed 24 May 2017

11

Computer vision methods for cranial sex estimation

Olasimbo Ayodeji Arigbabu[1], Iman Yi Liao[1*], Nurliza Abdullah[2] and Mohamad Helmee Mohamad Noor[3]

Abstract

The objective of this study is to demonstrate through empirical evaluation the potential of a number of computer vision (CV) methods for sex determination from human skull. To achieve this, six local feature representations, two feature learnings, and three classification algorithms are rigorously combined and evaluated on skull regions derived from skull partitions. Furthermore, we introduce for the first time the application of multi-kernel learning (MKL) on multiple features for sex prediction from human skull. In comparison to the classical forensic methods, the results in this study are competitive, attesting to the suitability of CV methods for sex estimation. The proposed approach is fully automatic.

Keywords: Forensic anthropology, Sex determination, Local feature representation, Kernel principal component analysis, Support vector machine, Multi-kernel learning

1 Introduction

Sex determination from human skull plays an essential role in forensic anthropology. In the literature, morphological assessment and morphometric analysis are the two main approaches, which have historically been demonstrated for capturing sexually dimorphic characteristics from cranial regions. Morphological assessment involves some procedural steps where a forensic expert visually examines the anatomical regions of the skull (such as the glabella, mastoid, nuchal crest, orbital, and mental eminence), reports the observed variations on the skull with standard semantic terms, quantifies the descriptions on an ordinal scale, and eventually uses discriminant function analysis (DFA) to predict the sex of the skull. Morphometric analysis, on the other hand, requires forensic experts to annotate and measure the distance between anatomical landmarks. These measurements are considered as input to a DFA model to determine the sex of the skull.

Though both techniques are generally acceptable concepts founded on well-grounded principles for forensic examination, they exhibit some limitations. For instance,

both estimation techniques are based on manual derivation of estimation parameters. Morphological assessment being a method that relies on visual perception is highly influenced by subjectivity of the observer. Besides, it necessitates a certain level of experience as well as familiarity of the forensic expert with the cranial samples in a population group that is being studied. Whereas, the process of morphometric analysis is laborious as it requires ample amount of time for accurate and precise landmark annotation. Moreover, variation in the shape of the skull is another limitation of morphometric analysis, which inhibits the generalization ability of the method to diverse population groups.

This paper presents an automatic estimation method which eschews the need for human manual assessment. We demonstrate with experimental evidence the potential of computer vision (CV) methods for cranial sex estimation. Of particular interest is application of different 3D local shape descriptors, feature learning, and classification methods. In addition, for the first time, we present multi-kernel learning on multiple features for cranial sex estimation. 3D local descriptors have been used in several CV and medical applications such as 3D object recognition [1, 2], face recognition [3], gender recognition [4, 5],

*Correspondence: iman.liao@nottingham.edu.my
[1] School of Computer Science, University of Nottingham Malaysia Campus, Semenyih, Malaysia
Full list of author information is available at the end of the article

diagnosis of cranial deformity, and detection of anatomical landmarks [6–8]. However, to the best of our knowledge, there are no related works on their application to 3D representation of skulls for sex determination.

The remainder of the paper is organized as follows. Section 2 presents the related works on cranial sex estimation. In Section 3, we describe the experimental dataset used for validating our work. Section 4 presents the CV framework for cranial estimation which includes sub-stages of pre-processing, 3D local shape representation, feature learning, and classification. In section 5, we demonstrate the usefulness of the proposed CV methods by the prediction results attained. Finally, discussion and conclusion are given in Section 6 to summarize this paper.

2 Related works

Morphological assessment and morphometric analysis are the two main techniques employed by forensic anthropolgists for sex determination [9]. The earliest studies using morphological assessment were reported in [10–12]. Studies in the 90's have established standardized quantification methods using ordinal scale to aid visual assessment of sexually dimorphic characteristics from five anatomical sites of the skull [13]. These traits include the robusticity of the nuchal crest, size of the mastoid process, sharpness of the supraorbital margin, prominence of the glabella, and projection of the mental eminence. A forensic expert would examine how the dimorphic characteristics are expressed in those five anatomical sites and their visual similarity to the diagram presented in [13]. With various ordinal scoring methods, forensic experts have been able to achieve estimation performance between 83 and 90% [12, 14]. It has also been demonstrated that specific cranial regions such as the shape of supraorbital margin [15] can be assessed for sex determination with prediction rate of 70%. This is made possible by forming the contour shape of the supraorbital with plasticine impression, which is then visually assessed and quantified on a 7-point ordinal scale. A modification of such technique has been presented in [16] replacing manual assessment with computer-aided method by using 2D wavelet transform on 3D reconstruction of the scanned supraorbital impression to study its shape variation.

Alternative sex estimation technique is based on morphometric analysis, which involves linear or geometric measurement of anatomical landmarks. The choice of landmarks to annotate varies among the methods reported in literature. Franklin et al. [17] reported using eight measurements of the 3D landmarks to perform morphometric analysis with discriminant function analysis, which yielded prediction rates between 77 and 80%. The author discovered high sexual dimorphism in the facial width (bizygomatic breadth) and the length and height of the cranial vault. Bigoni et al. [18] conducted a study

on 139 cranial samples of the Central European population, where 82 ecto-cranial landmarks were annotated from seven sub-regions (the configuration of the neurocranium, cranial base, midsagittal curve of vault, upper face, orbital region, nasal region, and palatal region) of the skull. Generalized procrustes analysis (GPA) was adopted for analyzing the shape configuration, and no sex difference were noticed in the sample set when landmarks from the whole cranium were used. However, through partial shape examinations on each of the seven regions, there were indications of strong sexual dimorphism in the midsagittal curve, the upper face, the orbital region, the nasal region, and the palatal region, but no sex variation in the cranium base and the neurocranium configuration. Another study has compared two discriminant function analysis methods on 17 craniometric variables from 90 Iberian skulls [19]. The authors observed higher metric variables in male samples than in female samples [19]. Luo et al. [20] presented statistical analysis of the holistic shape of the frontal part of the skull using principal component analysis (PCA) and linear discriminant analysis (LDA) on Chinese samples.

While morphological assessment and morphometric analysis appear to be technically simple, they have been demonstrated to be effective for cranial sex estimation. Moreover, they are concepts which have been established on well-grounded principles and universally acceptable as evidence in court cases and forensic investigation [21]. Nevertheless, there are a number of weaknesses in the two techniques that are worth mentioning:

- Subjective perception of the observer (forensic expert) affects the confidence of prediction [18, 22]. This is a natural phenomenon associated with visual assessment and verbal description of the observed variation, especially in a situation where the descriptions connoted from a particular group is unable to generalize to other groups due to discrepancies in the perception of the observers.

- Inter-observer variability is commonly experienced when observers select landmarks in the case of morphometric analysis. Furthermore, this influence of population difference affects the accuracy and precision of the traits used for identification. As a result, an estimation method used in a specific population may not generalize to other populations [23]

- Inaccurate and incomplete landmarks is another limitation of morphometric analysis. In fact, it has been shown that the inter-observer error is approximately 10% for most measurements [21]. Accurate annotation of anatomical landmarks requires ample amount of time and it often needs expensive, specialized anthropometric equipment. In addition, forensic expert usually face the challenge of performing measurements that capture subtle variations among cranial traits that are easy to see but very difficult to measure [14].

2.1 Main contributions

The main objective of this paper is to demonstrate the potential of computer vision methods for sex determination from human skull. Though it is accurate that the 3D feature descriptors adopted in this paper are well known, from a holistic point of view, a framework integrating several stages of pre-processing—feature extraction, multiregion representation, and classification—has not been reported in the literature (to the best of our knowledge), which indicates the novelty of this work. Such pipeline provides an incentive for forensic anthropologists to look at sex estimation problem from a totally different perspective. Moreover, the proposed approaches are completely automatic. We therefore summarize the contributions of the paper as follows:

- This paper proposes using computer vision approaches based on local feature representation, feature learning, and classification for sex prediction from human cranial data obtained from CT scans. The proposed method advances the conventional forensic methods as it does not rely on manually configured estimation parameters.
- We propose to partition the skull along the axial, coronal, and sagittal axes, extract 3D local shape features, and aggregate those features into compact representations that possess discriminative capabilities. To segment the skulls into smaller regions, we constrained the partitioning to the X-, Y-, and Z-axes, where accurate distribution of features in each local sub-region can be generated.
- Furthermore, comprehensive performance analysis of different combination of local features and feature learning methods with different number of regions from the three planes is presented.
- Finally, we introduce the concept of multi-kernel learning on multiple features for cranial sex prediction. To the best of our knowledge, this is the first study to approach the problem of skull sex estimation from this novel perspective.

3 Application of computer vision methods

This section introduces the proposed framework for sex classification, which is composed of four main stages: 3D data pre-processing, 3D feature representation, multiregion feature representation, and classification.

3.1 Experimental dataset

The experimental data is a 100 sample set of post-mortem computed tomography (PMCT) scan slices obtained from the Hospital Kuala Lumpur (HKL). There are 54 males and 46 females between the ages of 5 and 85 years from South East Asia. Seventy percent of the data are Malaysian (Malay, Chinese, Indian) and 30% non-Malaysian. The scanning device is a Toshiba CT scanner with scanning settings of 1.0 slice thickness and 0.8 slice interval. The data contain slices belonging to the head region with resolutions between $512 \times 512 \times 261$ and $512 \times 512 \times 400$, depending on the size of the skull of each subject. Legal consent for the use of the dataset was obtained prior to commencing this research.

3.2 3D data pre-processing

The consecutive 2D CT slices of each subject are stacked vertically to obtain 3D volumetric data, which are then filtered to reduce noise, local irregularities, and roughness using a discretized spline smoothing method [24]. The 3D smoothing technique utilizes 3D discrete cosine transform-based penalized least square regression (DCT-PLS) on equally spaced high-dimension data. The main idea of the algorithm is to reformulate PLS regression problem with DCT, where the data are expressed in the form of cosine functions oscillating at different frequencies [24].

Afterward, the denoised 3D volumetric data is reconstructed into 3D surface using marching cubes algorithm [25] as illustrated in Fig. 1. The reconstruction is achieved using an iso-value of (150) to obtain the regions containing hard tissues. As the reconstructed 3D surface is of high dimension ($> 650,000$ vertex points), mesh simplification is performed to reduce the surface to 13% of the original size [26]. The resulting downsampled skulls have $< 130,000$ vertices, with well-preserved structural details of the surface after downsampling, as shown in Fig. 1.

3.2.1 Background object removal

After surface reconstruction, we noticed some dynamic background objects scanned with the subjects, with the same isovalue as the hard tissue, around some skull samples (~ 27 samples). In order to remove these background objects, we propose a method based on online sequential least square (OLS) with Gaussian mixture model (GMM) sample initialization. We are able to design this method using 27 noisy samples; however, the same approach can be improved further when there is availability of larger noisy samples. Initially, a training data matrix is prepared by randomly selecting eight clean and eight noisy skull samples. For each noisy skull, we manually annotate and cut out the background objects. The set of background objects which have been manually segmented are considered to form the negative training samples, while the clean skulls are regarded as the positive training samples, as illustrated in Fig. 2. Therefore, the training set is composed of eight clean and eight segmented background

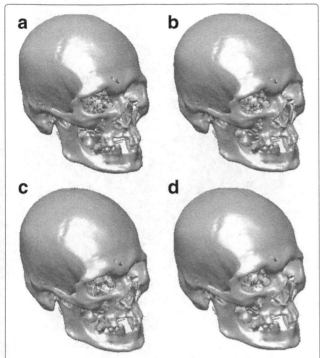

Fig. 1 Examples of reconstructed skull data. **a** Original skull. **b** Downsampled to 50% . **c** Downsampled to 25%. **d** Downsampled to 13%

objects resulting in $\sim 750,000$ training vertex points for the two classes. Due to the size of the training set, we used a sequential learning method where each time the training is performed in batches. However, the initial batch of data for training is initialized using a GMM to fit a mixture model composing of K components. Consider a training set $A = \{v_1, \ldots v_i\}$, where A is a matrix consisting of

clean and segmented background objects and v_i is a vertex point; GMM is used to cluster the set A into K clusters. Then, the OLS training process is initialized by choosing a cluster as the initial batch A_0. After selecting the initial batch, the following minimizing problem is solved:

$$\text{Minimize: } ||A_0 x_0 - b_0||^2 + \lambda ||x_0||^2 \tag{1}$$

where x_0 are the coefficients, λ is the regularization term, and $b_0 = \{+1, -1\}$ are the labels (+1 for clean skull, -1 for the background object) of the initial subsets. The initial solution x_0 can be obtained analytically using:

$$x_0 = \left(A_0^\top A_0 + \lambda \mathrm{I}\right)^{-1} A_0^\top b_0 \tag{2}$$

The coefficients x_0 are referred to as the least square solution to the minimization problem in Eq. (1). The inverse matrix M_0^{-1} can be obtained as: $M_0^{-1} = \left(A_0^\top A_0 + \lambda \mathrm{I}\right)^{-1}$ and the output coefficients $x_0 = M_0^{-1} A_0^\top b_0$.

3.2.2 Updating x_{k+1}

Having obtained the initial solution, the remaining subset of the data can be trained batch-by-batch without keeping the previously trained set to minimize computational time and complexity. Thus, it is necessary to use an efficient approach to update the initially learned coefficients, while solving new linear systems minimization problem [27]. A well-recognized method to sequentially update x_0 is the Sherman-Morrison Woodbury inverse formula [28]. When new sample subsets $A_{k+1} = \{v_1^{k+1}, \ldots, v_i^{k+1}\}$ are learned in batches, we can update x_0 from Eq. (2) as:

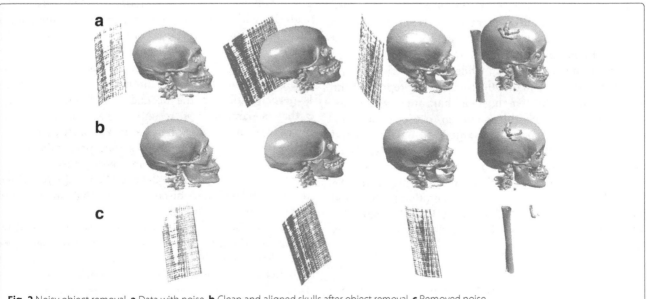

Fig. 2 Noisy object removal. **a** Data with noise. **b** Clean and aligned skulls after object removal. **c** Removed noise

$$x_{k+1} = x_k + M_{k+1}^{-1} A_{k+1}^T \left(b_{k+1} - A_{k+1} x_k \right) \tag{3}$$

$$M_{k+1}^{-1} = M_k^{-1} - M_k^{-1} A_{k+1} \left(I + A_{k+1}^T M_k^{-1} A_{k+1} \right)^{-1} A_{k+1}^T M_k^{-1} \tag{4}$$

where x_k is the output coefficients in the previous step, b_{k+1} is the newly collected labels and $M_{k+1}^{-1} = \left(A_{k+1}^T A_{k+1} + \lambda I \right)^{-1}$. Once x_{k+1} has been learned, each new skull sample containing noise, which were not included in the training phase are used to test the model. The results obtained are depicted in Fig. 2.

Afterward, skull alignment is performed using an iterative closest point (ICP) algorithm [29].

3.3 Skull representation with 3D local shape features

3.3.1 Mesh local binary pattern (MeshLBP)

MeshLBP is a local shape representation method for directly extracting local binary patterns from 3D mesh. Basically, the algorithm forms a set of ordered ring facets (ORF) [30, 31] and calculates the primitive functions such as mean or Gaussian curvature for each facet in the ring. Then, the binary patterns are obtained by thresholding the primitive function of neighboring facets by that of the centre facet. Given the primitive function $p(f)$, defined on a mesh, represents the Gaussian curvature. The MeshLBP can be derived as follows:

$$MeshLBP_m^r(f_c) = \sum_{k=0}^{m-1} s \left(p(f_k^r) - p(f_c) \right) \cdot \alpha(k) \tag{5}$$

$$s = \begin{cases} 1, & > 0 \\ 0, & \leq 0 \end{cases}$$

where r is the ring number and m is the number of facets available in the ring.

These two parameters in the Eq. (5) regulate the radial resolution and azimuthal quantization, while the discrete function $\alpha(k)$ is a weight which enables computation of other variants of LBP. Using $\alpha_1(k) = 1$ gives binary pattern in the range [0–12], while $\alpha_2(k) = 2^k$ gives patterns in the range [0–4096]. In order to represent the skull with MeshLBP, ten-ring neighbors are computed for each individual facet (this is chosen to provide a trade-off between fairly covering a large local neighbourhood and less computational time), $m = 12$ and $\alpha_2(k)$. Then, the MeshLBP is extracted by comparing the Gaussian curvature of center facet to the neighboring facets. An example of MeshLBP feature representation is illustrated in Fig. 3. The output of MeshLBP is V-by-10 matrix for each skull sample, with V denoting the number of vertex points.

3.3.2 Spin image

Spin image [1] is a point-based descriptor which is invariant to rotation and translation commonly used for object

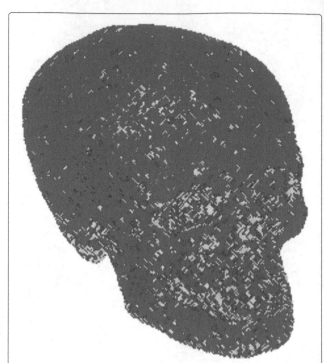

Fig. 3 Example of MeshLBP feature distribution by mapping the binary patterns to different color map. For illustration, we display the binary pattern of ring ($r = 2$). Red color indicates areas of small binary pattern (0) due to small variation in the curvature of the local regions. Blue represents patterns with values (1–16), green denotes patterns with values (32–256), and cyan represents patterns with values (512–4096), due to large variation in the curvature of the local regions. For instance, sharp curvature variation can be observed around the local regions of the orbital, nasal bone, and mandible, while the parietal bone exhibits mild variation in curvature

retrieval. Spin image generates 2D histogram for mesh point containing the representation of object geometry. To begin with, oriented points are initially computed for each point on the mesh according to location of the vertex p and its surface normal n, which results in a 2D basis (p, n). Then, to obtain the coordinate system, a tangent plane P passing through p is formed which is perpendicular to the normal n and line L through p that is parallel to n, resulting in a cylindrical coordinate system (α, β), where α is a non-negative distance to L and β is signed distance perpendicular to P. Finally, a spin map S_m is formed by projecting the 3D points x on a mesh to 2D coordinates (α, β), which are accumulated into discrete points that are updated incrementally.

The size (i_{max}, j_{max}) of a spin image is determined by the size of the bin and the maximum size of the object expressed in the spin map coordinates.

In this paper, a cell size of 10 and histogram bin of 10 are used for extracting the features, which result in 10×10 spin image for each vertex.

3.3.3 Local depth SIFT (LD-SIFT)

LD-SIFT [2] is an extension of SIFT [32] to mesh surface. The process of extracting the LD-SIFT features involves detecting a number of interest points representing the local maxima from difference of Gaussian (DoG) operation on the mesh. From each interest, a sphere support is constructed to cover the neighboring region. LD-SIFT then creates a 2D array that emanates from estimating a tangent plane T within the support region and computing the distance from each point in that region to the plane. Then, it makes the feature scale invariant by setting the viewport size to match the feature scale, as detected by the DoG detector. Further, it computes the principal component analysis (PCA) of the points surrounding the interest point and use their dominant direction as the local dominant angle. Similar to the standard SIFT, the depth map are rotated to a canonical angle with respect to the dominant angle to make the LD-SIFT rotation invariant. From the resulting depth maps, the standard SIFT feature descriptors are computed to create the LD-SIFT feature descriptor. The features represent 8-bin gradient histograms distributed in the local cells of 4×4 depth map. As a result, the dimensional of the final feature vector is 128 ($4 \times 4 \times 8$) for each detected vertex (interest) point.

3.3.4 Scale invariant heat kernel signature (SIHKS)

Heat kernel signature (HKS) is a type of spectral shape representation method which uses deformable shape analysis to create the point signature of a specific point [33]. The representation follows the concept of modeling shapes as Riemannian manifold and using their heat conduction characteristics as a descriptor.

Initially, heat kernel signature was proposed in [33] for shape representation, which is invariant to isometry and has gained popularity in shape retrieval application. However, the limitation of HKS is that the descriptor is not scale invariant. As a result, Bronstein et al. [34] introduced a method to remove the scale effect by sampling each point logarithmically in time ($t = \alpha^\tau$) and then computing the derivative based on the scale to undo the additive function with respect to the scale. They further utilized Fourier transform to remove the shift variation. In order to extract SIHKS, we used a logarithmic scale-space with base $\alpha = 2$ ranging from $\tau = 1 : 20$ with increments of 1/5. We then chose the first ten frequencies for feature representation. Each feature point in the 10-length vector denotes the heat kernel signature at a particular scale.

3.3.5 ShapeDNA

ShapeDNA initially proposed by Reuter et al. [35] computes the fingerprint of any 3D object by deriving the eigenvalues of Laplace-Beltrami operator of the shape model. It is isometry invariant and insensitive to noise. Normally, eigenvalues λ and eigenfunctions u are the solutions to the laplacian eigenvalue problem $\triangle u = -\lambda u$, where $\triangle u := div(grad(u))$, div is the divergence of the underlying Riemanian manifold and $grad$ represents the gradient. The first normed N eignevalues $0 < \lambda_1 < \lambda_2, \ldots \lambda_n$ are chosen as the shape descriptor. In this paper, we selected the first 100 eigenvalues as the shape descriptor. Figure 4 depicts some examples of ShapeDNA representation.

3.3.6 Area of skull regions

Finally, the surface area of each local sub-region of the skull is computed as additional features. The skull is initially partitioned in smaller regions along the X, Y, or Z, and the corresponding area is computed following the approach in [36]

3.4 Multiple-region feature representation

The common practice in computer vision applications is to directly concatenate features extracted from keypoints into long-tailed vector or, as an alternative, use the bag-of-word model to construct a compact representation. Nevertheless, we discovered that these approaches result in high possibility of the local features from a particular class to possess dissimilar representation. This inherently makes features from two different classes to exhibit the same or similar feature values, which reduces the informative characteristics of such methods. Hence, in this work, we employed a heuristic partitioning method, where each skull is divided into several regions along a particular orientation (axis). In each region, we stack the representations from each point on each other and aggregate the features into compact representation as shown in Fig. 5. It is essential to note that the partitioning could have been performed following the anatomic structure of the skull. However, such partitioning is itself a research topic, and there are currently no reported methods for anatomic partitioning in the literature. We intend to investigate this research aspect in our future works. Thus, such exploration would go beyond the scope of the current paper.

Assuming spin image of 10×10 size is extracted from $V = 10,000$ vertices, we stack the spin image from each vertex point on one another and calculate the aggregate, which results in a final spin image of 10×10 descriptor size and feature vector of 100 dimensions, as shown in Fig. 5. This makes the representation more distinctive than the long-tailed concatenated or bag-of-word representation. Similar approach is used for LD-SIFT by stacking the gradient features from the keypoints and taking aggregate, which results in a final feature vector of 128 dimensions. For MeshLBP, the descriptor extracted is 10

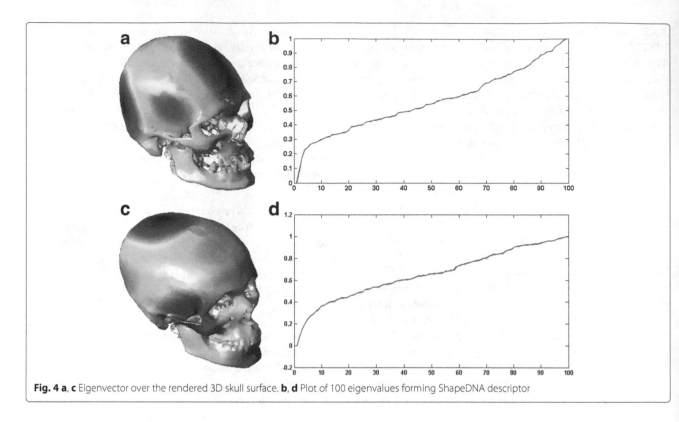

Fig. 4 a, c Eigenvector over the rendered 3D skull surface. **b, d** Plot of 100 eigenvalues forming ShapeDNA descriptor

scalar values from 10 rings for each vertex point, making a $V \times 10$ descriptor matrix; thus, a 32-histogram bin is aggregated for each ring along the vertices and the final feature vector is the concatenation of the histograms from the 10 rings ($32 \times 10 = 320$ feature descriptor). We used 32 bins to keep the dimension of the feature vector to a reasonable length. Also, SIHKS is compactly represented in this fashion, using 32-bin histogram bins to represent each frequency, which yields $32 \times 10 = 320$ descriptor. To obtain discriminant

representation from the extracted features, we used the Kernel principal component analysis (KPCA) [37] which is a dimensionality reduction method that generalizes the standard PCA to non-linear feature representation and K-SVD [38], a dictionary learning technique.

Furthermore, to make our evaluation comprehensive, the partition is performed along the X-, Y-, and Z-axes, as depicted in Fig. 6, and the number of regions N examined in each axis is $N = \{1 : 2 : 99\}$. The results attained from the regions in each axis are illustrated in Section 4.

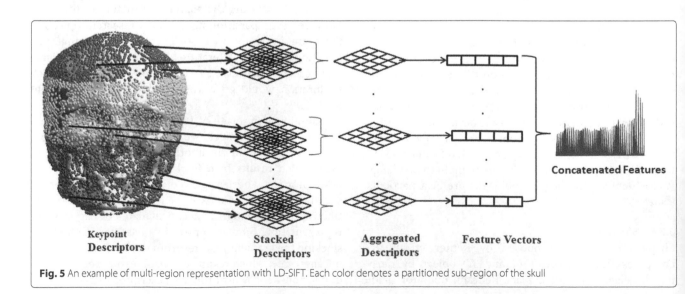

Fig. 5 An example of multi-region representation with LD-SIFT. Each color denotes a partitioned sub-region of the skull

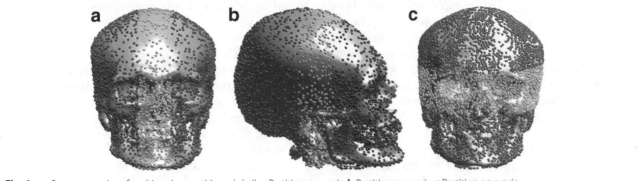

Fig. 6 a–c Some examples of multi-region partitioned skull. **a** Partition on x-axis. **b** Partition on y-axis. **c** Partition on z-axis

3.5 Multi-kernel learning (MKL) on multiple features

Besides testing the performance ability of the six local shape descriptors described in Section 4.2, we examine the potential of MKL to fuse multiple features with different representation properties. MKL has attracted significant amount of attention in CV research domain. In this paper, the soft margin MKL algorithm introduced by Xu et al. [39] is adopted, where a kernel slack variable is first introduced for each of the base kernels when learning the kernel. This approach is advancement over the MKL framework generally regarded as the hard margin MKL [40], which imposes sparsity on a category of features and selects the features that best optimize the object function. In fact, it has been pointed out in [39] that the hard margin MKL is a method which only selects the base kernels with minimum objective. This could easily lead to overfitting problem, particularly in a situation where the base kernels contain noisy features. Following the notion of standard hard margin SVM, it is believed that data from two classes can be separated by a hard margin. However, to enable usability of SVM in real applications the slack variables were introduced to the hard margin SVM, which allows some training errors to be incorporated to the training data, thereby minimizing the overfitting problem [39]. This concept inspired the development of soft margin MKL, which instead introduces kernel slack variable for each of the base kernels [39].

Futhermore, by conducting independent experiments on each local feature, we are able to figure out the best feature set in Section 4.1, where it turns out that MeshLBP > Spin Image > LD-SIFT > SIHKS > ShapeDNA > Region Area. Hence, the point of using MKL in this paper is to try to induce information from more than one feature source by different combination, which is why the soft margin MKL is more suitable for this purpose. As a result, it makes it unnecessary to select the best feature again or highlight the best set of features. Moreover combination of all features exhibited poor performance indicating that information cannot be induced from all features at the same time.

The motivation behind MKL is to combine or fuse multiple kernels or features rather than using a single feature representation to make prediction, with expectation that such combination leads to potential gain in performance. Assuming, we have a training set M consisting of $(h_i, g_i, w_i)_{i=1}^{M}$ where h_i is a type of local features of the ith sample and g_i is a another type of features of the same sample and $w = (-1, +1)$ are the class labels. We can map the features to the reproducing kernel hilbert space (RKHS) with a kernel function $k(\cdot, \cdot)$ defined over each of the two feature types. Without loss of generality, this notion applies to more than two feature types.

3.5.1 SVM-based MKL

Suppose we have a set of base kernels $K = \{K_1, \ldots K_N\}$ for our training set, the objective of the standard problem solved by the MKL introduced in [39] is:

$$\max_{\alpha \in \mathcal{A}} \min_{\mu \in \mathcal{M}} \sum_{n=1}^{N} \mu_n \mathbf{SVM}\{K_n, \alpha\} \tag{6}$$

where, $\mathbf{SVM}\{K_n, \alpha\} = -1/2(\alpha \odot w)' K_n(\alpha \odot w)$, α_i are the coefficients of the samples, and $\mu = [\mu_1, \ldots \mu_N]'^{1}$ are the coefficients measuring the importance of the nth base kernel. $\mathcal{A} = \{\alpha | \alpha' \mathbf{1} = 1, \alpha' w = 0, 0 \leq \alpha \leq C\}$ is the domain for α and $\mathcal{M} = \{\alpha | 0 \leq \mu, \sum_{n=1}^{N} \mu = 1\}$ is the domain for μ. For the solution in Eq. 6, a hard margin is constructed resulting in selection of only the most important base kernel, which eventually defeats the purpose of finding interaction between different feature sets. Therefore, in this work, we used the soft margin formulation, where a slack variable which is the difference between the target margin τ and the objective is introduced as:

$$\zeta = \tau - \mathbf{SVM}\{K_n, \alpha\} \quad \forall_n = 1, \ldots N \tag{7}$$

The loss incurred by the kernel slack can be expressed as

$$\xi_n = \ell(\zeta_n) \quad \forall_n = 1, \ldots N \tag{8}$$

where $\ell(\cdot)$ is a hinge loss function $\ell(\cdot) = max(0, \ell_n)$.

Besides using MKL to induce information from different features, it will be interesting to explore the interaction and joint contribution of different regions using MKL. However, as it itself is another research topic and our current focus is on evaluating the performances of different types of features and their combinations for sex identification of the cranial, we hope to include this direction in our future research.

4 Experimental results

In this section, two different experiments are reported to evaluate the described CV methods. Firstly, we test the effect of partition orientation on the four local descriptors, meaning that the prediction results attained are compared based on the regions in X-, Y-, and Z-axes. In addition to that the effect of number of partitions (regions) the skull is divided is tested. Secondly, we evaluate the performance of MKL for various feature combinations, similarly with respect to the three partition axes.

4.1 Sex determination using 3D local features

To evaluate the performance of the four local descriptors for sex determination, we have selected three baseline predictive models: (1) support vector machine (SVM) [41], (2) kernel extreme learning machine (KELM) [42], and (3) sparse representation classifier (SRC) [43]. The standard protocol used throughout this paper is that the input dataset is divided into 60 and 40% as training and testing set, respectively, by random sampling without replacement. In the training stage, a five-fold cross-validation is performed to derive the best regularization value C (between 2^{-10} and 2^{10}) for the three classifiers. Once training is completed, the skulls are classified into male or female using the separate unused testing set. The experiments are repeated 10 times, and the average is computed as the sex prediction rate.

4.1.1 Effect of number of regions and partition orientation on sex prediction

We now simultaneously demonstrate how the orientation of partition and the number of skull partition influence the results of sex prediction. These evaluations are divided into two categories, where the first evaluation involves using ordinary 3D local descriptors to train the three predictive models and the second evaluation involves using KPCA and KSVD to learn compact representation from the feature vectors before classification. In the first evaluation, the skulls are initially partitioned into different regions, and the local features are extracted, aggregated, and finally concatenated from all regions before serving as an input to the predictive models. It can be noticed in Fig. 7 that partitions derived from the z-axis generally provided the best prediction rates, particularly using

MeshLBP, as these results remain consistent across the three predictive models. When the MeshLBP features extracted from partitions in the z-axis are used to train the KELM classifier, the highest prediction rate obtained is 80.25%; SRC classifier showed similar performance with a prediction rate of 80%, while with SVM classifier, the highest prediction rate is 82%. Moreover, in all experiments, MeshLBP showed better performance than the region area, ShapeDNA, SI-HKS, LD-SIFT, and spin image local descriptors.

Whereas, the Y-axis in some cases showed comparable trend in performances, especially using LD-SIFT and Spin image local descriptors, which also remain consistent across the three classifiers. For instance the prediction results of spin image are 76.25, 73.5, and 73% using KELM, SRC, and SVM classifiers respectively.

However, for MeshLBP, it can be seen that the prediction results achieved from partitions in X- and Y-axes are lower than those from Z-axis. Besides that, we observed that the effect of increase in number of partitions is not so evident in all experiments, except for MeshLBP where the prediction results peaked at five regions before deteriorating as the number of partitions approach 99 regions. With region area, ShapeDNA, and SI-HKS, the performances are neither influenced by orientation of partition nor by number of regions as the prediction rate is generally less than 70% in the three predictive models, thus leading to the conclusion that the SI-HKS descriptor is not suitable for sex prediction from human skulls.

In the second evaluation, we used KSVD and KPCA to learn compact representations from the local features prior to classification, which significantly reduce the dimensionality of the feature vectors. Using KSVD, we noticed a slight improvement in the performance of the local descriptors. For instance, MeshLBP increased from 82 to 83% using KELM classifier, while the results using SRC and SVM also increase by at least 1%. Similarly, the prediction rates of LD-SIFT and spin image increased across the three classifiers. Meanwhile, a similar trend in prediction results with respect to the orientation of partitions can be observed from the results in Fig. 8, as the Y-axis tends to exhibit comparable performance to the Z-axis partitions.

Using KPCA, we further observed improvement in prediction results, especially in the case of spin image and MeshLBP where the prediction rates increased to 85.5 and 86% respectively, as depicted in Fig. 9. In addition, it is obvious that the partitions derived from the Z-axis provided better results than X- and Y-axes. Also, increasing the number of partitions resulted in reduced prediction results for MeshLBP; however, the trend is only slightly evident for spin image and LD-SIFT. Overall, SVM classifier showed better prediction performance than SRC and KELM.

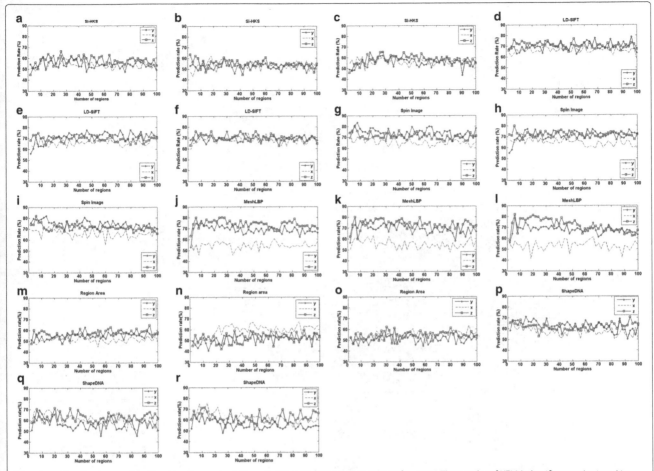

Fig. 7 a–r Results of sex estimation based on orientation of region partition and number of regions. The results of KELM classifier are depicted in (**a**, **d**, **g**, **j**, **m**, **p**). Results of SRC classifier are depicted in (**b**, **e**, **h**, **k**, **n**, **q**). Results of SVM classifier are depicted in (**c**, **f**, **i**, **l**, **o**, **r**)

4.2 Sex determination using MKL on multiple features

In this experiment, we used the linear kernel function for mapping each local feature, which are then combined in the MKL framework. We focus on LD-SIFT, spin image, and MeshLBP since these three feature representation methods showed better performance than region area, ShapeDNA, and SI-HKS in Section 4.1. Within this framework, four different sets of combination are performed with respect to the orientation of partition (X, Y, Z) and number of regions (1 : 2 : 99). Particularly, we have examined the integration of:

- LD-SIFT + MeshLBP
- Spin Image + MeshLBP
- Spin Image + LD-SIFT
- Spin Image + LD-SIFT + MeshLBP

The results attained are illustrated in Fig. 10. Learning a multi-kernel representation for LD-SIFT + MeshLBP, the best prediction rates attained are 72.5% (X-axis), 71.5% (Y-axis), and 78% (Z-axis). With spin image + MeshLBP, the prediction rates are 72% (X-axis), 70%

(Y-axis), and 86% (Z-axis), while the results of spin image + LD-SIFT are 79.5% (X-axis), 72.5% (Y-axis), and 85.5% (Z-axis). Similar to the case of single descriptor, it can be noted that the partitions derived from the Z-axis provided better performance than X- and Y-axes in all experiments.

Moreover, the influence of number of regions is slightly evident on the results of spin image + LD-SIFT and Spin + MeshLBP, as the peak recognition rate is achieved at five regions before receding as the partitions approach 99 regions. However, we observed no significant impact of number of region on the prediction rates of LD-SIFT + MeshLBP. Finally, we attempted to combine spin image + LD-SIFT + MeshLBP, but the prediction results decreased on the three orientations of skull partition, indicating less compatibility among the three features. Quite interestingly, spin + MeshLBP produced the most compatible combination as the prediction rate of 86% is comparable to the benchmark attained with single descriptor. We denote from these experiments that MKL is useful for sex prediction from human skulls albeit the selection of the most

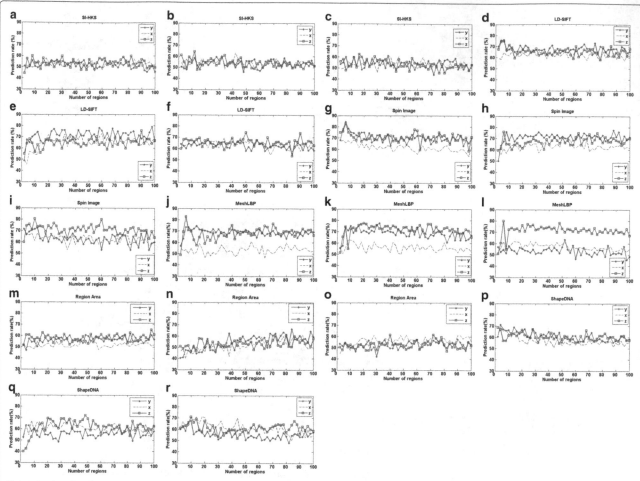

Fig. 8 a–r Results of sex estimation based on orientation of region partition and number of regions using KSVD. The results of KSVD-KELM are depicted in (**a, d, g, j, m, p**). Results of KSVD-SRC are depicted in (**b, e, h, k, n, q**). Results of KSVD-SVM are depicted in (**c, f, i, l, o, r**)

compatible 3D local descriptor seems to be necessary. Unlike the soft margin MKL which tries to induce information from multiple sources, we used the hard margin MKL based on primal formulation, which imposes penalty on the features and selects those that best optimize the objective. However, the results as shown in Fig. 11 are not so promising compared to the soft margin MKL. This can be attributed to the fact that the hard margin MKL tends to be dependent on the discriminative ability of the base kernels [44]. Thus, in a case where the single features are already discriminant, the hard margin MKL will be unable to exhibit any better performance than the single features. On the other hand, this indicates that if the single features are not discriminant such as heat kernel signature or ShapeDNA, their combination will have a negative impact on the performance unless they can be singled out.

4.3 Comparison with forensic approach

For the sake of completeness, we compared the performance of the proposed CV methods with conventional

forensic estimation method [45] as shown in Table 1. Prior to describing the forensic method, it is worth emphasizing that the objective of this paper is to demonstrate the potential of computer vision methods for sex determination from human skull. Despite the fact that the 3D feature descriptors adopted in this paper are commonly used in the domain of computer vision, from a general perspective, a framework which integrates several stages of pre-processing—feature extraction, multiregion representation, and classification—has not been reported in the literature. This differentiates the proposed framework from the existing forensic methods, and such framework serves as an incentive for forensic anthropologists to approach sex estimation problem from a completely different perspective.

The conventional forensic method [45] is based on traditional morphometrics, where 22 estimation parameters are measured covering anatomical locations of 87 cranial samples (45 males and 42 females). These 87 samples are drawn the same dataset we obtained from

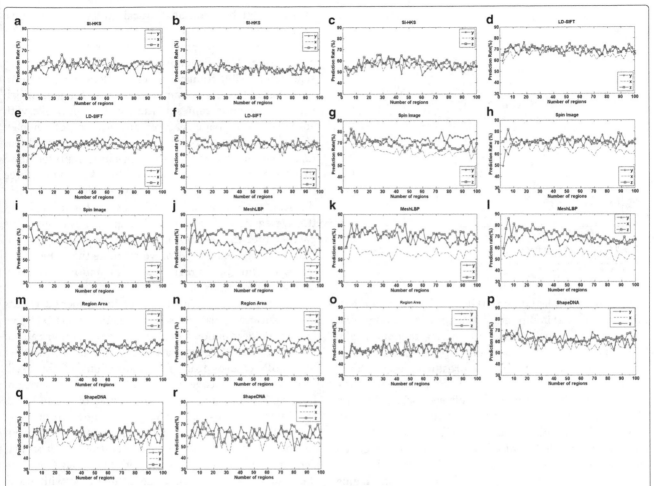

Fig. 9 a–r Results of sex estimation based on orientation of region partition and number of regions using KPCA. The results of KPCA-KELM are depicted in (**a**, **d**, **g**, **j**, **m**, **p**). Results of KPCA-SRC are depicted in (**b**, **e**, **h**, **k**, **n**, **q**). Results of KPCA-SVM are depicted in (**c**, **f**, **i**, **l**, **o**, **r**)

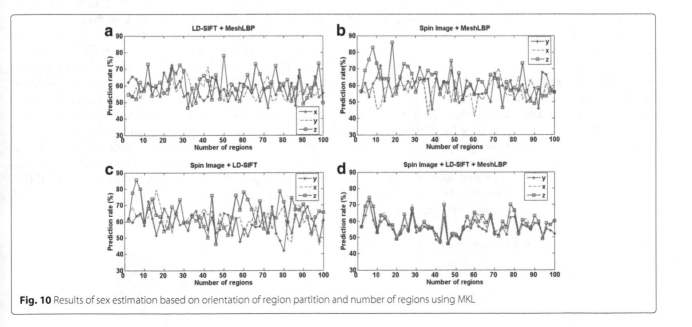

Fig. 10 Results of sex estimation based on orientation of region partition and number of regions using MKL

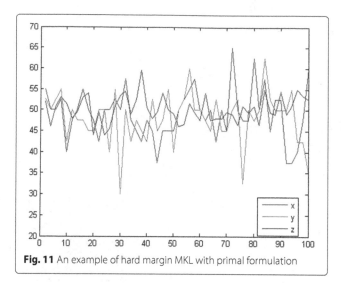

Fig. 11 An example of hard margin MKL with primal formulation

the Hospital Kuala Lumpur (HKL). The measurements include the maximum cranial length, maximum cranial breadth, cranial base length, basion-bregma height, bizygomatic breadth, maximum frontal breadth, minimum frontal breadth, basion prosthion, upper facial height, nasal height, nasal breadth, orbital height of the right eye, orbital height of the left eye, orbital breadth of the right eye, orbital breadth of the left eye, biorbital breadth, auriculo-bregmatic height of the right side, auriculo-bregmatic height of the left side, naso-occipital length, mastoidal bregma height of the right side, mastoidal bregma height of the left side, and nasion bregma height. Through independent t test, the authors were able to deduce the difference between male and female categories. Discriminant function analysis(DFA) is then used to generate equations for modeling the measurements and regression analysis to classify the samples into their respective classes. The prediction result from the study obtained through cross-validation is between 78.2 and 86.2%.

5 Discussion and conclusion

Sex determination from human skull is a very essential aspect of forensic examination. In the past few decades, forensic anthropologists have suggested two main approaches for determining sexual dimorphic characteristics from human skull, which are morphological assessment and morphometric analysis. These two methods either visually assess specific cranial sites that possess sexual dimorphism or perform inter-distance

measurement between anatomical landmarks that have been carefully annotated.

Probing from a different perspective and diverging completely from the conventional forensic approaches, we suggest a possible framework for sex determination from human skull based on computer vision techniques, which include automatic representation of human skulls with advanced local shape features and learning of compact and discriminant representation from the extracted features. We introduced multi-region-based representation that are derived from partitioning the skulls along three main axes (X, Y, Z) which are anatomically equivalent to the sagittal, coronal, and axial axes. Inclusive of this is the aggregation of several region descriptors into compact features that represent each region with better discriminant capabilities. Also, we examine the influence of increase in number of regions and orientation of partition on prediction results.

From a general perspective, our experimental results give indication that these CV methods are suitable for sex determination with the best prediction rate of 86% through KPCA subspace representation of compact MeshLBP features from five sub-regions of the skull. Intuitively, we discovered that orientation of partition have significant influence on the results of MeshLBP, as the difference between the results obtained from using partitions derived from Z-axis are superior to those from X- and Y-axes. However, this observation is not so evident in the case of LD-SIFT and spin image because the results of X-axis are quite competitive with those obtained from Z-axis. We mainly attribute this to the fact that spin image are LD-SIFT descriptors embodying rotation invariance property. It is also discovered from the experiments that increase in number of partition does not affect the performance of LD-SIFT and spin image, but MeshLBP seems to be sensitive to increase in number of regions. Furthermore, we presented the application of MKL on multiple feature set for cranial sex estimation. The framework provided possibility of integrating two or more 3D local shape descriptors with differing representation properties. It was discovered from the experiments that MKL is similarly suitable for cranial sex estimation with the fusion of spin image + MeshLBP, revealing the most compatibility with a prediction rate of 86%. Quite interestingly, similar trends observed from previous experiments with respect to orientation of partition and number of regions remain valid in the MKL framework.

Table 1 Performance comparison with traditional morphometrics

Estimation method	Cranial representation	Prediction model	Prediction rate (%)
Morphometrics	22 estimation parameters	DFA and regression analysis	78.2–86.2
Proposed	MeshLBP	KPCA-SVM	86

Comparing the results of CV methods with those of standard forensic approach, our results are within the often reported sex prediction range (70–90%) using morphometric or morphological assessment [14, 46]. This novel perspective has introduced an alternative and efficient approach in forensic anthropology, which could potentially set the path to bridging the semantic gap between visual assessment and perceived dimorphic characteristics. Besides, we are able to discard the challenge of incomplete anatomical landmarks, which affects the performance of morphometric analysis. From our experiments, we can make three fundamental suggestions for potential future studies:

- Extracting features from multiple regions is important for skull representation as it tends to out-perform holistic representation of the skull.
- Feature aggregation instead of long-tailed concatenation should be considered to compactly represent each local region of the skull as it makes the features more distinctive with less correlation among features from the same class.
- Prediction performance with respect to orientation of partition is highly dependent on the properties of the local shape descriptor. For instance, MeshLBP showed great performance along the Z-axis but deteriorated significantly along X- and Y-axes in all experiments, while the results of spin image and LD-SIFT on X- and Z-axes are quite comparable.

Abbreviations
CV: Computer vision; DFA: Discriminant function analysis; GMM: Gaussian mixture model; KPCA: Kernel principal component analysis; KSVD: K-singular value decomposition; KELM: Kernel extreme learning machine; MKL: Multi-kernel learning; OLS: Online sequential least square; RKHS: Reproducing kernel hilbert space; SVM: Support vector machine; SRC: Sparse representation classifier

Acknowledgements
This research is sponsored by the eScienceFund grant 01-02-12-SF0288, Ministry of Science, Technology, and Innovation (MOSTI), Malaysia. The project has received full ethical approval from the Medical Research & Ethics Committee (MREC), Ministry of Health, Malaysia (ref: NMRR-14-1623-18717), and from the University of Nottingham Malaysia Campus (ref: IYL170414). Iman Yi Liao would like to thank the National Institute of Forensic Medicine (NIFM), Hospital Kuala Lumpur, for providing the PMCT data and is grateful to Dr. Ahmad Hafizam Hasmi (NIFM) and Ms. Khoo Lay See (NIFM) for their assistance in coordinating the data preparation.

Authors' contributions
OAA and IYL designed the proposed method and drafted the manuscript. IYL and NA supervised the work. NA and MH coordinated the collection of the dataset. All authors reviewed and approved the manuscript.

Competing interests
The authors declare that they have no competing interests.

Author details
[1]School of Computer Science, University of Nottingham Malaysia Campus, Semenyih, Malaysia. [2]Department of Forensic Medicine, Hospital Kuala Lumpur, Kuala Lumpur, Malaysia. [3]Radiology Department, Hospital Kuala Lumpur, Kuala Lumpur, Malaysia.

References
1. Johnson AE, Hebert M (1999) Using spin images for efficient object recognition in cluttered 3D scenes. IEEE Trans Pattern Anal Mach Intell 21(5):433–449
2. Darom T, Keller Y (2012) Scale invariant features for 3D mesh models. IEEE Trans Image Process 21(5):1–32. doi:10.1109/TIP.2012.2183142
3. Tolga I, Halici U (2012) 3-D face recognition with local shape descriptors. IEEE Trans Inf Forensic Secur 7(2):577–587
4. Han X, Ugail H, Palmer I (2009) Gender classification based on 3D face geometry features using SVM. In: Proceedings of IEEE International Conference on CyberWorlds. pp 114–118. doi:10.1109/CW.2009.41
5. Ballihi L, Amor BB, Daoudi M, Srivastava A, Aboutajdine D (2012) Boosting 3-D-geometric features for efficient face recognition and gender classification. IEEE Trans Inf Forensic Secur 7(6):1766–1779
6. Shapiro LG, Wilamowska K, Atmosukarto I, Wu J, Heike C, Speltz M, Cunningham M (2009) Shape-based classification of 3D head data. In: International Conference on Image Analysis and Processing. Springer, Berlin. pp 692–700
7. Atmosukarto I, Wilamowska K, Heike C, Shapiro LG (2010) 3D object classification using salient point patterns with application to craniofacial research. Pattern Recognit 43(4):1502–1517
8. Yang S, Shapiro LG, Cunningham ML, Speltz ML, Birgfeld C, Atmosukarto I, Lee SI (2012) Skull retrieval for craniosynostosis using sparse logistic regression models. In: MCBR-CDS. pp 33–44
9. Franklin D, Cardini A, Flavel A, Kuliukas A (2012) The application of traditional and geometric morphometric analyses for forensic quantification of sexual dimorphism: preliminary investigations in a Western Australian population. Int J Legal Med 126(4):549–558. doi:10.1007/s00414-012-0684-8
10. Krogman WM (1962) The human skeleton in forensic medicine. Am Assoc Adv Sci. doi:10.1126/science.135.3506.782-a
11. Stewart TD, Kerley ER (1979) Essentials of forensic anthropology: especially as developed in the United States. Charles C. Thomas, Springfield
12. Konigsberg LW, Hens SM (1998) Use of ordinal categorical variables in skeletal assessment of sex from the cranium. Am J Phys Anthropol 107(1):97–112
13. Buikstra JE, Ubelaker DH (1994) Standards for data collection from human skeletal remains. In: Proceedings of a seminar at the Field Museum of Natural History (Arkansas Archaeology Research Series 44)
14. Walker PL (2008) Sexing skulls using discriminant function analysis of visually assessed traits. Am J Phys Anthropol 136(1):39–50. doi:10.1002/ajpa.20776
15. Graw M, Czarnetzki A, Haffner HT (1999) The form of the supraorbital margin as a criterion in identification of sex from the skull: investigations based on modern human skulls. Am J Phys Anthropol 108:91–96
16. Pinto SCD, Urbanová P, Cesar RM (2016) Two-dimensional wavelet analysis of supraorbital margins of the human skull for characterizing sexual dimorphism. IEEE Trans Inf Forensic Secur 11(7):1542–1548
17. Franklin D, Freedman L, Milne N (2005) Sexual dimorphism and discriminant function sexing in indigenous South African crania. HOMO - J Comparative Hum Biol 55(3):213–228. doi:10.1016/j.jchb.2004.08.001
18. Bigoni L, Velemínská J, Brůžek J (2010) Three-dimensional geometric morphometric analysis of cranio-facial sexual dimorphism in a Central European sample of known sex. HOMO- J Comparative Human Biol 61(1):16–32. doi:10.1016/j.jchb.2009.09.004
19. Jiménez-Arenas JM, Esquivel JA (2013) Comparing two methods of univariate discriminant analysis for sex discrimination in an Iberian population. Forensic science international 228:175.e1–175.e4. doi:10.1016/j.forsciint.2013.03.016
20. Luo L, Wang M, Tian Y, Duan F, Wu Z, Zhou M, Rozenholc Y (2013) Automatic sex determination of skulls based on a statistical shape model. Comput Math Methods Med 2013:1–7

21. Williams BA, Rogers TL (2006) Evaluating the accuracy and precision of cranial morphological traits for sex determination. J Forensic Sci 51(4):729–735. doi:10.1111/j.1556-4029.2006.00177.x

22. Lewis CJ, Garvin HM (2016) Reliability of the walker cranial nonmetric method and implications for sex estimation. J Forensic Sci 61(3):743–751. doi:10.1111/1556-4029.13013

23. Guyomarc'h P, Bruzek J (2011) Accuracy and reliability in sex determination from skulls: a comparison of Fordisc 3.0 and the discriminant function analysis. Forensic Sci Int 208:30–35. doi:10.1016/j.forsciint.2011.03.011

24. Garcia D (2010) Robust smoothing of gridded data in one and higher dimensions with missing values. Comput Stat Data Anal 54(4):1167–1178. doi:10.1016/j.csda.2009.09.020

25. Lorensen WE, Cline HE (1987) Marching cubes: a high resolution 3D surface construction algorithm. ACM SIGGRAPH Comput Graphics 21(4):163–169. doi:10.1145/37402.37422

26. Cignoni P, Montani C, Scopigno R (1998) A comparison of mesh simplification algorithms. Comput Graphics 22(1):37–54. doi:10.1016/S0097-8493(97)00082-4

27. Do TN, Fekete JD (2007) Large scale classification with support vector machine algorithms. In: Proceedings of the 6th International Conference on Machine Learning and Applications, ICMLA. pp 148–153. doi:10.1109/ICMLA.2007.25

28. Golub GH, Van Loan CF (1996) Matrix computations. Phys Today. doi:10.1063/1.3060478

29. Besl P, McKay N (1992) A method for registration of 3-D shapes. IEEE Trans Pattern Anal Mach Intell 14(2):239–256. doi:10.1109/34.121791

30. Werghi N, Rahayem M, Kjellander J (2012) An ordered topological representation of 3D triangular mesh facial surface : concept and applications. EURASIP J Adv Signal Process 2012(144):1–20

31. Werghi N, Berretti S, del Bimbo A (2015) The Mesh-LBP : a framework for extracting local binary patterns from discrete manifolds. IEEE Trans Image Process 24(1):220–235

32. Lowe DG (2004) Distinctive image features from scale-invariant keypoints. International Journal of Computer Vision 60(2):91–110

33. Sun J, Ovsjanikov M, Guibas L (2009) A concise and probably informative multi-scale signature based on heat diffusion. Eurographics Symposium on Geometry Processing 28(5):1383–1392. doi:10.1111/j.1467-8659.2009.01515.x

34. Bronstein AM, Bronstein MM, Ovsjanikov M (2012) Feature-based methods in 3D shape analysis. In: 3D Imaging, Analysis and Applications. Springer, London. pp 185–219

35. Reuter M, Wolter F, Peinecke N (2006) Laplace–Beltrami spectra as 'Shape-DNA' of surfaces and solids. Computer-Aided Design 38(4):342–366

36. Zhang C, Tsuhan C (2001) Efficient feature extraction for 2D/3D objects in mesh representation. In: Proceedings of the 2001 IEEE International Conference on Image Processing Vol. 3. pp 935–938

37. Schölkopf B, Smola A, Müller KR (1998) nonlinear component analysis as a kernel eigenvalue problem. Neural Comput 10(5):1299–1319. doi:10.1162/089976698300017467

38. Aharon M, Elad M, Bruckstein A (2013) K-SVD: an algorithm for designing overcomplete dictionaries for sparse representation. IEEE Trans Signal Process 54(11):4311–4322. doi:10.1109/TSP.2006.881199

39. Xu X, Tsang IW, Xu D (2013) Soft margin multiple kernel learning. IEEE Trans Neural Netw Learn Syst 24(5):749–761. doi:10.1109/TNNLS.2012.2237183

40. Gönen M, Alpaydın E (2011) Multiple kernel learning algorithms. J Mach Learn Res 12:2211–2268

41. Cortes C, Vapnik V (1995) Support vector networks. Mach Learn 297:273–297

42. Huang GB (2014) An insight into extreme learning machines: random neurons, random features and kernels. Cogn Comput 6(3):376–390

43. Wright J, Yang AY, Ganesh A, Sastry SS, Ma Y (2009) Robust face recognition via sparse representation. IEEE Trans Pattern Anal Mach Intell 31(2):210–227

44. Gehler P, Nowozin S (2009) On feature combination for multiclass object classification. In: Proceedings of 2009 IEEE 12th International Conference on Computer Vision. pp 221–228

45. Ibrahim A, Alias A, Nor FM, Swarhib M, Abu Bakar SN, Das S (2017) Study of sexual dimorphism of Malaysian crania: an important step in identification of the skeletal remains. Anat Cell Biol 50:86–92

46. Garvin HM, Sholts SB, Mosca LA (2014) Sexual dimorphism in human cranial trait scores: effects of population, age, and body size. Am J Phys Anthropol 154:259–269

12

Accurate laser scanner to camera calibration with application to range sensor evaluation

Peter Fuersattel[1,2]* (iD), Claus Plank[3], Andreas Maier[1] and Christian Riess[1]

Abstract

Multi-modal sensory data plays an important role in many computer vision and robotics tasks. One popular multi-modal pair is cameras and laser scanners. To overlay and jointly use the data from both modalities, it is necessary to calibrate the sensors, i.e., to obtain the spatial relation between the sensors.

Computing such a calibration is challenging as both sensors provide quite different data: cameras yield color or brightness information, laser scanners yield 3-D points. However, several laser scanners additionally provide reflectances, which turn out to make calibration to a camera well feasible. To this end, we first estimate a rough alignment of the coordinate systems of both modalities. Then, we use the laser scanner reflectances to compute a virtual image of the scene. Stereo calibration on the virtual image and the camera image are then used to compute a refined, high-accuracy calibration.

It is encouraging that the accuracies in our experiments are comparable to camera-camera stereo setups and outperform another of other target-based calibration approach. This shows that the proposed algorithm reliably integrates the point cloud with the intensity image. As an example application, we use the calibration results to obtain ground-truth distance images for range cameras. Furthermore, we utilize this data to investigate the accuracy of the Microsoft Kinect V2 time-of-flight and the Intel RealSense R200 structured light camera.

Keywords: Laser scanner, Range camera, RealSense R200, Kinect V2

1   Introduction

Finding the spatial relation between a laser scanner and a 2-D or 2.5-D camera is crucial for sensor data fusion. Knowing this relation enables a multitude of applications, for example coloring the point cloud, the generation of textured meshes, or the creation of high accuracy ground truth for range cameras. The method proposed in this work has been specifically designed for generating reference distances for range camera evaluation. Nonetheless, the approach is not limited to this application and can also be used to calibrate a common 2-D camera to a laser scanner.

Range cameras find widespread use, for example in the field of robotics [1], in space [2, 3], automation in

logistics [4] or in augmented reality devices like the Google Tango phones. The major problem with these sensors is their limited accuracy. This gives rise to thorough camera evaluations with respect to accuracy and other individual camera characteristics that influence the range measurements.

Several studies that investigate the accuracies and error characteristics of range cameras have been presented in the past. Rauscher et al. [5] analyze range cameras with respect to their applicability to robotics. Yang et al. presented a detailed study on the Kinect V2 [6]. Fuersattel et al. evaluated multiple time-of-flight cameras with respect to different error sources [7]. Wasenmüller and Stricker compare the structured light Kinect V1 camera to the time-of-flight-based Kinect V2 camera [8].

Quantitative evaluation of range cameras requires scenes with ground truth distance measurements. Nair et al. state three methods to acquire such ground truth [9]:

---

*Correspondence: peter.fuersattel@fau.de
[1] Pattern Recognition Lab, University of Erlangen - Nuremberg, Martensstrasse 3, Erlangen, Germany
[2] Metrilus GmbH, Henkestrasse 91, Erlangen, Germany
Full list of author information is available at the end of the article

- Computed from a calibration pattern and known camera intrinsic parameters
- Computed from a calibration pattern as seen from a second high-resolution camera with known intrinsic parameters and known spatial relation to the evaluated camera.
- Measured with an additional, highly accurate 3-D sensor (e.g., a laser scanner) with known spatial relation to the evaluated camera.

The first two approaches have limited information value as they typically provide reference distances only for planar regions. Moreover, the accuracy of the ground truth quickly degrades as the distance between camera and calibration pattern increases.

A laser scanner mitigates both issues. Laser scanners typically provide high-accuracy point clouds of a scene for larger operating ranges than camera-based solutions. Also, this distance information can be obtained for arbitrary, not necessarily planar, surfaces. However, to leverage laser scanner point clouds for range camera evaluation, it is necessary to calibrate the laser scanner to the camera.

In this paper we propose a method for solving this task. Starting from a scene that shows multiple calibration patterns, e.g., checkerboards, we show how stereo calibration methods can be used to obtain the rotation and translation between the sensors. We aim at calculating the spatial relation based on a single point cloud/camera image pair, as acquiring densely sampled point clouds can take up to multiple minutes.

First, a virtual image of the point cloud has to be generated. It is important that this image shows all calibration patterns without occlusions. Thus, we demonstrate how the laser scanner's unordered point cloud can be transformed such that it is approximately aligned with the coordinate system of the camera. From this transformed point cloud, a virtual image is generated. In this image, the pixel intensities are derived from the reflectivity data that is associated with the individual 3-D point measurements.

The reflectivity data quantifies the amount of light that is reflected from a point in the scene back to the laser scanner. Therefore, the strong contrast of the calibration patterns also results in strong variations of the reflectivity data. By detecting the calibration patterns in both the virtual and the camera image, point correspondences for the two sensors can be obtained with sub-pixel accuracy. Finally, these corresponding points are used as input to established stereo calibration algorithms to obtain the spatial relation between both sensors. Note that it is necessary that the scene is sampled densely, such that at least one 3-D point measurement can be mapped to each pixel of the virtual image. Dense point clouds are required

for example calculating accurate meshes of the scene, or like in our application, for generating ground-truth distance measurements for range cameras. In this work, we exploit the high sampling density to achieve even more accurate calibration results than current state-of-the-art methods.

The proposed method is evaluated with multiple data sets from four different range cameras. We show both qualitatively and quantitatively that the presented method aligns the coordinate systems accurately and, furthermore, considerably outperforms the baseline method. In image domain, misalignments of less than 0.2 pixels are achieved. For corresponding 3-D coordinates in the scene, the mean error is as small as 1.3 mm.

The contributions of this work consist of two parts.

1. We present an automatic method for calibrating a laser scanner to a camera. This method enables the user to estimate the spatial relation between the two sensors with a single shot of a scene, which contains only a small number of calibration patterns. The applicability of the proposed method is shown for four different camera-laser scanner setups.
2. We use the calibration technique to present accuracy evaluations for different range camera technologies: the Microsoft Kinect V2 time of flight camera and Intel RealSense R200 structured light cameras.

In Section 2 we present related work. Detailed information on the proposed algorithm can be found in Section 3. The evaluation of the performance of the presented approach and the range camera evaluation results are presented in Section 4. Section 5 summarizes and concludes this work.

2 Related work

Several approaches exist for calibration of laser scanners to cameras. Oftentimes, these methods are categorized by the type of laser scanner they operate on, namely methods for line scanners and methods for 2.5-D laser scanners.

For calibration of a 2-D laser line scanner to a camera, Zhang et al. [10] proposed a method that makes use of checkerboards for aligning the coordinate systems of both modalities. The method requires multiple acquisitions from different positions to establish sufficiently many constraints for nonlinear optimization. More recently, Kassir et al. [11] propose an automatic toolbox that builds on top of the well-known Camera Calibration Toolbox for Matlab. The toolbox is extended by detection algorithms for both checkerboards in the camera images and lines in the laser scanner data. In an iterative process, the spatial relation is optimized such that the detected lines match the planes of the calibration pattern. Zhou [12] presented a numerically more stable approach that also uses plane-line correspondences to constrain the estimation. This method also requires fewer plane-line pairs than the method by Zhang et al. [10].

Line laser scanners obtain range information only for a single scanline. In the context of range camera evaluation, this information is not sufficient. Instead, dense 2.5-D point clouds are preferable. For example, Unnikirshnan et al. [13] published an interactive Matlab toolbox to calculate the spatial relation between a camera and a 2.5-D dense point cloud. The authors recommend using at least 15 to 20 images. In each of the images, the calibration pattern region has to be delimited manually by drawing a polygon that encloses the area. In contrast, we find the planar segments of the calibration pattern automatically. With multiple patterns in the scene, an accurate calibration from a single shot is possible. The method proposed by Geiger et al. [14] obtains the spatial relation based on a single shot of a scene that shows multiple checkerboard patterns. Based on the checkerboards and planar segments in the scene, an initialization for a subsequent iterative closest point-based refinement is calculated. In contrast to their work, we incorporate the laser scanner amplitudes to reduce the impact of inaccuracies of the plane detection.

Ha et al. [15] propose a new, specifically constructed calibration pattern with a triangular hole to reduce the number of calibration images. While other methods typically require at least three different poses of calibration patterns, this method requires only two. Hoang et al. [16] also use a calibration pattern with a triangular hole. Their pattern is used to obtain 3-D/2-D correspondences for solving the perspective-n-point problem. Gong et al. [17] propose to use as a calibration target three planes that form a trihedral. Based on at least two shots on such scenes, the relative transformation between the two sensor coordinate systems is estimated via nonlinear optimization. Although the method does not require special calibration targets, it still requires the user to define the planar region in the camera image. Our method requires three patterns, but these are off-the-shelf patterns without particular manufacturing requirements.

Moghadam et al. [18] estimate the spatial relation from line segments that can be detected both in the point cloud and in the camera image. Taylor and Nieto [19] find the spatial relation by maximizing the mutual information between the camera image and a virtual image, which is colored according to the direction of the point cloud's normals. The work presented in [20] extends this method by a more robust normal estimation algorithm. However, both methods share the same drawbacks: the usage of particle swarm optimization requires (a) the initial knowledge of the range of the extrinsic parameters and (b) a computationally expensive rendering

of a virtual image for each particle in each iteration. In contrast, we propose to use scene reflectivity to generate virtual views, which enables the use of highly accurate calibration targets. Pandey et al. [21] also do not require a calibration target. The authors propose a calibration via minimizing the mutual information between the camera pixels and the laser scanner reflectivity information. This approach requires multiple views in order to obtain a smooth cost function that can be optimized robustly. Levinson and Thrun proposed a framework that monitors the accuracy of a calibrated camera-laser scanner setup while being in use [22]. If a miss-calibration is observed, the extrinsic parameters are corrected by finding the transformation which maximizes the overlap between edges in the image and in the point cloud. This approach requires multiple frames and varied scene geometry such that sufficient corresponding edges can be found and a smooth cost function can be obtained. Scott et al. [23] presented an approach for the calibration of a laser scanner and cameras setup that also exploits reflectivity information. The method is suited for setups that move through an environment, e.g., in an autonomous driving scenario. The authors relax the constraint that field of views at a single point in time must overlap. Instead, the authors assume that some overlap will occur at some later point in time due to motion of the rigid sensor setup. The abovementioned methods are particularly useful if no calibration pattern is present, e.g., outside a lab environment. However, the disadvantage of these approaches is the reduced accuracy compared to controlled lab setups.

3 Laser scanner to camera calibration

The basic concept of the proposed method is that we use stereo calibration on the camera intensities and the laser scanner reflectivities. Thus, the large reflectivity differences of checkerboards allow to compute rotation and translation between the coordinate systems of both sensors. Classic stereo calibration expects two input images. The first input image is the intensity image from the range camera. The second input image, from the laser scanner, needs to be computed: the laser scanner measures an unordered 2.5-D point cloud that has to be rendered to a virtual image. In order to perform the rendering, a viewing direction onto the point cloud has to be defined. Good viewing directions avoid occlusions, and yield a balanced, unencumbered picture of the checkerboards in the scene. Figure 1 shows a negative example, i.e., a virtual image computed from a bad viewing direction. Here, only two of the checkerboard patterns can be detected completely. The corners of the left checkerboard cannot be found automatically due to the pose of the pattern. Additionally, this pattern occludes some parts of the big pattern in its background. Such occlusions can make calibration

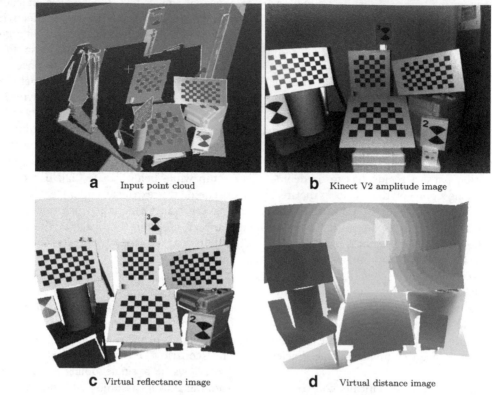

a Input point cloud   **b** Kinect V2 amplitude image

c Virtual reflectance image   **d** Virtual distance image

Fig. 1 Examples from a Kinect V2 / laser scanner setup. **a** Laser scanner data, visualized in a point cloud viewer. **b** Amplitude image of the Kinect V2 for reference. **c**, **d** Virtual reflectance and distance images of the point cloud as seen from the camera position

much more difficult or even cause complete failure. We mitigate this problem by computing a virtual image that shows the calibration patterns from an angle similar to the observing camera. It is likely that there is considerable overlap between such computed virtual image and the camera image. Thus, we seek a transformation that approximately aligns the camera and laser scanner coordinate systems.

In the next subsections, we present the full calibration algorithm in three steps, i.e.,

1. Finding the plane segments of the calibration patterns in the unordered point cloud
2. Calculation of an initial alignment for the two coordinate systems
3. Virtual image generation and estimation of a spatial relation via stereo calibration

3.1 Finding the calibration patterns in the point cloud
We assume that planes within certain size boundaries stem from calibration patterns. We first search such planes in the unordered point cloud obtained from the laser scanner. The algorithm uses the idea that a plane is characterized by a set of co-located points with surface normals pointing towards the same direction. We define neighborhoods for individual points and normal-based region growing.

In organized point clouds, the term neighborhood is often defined as the 4-connected or 8-connected neighborhood of a (x, y) coordinate of a 2-D array. This association is not available with unorganized point clouds. In this work, we define the neighborhood of a point p_i as its N_o closest points in a L_2 sense. These neighbors can be efficiently looked up by organizing the point cloud in a suitable data structure, for example an Octree. The normal n_i for a point p_i can be approximated by fitting a plane to the point and its N_o neighbors. This can be done efficiently by calculating the eigenvalue decomposition of the covariance matrix of these points [24].

Laser scanner data exhibits a relatively low noise level, and computing n_i from multiple points further reduces noise in the estimated normals. Yet, inspection of the normals still exhibits some unwanted variations. Therefore, we apply a modified version of a bilateral smoothing filter for organized point clouds [25]. The filter can be rewritten such that it operates on neighborhoods in unorganized point clouds. The smoothed 3-D point p_i' is given by

$$\boldsymbol{p}_i' = \left(\boldsymbol{p}_i + \sum_{j=0}^{N_o} w_{ij}\boldsymbol{p}_j \right) \Big/ \left(1 + \sum_{j=0}^{N_o} w_{ij} \right), \qquad (1)$$

$$\text{where } w_{ij} = \mathrm{e}^{\left(\alpha \| \boldsymbol{p}_i - \boldsymbol{p}_j \|_2 \right)} \mathrm{e}^{\left(\beta \| \boldsymbol{n}_i - \boldsymbol{n}_j \|_1 \right)}, \qquad (2)$$

and $\boldsymbol{p}_j$ denotes the jth neighbor of $\boldsymbol{p}_i$. The same smoothing can also be applied to each normal $\boldsymbol{n}_i$. The influence of the distance between points and the difference between normals is controlled with the parameters α and β.

The computed normals are used to segment planar segments in the point cloud. The algorithm begins with a random seed point to define a new planar segment. The seed point consists of a point coordinate and its associated normal. We perform breadth-first region growing on points with similar normals. In other words, all points in the neighborhood of the segment that have a similar normal are iteratively added to the current segment. Every time a new point has been added to a segment, its normal is updated to be the average normal of all supporting points. The similarity of two normals is determined by thresholding on their angular difference. In our experiments, a conservative threshold of 10° has proven to work well. Segmentation stops if all points have been assigned to a segment label. The segmentation is similar to a previous method for approximate plane segmentation for organized point clouds [25].

With all points assigned to a planar segment, we select those segments that may represent calibration patterns. Assuming that the dimensions of the calibration patterns are known, it suffices to threshold on the sizes of the minimum oriented bounding boxes of all segments.

3.2 Estimation of the initial spatial relation

The initial transformation approximately aligns the coordinate system of the laser scanner and the camera. The initialization is calculated from the candidate planes and the planes derived from the checkerboard patterns visible in the camera image.

First, the checkerboard patterns have to be detected as accurately as possible in the camera image. In this work we use the detector proposed in [26]. With the known dimensions of the patterns and the intrinsic parameters of the camera, the 3-D coordinates of the calibration features (e.g., checkerboard corners) can be calculated. Correspondences between planes in the laser scanner and detected patterns in the camera image can be directly established if the calibration patterns can be uniquely identified by their size, and if the number of plane candidates matches the number of calibration patterns. Otherwise, these correspondences have to be estimated. The naive solution is to evaluate all possible permutations K for planes and patterns and to choose the permutation that minimizes some error metric. If N_c calibration patterns are used, then

N_c plane candidates are drawn from all found plane candidates. The centroids of the plane segments $\boldsymbol{m}^{(p)}$ and the calibration patterns $\boldsymbol{m}^{(c)}$ are used as candidate correspondences to estimate a transformation $\mathcal{R}$. The optimum transformation $\mathcal{R}^*$ is the one that minimizes the following error metric

$$\mathcal{R}_i^* = \underset{K}{\arg\min} \sum_i^{N_c} \left\| \mathcal{R}\left(\boldsymbol{m}_i^{(c)}\right) - \boldsymbol{m}_i^{(p)} \right\|. \qquad (3)$$

The quality of a permutation is measured as the sum of the distances between the transformed centroids $\mathcal{R}\left(\boldsymbol{m}_i^{(c)}\right)$ and the centroids of the respective planar segments $\boldsymbol{m}_i^{(p)}$. Under the assumption that calibration patterns and planes have been accurately detected, then the minimum of the error metric corresponds to the best initialization. Note that other metrics could be employed here as well, e.g., metrics based on normal directions or combinations of normal directions and centroids. However, we found the metric in Eq. (3) to be sufficient, since the initialization requires only a rough estimate of the spatial relation. In our experiments, the number of permutations K to search through was always low, since most plane candidates are already filtered out using the sizes of the calibration patterns.

The calculation above imposes mild constraints on the positions and orientations of the calibration patterns. These constraints are identical to the requirements for a robust stereo calibration and typically not difficult to satisfy: to obtain the most accurate results, the checkerboard poses must constrain all six degrees of freedom of the rigid body transformation. In practice, this means that the checkerboards need to point into different directions (see, e.g., Fig. 1b) and should cover as much area of the field of view as possible.

3.3 Virtual view generation and refinement transformation via stereo calibration

The initial, approximate alignment of the point cloud with the camera image can be used to perform stereo calibration. To this end, a virtual image is computed from the point cloud. Virtual image and camera image together are then used to obtain a second transformation that refines the initial relation between the sensors.

Brightness differences in the virtual image are created from reflectivity information at each point from the laser scanner. Strong reflectivity variations within the calibration pattern result in strong contrasts in the virtual image. This is particularly useful at the transition between black and white quads of the checkerboard pattern for calibration.

For generating the virtual view, a set of intrinsic parameters for the virtual camera is required. These parameters have to be defined such that the calibration patterns can be detected reliably. In this work, $\Pi(\boldsymbol{p})$ will be used to denote the projection from a point $\boldsymbol{p}$ in 3-D space onto a point (u, v) image plane, with Π containing the pinhole camera parameters as well as potential lens distortion parameters.

If the camera itself has a reasonable resolution, then their intrinsic parameters can also be used for the virtual camera. Otherwise, these parameters need to be selected manually. It is possible to distinguish two cases: first, if the camera resolution is very low, for example with time-of-flight cameras, then a higher image resolution should be chosen. In contrast, if the image resolution of the camera is very high (e.g., $> 1280 \times 1024$), the point cloud might not be dense enough to provide good amplitude values for each pixel. In the latter case, the resolution needs to be adjusted to a smaller value.

The simplest method to obtain the intensity information for each pixel is to project all points of the point cloud onto the image plane. First, the intensities $C(\boldsymbol{p})$ of all points which are projected onto a single pixel coordinate (u, v) have to be obtained. To this end, we define a function $\gamma(u, v, \boldsymbol{p})$, which indicates whether a point $\boldsymbol{p}$ is projected onto a particular (u, v) coordinate or not.

$$\gamma(u, v, \boldsymbol{p}) = \begin{cases} \text{true} & \text{if } \Pi(\boldsymbol{p}) \mapsto (u', v'), \\ & |u' - u| \leq 0.5 \wedge |v' - v| \leq 0.5 \\ \text{false} & \text{otherwise} \end{cases}$$

Let $\mathcal{N} = \left\{ \boldsymbol{p}_j \mid \gamma(u, v, \boldsymbol{p}_j) \right\}$ be the set of all points that are projected on pixel (u, v). As a simple heuristic to mitigate issues from occlusions, we limit the size of $\mathcal{N}$ to a maximum of 8. If more than 8 points map onto (u, v), we select only the 8 points that are closest to the camera. Then, the intensity $V(u, v)$ of the virtual image is given as the average of N_c laser scanner intensity values $C(\boldsymbol{p}_j)$,

$$V(u, v) = \frac{1}{N_c} \sum_{p_j \in \mathcal{N}} C(\boldsymbol{p}_j) . \tag{4}$$

Instead of the naive approach, more sophisticated methods can be used to obtain intensity values, for example ray casting. However, this is beyond the scope of this work.

Next, the calibration patterns are detected in the virtual image and matched to the keypoints from the camera image. These correspondences can be used to compute a second rigid body transformation $\mathcal{R}_r^*$, which we call refinement transformation. $\mathcal{R}_r^*$ is obtained by minimizing the reprojection error between corresponding keypoints as given in Eq. (6). The cost function measures the

2-D distance between a keypoint $\boldsymbol{x}_i$ and its corresponding transformed and projected keypoint $\hat{\boldsymbol{x}}_i$ in the other image.

$$\mathcal{R}_r^* = \underset{\mathcal{R}_r}{\arg\min} \sum_i \left\| \boldsymbol{x}_i - \Pi \mathcal{R}_r \hat{\Pi}^{-1}(\hat{\boldsymbol{x}}_i) \right\| \tag{5}$$

$$+ \left\| \hat{\boldsymbol{x}}_i - \hat{\Pi} \mathcal{R}_r^{-1} \Pi^{-1}(\boldsymbol{x}_i) \right\| , \tag{6}$$

where $\hat{\Pi}$ denotes the projection from the point cloud to the virtual image. The inverse projections Π^{-1} and $\hat{\Pi}^{-1}$ are obtained by solving the perspective-n-point problem. Note that there are also direct solutions to calculate rotations and translations for 3-D point correspondences, for example the method by Horn [27]. By choosing the nonlinear optimization approach, we can jointly optimize both for $\mathcal{R}_r^*$ and the transformation which relates the calibration pattern coordinate system and the camera coordinate system, thereby achieving a more accurate refinement transformation. By concatenating $\mathcal{R}_i^*$ and $\mathcal{R}_r^*$, the final spatial transformation $\mathcal{R}_f$ is obtained. Knowing the final rigid body transformation, it is possible to directly transform any point cloud into the coordinate system of the camera. This transformed point cloud allows the calculation of virtual amplitude images or virtual distance images that are accurately aligned with the camera image.

4   Evaluation

A particular benefit of a laser scanner-to-camera calibration is the ability to create ground truth for evaluating range sensors. To this end, we use two classes of range sensors as cameras: time-of-flight (ToF) sensors (Microsoft Kinect V2 and PMD CamBoard Pico Flexx) and structured light sensors (Intel RealSense R200 and the Orbbec Astra). The laser scanner is a Leica ScanStation P20 scanner.

In case of the ToF cameras, the amplitude channel is used to capture the calibration scene. For calibrating the structured light cameras to the laser scanner, we use the infrared channels with the pattern emitter either being covered or disabled. Of the RealSense R200's two infrared channels, we choose the left one as it is aligned with the distance map.

Whenever possible, we used the factory calibration of the range cameras as provided by the individual camera SDKs. For all cameras, except the Astra, these parameters could be obtained. The latter was calibrated with 60 checkerboard images using the method by Zhang [28].

In this evaluation we use the approach proposed by Geiger et al. [14] as baseline. It consists of an initialization and a refinement stage, similarly as the proposed method. Initialization is performed in a similar way as the proposed method and results in a set of rotations and translations, one of which approximately aligns the two coordinate systems. Different from our method, Geiger et al. propose to use the iterative closest point algorithm (ICP) for refining the initial alignment. In order to create common basis for comparison, we replace the proposed stereo calibration-based refinement with the ICP-based refinement. To this end, we generate 3-D coordinates from the camera intrinsics and the checkerboard coordinates as suggested by the authors.

The setup of our experiments and the used data is described in Section 4.1. In Section 4.2, we present qualitative results for the proposed method. In Section 4.3, we present quantitative results on the evaluation scenes. Section 4.4 provides additional insights on the impact of the proposed refinement step. An evaluation of the measurement accuracy of a ToF (Kinect V2) and a structured light camera (RealSense R200) conclude the evaluation in Section 4.5.

4.1 Experimental setup and data

We captured five different scenes with the same spatial relation: a calibration scene that shows the four patterns, an evaluation scene with rearranged patterns, and three general scenes with different objects. The individual point clouds contain $\approx$ 6.2 million points, sampled from a volume of approximately $230 \times 150 \times 95$ cm.

In the calibration and evaluation scene, four checkerboard patterns with different dimensions and a different number of corners are captured:

- 6×5 inner corners, 66.67 mm corner spacing
- 6×7 inner corners, 50 mm corner spacing
- 6×9 inner corners, 44 mm corner spacing
- 8×7 inner corners, 50 mm corner spacing

All patterns are printed on rigid boards to avoid errors from bending calibration patterns. Captured images are averaged for 100 frames to reduce the impact of measurement noise. The spatial relation between the laser scanner and the cameras is calculated on the first scene.

In all amplitude, intensity, and virtual images shown in the evaluation, the pixel values are normalized to values between 0 and 1 for better comparison.

4.2 Qualitative evaluation results

We illustrate the performance of the proposed method by comparing virtual reflectance images with observed images. The calibrations between the individual cameras and the point cloud are calculated on the first scene. Then, calibration data is used to generate virtual images of the evaluation scene for each camera. For comparison, each camera has been calibrated with the proposed method and the baseline method to the point cloud.

Figure 2 shows the difference between the observed camera images and the virtual images for the baseline method (denoted as "ICP") and for the proposed method (denoted as "Proposed"). Wrong spatial relations show

as additional edges in the scene, whereas all edges in the scene coincide for an accurate transformation. It is important to emphasize that the magnitude of the pixel differences is not caused by misalignments, but by the internal conversion of the incoming light to intensities of the different sensors.

When calculating the spatial parameters with the baseline method, small offsets between corresponding edges can be observed (see Fig. 2a, e, and g). In contrast, for the proposed method, the virtual and observed images accurately coincide for all cameras. A visual comparison of the calibration results of the CamBoard Pico Flexx is difficult due to the low sensor resolution and the low reflectance of the black checkerboard patches. In these areas, the CamBoard Pico Flexx does not provide amplitude values, as only a small portion of the emitted light is reflected back to the sensor.

4.3 Quantitative results

The reprojection error is a common choice to evaluate the quality of a stereo calibration result. Thus, we compare the checkerboard positions in the camera image and in the virtual image. In this experiment, the system is calibrated on the first scene. Hereafter, the reprojection errors are calculated on the evaluation scene. As the virtual image is generated from the perspective of the camera, we can directly compare the 2-D positions of the keypoints which are returned by the checkerboard detection algorithm.

For assessing the impact of the misalignments in 3-D, we reproject the keypoints based on the intrinsic parameters and known pattern dimensions. Similarly, as in the 2-D case, we can directly compute the differences between corresponding 3-D world coordinates.

The results of this comparison are shown in Table 1. With the proposed method, we observe mean errors in corresponding 3-D coordinates between $\approx$ 1 to 3 mm, depending on the used camera. When relying only on 3-D information, like in the ICP variant, the measured errors are at least three times as large as for the proposed approach.

The calibration errors of the proposed method are within the expectation of typical stereo calibrations. The authors of the pattern detector report 3-D measurement errors between 1 and 7 mm, depending on the sensor resolution [26].

4.4 Influence of the refinement transformation

In this section we demonstrate the importance of the refinement via stereo calibration. During initialization, the centroids of the planar segments that represent the checkerboard patterns in the laser scanner's point cloud are used to calculate the initial transformations. If these centroids are not perfectly accurate, then the resulting

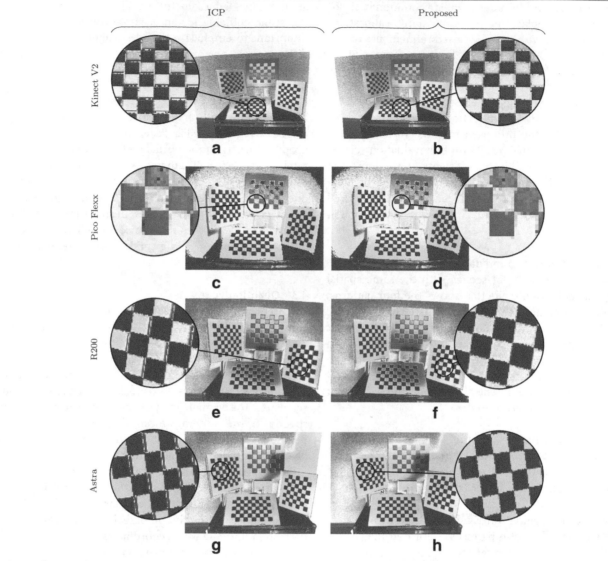

Fig. 2 Difference of observed image and the corresponding virtual images for the two evaluated approaches. The difference images (**a**), (**c**), (**e**) and (**g**) have been calculated with virtual images generated with calibrations from the ICP-based approach. The figures (**b**), (**d**), (**f**) and (**h**) show overlays which have been calculated with calibrations from the proposed method. For the baseline method, misalignments can be observed in examples (**a**), (**e**) and (**f**). In contrast, no misalignments identified if the proposed method is used for calibration

initial transformation has only limited accuracy. The centroid is given by the mean coordinate of all points that belong to the segment, and thus sensitive to segmentation errors. If the segmentation for example contains points of the supporting surface of the calibration pattern, or if the segmentation is not completely homogeneous, then the centroid will be off-center.

In Fig. 3a, double edges at the checkerboard quads indicate that the two images are not accurately aligned. Figure 3b shows the difference image of the Kinect's

Table 1 Mean calibration error and standard deviation for four cameras in 2-D and 3-D for two calibration approaches

Camera	ICP 2-D (px)	Proposed 2-D (px)	ICP 3-D (cm)	Proposed 3-D (cm)
Kinect V2	1.172 ± 0.492	0.176 ± 0.084	1.113 ± 0.108	0.267 ± 0.064
CamBoard Pico Flexx	2.309 ± 0.509	0.305 ± 0.125	0.930 ± 0.124	0.319 ± 0.134
Astra	0.491 ± 0.232	0.418 ± 0.119	1.135 ± 0.444	0.126 ± 0.038
RealSense R200	1.124 ± 0.653	0.252 ± 0.121	0.880 ± 0.285	0.160 ± 0.109

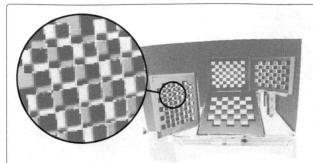

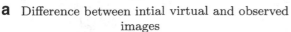

a Difference between intial virtual and observed images   **b** Difference between refined virtual and observed images

Fig. 3 Impact of refinement for the calibration scene and the Kinect V2. **a** Difference between the virtual reflectance image and the observed image. Inaccuracies in the initialization cause edges to appear twice. **b** Difference image between the final reflectance image and the amplitude image of the camera: all edges accurately coincide

amplitude image and the virtual reflectance image after refinement. In the refined result, no double edges can be observed. Instead, all checkerboard quads as well as the borders of the pattern boards are accurately aligned.

4.5 Range camera evaluation

For this experiment, we use the calibration results to generate ground truth distance data for the three general scenes. Depending on the focus of the study, the scenes have to be designed differently. The primary interest of the following experiment is to evaluate the absolute measurement accuracy of the range cameras with a certain volume of interest. Furthermore, we set up the scene such that several characteristics of the different range camera technologies can be illustrated. In this evaluation, we present as an example evaluation results for the Kinect V2 and the RealSense R200 camera, i.e, representatives of both classes of range cameras.

The setup consists of several objects which are positioned in front of the sensors: boxes, cylinders, etc. Each scene is captured first with the laser scanner then with the two cameras, to exclude mutual interference. Then, the individual range camera measurements are compared to the reference distance images which have been generated from laser scanner data. For visualizing the measurement errors, we subtract the observed distance image from the virtual distance image.

In Fig. 4 we demonstrate some of the characteristic properties of each sensor type on one of the general scenes. To investigate the dependency of measurement error and distance, we combine the result of the three general scenes and plot the errors for a region of interest as shown in Fig. 5. The mean accuracy is calculated for 1-cm bins and plotted in black. Gray dots represent individual measurements.

4.5.1 Kinect V2

The ToF sensor provides dense distance measurements for all pixels which are properly illuminated (see Fig. 4b). In Fig. 4c, the measurement errors for all pixels which lie in the common field of view of the laser scanner and the range camera are illustrated. Two characteristic errors can be observed in this figure: an amplitude-dependent error and multi-path effects [7]. The amplitude-dependent error can be observed best in the lower right corner of the image in the area of the calibration target. Even though the surface of this target is flat, a clear change of distances can be observed between high- and low-reflectivity regions. Multi-path can be observed best in the central image region. In this area, the emitted light can easily hit multiple regions one after another before being reflected back to the camera. Especially for pixels that belong to the flat surface of the box, the acute viewing angle fosters a comparably large impact of multi-path effects.

The results shown in Fig. 5 support this insight. Most of the objects in the scene can be found within the range from 1.5 to 1.85 m. The objects in the first row of the scene can be expected to suffer only marginally from multi-path effects as there are only very few small surfaces which could reflect the light such that it will return to the camera. In contrast, the central region of the scene contains more objects, and thus more surfaces which can create non-direct paths back to the camera. This can also be observed in Fig. 4g, where the absolute mean error changes drastically for distances that contain the center of the scene (see highlighted areas in Fig. 5a–c). For larger distances, which contain the well-reflecting background, the measurement accuracy increases again. For all areas which are not affected by multi-path, and which are well illuminated, the measurement error matches earlier reported values [7].

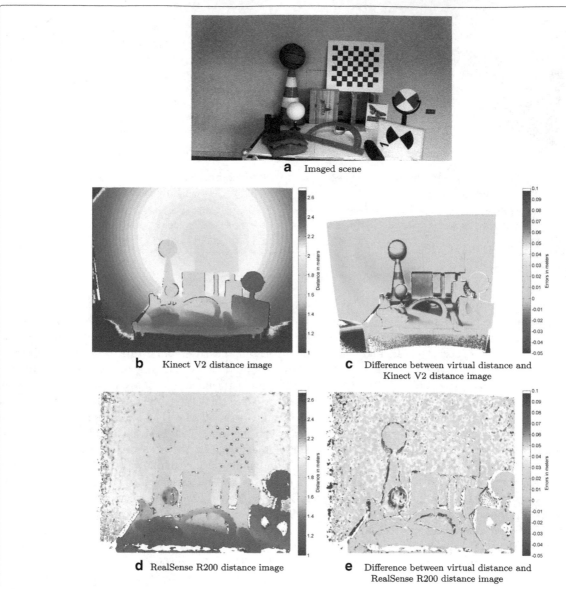

Fig. 4 Per-pixel accuracy evaluation for one of the general scenes. Distances and measurement errors are given in meters and encoded as colors. **a** Imaged scene. **b** Kinect V2 distance image **c** depth error for Kinect V2. **d** RealSense R200 distance image. **e** depth error for RealSense R200

4.5.2 RealSense R200

In this section, characteristic errors of the RealSense R200 structured light camera are investigated. Stereo block matching and the subsequent internal processing causes the speckle-like pattern that can be observed best in the planar background region of Fig. 4e. Block matching also causes fringes at sharp borders, e.g., at the borders of the spheres. Similarly as the time-of-flight camera, this sensor also relies on the requirement that the emitted light is reflected back to the cameras. If the imaged surface does not reflect the light in the spectrum of the emitter, then no or only inaccurate measurements are possible. These effects can be observed in the lower left sphere (inaccurate

measurements) and at the lower right calibration target. A characteristic of structured-light cameras is that the baseline between projector and observing camera introduces occluded image regions, seen best at the disc on the right side of the image.

Another error characteristic of stereo structured light cameras is the fact that the theoretical depth resolution decreases with the distance between camera and measured point [29]. This observation can also be made in Fig. 4h. While the accuracy for near regions is approximately 1 cm, it decreases steadily as the distance increases. For background pixels, the average accuracy drops to ≈ 3.5 cm (highlighted in blue).

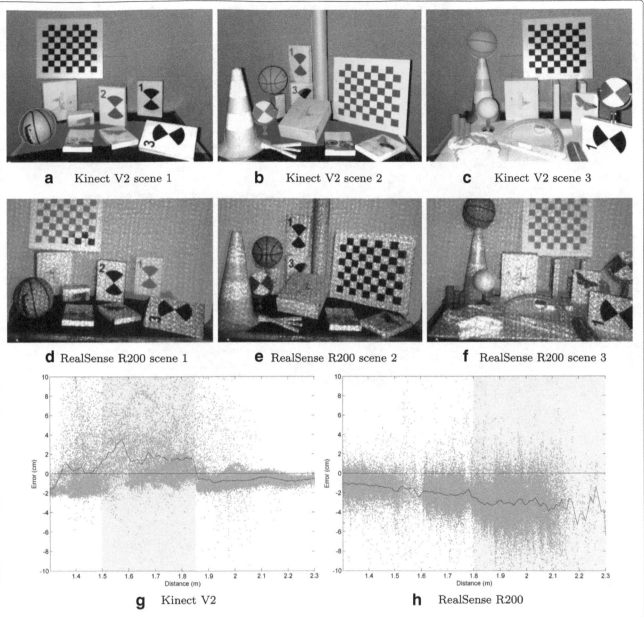

Fig. 5 Measurement error with respect to distance. **a–c** Evaluated ROI of the three scenes from the perspective of the Kinect V2 camera. **d–f** Respective ROIs for the RealSense R200 sensor. **g, h** Mean measurement error with respect to distance. Gray dots depict individual measurements. The black line represents the mean measurement error within 1 cm. The red line marks the zero-level to help reading the plots. The light blue overlays highlight interesting distance ranges which are discussed in the evaluation. (Kinect V2: 1.5 to 1.85 m, RealSense R200: 1.8 to 2.3 m)

5 Conclusion

We presented a novel method for finding the spatial relation between a camera and laser scanner based on stereo calibration. The algorithm enables the user to calibrate the laser scanner to a camera with high accuracy using only a single shot of a calibration scene.

In our evaluation, we compare the proposed method to a similar, calibration pattern-based approach and show that our method achieves notably more accurate calibration results. In terms of the reprojection error, our method outperforms the baseline at least by a factor of three. Furthermore, we show that the calibration results compare very well to standard stereo calibration algorithms, although the sensory data to our method is very heterogeneous. For corresponding keypoints of the observed and virtual images, the misalignments account for less than 0.2 pixels. In world coordinates, this results in errors of less than 1.3 mm.

The applicability of the method is demonstrated in the context of range camera evaluation. Here, we use the method to investigate the measurement errors of a time-of-flight and a structured light camera: the Microsoft Kinect V2 and the Intel RealSense R200. In this evaluation, we can showcase several error sources which are characteristic to the different range sensing technologies.

Acknowledgements
We thank PMD technologies for providing the Camboard Pico Flexx time-of-flight camera which has been used in this evaluation.

Authors' contributions
PF performed the primary development of the algorithm, designed the evaluation, and wrote the intial draft of the manuscript. CP helped with the data acquisition and provided the laser scanner. AM and CR supervised the work. CR also played an essential role in drafting and refining the final manuscript. All authors read and approved the manuscript.

Competing interests
The authors declare that they have no competing interests.

Author details
[1]Pattern Recognition Lab, University of Erlangen - Nuremberg, Martensstrasse 3, Erlangen, Germany. [2]Metrilus GmbH, Henkestrasse 91, Erlangen, Germany. [3]Ostbayerische Technische Hochschule Regensburg, Pruefeninger Strasse 58, Regensburg, Germany.

References
1. Buck S, Hanten R, Bohlmann K, Zell A (2016) Generic 3D obstacle detection for AGVs using time-of-flight cameras. In: 2016 IEEE/RSJ International Conference on Intelligent Robots and Systems (IROS). pp 4119–4124
2. Smith T (2016) Astrobee: A New Platform for Free-Flying Robotics on the International Space Station. In: Proceedings of the International Symposium on Artificial Intelligence, Robotics and Automation in Space (i-SAIRAS 2016)
3. Klionovska K, Benninghoff H (2017) Initial Pose Estimation using PMD Sensor during the Rendezvous Phase in On-Orbit Servicing Missions. In: 27th AAS/AIAA Space Flight Mechanics Meeting
4. Leo M, Natale A, Del-Coco M, Carcagnì P, Distante C (2017) Robust Estimation of Object Dimensions and External Defect Detection with a Low-Cost Sensor. J Nondestruct Eval 36(1)
5. Rauscher G, Dube D, Zell A (2014) A Comparison of 3D Sensors for Wheeled Mobile Robots. In: 2014 International Conference on Intelligent Autonomous Systems (IAS-13). Padova
6. Yang L, Zhang L, Dong H, Alelaiwi A, Saddik AE (2015) Evaluating and Improving the Depth Accuracy of Kinect for Windows v2. EEE Sensors J 15(8):4275–4285
7. Fuersattel P, Placht S, Balda M, Schaller C, Hofmann H, Maier A, et al. (2016) A Comparative Error Analysis of Current Time-of-Flight Sensors. IEEE Trans Comput Imaging 2(1):27–41
8. Wasenmüller O, Stricker D (2017) Comparison of Kinect v1 and v2 Depth Images in Terms of Accuracy and Precision. In: Asian Conference on Computer Vision Workshop Asian Conference on Computer Vision Workshop (ACCV)
9. Nair R, Meister S, Lambers M, Balda M, Hofmann H, Kolb A, et al. (2013) Ground Truth for Evaluating Time of Flight Imaging. In: Time-of-Flight and depth imaging: Sensors, algorithms, and applications : Dagstuhl 2012 Seminar on Time-of-Flight Imaging and GCPR 2013 Workshop on Imaging New Modalities. pp 52–74
10. Zhang Q, Pless R (2004) Extrinsic calibration of a camera and laser range finder (improves camera calibration). In: 2004 IEEE/RSJ International Conference on Intelligent Robots and Systems (IROS). pp 2301–2306
11. Kassir A, Peynot T (2010) Reliable automatic camera-laser calibration. In: Proceedings of the 2010 Australasian Conference on Robotics & Automation
12. Zhou L (2014) A New Minimal Solution for the Extrinsic Calibration of a 2D LIDAR and a Camera Using Three Plane-Line Correspondences. IEEE Sensors J 14(2):442–454
13. Unnikrishnan R, Hebert M (2005) Fast Extrinsic Calibration of a Laser Rangefinder to a Camera. Pittsburgh
14. Geiger A, Moosmann F, Car O, Schuster B (2012) Automatic camera and range sensor calibration using a single shot. In: 2012 IEEE International Conference on Robotics and Automation (ICRA). pp 3936–3943
15. Ha JE (2012) Extrinsic calibration of a camera and laser range finder using a new calibration structure of a plane with a triangular hole. Int J Control Autom Syst 10(6):1240–1244
16. Hoang VD, Cá D, Jo KH (2014) Simple and Efficient Method for Calibration of a Camera and 2D Laser Rangefinder. In: Hutchison D, Kanade T, Kittler J, Kleinberg JM, Mattern F, Mitchell JC, et al (eds). Intelligent Information and Database Systems, vol 8397 of Lecture Notes in Computer Science. Springer International Publishing. pp 561–570
17. Gong X, Lin Y, Liu J (2013) 3D LIDAR-camera extrinsic calibration using an arbitrary trihedron. Sensors 13(2):1902–1918
18. Moghadam P, Bosse M, Zlot R (2013) Line-based extrinsic calibration of range and image sensors. In: 2013 IEEE International Conference on Robotics and Automation (ICRA). pp 3685–3691
19. Taylor Z, Nieto J (2012) A Mutual Information Approach to Automatic Calibration of Camera and Lidar in Natural Environments. In: Proceedings of Australasian Conference on Robotics and Automation (ACRA). pp 31–39
20. Taylor Z, Nieto J (2013) Automatic calibration of lidar and camera images using normalized mutual information. University of Sydney, Australia
21. Pandey G, McBride JR, Savarese S, Eustice RM (2015) Automatic Extrinsic Calibration of Vision and Lidar by Maximizing Mutual Information. J Field Robot 32(5):696–722
22. Levinson J, Thrun S (2013) Automatic Online Calibration of Cameras and Lasers. In: Proceedings of Robotics: Science and Systems. Berlin
23. Scott T, Morye AA, Pinies P, Paz LM, Posner I, Newman P (2015) Exploiting known unknowns: Scene induced cross-calibration of lidar-stereo systems. In: 2015 IEEE/RSJ International Conference on Intelligent Robots and Systems (IROS). pp 3647–3653
24. Poppinga J, Vaskevicius N, Birk A, Pathak K (2008) Fast plane detection and polygonalization in noisy 3D range images. In: 2008 IEEE/RSJ International Conference on Intelligent Robots and Systems. pp 3378–3383
25. Holz D, Behnke S (2014) Approximate triangulation and region growing for efficient segmentation and smoothing of range images. Robot Auton Syst 62(9):1282–1293
26. Placht S, Fürsattel P, Mengue EA, Hofmann H, Schaller C, Balda M, et al. (2014) ROCHADE: Robust Checkerboard Advanced Detection for Camera Calibration. In: Fleet D, Pajdla T, Schiele B, Tuytelaars T (eds). Computer Vision – ECCV 2014. vol 8692 of Lecture Notes in Computer Science. Springer International Publishing, Cham. pp 766–779
27. Horn BKP (1987) Closed-form solution of absolute orientation using unit quaternions. J Opt Soc Am A 4(4):629–642
28. Zhang Z (2000) A flexible new technique for camera calibration. IEEE Trans Pattern Anal Mach Intell 22(11):1330–1334
29. Kytö M, Nuutinen M, Oittinen P (2011) Method for measuring stereo camera depth accuracy based on stereoscopic vision. In: Beraldin JA, Cheok GS, McCarthy MB, Neuschaefer-Rube U, Baskurt AM, McDowall IE, et al. (eds). Three-Dimensional Imaging, Interaction, and Measurement. SPIE Proceedings. SPIE. p 78640I

13

Generic and attribute-specific deep representations for maritime vessels

Berkan Solmaz[*†] (iD), Erhan Gundogdu[†], Veysel Yucesoy and Aykut Koc

Abstract

Fine-grained visual categorization has recently received great attention as the volumes of labeled datasets for classification of specific objects, such as cars, bird species, and air-crafts, have been increasing. The availability of large datasets led to significant performance improvements in several vision-based classification tasks. Visual classification of maritime vessels is another important task, assisting naval security and surveillance applications. We introduced, MARVEL, a large-scale image dataset for maritime vessels, consisting of 2 million user-uploaded images and their various attributes, including vessel identity, type, category, year built, length, and tonnage, collected from a community website. The images were categorized into vessel type classes and also into superclasses defined by combining semantically similar classes, following a semi-automatic clustering scheme. For the analysis of the presented dataset, extensive experiments have been performed, involving several potentially useful applications: vessel type classification, identity verification, retrieval, and identity recognition with and without prior vessel type knowledge. Furthermore, we attempted interesting problems of visual marine surveillance such as predicting and classifying maritime vessel attributes such as length, summer deadweight, draught, and gross tonnage by solely interpreting the visual content in the wild, where no additional cues such as scale, orientation, or location are provided. By utilizing generic and attribute-specific deep representations for maritime vessels, we obtained promising results for the aforementioned applications.

Keywords: Fine-grained object categorization, Naval surveillance, Deep representations for maritime vessels, Maritime vessel attributes, Convolutional neural networks, Deep learning

1 Introduction

The coastal and marine surveillance systems are mainly based on sensors such as radar and sonar, which allow detecting marine vessels and taking responsive actions. Vision-based surveillance systems containing electro-optic imaging sensors can also be exploited for developing robust and cost-effective systems. Categorization of maritime vessels is of utmost importance to improve the capabilities of such systems. For a given image of a ship, the goal is to automatically identify it using computer vision and machine learning techniques. Vessel images include important clues regarding different attributes such as vessel type, category, gross tonnage, length and draught. A large-scale dataset would be beneficial for extracting such clues and learning compelling models from images containing several types of vessels.

Presence of benchmark datasets [1] with large quantities of images and manual labels with meaningful attributes has resulted in a significant increase in visual object categorization performance by allowing the use of convenient machine learning methods such as deep architectures [2]. Later, these powerful deep architectures have been employed in a more challenging problem, fine-grained visual categorization, by either training on datasets from scratch [3], by fine-tuning deep architectures trained on large-scale datasets [4], or by exploiting the previously trained architectures with specific modifications [5].

To classify images with a fine-grained resolution, a considerable amount of training data is necessary for a respectable model generalization. Thus, fine-grained datasets were collected for specific object categories. Some examples are aircraft datasets [6, 7]; Caltech-UCSD bird species dataset [8] consisting of 12 K images, car

*Correspondence: bsolmaz@aselsan.com.tr
†Equal contributors
Aselsan Research Center, Ankara, Turkey

make, and model datasets; Standford cars dataset [9] containing 16 K car images; and CompCars dataset [10] of 130 K images. One work related to marine vessel recognition is [11], where 130,000 random example images from the *Shipspotting* website [12] is utilized and a convolutional neural network [2] is trained for classifying vessel types. In our dataset, 140,000 images are engaged for vessel type classification among 26 superclasses constructed using a semi-supervised clustering approach. Furthermore, constructed vessel superclasses are balanced; the training set is arranged to have an equal number of examples from each superclass, after augmenting data for vessel type classes with lower number of examples. However, there is a significant imbalance of examples among the classes in [11], which may result in a bias in classification towards the dominant classes with more examples. Hence, imbalance makes it more difficult to validate the performance of different classifiers. In this work, for measuring vessel classification performance, we report mean per class accuracies. In addition, we accomplish further important tasks with a vast amount of vessel images and obtain pleasing results, which will be described in details in the following sections.

In order to utilize the-state-of-the-art fine-grained visual classification methods for maritime vessel categorization, we collected a dataset consisting of a total of 2 million images downloaded from the Shipspotting website [12], where hobby photographers upload images of maritime vessels and corresponding detailed annotations including types, categories, tonnage, draught, length, summer deadweight, year built, and International Maritime Organization (IMO) numbers, which uniquely identify ships. To the best of our knowledge, the collected dataset, MARitime VEsseLs (MARVEL) [13, 14], is the largest-scale dataset with meta-data composed of the aforementioned attributes, suited for fine-grained visual categorization, recognition, retrieval, and verification tasks, as well as any possible future applications.

In addition to the introduced large-scale dataset, our other major contributions are presenting generic representations for maritime vessels, as well as targeting visual vessel analysis from five different aspects: (1) *vessel type classification*, (2) *vessel identity verification*, (3) *vessel retrieval*, (4) *vessel identity recognition with and without prior type knowledge*, and (5) *specific vessel attributes (draught, length, gross tonnage, and summer deadweight) prediction and classification*. To verify the practicality of MARVEL and encourage researchers, we present baseline results for these tasks. By providing relevant splits of the dataset for each application and inspecting the consistency of associated labels, we form a comparison basis for visual analysis of maritime vessels. Moreover, we believe our structured dataset will be a benchmark for evaluating approaches designed for fine-grained recognition.

The researchers may also develop several new applications with the help of this dataset in addition to the aforementioned applications.

2   MARVEL dataset properties

MARVEL dataset consists of 2 million marine vessel images collected from Shipspotting website [12]. For most of the images in the dataset, the following attributes are available: *beam, year built, draught, flag, gross tonnage, IMO number, name, length, category, summer deadweight, MMSI, vessel type.*

Among the above attributes, we observe that the most useful and visually relevant categories are as follows: (1) *Vessel type*, (2) *category*, (3) *draught*, (4) *gross tonnage*, (5) *length*, (6) *summer deadweight*, and (7) *IMO number*. *Vessel type* is assigned based on the type of cargo a vessel will be transporting. For instance, if a vessel carries passengers, its type is very likely to be a *Passengers Ship*. The dataset contains 1,607,190 images with valid annotated type labels belonging to one of 197 categories. *Vessel type* histogram, highlighting the major categories, is depicted in Fig. 1c. Another available attribute is *category*, which is another vessel description. Example *categories* with a substantial number of members are *chemical and products tankers, containerships built 2001–2010*, and *Tugs* (please see Fig. 1a). All collected images have been assigned a *category* out of 185 categories in MARVEL dataset. *IMO number* is another category, which is an abbreviation for International Maritime Organization number. Similar to the chassis numbers of cars, IMO numbers of vessels uniquely identify the ships registered to IMO regardless of any changes made in their names, flags, or ownerships. Of the collected images, 1,628,056 are annotated with IMO numbers (please refer to Fig. 1b). There are a total of 103,701 unique IMO numbers in MARVEL dataset.

Considering the fact that images which have been assigned identical IMO numbers belong to the same vessels, we are able to check the consistency of other attribute annotations and fill out the missing entries when necessary. First, zero or invalid entries are discarded. Next, we convert all attribute labels to metric unit system to account for the presence of some labels in an imperial system. Finally, we maintain the consistency of labels for each vessel separately by applying median filters on available annotations. Engaging such preprocessing procedures, we obtain very large groups of images that include valid attribute labels. The attributes we focus on are IMO number, vessel type label, draught, gross tonnage, length, and summer deadweight (Fig. 2). For *draught*, an attribute which is defined as the vertical distance between the bottom of vessel hull and waterline, there are 1,067,946 images carrying validated labels. *Gross tonnage* is a unitless index calculated using the internal volume of vessels.

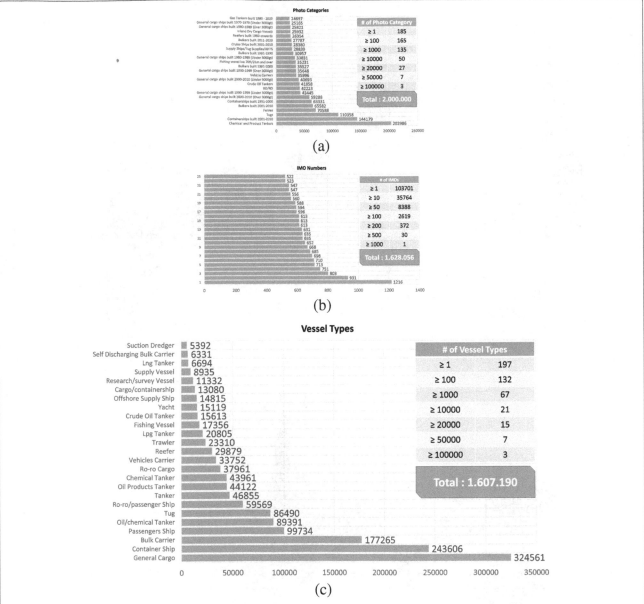

Fig. 1 Distribution of collected vessel images: Number of images belonging to each photo category, individual vessel, and vessel type are depicted in **a**, **b**, and **c**, respectively. The largest group among photo categories is chemical and product tankers. General cargo is the vessel type including highest number of images. Further statistics are provided on the right columns: In **b**, 8388 marine vessels are present containing at least 50 images. In **c**, there are 132 vessel type categories including at least 100 images

There are 1,583,882 images with valid annotated labels for gross tonnage. Validated annotations for *summer dead-weight*, a measure of carrying capacity of a ship, are provided for 1,508,974 of all images. *Length* data of the maritime vessels are made available for 1,107,907 images. In summary, when combined, a total of 1,006,868 images retain valid annotated labels for all vessel type, IMO number, draught, length, summer deadweight, and gross tonnage attributes.

3 Potential computer vision tasks on MARVEL dataset

Huge quantity of images and their annotations, existing in MARVEL, makes it applicable to directly employ recent methods utilizing deep architectures such as AlexNet [2] for vessel categorization. One may choose one of the provided vessel attributes such as *vessel type* or *category* and apply classification methods for categorizing images according to the selected attribute.

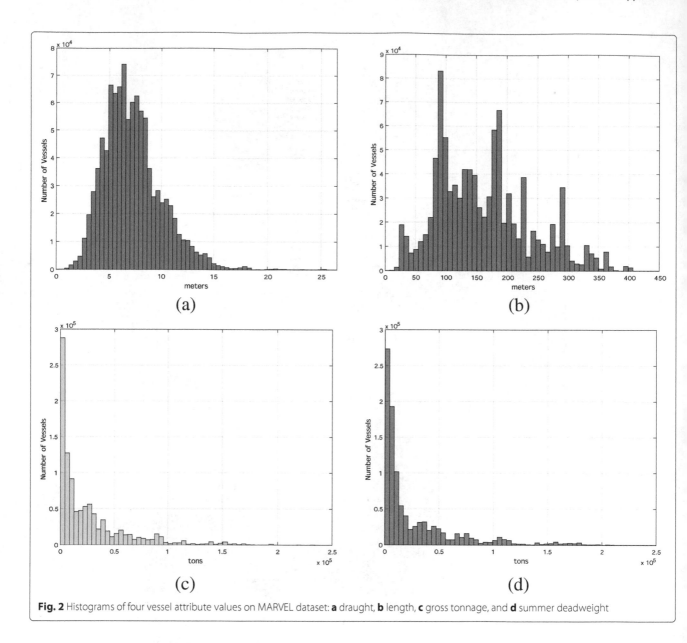

Fig. 2 Histograms of four vessel attribute values on MARVEL dataset: **a** draught, **b** length, **c** gross tonnage, and **d** summer deadweight

In MARVEL there are more than 8000 unique vessels (carrying unique IMO numbers) having more than 50 example images as shown in Fig. 1b. It is also feasible to use the dataset for both vessel verification and identity recognition, which could be a vital part of a maritime security system, analogous to a scenario where vehicle make and model recognition is crucial for a traffic security system.

The main foci of this study on MARVEL dataset are five folds: (1) *vessel classification* since content of cargo that a ship carries, specified by its type, is crucial for maritime surveillance, (2) *identity verification* where the ultimate goal is to find out if a pair of images belong to the same vessel with a unique IMO number, (3) *retrieval* where one might desire to query a vessel image and retrieve a certain

number of similar images from a database, (4) *identity recognition* which is a challenging though interesting task which aims at recognizing a specific vessel within vessels of same type or among all other vessels (This might be likened to a facial recognition task.), and finally (5) *specific attribute prediction and classification*, where the objective is to grasp draught, length, gross tonnage, and summer deadweight of a vessel by simply analyzing the 2-D visual content. With an aim to achieve these goals, we design generic and attribute specific representations which are powerful in describing marine vessel images.

For *vessel classification*, one of the most important tasks, we first generate a set of superclasses which may contain vessels of more than one type, since some subsets of *vessel types* are not visually distinguishable even with human supervision. The sole differences within the subsets arises from the invisible content of cargo rather than the visual appearance of ships. A concrete example of such a case arises for the pair of vessel types: *crude oil tanker* and *oil products tanker*, which is illustrated in Fig. 3. Although the two vessel types have distinct functional differences, their visual characteristics are congruent especially when images are captured by cameras located far away from these vessels; when the vessels occupy a small portion of images and their decks are not visible from such a view point, it is tough to distinguish them. Hence, we merge some of the types to generate superclasses which are semantically correct and visually discriminable. In Section 4, we describe the details for combining *vessel types*. As inspired by [15], the presence of multi-level relevance information and hierarchical grouping of vessels may allow exploitation of MARVEL dataset for a further performance improvement for particular marine vessel recognition tasks in the future.

Vessel verification task serves for deciding whether a pair of vessel images belong to the same vessel or not. This may be beneficial for a naval surveillance scenario, where a specific vessel is required to be tracked using an electro-optic imaging system.

For the task of *vessel retrieval* relating to *vessel classification*, the goal is to retrieve images belonging to providing a query image, several images with similar content are retrieved from the database.

Vessel recognition aims at revealing the accurate identity of a vessel by analyzing an unseen example image of it and finding out the matching vessel within a group of vessels. This task may be particularly useful for scenarios of marine surveillance and port registration. For this task, first, we performed recognition for vessels considering their type labels, for instance, identifying a passenger ship among other passenger ships. Next, we attempt a more challenging recognition problem, identifying vessels where no additional cues such as *vessel type labels* or *category labels* are given.

Moreover, as novel problems, we attempt tasks of *predicting and classifying vessel attributes*: draught, gross tonnage, length, and summer deadweight. The objective here is to quantify these attributes based on 2-D visual content only, which may ameliorate the practicality of coastal surveillance systems, since that avoids the need for retaining meta-data for optical systems, namely camera parameters, camera position, and distance to the vessel, while estimating physical dimensions of a vessel based on its appearance. Another beneficial use of this task may be for safe marine traffic routing as well as for the calculation of port access and transit fees, when vessel dimensions need to be known. Furthermore, there are studies, proving that presence of attribute-based representations are helpful for several computer vision tasks including object recognition [16], detection [17], and identification [18]. The attribute-based learned representations for marine vessels in this work may be utilized in a similar fashion aiding other visual analysis tasks.

4 Superclasses for vessel types

To generate superclasses from *vessel types*, the first 50 major *vessel types* containing the largest amount of

Fig. 3 Visual comparison of two very similar classes: *crude oil tanker* (top row) and *oil products tanker* (bottom row)

example images are selected and sorted according to their quantity. The *vessel type* with the largest number of images which is employed in our superclass generation, is *general cargo*, consisting of 324,561 example images. The class with the smallest number of images is the *timber carrier*, accommodating only 1837 images. In this work, to investigate the visual similarities among *vessel types*, MatConvNet Toolbox [19] implementation of a pre-trained convolutional neural network (CNN) architecture, VGG-F [20], is adopted. Features are extracted posterior to resizing images to 224 × 224. Utilizing the penultimate layer acctivations of VGG-F [20] as visual representations of images, each image is described by a 4096-dimensional feature vector. Based on these feature vectors, we calculated a dissimilarity matrix for the 50 major vessel classes. To generate superclasses, 1/10 of all collected images belonging to 50 major classes are randomly selected (approximately 130,000 images) and individual class statistics are estimated. Prior to calculating a dissimilarity matrix, we removed outliers following the preprocessing step explained below.

4.1 Outlier removal

Although image annotations for most categories are valid and correct, interior images of vessels are also present in MARVEL dataset. Thus, we prune outliers within individual *vessel types* and avoid them while computing the dissimilarity matrix. First, feature vector dimensionality is reduced to 10 by principal component analysis (PCA) using all examples of 50 major vessel type classes, since Kullback-Leibler divergence is utilized in dissimilarity computation and determinants of very high dimensional matrices become unbounded. After dimensionality reduction, each vessel type class is processed independently and Gaussian distributions are fitted; means and covariances of each distribution are estimated. The feature vectors of corresponding classes are whitened to obtain unit variance within each class. We intent to filter out unlikely examples in the dataset to obtain a clear dissimilarity matrix. Next, we utilize χ^2 distribution since the dataset is already whitened. For each example in individual classes, the sum of the square values of the 10-dimensional feature vectors are used as samples drawn from the χ^2 distribution with 10° of freedom. Cumulative distribution function (cdf) value for each sample is calculated and removed from the class set if the cdf value is greater than 0.95, which corresponds to the samples drawn from the 5% tail of the χ^2 distribution.

4.2 Dissimilarity matrix and superclass generation

Once outliers are removed from each vessel type class by the above procedure, the remaining examples are used to compute a dissimilarity matrix. We compute symmetrized divergence as the dissimilarity index. Symmetrized divergence $D_S(P, Q)$ of two classes, namely P and Q, is defined as $D_S(P, Q) = \frac{1}{2}D_{KL}(P||Q) + \frac{1}{2}D_{KL}(Q||P)$, where $D_{KL}(.||.)$ stands for Kullback-Liebler divergence of two multivariate Gaussian distributions. The computed dissimilarity matrix is depicted in Fig. 4.

By exploiting the dissimilarity matrix, we merge similar vessel type classes using a threshold. Prior to thresholding, we applied spectral clustering methods with the help of the dissimilarity matrix. Nevertheless, the resulting groups were not semantically meaningful. Hence, we opt to continue by increasing the threshold for the similarities of the pairs of classes (i.e., this corresponds to each entry of the dissimilarity matrix). If dissimilarity index of a pair of classes is below a threshold, the pair is assigned to the same superclass. We keep increasing the threshold before it reaches to a point where semantically irrelevant classes (human supervision is adopted here) start to merge, and we define it as the final threshold for clustering. The majority of the resulting superclasses contain reasonable classes. The generated vessel type superclasses with more than one *vessel type* are (1) *tankers* (consisting of *oil products tanker, oil/chemical tanker, tanker, chemical tanker, crude oil tanker, lpg tanker, lng tanker, ore carrier*), (2) *carrier/floating* (consisting of *timber carrier, floating storage production, self discharging bulk carrier*), (3) *supply vessels* (which contain *offshore supply ship, supply vessel, tug/supply vessel, anchor handling vessel, multi purpose offshore vessel*), (4) *fishing vessels* (which include *trawler, fishing vessel, factory trawler, fish carrier*), and (5) *dredgers* (which contain *suction dredger, hopper dredger*). Finally, marginal adjustments are done manually to make all superclasses as meaningful as possible. These adjustments include merging superclass containing only *trailing suction hopper dredger* with superclass consisting of *Suction Dredger* and *Hopper Dredger*. In addition, seven *vessel types* are removed entirely from the set of superclasses. The classes to be eliminated are decided according to the average dissimilarity of the classes to the rest. The salient overall dissimilarity scores are detected manually. The removed classes are, namely (1) *general cargo* (it is significantly confusing with the *container ship* and *ro-ro cargo*), (2) *cargo/containership*, (3) *research/survey vessel*, (4) *cement carrier*, (5) *multi purpose offshore vessel*, (6) *passenger/cargo ship*, and (7) *cable layer*. The removed classes both visually and functionally contain more than at least two separate classes, i.e., *passenger/cargo ship* involve both passenger vessels and general cargo vessels. The merged classes with thresholding also contain visually very meaningful *vessel types*, i.e., all of the fish-related vessels are clustered within the same superclass. The distribution of final 26 superclasses can be viewed in Fig. 5.

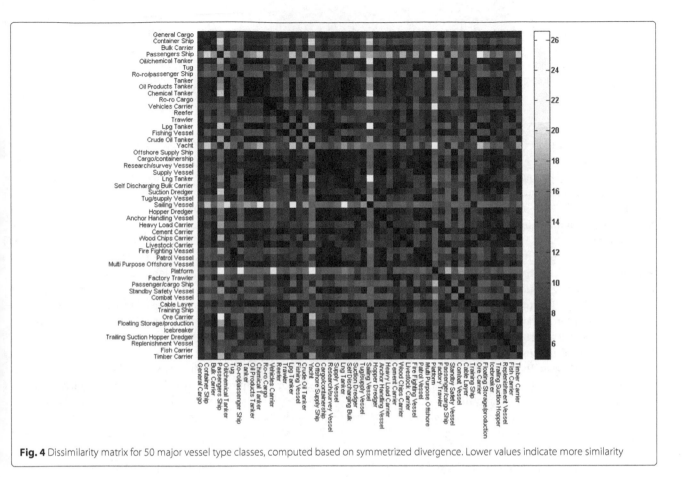

Fig. 4 Dissimilarity matrix for 50 major vessel type classes, computed based on symmetrized divergence. Lower values indicate more similarity

4.3 Superclass classification

As demonstrated in Fig. 5, there exists an imbalance between superclasses. Nevertheless, even the superclass with the least amount of examples has a large quantity of examples. Therefore, to classify superclasses of vessels, it is feasible to train a deep CNN architecture AlexNet [2]. To avoid the imbalance between superclasses, we acquire equal numbers of samples from each class for both training and testing, as 8192 and 1024 images,

respectively. For superclasses with examples less than the required amount, we generate additional examples by data augmentation (using different croppings of images). Consequently, our training and test sets contain 212,992 and 26,624 examples, respectively, although we have 140,000 unique examples. We should also note that no images of the same vessels appear in both training and test sets. The classification performance is quantified by the help of a normalized confusion matrix [7]. The practical +

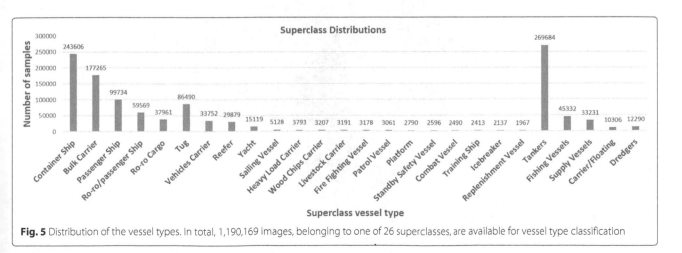

Fig. 5 Distribution of the vessel types. In total, 1,190,169 images, belonging to one of 26 superclasses, are available for vessel type classification

metric for a fine-grained classification task can be the class-normalized average classification accuracy, which is calculated as the average of diagonal elements of a normalized confusion matrix, C, entries of which are defined as follows [6]:

$$C_{pq} = \frac{|\{i : \hat{y}_i = q \wedge y_i = p\}|}{|\{i : y_i = p\}|},$$ (1)

where $|.|$ denotes the cardinality of the set, $\hat{y}_i$ indicates the estimated class label, and y_i is the actual label for the ith training example. The final performance measure is the mean of the diagonal elements of the matrix C. This value for 26 superclasses is 73.14% for the normalized confusion matrix depicted in Fig. 6. To emphasize the validity and efficacy of the learned network, we also compare it with another method utilizing multi-class support vector machine (SVM) with the Crammer and Singer multi-class SVM [21] implementation of [22] in LIBLINEAR [23] library. The feature vectors for training SVM are extracted from the VGG-F network of [20], their dimensionality is reduced to 256, and PCA whitening is applied. Due to memory requirements and computational complexity in optimization, we use half of the training set. We report the class-normalized average classification accuracy in testing as 53.89%. Compared to the use of pre-learned VGG-F weights with an SVM classifier, AlexNet trained from scratch has 35% improvement in accuracy.

5 Experiments on potential applications

In this section, we make use of our dataset, MARVEL, for potential maritime applications and vessel verification, retrieval, identity recognition, and attribute prediction and classification. In the following subsections, these applications and necessary experimental settings are explained.

During all experiments, we follow training and testing strategies similar to [10]. First, 8000 vessels with unique IMO numbers are selected such that each vessel will have 50 example images, resulting in a total of 400,000 images. This data is divided into two splits: training and testing. The training set consists of 4035 vessels (201,750 example images in total), and the test set contains 3965 vessels (198,250 example images in total). There exist 109 vessel type labels among 400,000 examples, and training and test sets are split in a way that the number of vessel types are identical in both sets. In the rest of the paper, we call the training split of this subset as IMO training set, and the test split as IMO test set.

We propose three deep CNN-based generic representations for marine vessels on IMO training set by making use of *vessel type* and/or *vessel IMO* labels . Hence, we train the same architecture of [2] as in *vessel classification* task and modify it accordingly with an aim to capture more details in vessel images: For the last layer, rather than 26 label classes, we use 109, 4035, and 4144 label classes.

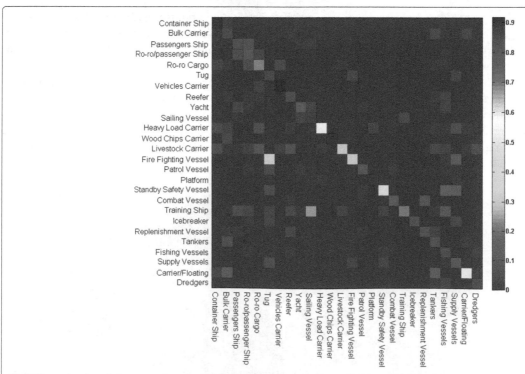

Fig. 6 Normalized confusion matrix for categorization of 26 superclasses representing vessel types. Accuracy, computed by averaging diagonal entries, is 73.14%

These three different classifiers focus on discriminating vessel types, vessel IMO numbers (classifying individual vessels on IMO training set), and both vessel types and IMO numbers (jointly classifying type and IMO numbers of vessels on IMO training set), respectively. We compare the performances of these three representations over computer vision tasks, which are described below in details.

Deep representations for example images are extracted as the penultimate layer activations of the trained networks (as in the superclass generation part in Section 4) with 4096 dimensions. More discriminative features being desired, we extract the penultimate layer activations prior to the rectified linear unit (ReLU) layer, which carry more information than the layer after ReLU since the negative values are cast to zero after ReLU. This choice makes our vessel verification performance better than the case with the deep representations after ReLU case.

During all experiments utilizing convolutional neural networks, we select batch sizes as 256 without normalization and decaying learning rates, consisting of logarithmically equally spaced values between 0.01 and 0.0001. For superclass classification, we train the networks for 60 epochs and for attribute classification and prediction, we train the networks for 50 epochs, since we notice that the training error does not decrease with further training. The implementation of the networks are based on the MatConvNet Toolbox [19].

5.1 Vessel verification, retrieval, and recognition

5.1.1 Vessel verification

Akin to face verification [24], car model verification is applied in CompCars dataset [10] to serve for conceivable purposes in transportation systems. That kind of task is claimed to be more complicated compared to face verification, since car model verification is performed on images with unconstrained viewpoints. On MARVEL dataset, we perform maritime *vessel verification* where the attribute to be verified is the vessel identity. *Please note that our task is more challenging compared to identifying other attributes such as category or vessel type.* Furthermore, this problem is more challenging than both car model and face verification tasks, since it is desired to identify/verify pairs of individual vessels by looking only at their appearances which have more diversity.

After extracting the generic deep representations (109 and 4144-dimensional output based), 50,000 positive pairs (belonging to same vessels) and 50,000 negative pairs (belonging to different vessels) are picked randomly from both training and test splits out of 201,750 training examples and 198,250 test examples, respectively[1]. For all 400,000 training and testing examples, feature vector dimensionality is reduced to 100 by PCA exploited with only training examples. Moreover, all 100-dimensional

examples are PCA whitened since whitening increases performance of SVM classifier. Concatenating two 100-dimensional vectors, we describe each pair of vessel during verification experiments. Finally, for each generic representation, we train a binary SVM classifier with a radial basis function kernel on the generated training set by using the implementation of LIBSVM library [25]. Additionally, we attempt end-to-end learning for verification. For this experiment, we construct a Siamese neural network, based on AlexNet architecture, with shared weights, and added a contrastive loss layer after the last fully connected layers. Contrastive loss [26], incurring for similar and dissimilar pairs of images is defined as,

$$L = (1 - Y)\frac{1}{2}(D_W)^2 + Y\frac{1}{2}\{max(0, m - D_W)\}^2 \quad (2)$$

where Y is a binary label, assigned to 1 for similar images, otherwise set to 0. $m > 0$ is a margin set for dissimilar pairs, and D_W is the distance to be learned for pairs of images, $\vec{X_1}$ and $\vec{X_2}$. D_W is calculated as the Euclidean distance between outputs of parametrized function G_W.

$$D_W(\vec{X_1}, \vec{X_2}) = \left\| G_W(\vec{X_1}) - G_W(\vec{X_2}) \right\|_2 \quad (3)$$

The precision recall curves for the two generic representations and the Siamese network-based representation, obtained by varying the classification thresholds, are plotted in Fig. 7. We also compare the performance of SVMs with the nearest neighbor (NN) classifiers. For NN classifier, each test pair is assigned the label of the training pair for which the Euclidean descriptor distances are the smallest. The resulting precision and recall values of SVM and NN classifier are presented in Table 1. All classifiers

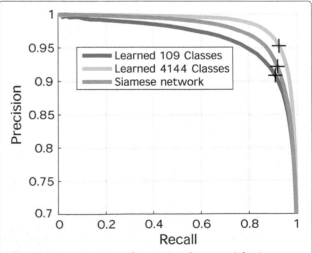

Fig. 7 Precision-recall curves for vessel verification task for three representations designed for marine vessels: 109 (shown in blue), 4144 (shown in green) dimensional output, and Siamese network based (shown in orange)

Table 1 Vessel verification results on 50,000 positive pairs and 50,000 negative pairs of vessels for the nearest neighbor and SVM classifiers by utilizing the generic and end-to-end learning-based vessel representations learned in IMO training set, which does not contain any images of the vessels in IMO test set

	Representation	True positives	True negatives	False positives	False negatives	Accuracy	Precision	Recall
NN	109-dimensional output based	44,978	40,198	9,802	5,022	85.18%	0.82	0.90
SVM	109-dimensional output based	45,503	45,422	4,578	4,497	90.93%	0.91	0.91
NN	4144-dimensional output based	47,305	41,148	8,852	2,695	88.45%	0.84	0.95
SVM	4144-dimensional output based	46,225	47,744	2,256	3,775	93.97%	0.95	0.92
NN	Siamese network based	44,459	40,390	9,610	5,541	84.85%	0.82	0.89
SVM	Siamese network based	45,869	46,150	3,850	4,131	92.02%	0.92	0.92

are quite satisfactory, which is very promising for a real-world verification application. SVM performs better than NN for all tested representations, since it generalizes better, making use of all training data while learning support vectors. The 4144-dimensional output-based generic representation, carrying finer details for the vessels performs the best for both classifiers. Verification performance is slightly lower for end-to-end learning -based representation compared to the 4144-dimensional output-based vessel representation. One reason may be the limitation in random and insufficient sampling of image pairs out of 4035 different vessels during training.

5.1.2 Vessel retrieval

Compelling amount of research efforts [27–30] have been put on content-based image retrieval (CBIR) as volumes of image databases are dramatically growing. Particularly, vessel retrieval is another promising application, potentially required in a maritime security system, where a user would like to query a database with a vessel image and retrieve similar images. It may also help annotating vessel images uploaded to a database when no meta-data is present. In our application, the retrieved content is not chosen as either the superclasses of *vessel types* that we

constructed as the coarse attribute in Section 4.3, or the IMO number (aiming to identify the exact vessel), which is too fine for a retrieval task (This is studied as a recognition problem in Section 5.1.3.). Instead, we use 109 *vessel types* of the 8000 unique vessels with 50 example images, as the content for the retrieval task. We perform content based vessel retrieval (CBIR), using Euclidean (L^2) and chi-squared (χ^2) distances as the similarity metric for four different vessel representations.

The first representation is one of the presented generic descriptions for marine vessels, a 109-dimensional classifier output of the network, trained on IMO training set. The second representation is the 4144 dimensional output-based generic description designed for distinguishing both vessel types and identities. Third representation is based on a Siamese network similar to the one, end-to-end trained in Section 5.1.1. However, this network focuses on matching vessel types. On the other hand, we also compare these learned deep representations (employing the content information) with another effective representation, designed for object classification. Hence, we use pre-learned VGG-F weights to extract 4096-dimensional features. We train a multi-class SVM to train a classifier for 109 vessel types on the IMO training

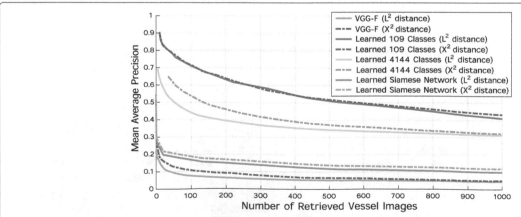

Fig. 8 Vessel retrieval results for four representations: the feature vectors of pre-trained VGG-F network (shown in magenta), AlexNet network based 109 (shown in blue), 4144 (shown in green) dimensional output based, and Siamese network (shown in orange) representations

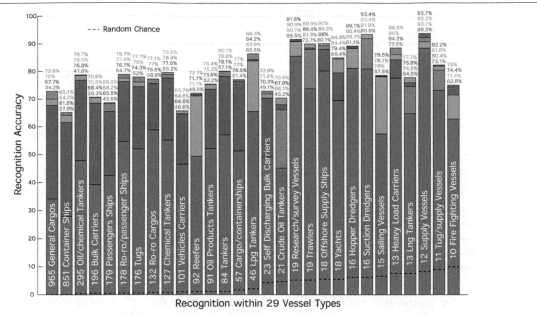

Fig. 9 Vessel type specific recognition: Average recognition accuracies computed within each of the 29 vessel types on IMO testing set are depicted for extracted 109- (blue), 4035- (red), and 4144- (green) dimensional output-based representations and VGG-VD-19-based 4144-dimensional output-based representation (gray) learned in IMO training set

set. For each example, classifier responses of dual combinations of 109 classes (generated during the multi-class SVM phase) are utilized as $\binom{109}{2}$ dimensional feature vectors. By utilizing these four representations, various numbers of images are retrieved and mean average precision curves are generated, as depicted in Fig. 8.

Here, the deep representations learned specifically for maritime vessels significantly outperform the deep representation (VGG-F) learned for general object categorization for 1000 classes [2, 20] for both distance metrics. In addition, χ^2 distance is superior in CBIR than L^2 distance, for the tested representations. A 109-dimensional output-based generic representation performs the best in this experiment, since it is specifically designed for learning vessel types. The retrieval performance of Siamese network, utilizing end-to-end learning, is lower, compared to 109 and 4144-dimensional representations.

5.1.3 Vessel recognition
Visual object recognition is one of the most crucial topics of computer vision. Especially, face recognition has been studied extensively, and state-of-the-art methods [31, 32],

which perform effectively on the benchmark datasets [33–35], have been proposed. Since encouraging performance results are obtained with recent methods, another application performed, utilizing MARVEL, is *vessel recognition* task, where the ultimate goal is to perceive a vessel's identity by its visual appearance. It might not be meaningful for object types, other than maritime vessels or faces, such as cars, since same car models with same color have no visual differences and technically are not distinguishable. Nevertheless, individual vessels generally carry distinctive features, as shapes of vessels belonging to the same *vessel type category* may vary significantly due to their customized construction processes. Here, we utilize the learned generic vessel representations as feature vectors for vessels.

We perform *identification* for two scenarios. First, we assume the vessel type labels are provided. Hence, recognition is performed among individual classes separately, e.g., vessels belonging to the *passenger ships* class are learned and recognized. Multi-class SVMs are trained for images belonging to each vessel type and classification is done. Among the 3965 vessels in IMO test set, there exist 29 *vessel types* that have at least 10

Table 2 Vessel recognition performance on IMO testing set, composed of 3965 marine vessels, by utilizing nearest neighbor search on 109-, 4035-, and 4144-dimensional output-based representations learned in IMO training set

	109-dim. output based representation	4035-dim. output based representation	4144-dim. output based representation	4144-dim. output based representation (VGG-VD-19)
Recognition accuracy	23.87%	59.25%	65.13%	65.78%

Table 3 Vessel attribute prediction performance, measured as correlation of manual truth and predicted labels for 158,850 images in IMO testing set

	Draught	Gross tonnage	Length	Summer deadweight
SVM	0.7556	0.8301	0.8696	0.7930
CNN	0.7911	0.2699	0.9042	0.0830

unique vessels, and each unique vessel has 50 example images. For recognition, we first divide the examples of each vessel into fivefolds where each fold has 10 examples per vessel. The training and testing sets contain fourfolds (40 examples) and onefold (10 examples) per vessel, respectively. We perform fivefold cross-validation for classifying all 50 example images of each vessel. For each multi-class SVM, the number of classes equals the number of unique vessels of that particular *vessel type*. In Fig. 9, the recognition performances are illustrated for each *vessel type* and by using each generic vessel representation as feature vectors. Representations trained over 4035- and 4144-dimensional output labels, which aim to learn specific vessels in IMO training set, perform significantly better than the representation trained on 109-dimensional output labels which only learns vessel types on IMO training set. Being able to learn both, hence extracting both coarse and fine details, 4144 dimensional output-based representation is the best of three for generic vessel description. Random chance for recognition is also depicted in the figure in order to prove the success of the presented generic marine vessel representations. Additionally, we tested the performance of 4144 dimensional representation when employing a deeper neural network VGG-VD-19 [20], and we obtain high performance similarly.

Vessels belonging to *research survey vessels*, *suction dredgers*, and *supply vessels* type classes of are the most distinguishable ones with recognition accuracies above 90%. On the other hand, vessels of *crude oil tankers*, *vehicle carriers*, and *containership* classes have less distinct differences and a slightly lower recognition performances are achieved, compared to the rest of the classes. Please note that, as number of unique vessels increase in a vessel type group, the random chance and recognition rates slightly decrease as expected, since it becomes a more challenging recognition problem. Yet, recognition accuracies over 77% can be obtained even though the number of unique vessels exceeds a hundred, such as in *ro-ro cargo* and *chemical tanker* vessel types.

As a second scenario for recognition, we attempt recognition of vessels when there is no prior information, namely, when type labels are not present. Here, the goal is to classify images of 3965 vessels in IMO testing set by the use of generic vessel representations learned on images of IMO training set. Large number of classes makes it computationally infeasible to train models with a SVM; thus, we employ a nearest neighbor classifier for this experiment. In a similar setting, we split images of individual vessels in IMO testing set into five non-overlapping folds (fourfolds as a training and onefold as a testing split), and we perform fivefold cross-validation for and classify all 50 example images of each vessel. For each image in a testing fold, we find the best matching image among training images and assign its label for the test image. Repeating the same experiment for four generic representations, we conclude that 4144-dimensional output-based representations (AlexNet based and VGG-VD-19 based) perform better than the other two. The recognition rates are listed in Table 2.

5.2 Vessel attribute prediction and classification

MARVEL dataset includes several labeled vessel attributes some of which relate to the visual content. Here, as interesting applications, by studying only the visual content, we targeted predicting and classifying four important attributes: draught, gross tonnage, length, and summer deadweight.

The draught of a vessel is a measure describing the vertical distance between the waterline and the bottom of vessel hull. Draught, defining the minimum depth of water a vessel can operate, is an important factor for navigating and routing vessels while avoiding shallow water pathways. Length of a vessel does matter for navigation and marine traffic routing, as well as for calculating fees during vessel registration. Consequently, estimating length of a vessel effectively from a single image may be very beneficial for maritimeapplications. Gross tonnage is a nonlinear measure calculated based on overall interior volume (from keel to funnel) of a vessel. It is important in determining the number of staff, safety rules, registration fees, and port dues. Summer deadweight defines how much mass a ship can safely carry. It excludes the weight of the ship and includes the sum of the weights of cargo, fuel, fresh water, ballast water, provisions, passengers, and crew [36].

Table 4 Vessel attribute prediction performance, measured as coefficient of determination between manual truth and predicted labels for 158,850 images in IMO testing set

	Draught	Gross tonnage	Length	Summer deadweight
SVM	0.598	0.554	0.743	0.481
CNN	0.770	0.419	0.863	0.466

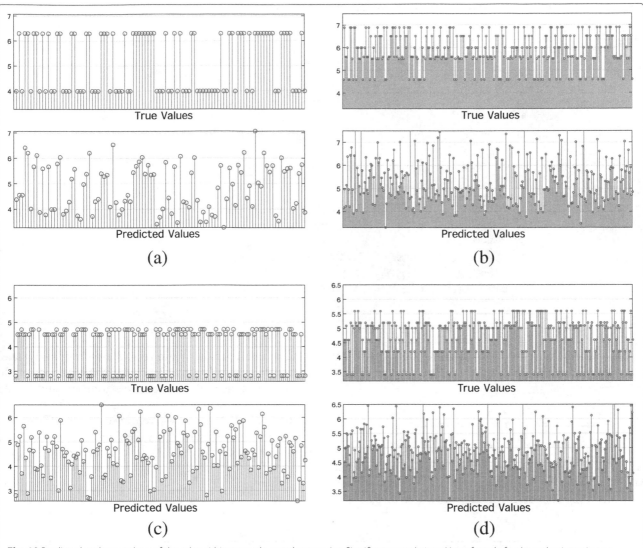

Fig. 10 Predicted and true values of draught within example vessel categories: Significant correlations (*r*) are found after hypothesis testing as indicated by *p* values for asphalt/bitumen tankers (**a**), cable layer (**b**), patrol vessels (**c**), and supply vessels (**d**)

Such efforts of attribute estimation is especially valuable for coastal guarding and surveillance, since it allows grasping the physical specifications of a vessel remotely and only by a captured image. In order to achieve these objectives, we both test the use of our powerful 4144-dimensional output-based generic vessel representation and also employ specific attribute-based deep representations. *Please note that estimating these attributes are very challenging due to the lack of notion of scale, pose, perspective, camera parameters, etc. The only available information is the appearance of a vessel.* For all experiments of attribute prediction, we learn models in IMO training set and evaluate performances of the learned models in IMO testing set. Images missing valid attribute labels were not used in these experiments. Attribute labels, as opposed to being discrete numbers as in vessel type labels or IMO number labels, are continuous and might be unique for each vessel.

We design two sets of experiments: regression and classification. Approaching the problem as a regression task, we represent vessel images by either generic deep models we designed for marine vessels or deep models trained for estimating specific attributes. As in the previous experiments, we extract the penultimate layer activations of the trained networks as feature vectors and utilize a support vector regressor [25, 37] for prediction. For learning attribute-specific deep models, we use AlexNet as a base CNN architecture and modify the last loss layer with an objective to minimize an $L2$-norm loss, approaching the problem as a least squares regression. For performance evaluation, we compute two measures.

Table 5 Vessel attribute classification performance of generic and attribute-specific representations, calculated for four attributes on 158,850 images of IMO testing set

Classified attribute	Employed representation	Top 1 accuracy	Top 2 accuracy	Top 3 accuracy	Top 4 accuracy	Top 5 accuracy
Draught	Generic model + SVM	0.1302	0.3104	0.4432	0.5506	0.6320
Gross tonnage	Generic model + SVM	0.4755	0.6393	0.7418	0.8178	0.8678
Length	Generic model + SVM	0.4539	0.6345	0.7317	0.8019	0.8510
Summer deadweight	Generic model + SVM	0.4304	0.6209	0.7310	0.7998	0.8525
Draught	Attribute-specific trained CNN	0.1834	0.4159	0.5761	0.6884	0.7774
Gross tonnage	Attribute-specific trained CNN	0.5515	0.7492	0.8556	0.9131	0.9454
Length	Attribute-specific trained CNN	0.5289	0.7266	0.8257	0.8896	0.9328
Summer deadweight	Attribute-specific trained CNN	0.5155	0.7364	0.8317	0.8938	0.9288

The first measure is Pearson correlation coefficient between predicted labels and manual truth. It is defined as,

$$r = \frac{\sum_{i=1}^{N}(\hat{y}_i - \bar{\hat{y}})(y_i - \bar{y})}{\sqrt{\sum_{i=1}^{N}(\hat{y}_i - \bar{\hat{y}})^2}\sqrt{\sum_{i=1}^{N}(y_i - \bar{y})^2}}, \tag{4}$$

where $\hat{y}_i$ and y_i are single indexed samples of predicted labels and true labels, respectively. N is the sample size, which is 158,850, corresponding to all test images with valid attribute labels. These results are given in Table 3. The highest correlations obtained are 0.9042 for length, 0.7911 for draught, 0.8301 for gross tonnage, and 0.7930 for summer deadweight.

The second measure we report is the coefficient of determination, namely R^2, which quantifies how well regression model fits the data. It is calculated as,

$$R^2 = \frac{\sum_{i=1}^{N}(\hat{y}_i - \bar{y})^2}{\sum_{i=1}^{N}(y_i - \bar{y})^2}. \tag{5}$$

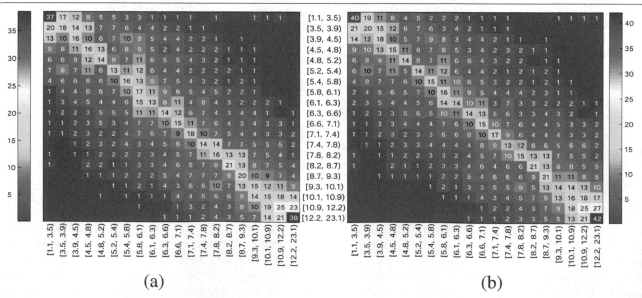

(a)   (b)

Fig. 11 Confusion matrices for classifying draught: **a** generic vessel features combined with a support vector machine classifier and **b** learned draught-specific representation combined with a softmax classifier

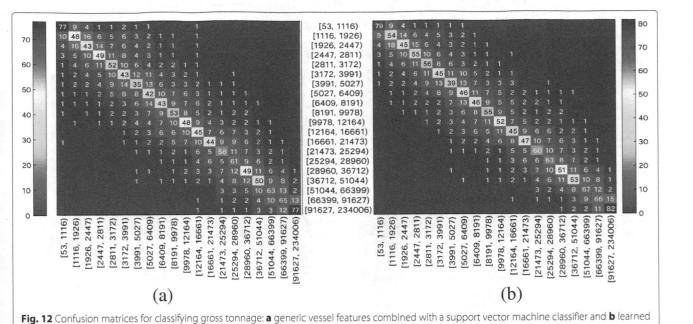

Fig. 12 Confusion matrices for classifying gross tonnage: **a** generic vessel features combined with a support vector machine classifier and **b** learned gross tonnage-specific representation combined with a softmax classifier

Table 4 shows the R^2 values when predicting four attributes. SVM classifier employs the generic representation learnt for vessel type classification, whereas CNN employs a representation specifically learnt for predicting attributes. Table 4 shows that attribute-based representation performs better for predicting length and draught; nevertheless, it performs slightly worse for gross tonnage and summer deadweight. Thus, we may conclude that for predicting physical attributes, values of which are visually explicit, specific representations are more effective. For predicting attributes such as weight, our method relies on vessel type classification.

For further analysis, we plot predicted draught values for four example vessel categories separately in Fig. 10. The annotated attributes differ for individual vessels within specific vessel categories. However, the significant correlations, between the true values and predicted values for vessels belonging to the same types, show that learnt representations, capturing visual cues, are effective in attribute prediction. The trained neural networks simply try to estimate vessel attributes similar to how human can do, based on clues such as vessel type and also appearance (visible parts of a vessel).

As another experiment, we quantize the attribute labels and relabel and assign the images in IMO training set accordingly to 20 distinct classes such that each class has equivalent number of examples for a balanced training. Next, we train a multi-class classifier, using both the generic vessel representation (combined with a nonlinear SVM) and also specific deep representations (softmax classifier) for each attribute. For instance, in training, we

use a total of 134,000 images for draught, 142,000 images for gross tonnage, 140,000 images for length and 148,000 images for summer deadweight. For testing, we use all 158,850 images of IMO test set for which all attribute annotations are present. Top five classification accuracies for the attributes and employed representations are summarized in Table 5. Though generic vessel representation performs reasonably well, trained deep models which focus on specific attributes are significantly better in attribute categorization. The classification results are also depicted as normalized confusion matrices in Figs. 11, 12, 13, and 14. The imbalance of the training set results in coarser ranges for classes around the extrema values and very fine classes otherwise. The entries of the confusion matrices are high valued along the diagonal entries, which shows that the learned models are effective in capturing the desired attribute information.

6 Discussions

Introducing MARVEL, a large-scale dataset for maritime vessels, our goal is to point out several research problems and applications for maritime images. MARVEL dataset, composed of a massive number of images and their metadata, carries interesting attributes to be considered for visual analysis tasks. In this work, we presented our efforts for visual classification of maritime vessel types, retrieval, identity verification, identity recognition, and estimation of physical attributes such as draught, length, and tonnage of vessels. For each of these tasks, we provide the details (experimental settings, labels, training and testing splits) to make results reproducible.

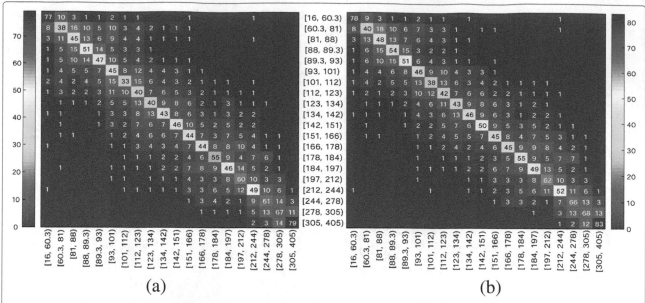

Fig. 13 Confusion matrices for classifying length: **a** generic vessel features combined with a support vector machine classifier and **b** learned length-specific representation combined with a softmax classifier

For organizing the dataset, first, we performed semantic analysis and combined vessel type classes which are visually indistinguishable. Next, we pruned annotations for attributes semi-automatically, converting them to certain metric units, filtering out the missing and wrong entries and ensured reliability of the labels. We also present baseline results for several computer vision tasks to inspire future applications on MARVEL. Moreover, we provide generic deep representations for maritime vessels and prove their success in aforementioned tasks by performing extensive experiments. We achieve promising performance in vessel classification, recognition, and retrieval. Moreover, we observe that attributes are predictable as long as they are visually distinguishable. Hence, attributes such as length and draught can be estimated accurately and by solely exploiting visual data. What remains of key interest for future work is the enhancement of performance for the aforesaid tasks, which can be fulfilled by utilizing more powerful visual representations, developing sophisticated methods.

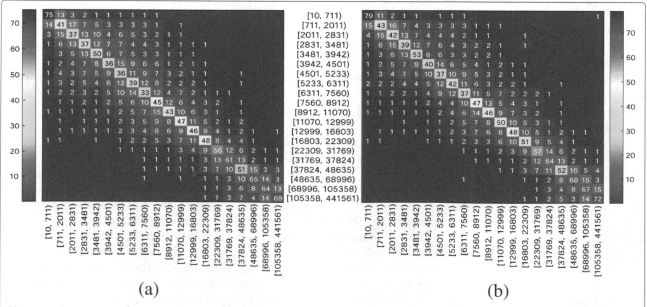

Fig. 14 Confusion matrices for classifying summer-deadweight: **a** generic vessel features combined with a support vector machine classifier and **b** learned summer deadweight-specific representation combined with a softmax classifier

Endnote

[1] A negative pair indicates a pair of different vessel images, whereas a positive pair corresponds to a pair of vessel images belonging to a unique vessel.

Acknowledgements
We would like to thank to Koray Akçay for his invaluable support and special consultancy for maritime vessels.

Authors' contributions
VY took charge of data collection and organization. VY and EH generated the statistics of the collected dataset. EH implemented and performed the representation learning for marine vessels and carried out vessel type classification experiments. BS designed the marine vessel applications (verification, retrieval, recognition, attribute estimation) and implemented and carried out the related experiments. BS proposed superclass generation and EH implemented and executed the task. EH organized the initial manuscript and BS created the supplemental. BS later revised and extended the work and writing. AK coordinated the work during the study and did English revising. All authors read and approved the final manuscript.

Competing interests
The authors declare that they have no competing interests.

References
1. Russakovsky O, Deng J, Su H, Krause J, Satheesh S, Ma S, Huang Z, Karpathy A, Khosla A, Bernstein M, Berg AC, Fei-Fei L (2015) ImageNet large scale visual recognition challenge. Int J Comput Vis (IJCV) 115(3):211–252. doi:10.1007/s11263-015-0816-y
2. Krizhevsky A, Sutskever I, Hinton GE (2012) Imagenet classification with deep convolutional neural networks. In: Proceedings of the 25th International Conference on Neural Information Processing Systems - Volume 1. Curran Associates Inc., Lake Tahoe, Nevada. pp 1097–1105. http://dl.acm.org/citation.cfm?id=2999134.2999257
3. Lin D, Shen X, Lu C, Jia J (2015) Deep lac: Deep localization, alignment and classification for fine-grained recognition. In: 2015 IEEE Conference on Computer Vision and Pattern Recognition (CVPR). pp 1666–1674. doi:10.1109/CVPR.2015.7298775
4. Xie S, Yang T, Wang X, Lin Y (2015) Hyper-class augmented and regularized deep learning for fine-grained image classification. In: 2015 IEEE Conference on Computer Vision and Pattern Recognition (CVPR). pp 2645–2654. doi:10.1109/CVPR.2015.7298880
5. Liu L, Shen C, van den Hengel A (2015) The treasure beneath convolutional layers: Cross-convolutional-layer pooling for image classification. In: 2015 IEEE Conference on Computer Vision and Pattern Recognition (CVPR). pp 4749–4757. doi:10.1109/CVPR.2015.7299107
6. Maji S, Rahtu E, Kannala J, Blaschko M, Vedaldi A (2013) Fine-grained visual classification of aircraft. arXiv preprint arXiv:1306.5151
7. Vedaldi A, Mahendran S, Tsogkas S, Maji S, Girshick R, Kannala J, Rahtu E, Kokkinos I, Blaschko MB, Weiss D, Taskar B, Simonyan K, Saphra N, Mohamed S (2014) Understanding objects in detail with fine-grained attributes. In: Proceedings of the IEEE Conference on Computer Vision and Pattern Recognition. Institute of Electrical and Electronics Engineers, USA. pp 3622–3629
8. Wah C, Branson S, Welinder P, Perona P, Belongie S (2011) The Caltech-UCSD Birds-200-2011 Dataset. Technical Report CNS-TR-2011-001. California Institute of Technology
9. Krause J, Stark M, Deng J, Fei-Fei L (2013) 3d object representations for fine-grained categorization. In: Computer Vision Workshops (ICCVW), 2013 IEEE International Conference On. pp 554–561. doi:10.1109/ICCVW.2013.77
10. Yang L, Luo P, Loy CC, Tang X (2015) A large-scale car dataset for fine-grained categorization and verification. In: 2015 IEEE Conference on Computer Vision and Pattern Recognition (CVPR). pp 3973–3981. doi:10.1109/CVPR.2015.7299023
11. Dao-Duc C, Xiaohui H, Morère O (2015) Maritime vessel images classification using deep convolutional neural networks. In: Proceedings of the Sixth International Symposium on Information and Communication Technology. SoICT 2015. ACM, New York. pp 276–281. doi:10.1145/2833258.2833266. http://doi.acm.org/10.1145/2833258.2833266
12. Ship Photos and Ship Tracker. www.shipspotting.com. Accessed 1 May 2017
13. Gundogdu E, Solmaz B, Yücesoy V, Koç A (2016) MARVEL: a large-scale image dataset for maritime vessels. In: Asian Conference on Computer Vision. Springer International Publishing, Cham. pp 165–180
14. Solmaz B, Gundogdu E, Karaman K, Koç A, et al (2017) Fine-grained visual marine vessel classification for coastal surveillance and defense applications. In: Electro-Optical Remote Sensing XI. vol. 10434. International Society for Optics and Photonics, USA. p 104340A
15. Zhang X, Zhou F, Lin Y, Zhang S (2016) Embedding label structures for fine-grained feature representation. In: Proceedings of the IEEE Conference on Computer Vision and Pattern Recognition. Institute of Electrical and Electronics Engineers, USA. pp 1114–1123
16. Farhadi A, Endres I, Hoiem D, Forsyth D (2009) Describing objects by their attributes. In: 2009 IEEE Conference on Computer Vision and Pattern Recognition. Institute of Electrical and Electronics Engineers, USA. pp 1778–1785. doi:10.1109/CVPR.2009.5206772
17. Lampert CH, Nickisch H, Harmeling S (2009) Learning to detect unseen object classes by between-class attribute transfer. In: Computer Vision and Pattern Recognition, 2009. CVPR 2009. IEEE Conference On. pp 951–958. doi:10.1109/CVPR.2009.5206594
18. Sun Y, Bo L, Fox D (2013) Attribute based object identification. In: 2013 IEEE International Conference on Robotics and Automation, Karlsruhe, Germany, May 6-10, 2013. pp 2096–2103. doi:10.1109/ICRA.2013.6630858
19. Vedaldi A, Lenc K (2015). In: Proceedings of the 23rd ACM international conference on Multimedia. ACM. pp 689–692
20. Chatfield K, Simonyan K, Vedaldi A, Zisserman A (2014) Return of the devil in the details: delving deep into convolutional nets. arXiv preprint arXiv:1405.3531
21. Crammer K, Singer Y (2002) On the learnability and design of output codes for multiclass problems. Mach Learn 47(2):201–233. doi:10.1023/A:1013637720281
22. Keerthi SS, Sundararajan S, Chang KW, Hsieh CJ, Lin CJ (2008) A sequential dual method for large scale multi-class linear svms. In: Proceedings of the 14th ACM SIGKDD International Conference on Knowledge Discovery and Data Mining. KDD '08. ACM, New York. pp 408–416. doi:10.1145/1401890.1401942. http://doi.acm.org/10.1145/1401890.1401942
23. Fan RE, Chang KW, Hsieh CJ, Wang XR, Lin CJ (2008) LIBLINEAR: a library for large linear classification. J Mach Learn Res 9:1871–1874
24. Sun Y, Wang X, Tang X (2014) Deep learning face representation from predicting 10,000 classes. In: 2014 IEEE Conference on Computer Vision and Pattern Recognition. Institute of Electrical and Electronics Engineers, USA. pp 1891–1898. doi:10.1109/CVPR.2014.244
25. Chang CC, Lin CJ (2011) LIBSVM: a library for support vector machines. ACM Trans Intell Syst Technol 2:27–12727. Software available at http://www.csie.ntu.edu.tw/~cjlin/libsvm
26. Hadsell R, Chopra S, LeCun Y (2006) Dimensionality reduction by learning an invariant mapping. In: Computer Vision and Pattern Recognition, 2006 IEEE Computer Society Conference On. vol. 2. IEEE, USA. pp 1735–1742
27. Guo JM, Prasetyo H (2015) Content-based image retrieval using features extracted from halftoning-based block truncation coding. IEEE Trans Image Process 24(3):1010–1024. doi:10.1109/TIP.2014.2372619
28. Qiu G (2003) Color image indexing using btc. IEEE Trans Image Process 12(1):93–101
29. Lai CC, Chen YC (2011) A user-oriented image retrieval system based on interactive genetic algorithm. IEEE Trans Instrum Meas 60(10):3318–3325. doi:10.1109/TIM.2011.2135010
30. Gordo A, Almazan J, Revaud J, Larlus D (2017) End-to-end learning of deep visual representations for image retrieval. Int J Comput Vis 124(2):237–254
31. Lai J, Jiang X (2016) Classwise sparse and collaborative patch representation for face recognition. IEEE Trans Image Process 25(7):3261–3272. doi:10.1109/TIP.2016.2545249

32. Gong D, Li Z, Tao D, Liu J, Li X (2015) A maximum entropy feature descriptor for age invariant face recognition. In: 2015 IEEE Conference on Computer Vision and Pattern Recognition (CVPR). Institute of Electrical and Electronics Engineers, USA. pp 5289–5297. doi:10.1109/CVPR.2015.7299166

33. Lee KC, Ho J, Kriegman DJ (2005) Acquiring linear subspaces for face recognition under variable lighting. IEEE Trans Pattern Anal Mach Intell 27(5):684–698. doi:10.1109/TPAMI.2005.92

34. Sim T, Baker S, Bsat M (2003) The cmu pose, illumination, and expression database. IEEE Trans Pattern Anal Mach Intell 25(12):1615–1618. doi:10.1109/TPAMI.2003.1251154

35. Ricanek K, Tesafaye T (2006) Morph: a longitudinal image database of normal adult age-progression. In: 7th International Conference on Automatic Face and Gesture Recognition (FGR06). pp 341–345. doi:10.1109/FGR.2006.78

36. Turpin EA, McEwen WA (1980) Merchant Marine Officers' Handbook. 4th edn.. Cornell Maritime Press, Centreville, Maryland

37. Schölkopf B, Smola AJ, Williamson RC, Bartlett PL (2000) New support vector algorithms. Neural computation 12(5):1207–1245

14

Efficient video collection association using geometry-aware Bag-of-Iconics representations

Ke Wang[1][*] (iD), Enrique Dunn[2], Mikel Rodriguez[3] and Jan-Michael Frahm[1]

Abstract

Recent years have witnessed the dramatic evolution in visual data volume and processing capabilities. For example, technical advances have enabled 3D modeling from large-scale crowdsourced photo collections. Compared to static image datasets, exploration and exploitation of Internet video collections are still largely unsolved. To address this challenge, we first propose to represent video contents using a histogram representation of iconic imagery attained from relevant visual datasets. We then develop a data-driven framework for a fully unsupervised extraction of such representations. Our novel *Bag-of-Iconics* (BoI) representation efficiently analyzes individual videos within a large-scale video collection. We demonstrate our proposed BoI representation with two novel applications: (1) finding video sequences connecting adjacent landmarks and aligning reconstructed 3D models and (2) retrieving geometrically relevant clips from video collections. Results on crowdsourced datasets illustrate the efficiency and effectiveness of our proposed Bag-of-Iconics representation.

Keywords: Video collection, Video representation, Video retrieval, 3D reconstruction

1 Introduction

Taking photos and video clips has never been easier. One can record videos at high frame rates (e.g., 240 fps are available on the iPhone), in high resolution (4K resolution available on GoPros), or even in 360° [1]. Such technical convenience yields a sheer amount of user-generated visual data being shared over the Internet. For example, over 400 h of videos are uploaded to YouTube every minute [2]. Accordingly, such a huge amount of visual data poses great challenges on storing, analyzing, indexing, and searching these unstructured photo/video collections. To unleash the wealth of information embedded within the ever expanding corpora of visual media, we need efficient and effective content-based data association algorithms for large-scale unordered photo/video collections.

Developing technologies for large-scale visual data collections is at the core of computer vision research. Today,

state-of-the-art methods can process static Internet photo collections for different vision tasks. For example, 3D modeling methods have striven to handle large datasets [3–6], as well as improving model robustness and completeness [7]; modern visual recognition systems can build rich feature hierarchies from large annotated image datasets [8] and perform complicated recognition tasks like image classification [9], object detection [10], and semantic segmentation [11].

Compared to photo collections, the current scope of video analysis mostly focuses on the per-sequence level analysis, with examples of video summarization [12] and action recognition [13]. Discovering inter-sequence relationships among collections of videos is still a largely unaddressed problem.

To tackle such challenge, we propose a novel algorithm that first summarizes common visual elements/entities within the internet video collections as *"iconics."* Iconic images, as used in Frahm et al. [6] and Heinly et al. [7], provide a compact yet informative summarization of the common visual elements occurring within a visual dataset. By representing videos as a histogram of *iconic* occurrences, we can develop efficient algorithms

*Correspondence: kewang@cs.unc.edu
[1]Department of Computer Science, UNC Chapel Hill, 201 S Columbia Street, Chapel Hill 27599, USA
Full list of author information is available at the end of the article

to discover inter-sequence relationships within a video collection. In this paper, we apply the proposed Bag-of-Iconic video representation for novel video analysis applications: in addition to the 3D model alignment task as in our earlier work [14], we demonstrate the usefulness of the Bag-of-Iconic video representation with a novel geometry-aware video retrieval task.

Our major innovations include:

1. A global *Bag-of-Iconics* video representation for collection level video content analysis;
2. A fully automatic and unsupervised framework to find iconic images and build the BoI video representations;
3. Application of the BoI video representation to discover observational connectivities among known 3D landmark models for model alignment;
4. Employing the BoI video representation for geometry-aware video retrieval.

Our paper is organized as follows: Section 2 reviews relevant related works. Section 3 introduces our proposed video representation and explains how to establish it. Section 4 demonstrates how to use the video representation to further enhance model completeness from Internet 3D reconstructions. Section 5 shows geometry-aware video retrieval using the proposed representation. Section 6 concludes our paper.

2 Related work

Large-scale crowdsourced visual data collections have long driven the development of computer vision research. The scope of research covering large-scale visual datasets is broad. In this paper, we mainly focus on discovering inter-sequence relationships within unordered video collections. Thus, we only review relevant solutions to our problem.

2.1 Photo collections

3D modeling first needs to establish pairwise epipolar geometry relationships within photo collections, thus provides a good example for mining inter-element connections within unordered visual datasets. Large-scale structure-from-motion systems started with datasets of a few thousand images [3, 4]. Using image retrieval techniques for overlap prediction, Agarwal et al. [5] processed 150 thousand images in a single day on a computer cluster. Frahm et al. [6] reconstructed 3 million images in one day on a single computer utilizing a compact binary image representation for clustering. Recently, Heinly et al. [7] pushed the envelope to tackle a world-scale dataset (100 million images) by using a streaming paradigm to identify connected images by looking at each image only once.

One of the core computational challenges and the key to improved scalability for large-scale structure-from-motion systems is the efficient mining for element connectivities within photo collections. Li et al. [15] introduced the concept of *iconic images* to model the relationship between different image clusters via iconic scene graphs. Frahm et al. [6] and Heinly et al. [7] further utilized the iconic representation for better scalability. Similarly, our method extends the concept of iconic images to represent visual video contents.

Compared to photo collections, video datasets can contain a much larger number of frames even for small collections. For example, our experiments are conducted on two video collections with more frames than the largest photo collection in [7]. Methods designed for photo collections do not consider the video temporal redundancy, thus cannot scale to video collection problems easily.

2.2 Video collections

As a dual concept to unstructured photo datasets, unordered Internet video collections also exhibit sparsity and lack of structures in the dataset. Tompkin et al. [16] proposed to identify common scenes as "portals" to explore the structure and relationship within a video collection. Using such "portals" as nodes, a connectivity graph can be built from a video collection for interactive visualization and exploration. Our work also identifies common scene elements ("iconics"), but we aim at using a fully unsupervised approach to creating Bag-of-Iconic video representations, which can enable more interesting applications.

2.3 Video summarization

Compared to photo collections, the additional temporal domain in video data, not only provides more information than static images but also brings high redundancy. Selecting informative frames/segments from the videos is essential to achieve high scalability and throughput for real-world large-scale applications. Motion information is a common cue for keyframe selection [17] in video processing. Ahmed et al. [18] explicitly consider epipolar geometry when selecting keyframes for 3D modeling. Compared to keyframe selection, video summarization aims to find the most meaningful/interesting video segments, which can help users to skim long video sequences. Ajmal et al. [19] gives an anatomy of video summarization methods, we refer interested readers to [19] for more details.

2.4 Video retrieval

One application for large video collections is to retrieve *relevant* videos for a given query video. Hu et al. [20] provided a detailed survey on the indexing and retrieval of content-based video retrieval. In this paper, we propose the concept of "geometry-aware" video retrieval: i.e., finding videos that have the same background/entities for a given query video. Such rigid geometric constraints are hard to fulfill by existing video indexing schemes, while our proposed Bag-of-Iconics representation provides a direct solution.

Considering the large volume of the video collections, high-dimensional feature representations can be slow to search/retrieve. Binary hashing [21] together with Hamming space indexing and searching [22] provides a computationally efficient way to scale-up to the size of video databases.

2.5 Camera trajectories

To align separate 3D models into a joint model, we need a camera trajectory that links multiple 3D models. Visual odometry [23] provides a solution of reconstructing such camera trajectories from visual data. Different from visual odometry techniques, Zheng et al. [24] jointly estimates the topology of the objects motion path and reconstructs the 3D object points for dynamic objects in a static scene. In contrast, our work needs to recover the camera motion trajectory to align 3D models and is focused on identifying relevant video (sub)-sequences from a large video collection rather than obtaining the camera motion trajectories.

3 Bag-of-Iconic representation

To build the proposed Bag-of-Iconic representation for videos, we first need to distill the temporal redundancy in the videos by selecting only keyframes (Section 3.1). Visually similar keyframes are then grouped together and each keyframe cluster represents some commonly captured visual entities or structures. An *iconic* image is selected to represent each keyframe cluster (Section 3.2). The set of representing iconic images, when viewed in aggregation, forms a "*visual codebook*" describing the captured visual contents. At individual video sequence level, it encodes how frequently each visual element occurs in a video, and it characterizes and summarizes the video's content. To utilize the visual codebook, we perform geometric verification between the video keyframes and the iconic images to accumulate the histogram of iconic image occurrences (Section 3.3).

3.1 Video keyframe selection

Different from images, the additional temporal domain in videos brings more visual information at the cost of high redundancy and enormous data volumes. Selecting only keyframes from the raw video streams achieves a balance between keeping visual information and lowering computational overhead. To this end, we divide each video $\mathbf{v} = \{f | f \in \mathbf{v}\}$ into small non-overlapping segments $\mathbf{vs} \subseteq \mathbf{v}$ where each segment is represented by one keyframe $kf \in \mathbf{vs} \subseteq \mathbf{v}$.

$$\mathbf{vs}_i \cap \mathbf{vs}_j = \emptyset, \quad \forall i, j, i \neq j \tag{1}$$

Ideally, different keyframes should represent distinct visual elements. The keyframe extraction process must take geometric information into consideration. In addition, the high volume of video collections requires the keyframe selection algorithm to be computationally efficient. With such goals in mind, we choose a GPU-accelerated KLT tracker [25] to select keyframes.

For a new video $\mathbf{v}$, we start processing the first video segment from the beginning and we select the first frame as the first keyframe kf_1. Shi-Tomasi's corner points $\mathbf{x}_1$ [26] are detected within kf_1. At any given timestamp $t + 1$, we keep track of the previous frame f^t and the previous keypoints $\mathbf{x}^t$. The KLT tracker then computes the tracked feature points $\mathbf{x}^{t+1}$ for the current frame f^{t+1}. If the ratio of tracked feature points $\mathbf{x}^{t+1}$ over the current keyframe feature points $\mathbf{x}_i$ falls below the pre-defined threshold of $|\mathbf{x}^{t+1}|/|\mathbf{x}_i| < 20\%$, the current frame f^{t+1} is selected as the new keyframe for the new video segment. Shi-Tomasi's corner points are then re-detected for the new keyframe kf_{i+1} and KLT tacker is re-initialized. Please refer to Fig. 1 for examples of selected video keyframes.

We add the following processing to increase the robustness of the KLT tracker: (a) To compensate for the camera exposure changes, we estimate a global gain ratio β between successive frames f^t and f^{t+1} [27]. Given corresponding pixels $\mathbf{x}^t$ and $\mathbf{x}^{t+1}$ in the frame pair, pixel intensities are related by the multiplicative camera gain model:

$$f^{t+1}\left(\mathbf{x}^{t+1}\right) = \beta f^t\left(\mathbf{x}^t\right) \tag{2}$$

Fig. 1 Examples of extracted keyframes. For visualization purposes, video frames are shown in grayscale and only subset of feature tracks are visualized in color

(b) In crowdsourced video collections, watermarks on border regions of video frames can lead to constantly tracked feature points. Such consistent feature tracks do not help to distinguish the actual visual content between frames. We discard the detection and tracking in video border regions to suppress watermarks. (c) We apply additional forward and backward tracking consistency checks to remove bogus feature tracks.

3.2 Codebook extraction

Similar to large-scale structure-from-motion systems, we enforce a strict epipolar geometry relationship (fundamental matrix or essential matrix [28]) when grouping keyframes together. However, pairwise geometric verification is computationally infeasible for large keyframe collections. Inspired by Heinly et al. [7], we adopted a streaming clustering approach.

Each image cluster has a representing iconic image. SIFT features [29] of all belonging images within the cluster are grouped into a Bag-of-Visual-Word (BoVW) vector. Such augmented BoVW vector is used as the feature representation of the iconic images. Iconic images are indexed in a vocabulary tree [30] for fast retrieval. For each new image I, a small set of iconic images (2 in our case) is retrieved using vocabulary trees. Geometric verification is performed between the unseen image I and every retrieved iconic image. Based on the registration results, different actions are taken: (1) if the new image I fails to register to any retrieved iconic images, it will form its own new cluster with itself being the iconic image; (2) if I registers to multiple iconic images, the registered clusters are merged together as a connected component; and (3) if the new image registers to only one iconic image, image I is added to that cluster.

The first image for each image cluster is chosen as the initial iconic image. Then for each image cluster, the iconic images are updated when different clusters merge together or the size increase of the cluster exceeds a certain threshold. The image that contains the most visual words is selected as the new iconic image in that cluster.

Such process, although with great scalability and throughput, has two issues for extracting compact codebooks. First of all, Heinly et al. [7] constrain the resource consumption by discarding slowly growing image clusters. Depending on the processing ordering of images, such early-stopping strategy can leave similar images in disjoint clusters. Since we treat each iconic image as one entry in the codebook, different codebook elements representing the same visual content can cause ambiguity for later processing. In addition, the total number of discovered image clusters is theoretically unbounded. This causes little practical trouble for the 3D reconstruction problems in Heinly et al. [7], but high dimensionality of the codebook can significantly threaten the efficiency of storing, indexing, and searching large video datasets.

To address such issues, we run a second pass of the clustering algorithm on the keyframe collection to regularize the extracted codebook. Keyframes are randomly shuffled into different orders before the second pass streaming process. By processing the images one more time in different order, separated image clusters due to ordering and discarding reasons can be agglomerated together. Furthermore, image clusters with less than 200 entries are removed from the codebook to reduce the codebook cardinality. Iconic images from all discovered image clusters after the second streaming pass will form the codebook $\mathcal{C} = \{ic_0, ic_1, \ldots, ic_m\}$ together. Examples of iconic images and corresponding image clusters are shown in Fig. 2.

3.3 Video representation extraction

Having extracted keyframes from videos and built codebook $\mathcal{C}$, by generalizing the Bag-of-Visual-Words concept we can build a global descriptor $H(\mathbf{v})$ for each video $\mathbf{v}$. Video keyframes are assigned to high-level "words" in

Fig. 2 Visualization of image clustering on London Flickr dataset (see Section 4.4). First row: iconic views for different connect components. From left to right: Big Ben, Westminster Abbey, London Eye, Buckingham Palace, and Tower Bridge. Second row: selected images from one of the Big Ben image clusters. Images cropped for visualization purposes. Best view in color

the codebook (iconic images). TF-IDF (term frequency-inverse document frequency) weighted numbers of occurrence of each iconic view $ic \in \mathcal{C}$ are then accumulated into a histogram, which is our proposed video descriptor $H(\mathbf{v}) = [h(0), h(1), \ldots, h(m)]$. Strictly speaking, occurrence means a valid geometric registration exists between an iconic image ic and a given keyframe kf.

$$h(i) = W_{TFIDF} \left(\sum_{kf \in \mathbf{v}} GV(kf, ic_i) \right), ic_i \in \mathcal{C}. \qquad (3)$$

where $GV(kf, ic)$ is an indicator function that returns 1 upon successful geometric verification between keyframe kf and iconic image ic, and 0 otherwise. $W_{TFIDF}()$ is the term frequency-inverse document frequency weighting function $w.r.t.$ elements in the iconic codebook $\mathcal{C}$. Weighted histogram $H(\mathbf{v})$ are then normalized to unit length. Compared to using the L_2 normalization scheme alone in Wang et al. [14], adding the TF-IDF weight scheme can better adjust to the bias that some visual elements appear more frequently in general.

Considering the potentially large number of iconic images, to make the video representation extraction process practical, we only perform geometric verification for each keyframe kf with only the two most similar iconic images retrieved using the indexed vocabulary tree, similar to the codebook extraction process (Section 3.2),

The similarity between the visual content of two videos $\mathbf{v}_i$ and $\mathbf{v}_j$ can be computed as the sum of intersections between their histogram representations $H(\mathbf{v}_i)$ and $H(\mathbf{v}_j)$:

$$S\left(H(\mathbf{v}_i), H(\mathbf{v}_j)\right) = \sum_{k=0}^{m} \min\left(h_i(k), h_j(k)\right), \qquad (4)$$

4 3D model connection

Recent advances in large-scale structure-from-motion have striven to handle larger photo collections [5, 6], while improving model robustness and completeness [7]. However, existing methods usually generate 3D models restricted to individual landmarks. We notice two data deficiencies issues that lead to this lack of geospatial connectivity of the 3D models attained from photo collections. Firstly, crowdsourced photos tend to be highly redundant. The viewing directions also tend to converge to a given landmark's most salient regions. Secondly, sampling density erodes towards the model's periphery. Such sampling deficiencies lead to much fewer images in the photo collection depicting scenes in-between landmarks of interest. In addition, state-of-the-art structure from motion systems do not use exhaustive pairwise matching for large-scale datasets. Under-sampled connectivities are more likely to be discarded during the 3D reconstruction process [31].

Auxiliary data sources, like videos, are thus necessary to overcome the data deficiency in photo collections and to obtain more complete models. Intuitively, many sight-seeing videos captured with wearable cameras or

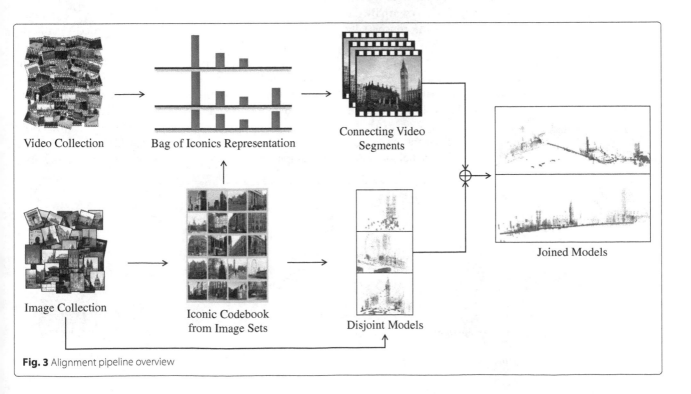

Fig. 3 Alignment pipeline overview

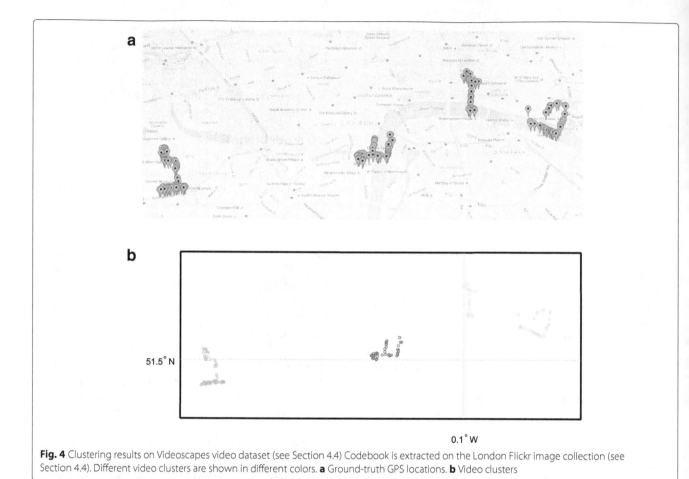

Fig. 4 Clustering results on Videoscapes video dataset (see Section 4.4) Codebook is extracted on the London Flickr image collection (see Section 4.4). Different video clusters are shown in different colors. **a** Ground-truth GPS locations. **b** Video clusters

mobile phones, directly record such missing connectivity information between landmarks, e.g., GoPros worn by the user that continuously capture video. Such geospatially connecting video sequences can be used to join separate 3D models by aligning them to the common camera trajectories. Here, we propose to use our Bag-of-Iconic video representation to efficiently identify such video liaisons from a video collection. An overview can be found in Fig. 3.

Crowdsourced video and image collections can differ greatly in their visual content. Common visual elements

(scenes, structures, objects, be identified to bridge this gap. We use [7] to obtain 3D models from photo collections. The streaming clustering process naturally provides us with a set of *"iconic"* images, which we can use as the codebook $\mathcal{C}$. We propose to uncover the hidden visual connections by reusing the photo collection iconics to represent video contents. Frequent co-occurrences of different visual elements in video sequences strongly indicate the possible connections between different landmarks. Such co-occurrence relationships are efficiently uncovered via clustering over

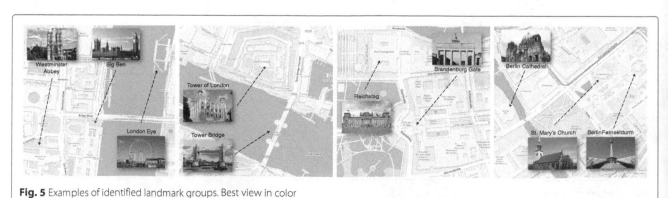

Fig. 5 Examples of identified landmark groups. Best view in color

Table 1 Statistics on crowdsourced image and video collections (Section 4.4)

Dataset	Number of images			Processing time (h)			
	Registered	Iconics	Total	Stream	Densify	SfM	Total
Berlin Flickr	865,699	37,544	2,661,327	18.46	1.89	5.57	25.92
London Flickr	3,716,916	103,290	12,036,991	90.75	7.09	33.83	131.67
	Videos	Length (h)	Frames	Keyframes	Registered	Clusters	
London YouTube	19,217	2,195.96	245,586,526	5,648,490	734,303	4,937	
Berlin YouTube	17,480	2,068.41	223,388,274	4,244,377	636,689	4,135	

Iconics are for clusters of size $\geq$ 200 (Section 3.2). SfM timings are reported on components with $\geq$ 400 images. Video clusters with more than 50 videos are reported. Reported numbers are based on two passes of the dataset

the Bag-of-Iconics representation (Section 4.1). Finally, we pick smoothly transitioning video sub-sequences (Section 4.2) to align separately reconstructed 3D models together (Section 4.3).

4.1 Video representation clustering

Given a collection of 3D models, we need to first identify from video data which of those models are geospatially adjacent. Following the intuition that spatially nearby landmarks appear more often with each other, we cluster the video BoI histograms to uncover the frequently co-occurring iconics. Videos covering the same set of iconics will have a higher similarity score (Eq. 4). If such small groups of geospatially nearby landmarks exist, the video BoI representation should be close to each other within the BoI space. We adopted the mean shift clustering algorithm [32] to identify such landmark groups. An empirical value of 0.1 is used as the clustering bandwidth d. The histogram intersection kernel (Eq. 4) is used as the weighting function. As shown in Fig. 4, clustering videos in the BoI space can successfully group them by geospatial proximity.

Geospatially adjacent landmarks can then be identified from the clustered video histograms as common high peaks in the histogram representations (Fig. 5). To suppress noise, we compute the average histogram $\tilde{H}$ of the descriptor cluster $\mathcal{H} = \{H(\mathbf{v}_1), \ldots, H(\mathbf{v}_l)\}$ as:

$$\tilde{H} = \left[\tilde{h}(0), \tilde{h}(1), \ldots, \tilde{h}(m)\right], \tilde{h}(i) = \frac{\sum_{H \in \mathcal{H}} h_H(i)}{|\mathcal{H}|}. \quad (5)$$

The underlying landmark group corresponds to a minimal subset of histogram bins $\{c | c \in \mathcal{C}_\mathcal{H} \subseteq \mathcal{C}\}$ that sum

up to a pre-defined threshold $\sum_{c \in \mathcal{C}_\mathcal{H}} \tilde{h}(c) \geq \tau$. Without loss of generality, we sort the bins of the average histogram $\tilde{H}$ into descending order H', where $h'(0) \geq h'(1) \geq \cdots \geq h'(m)$. Then we can select the minimal subset of bins $\mathcal{C}_\mathcal{H} = \{0, 1, \ldots, S\}$ such that $\sum_{i=0}^{S} h'(i) \geq \tau$, where $\tau = 0.70$.

4.2 Optimal video sequence selection

To align disjoint reconstructed 3D models together, smooth and continuous camera motion trajectories are preferred. The BoI histogram representation does not contain temporal information, thus we need to inspect the videos again to pick suitable video sequences.

Given a group of adjacent landmarks $\mathcal{C}_\mathcal{H}$ and the corresponding set of videos $\{\mathbf{v}_H | H \in \mathcal{H}\}$, we first need to filter out invalid video sequences $\mathbf{v}_H$ that cannot connect the separately reconstructed 3D models. A valid video path is a set of consecutive video segments $Path(\mathbf{v}) = \{vs_i, vs_{i+1}, vs_{i+2}, \ldots, vs_{i+k}\}$ where the keyframes (kf_i and kf_{i+k}, respectively) of the ending video segments (vs_i and vs_{i+k}, respectively) have valid registrations with respect to the landmark iconic image set $\mathcal{C}_\mathcal{H}$. We loosen the registration constraints on the in-between video segments $vs_{i+1}, \ldots, vs_{i+k-1}$ because of the photo collection data sampling density decrease towards the periphery of landmark models.

To reconstruct the camera motion trajectory Path(**v**) of the video **v**, we uniformly re-sample the video sequence Path(**v**) and obtain a frame sequence F. A good frame sequence $F(Path(\mathbf{v})) = [f_0, f_1, \ldots, f_M]$ should exhibit smoothness in camera motion without abrupt motion or motion discontinuities. To pick better frame sequences,

Table 2 Processing time (in hours) of each stage of our proposed 3D model alignment algorithm

Dataset	Keyframe	Histogram	Clustering	Scoring	SfM	Merging	Total
London YouTube	227.34	11.73	6.10	132.17	4.37	2.25	383.96
Berlin YouTube	206.84	9.12	5.37	146.84	3.10	1.12	372.39

SfM timing reported on top 30 video sub-sequences

we use the geometric mean of the inlier ratio of the tracked features between every consecutive frame pair in the sequence F as the smoothing score for F:

$$\text{Score}(F) = \sqrt[M+1]{\prod_{i=1}^{M} T(f_{i-1}, f_i)}, \tag{6}$$

where $T(f_{i_1}, f_i)$ is the ratio of tracked features between frame f_{i-1} and frame f_i, computed by the bi-directional KLT tracker as in Section 3.1. The KLT tracker is re-initialized for at frame f_i for each frame pair (f_i, f_{i+1}).

4.3 Model reconstruction and merging

Having obtained the frame sequence F and the 3D models, a simple solution to align the 3D models together is to run structure from motion on all the registered images belonging to 3D models and the frame sequence F together. Such direct approach is computationally too heavy, especially for larger models. Instead, we propose a significantly more efficient approach: we first reconstruct the camera motion trajectory from selected video sequences alone, and then align the 3D models to the camera trajectory model.

Colmap [33] is used to obtain the 3D model V from the video frame sequence F (Section 4.2). Landmark 3D

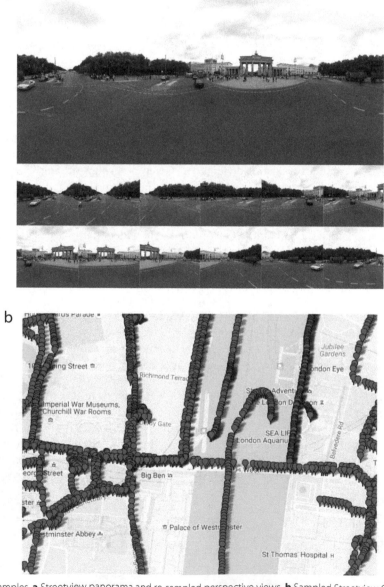

Fig. 6 Streetview images examples. **a** Streetview panorama and re-sampled perspective views. **b** Sampled Streetview GPS locations

models $L_0, L_1, \ldots, L_n$ from photo collections are obtained as in Heinly et al. [7]. To align a landmark 3D model L_i to the camera motion trajectory V, we need to estimate a similarity transformation: a rotation $\mathbf{R} \in \mathbb{R}^{3 \times 3}$, a translation $\mathbf{t} \in \mathbb{R}^3$, and a scaling factor $s \in \mathbb{R}$.

The key to obtaining the similarity transformation lies in the fact that frames within the camera frame sequence F can register to both the camera trajectory model V and the landmark model L_i. Given a video frame f, let $\mathbf{R}_i^L, \mathbf{t}_i^L$ be its rotation and translation of video frame f_i w.r.t. landmark model L, and R_i^V, t_i^V be its rotation and translation against video trajectory model V. The desired similarity transformation aligning the model L to the video camera trajectory model V can be calculated as:

$$\mathbf{R} = \mathbf{R}_i^{V^T} \cdot \mathbf{R}_i^L, s = \frac{\left\| \mathbf{c}_i^V - \mathbf{c}_j^V \right\|_2}{\left\| \mathbf{c}_i^L - \mathbf{c}_j^L \right\|_2}, \mathbf{t} = \mathbf{c}_i^V - s\mathbf{R}\mathbf{c}_i^L. \quad (7)$$

where $\mathbf{c} \in \mathbb{R}^3$ is the camera location. Transformations obtained from multiple video frames are averaged and further optimized by bundle adjustment [34].

4.4 Datasets and setup

We demonstrated the effectiveness of our proposed model alignment on multiple crowdsourced datasets. Two unordered Internet photo collections from Flickr covering London and Berlin are obtained from the authors of [6] (see Table 1 for the dataset statistics). Two crowdsourced video collections and one manually collected video collection are then used to separately align the disjoint models. Two Internet video collections (covering London and Berlin respectively) are obtained from YouTube by text and geo-location-based queries within the "travel" and "events" video subcategory s. The crowdsourced video collections contain great variances in video resolutions, frame rates, bit rates, etc. We limit the maximum resolution of download for YouTube videos to be 1080P for efficient storage and processing. The Videoscapes dataset [16] is a manually collected video dataset, covering major landmarks in London with ground-truth GPS trajectories.

We implemented the proposed pipeline in C++ & Python. A single computer with 192 GB memory, a 32-core 2 GHz Intel Xeon CPU, and three nVidia Tesla K20c GPUs, is used for our experimental evaluations. Detailed

timings can be found in Tables 1 and 2, respectively. To the best of our knowledge, processing such large-scale hybrid visual datasets on a single computer in a few days is unprecedented.

4.5 Inter-model alignment results

Registration can only be achieved on 15% videos of the Berlin video dataset and 13% videos of the London video dataset. While [7] registered 26% images on Berlin image dataset and 25% on London image dataset, the different characteristics of the video dataset are the main reason for lower registration rate on video collections. We borrowed the iconic codebook from the image dataset to search for video segments connecting landmarks. Considering the vast differences between photo and video datasets, the visual content of videos cannot be fully summarized by the iconic codebook from photo collections. Lower registration rate on video collections actually reveals the fact that by using the photo collection codebook, only relevant video contents are considered for our model alignment problem.

Our proposed pipeline has smaller throughput compared to state-of-the-art [7] (Table 1) because (1) we iterate the dataset for an additional pass; and (2) we have inferior computation capability with our hardware platform compared to [7].

Qualitative results are presented in Figs. 11 and 12. All results in London are reported on the crowdsourced YouTube video dataset. We then utilize geo-registered streetview (SV) images for a quantitative evaluation (Fig. 6). Although many crowdsourced images contain geo-tags, we did not utilize such information for registration in our algorithms. In addition, streetview images have higher GPS accuracy [35]. Google streetview images are stored as equirectangular panoramas. We re-sampled perspective images from 12 uniformly distributed viewing angles of each panorama. The obtained perspective views are then registered to the 3D SfM models (from Section 4.3) to get ground-truth inter-model transformations.

For quantitative evaluation, the coordinate system of one 3D landmark model is used as the reference coordinate system. The similarity transformations (rotation $\mathbf{R}$, translation $\mathbf{t}$, and scaling s) of other landmark models with

Table 3 Quantitative evaluations of model alignment. Euclidean distance in meters are reported for positional errors

Evaluated model	London eye	Westminster Abbey	Tower of London	Brandenburg gate	Average
Reference model	Big Ben	Big Ben	Tower Bridge	Reichastag	
Orientation error (°)	6.94	5.46	4.38	8.34	6.28
Position error (m)	1.71	0.96	3.15	2.76	2.15
Scaling error (%)	3.42	4.67	9.19	2.47	4.94

Rotations are converted to axis-angle representation, and errors are reported as average angle differences in degrees. Relative errors in percentage are reported for scaling

Table 4 Comparison of different keyframe extraction algorithms. Experiments are performed on the Videoscape dataset 4.4

Method	Speed (Hz)	Keyframes	Iconics	Clustering time (min)
Intensity	1057.2	2784	759	9.8
Tracking	301.8	1298	622	6.6
[18]	15.76	962	619	6.1

respect to the reference model is computed as Eq. (7). As shown in Table 3, our proposed method successfully discovered the geospatial relationships from the video collections and produced accurate spatial transformations to align separate 3D landmark models.

4.6 Discussions

4.6.1 Keyframe selection

As seen in Table 2, keyframe extraction takes the majority of the video processing time. But the quality of selected video keyframes is critical for extracting meaningful BoI representations and controlling the keyframe collection sizes.

Notice in Table 1 that the total number of raw frames exceeds even the 100 million images dataset in [7]. To make the entire pipeline feasible with limited computational resources, it is necessary to reduce redundant video data to distinctive and representative keyframes. Though keyframe extraction is taking a majority of the processing time, without it later stages would suffer from intractably high volumes of data.

To further justify our choice of KLT tracking, we compare our GPU-based KLT tracker with two different keyframe selection strategies. One is a fast frame intensity based keyframe selection algorithm: where each frame is represented as the concatenation of the integrated row and column pixel intensities; frame vectors are normalized to unit length; subsequent frame vector is compared against the previous keyframe vector, whenever significant changes are detected (Euclidean distance larger than 0.2) the current subsequent frame is selected as a new keyframe. The other method [18] explicitly evaluates frame-to-frame point correspondence sets as well as frame-to-frame epipolar geometries (homography and

fundamental matrix), thus avoiding motion and structure degeneracy to select more robust keyframes for 3D reconstruction purposes.

As can be seen in Table 4, the appearance based keyframe extraction algorithm is much faster, but it produced significantly more keyframes and thus greatly burdens the later clustering stage. The more expensive keyframe selection method [18] generated fewer keyframes but a similar number of iconics, which means it summarized the visual dataset with fewer iconic images. However, the superiority of its keyframe quality cannot compensate for its huge computation overhead when seen in the context of the overall method.

4.6.2 Histogram clustering

Our proposed method can successfully discover the geospatial relationships from video collections and align the corresponding 3D landmark models, as shown in Figs. 11 and 12. However, our method empirically finds small groups of landmarks. We contribute this to the following reasons:

1. Many video clusters have a single major peak. Single mode descriptors correspond to videos that describe a single landmark. Such video clusters do not bring extra information for model alignment tasks.
2. The smaller bandwidth parameter d used in the mean shift clustering algorithm prefers more tightly coupled video clusters. But greater bandwidth d is more error-prone to noise in the BoI descriptors. Further exploration is needed on how to select the bandwidth d.
3. There exists a limited number of geospatially adjacent landmarks. The farther away the landmarks

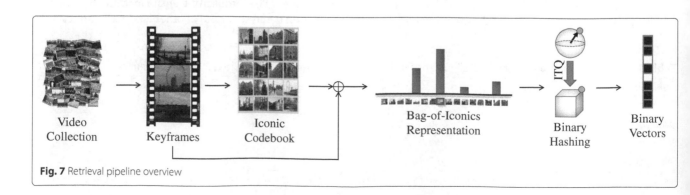

Fig. 7 Retrieval pipeline overview

Table 5 Statistics of video retrieval datasets

Training dataset	Video		Frame				Time (h)	
	Total	Registered	Total	Keyframe	Registered	Iconics	Keyframe	Clustering
Augmented Videoscape	901	659	605,544	2784	2575	622	0.05	0.11
London YouTube	15,417	4691	184,189,894	4,518,792	1,402,825	97,048	179.58	4.68
Berlin YouTube	13,984	4317	179,380,784	3,395,501	1,086,560	83,262	165.47	4.30

are, the longer videos need to be to capture the necessary trajectories. Such verbose and long videos are generally of less interest to the general public and more burdensome to capture, thus are harder to find in the public domain.

5 Geometry-aware video retrieval

Given an example video, finding relevant or similar videos that share the same geometry background or geometric entity can be helpful for many applications: duplicate detection, surveillance, and geo-localization, to name a few. Our BoI representation makes it possible to retrieve geometrically similar videos in large-scale datasets. To further scale-up the target database, we demonstrate that through state-of-the-art binary hashing [21], indexing, and searching techniques [22], our proposed BoI representations can perform geometry-aware video retrieval very effectively and efficiently. An overview of the geometry-aware retrieval pipeline is shown in Fig. 7.

For searching the video database, we first follow Section 3 to extract the iconic codebook and build the BoI representations for all database videos. For a given query video, we follow the same algorithm (Section 3.3) and build the corresponding BoI vector. Finding geometrically relevant videos is then equivalent to performing a nearest neighbor search in the BoI space using the histogram intersection kernel (Eq. 4) [36].

It would be challenging to index and search the BoI vector databases if the extracted codebook $\mathcal{C}$ contains a large number of iconic images for a very large video collection. Compact binary representations provide opportunities to easily scale up the target database. We leverage one of the state-of-the-art binary hashing techniques: iterative quantization (ITQ) [21] to hash the BoI vector representation

Table 6 Speed for geometry-aware video retrieval tasks. Time is given in milliseconds

Target dataset	Size	Search space	
		Original BoI	Binary BoI
London training	15,417	1425.18	9.82
Berlin training	13,984	1251.76	8.79

into a fixed-length binary string (128 bit in our example, two words on modern 64-bit architectures). Geometry-aware video retrieval is first done in the binary Hamming space with multi-indexed hashing [22]. Then re-ranking in the original BoI space is performed for top 128 retrieved results in the binary space.

5.1 Datasets and setup

We use the same hardware platform as in Section 4.4 to perform experimental evaluations for the geometry-aware video retrieval tasks. The same datasets used in Section 4.4 are also employed for our retrieval evaluation.

For the crowdsourced London and Berlin datasets, no ground-truth GPS annotation is available. The Videoscapes dataset [16], however, recorded the ground-truth GPS trajectories for each video within the dataset. The original Videoscapes dataset provides less than 300 hundred videos, with a total length of around 3 h. To demonstrate the scalability of our proposed retrieval approach, we augmented the original Videoscapes dataset by randomly partitioning the original video sequences into shorter but temporally overlapping video sequences. In this way, we can increase the cardinality of the video collections with known geometric connections.

For each of the datasets (London YouTube, Berlin YouTube, and augmented Videoscape), we randomly split the video collection into a disjoint 80% training dataset and a 20% testing dataset. Please refer to Table 5 for training set statistics. We follow Section 3 to extract the codebook and build the BoI representation for the database videos for each training dataset.

For a given query video, each keyframe takes 30 ms to test for occurrence in the BoI histogram, including SIFT [29] feature extraction, visual world quantization, vocabulary tree querying, and geometric verification. Detailed retrieval speed in given in Table 6. For example, the London YouTube training dataset contains 15,417 training videos. Our direct video retrieval in BoI space takes less than 1.5 s after the BoI vector is obtained for the query video. Once binary representation is obtained, similar videos can be retrieved within 10 ms. By compressing and indexing the original BoI vector into binary hamming space, we can achieve significant speedup for the retrieval tasks.

Fig. 8 Examples of identified *iconic* images on YouTube video keyframes. Best view in color

5.2 Results

Identified iconic images are visualized in Fig. 8. Iconic images from the London YouTube training dataset demonstrated greater variety in terms of visual content. The variety in iconic views can form a better group of *bases* for representing individual videos. Compared to *borrowing* codebook from photo collections (Section 4), directly extracting iconic codebook from video keyframes can lead to higher registration rate. Thirty percent of videos are registered in the London training dataset (Table 5) using the video iconic codebook, while only 13% of videos are registered in the London dataset (Table 1) using the photo iconic codebook. Being able to find a group of well-formed bases from noisy crowdsourced data further demonstrated the robustness and effectiveness of our proposed BoI representation.

Qualitative retrieval results from the two YouTube datasets are shown in Fig. 10. Although the dataset is large and noisy, we can successfully retrieve geometrically relevant videos. This underlines the efficiency, effectiveness, and scalability of our proposed representation for large-scale video retrieval tasks.

Quantitatively evaluations of the retrieval performance of our BoI representation are performed on the augmented Videoscapes dataset. For each query video, training videos that lie in a 50-m radius are defined as the ground truth. We achieve a precision of over 0.90 at a recall rate of 0.36 with BoI vectors, and a precision of 0.85 with binary codes at the same recall rate. Detailed precision-recall curves can be found in Fig. 9. By compressing the original high-dimensional sparse BoI vectors into compact binary descriptors, over $100\times$ speed up can be achieved with sacrificing 0.05 precision at 0.30 recall. In general, our proposed Bag-of-Iconics representation is effective for video retrieval tasks, and robust under different distance metrics.

We further explored different options for building BoI histograms with extracted codebooks. For example, BoI histograms are built with a different number of similar iconic images, with/without geometric verification. Quantitative evaluations can be found in Fig. 9. With geometric verification enabled, increasing the number of the nearest neighbors has a negligible impact on retrieval performance (see 2-NN-GV and 5-NN-GV precision-recall curves). Similar iconic images without rigid geometric transformations are filtered out in the histogram, and thereby removing the noise. Without geometric verification, the iconic image retrieval error will be amplified with an increasing number of nearest neighbors. For

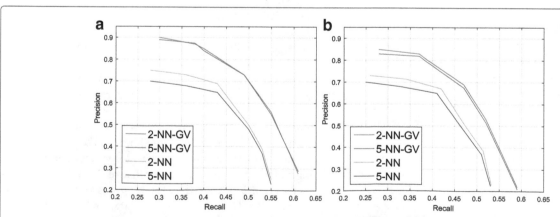

Fig. 9 Precision-recall curves for retrieval tasks. 2-NN-GV: BoI vectors are obtained with two nearest neighbor search followed by geometric verification; 5-NN-GV: 5 nearest neighbor search followed by geometric verification; 2-NN, 5-NN: nearest neighbor search without geometric verification. Geometric verification is critical for accurate retrieval. **a** Precison-recall for video retrieval on BoI vectors. **b** Precison-Recall for video retrieval on binary BoI vectors

Table 7 Performance evaluation for geometry-aware video retrieval tasks

Feature	SIFT-BOW	BOI	CNN
Precision	0.81	0.90	0.69
Recall	0.35	0.36	0.28

example, 5-NN have lower accuracy than 2-NN in both BoI histogram and binary retrieval. Thus, geometric verification is critical for our proposed representation to achieve high quality results.

We also compare our proposed BOI feature representation against other feature representations for the geometry-aware video retrieval task. Experimental comparisons are performed on the augmented Videoscapes dataset. For each query video, training videos within a 50-m range are considered as ground truth.

Convolutional neural networks (CNN) have demonstrated their successes in extracting feature representations from visual inputs. Thus we also compare our BoI representation with CNN based features. The ResNet-50 network pretrained on ImageNet dataset [37] is used as feature extractor. Output from the last fully-connected layer is used as the visual feature representation. For a given video, keyframes are extracted as described in Section 3.1. The convolutional feature representation for each keyframe is obtained by feeding the keyframe into the ResNet-50 neural network. Then, feature vectors for all keyframes are averaged together to get the video feature representation. We also compare our BoI representation with the traditional Bag-of-Visual-words representation. For each video, SIFT features from all extracted keyframes are aggregated into the Bag-of-Words histogram to build the global feature representation.

Detailed performances can be found in Table 7. For our novel geometry-aware video retrieval task, our proposed BoI representation exceeds the traditional BoW. Surprisingly, CNN based features do not show strong performances. For one thing, the pre-trained network is not fine-tuned on our video data, thus may not be able to provide the optimal feature representation for this task. For another, CNNs are great at high level semantic visual tasks. However, our proposed geometry-aware video retrieval task enforces low-level geometric constraints, which the CNN is not exposed to during its training process. We leave as future work integrating such geometry constraints into the end-to-end learning framework of CNN models.

Fig. 10 Qualitative video retrieval results on YouTube dataset. Each row represents a query, with first column showing an example keyframe of the query video and other columns showing keyframes of retrieved videos. Correct retrieval results highlighted in blue, incorrect in red. Best view in color

5.3 Discussions

We have proposed a "Bag-of-Iconics" representation for the analysis of large-scale unstructured video collections. Our results reveal the importance of geometric verification. On the "scene" level of abstraction, the detection of scene similarity/overlap among videos provides a shared context among visual data that is robust to a certain class of scene dynamic content, e.g., we can associate different events recorded in a common setting through background co-occurrence (see Fig. 10).

The experimental results in Section 5.2 show the effectiveness of our proposed BoI representation, but also reveal several opportunities for further improvements and research efforts (Figs. 11 and 12).

5.3.1 Association completeness

Constructing the iconic codebook through a combination of keyframe-based processing and our aggressive reduction of the image association space will inevitably compromise completeness. Going forward, we will explore the use of recent efficiency-driven pairwise geometric verification methods, e.g., [38, 39], to expand the scope of image associations within our streaming framework.

5.3.2 Spatio-temporal representation

Our implementation focuses on geometric similarity as an association cue. However, for tasks like video semantic classification, or action recognition, the temporal ordering of the observation provides valuable information not currently integrated into our framework. We will explore

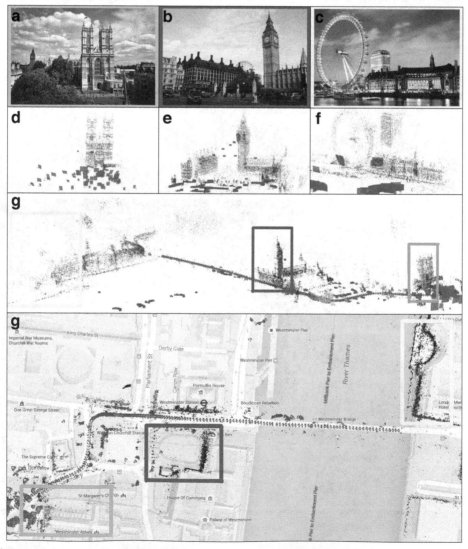

Fig. 11 Example of 3D model alignment. Separate 3D models (**d–f**), for Westminster Abbey (**a**), Big Ben (**b**), and London Eye (**c**) can be obtained from image collections. Our proposed method can find video segments that links these three models together, as shown in (**g, h**). Best view in color

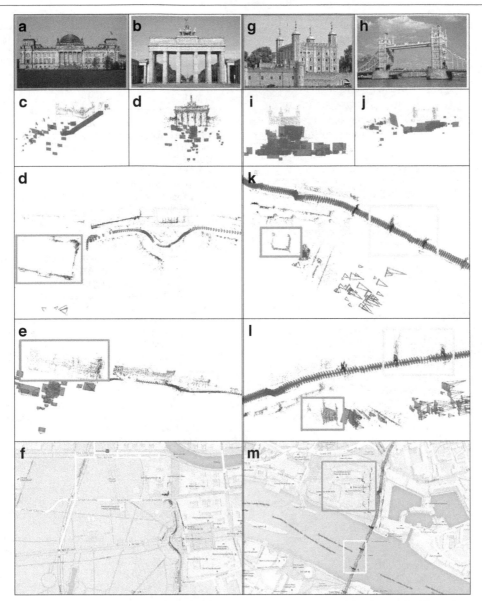

Fig. 12 Example of 3D model alignment. Visualizations obtained from the Berlin and London YouTube dataset. Reichastag (**a, c**) and Brandenburg Gate (**b, d**) are aligned by video trajectory (**f**) as shown in (**d, e**). Tower of London (**g, i**) and Tower Bridge (**h, j**) are aligned by the video trajectory (**m**) as shown in (**k, l**). Best view in color

possible extensions to our current BoI representation to incorporate temporal information.

6 Conclusions

In this paper, we tackle the problem of understanding inter-sequence relationships within a large-scale video datasets. To this end, we propose to represent videos as a bag of iconic images. We develop a fully automatic and unsupervised approach to summarize a crowdsourced video collection by a compact set of representative iconic images. We further demonstrate the effectiveness of our proposed BoI representation through two novel applications: (1) retrieving geometry-aware relevant videos from a video collection and (2) mining geospatially adjacent landmarks and align reconstructed 3D models together using common video motion trajectories. For future research, we plan to apply the Bag-of-Iconic representation for new video analysis tasks.

Acknowledgements
Supported in part by the NSF No. IIS-1349074, No. CNS-1405847. Partially funded by MITRE Corp.

Authors' contributions
All authors read and approved the final manuscript.

Competing interests
The authors declare that they have no competing interests.

Author details
[1] Department of Computer Science, UNC Chapel Hill, 201 S Columbia Street, Chapel Hill 27599, USA. [2] Department of Computer Science, Stevens Institute of Technology, 1 Castle Point Terrace, Hoboken 07030, USA. [3] MITRE Corporation, 202 Burlington Rd, Bedford 01730, USA.

References

1. Anderson R, Gallup D, Barron JT, Kontkanen J, Snavely N, Hernández C, Agarwal S, Seitz SM (2016) Jump: virtual reality video. ACM Trans Graphics (TOG) 35(6):198

2. (2017) 160 Amazing YouTube Statistics. http://expandedramblings.com/index.php/youtube-statistics/. Accessed May 2017

3. Snavely N, Seitz SM, Szeliski R (2006) Photo tourism: exploring photo collections in 3D. ACM Trans. Graph. 25(3):835–846. doi:10.1145/1141911.1141964. http://doi.acm.org/10.1145/1141911.1141964

4. Snavely N, Seitz SM, Szeliski R (2008) Modeling the world from internet photo collections. IJCV 80(2):189–210

5. Agarwal S, Furukawa Y, Snavely N, Simon I, Curless B, Seitz SM, Szeliski R (2011) Building rome in a day. Commun ACM 54(10):105–112

6. Frahm JM, Fite-Georgel P, Gallup D, Johnson T, Raguram R, Wu C, Jen Y-H, Dunn E, Clipp B, Lazebnik S, Pollefeys Marc (2010) Building Rome on a cloudless day. In: Daniilidis K, Maragos P, Paragios N (eds) Computer Vision – ECCV 2010: 11th European Conference on Computer Vision, Heraklion, Crete, Greece, September 5-11, 2010, Proceedings, Part IV. Springer Berlin Heidelberg, Berlin. pp 368–381. doi:10.1007/978-3-642-15561-1_27. https://doi.org/10.1007/978-3-642-15561-1_27

7. Heinly J, Schönberger JL, Dunn E, Frahm JM (2015) Reconstructing the world* in six days. In: 2015 IEEE Conference on Computer Vision and Pattern Recognition (CVPR). pp 3287–3295. doi:10.1109/CVPR.2015.7298949

8. Russakovsky O, Deng J, Su H, Krause J, Satheesh S, Ma S, Huang Z, Karpathy A, Khosla A, Bernstein M, Berg AC, Fei-Fei L (2015) ImageNet large scale visual recognition challenge. Int J Comput Vis (IJCV) 115(3):211–252. doi:10.1007/s11263-015-0816-y

9. Krizhevsky A, Sutskever I, Hinton GE (2012) Imagenet classification with deep convolutional neural networks. In: Pereira F, Burges CJC, Bottou L, Weinberger KQ (eds). Advances in Neural Information Processing Systems 25. Curran Associates, Inc. pp 1097–1105. http://papers.nips.cc/paper/4824-imagenet-classification-with-deep-convolutional-neural-networks.pdf

10. Girshick R, Donahue J, Darrell T, Malik J (2014) Rich feature hierarchies for accurate object detection and semantic segmentation. In: 2014 IEEE Conference on Computer Vision and Pattern Recognition. pp 580–587. doi:10.1109/CVPR.2014.81

11. Shelhamer E, Long J, Darrell T (2017) Fully convolutional networks for semantic segmentation. IEEE Trans Pattern Anal Mach Intell 39(4):640–651. doi:10.1109/TPAMI.2016.2572683

12. Zhao B, Xing EP (2014) Quasi real-time summarization for consumer videos. In: 2014 IEEE Conference on Computer Vision and Pattern Recognition. pp 2513–2520. doi:10.1109/CVPR.2014.322

13. Simonyan K, Zisserman A (2014) Two-stream convolutional networks for action recognition in videos. In: Ghahramani Z, Welling M, Cortes C, Lawrence ND, Weinberger KQ (eds). Advances in Neural Information Processing Systems 27. Curran Associates, Inc. pp 568–576. http://papers.nips.cc/paper/5353-two-stream-convolutional-networks-for-action-recognition-in-videos.pdf

14. Wang K, Dunn E, Rodriguez M, Frahm JM (2017) Computer Vision – ACCV 2016: 13th Asian Conference on Computer Vision, Taipei, Taiwan, November 20-24, 2016, Revised Selected Papers, Part IV. In: Lai S-H, Lepetit V, Nishino K, Sato Y (eds). Springer, Cham. pp 408–23

15. Raguram R, Wu C, Frahm J-M, Lazebnik S (2011) Modeling and recognition of landmark image collections using iconic scene graphs. Int J Comput Vis 95(3):213–239. doi:10.1007/s11263-011-0445-z. https://doi.org/10.1007/s11263-011-0445-z

16. Tompkin J, Kim KI, Kautz J, Theobalt C (2012) Videoscapes: exploring sparse, unstructured video collections. ACM Trans Graph 31(4):68:1–68:12. doi:10.1145/2185520.2185564. http://doi.acm.org/10.1145/2185520.2185564

17. Wolf W (1996) Key frame selection by motion analysis. In: Acoustics, Speech, and Signal Processing, 1996. ICASSP-96. Conference Proceedings., 1996 IEEE International Conference On, vol. 2. IEEE. pp 1228–31

18. Ahmed MT, Dailey MN, Landabaso JL, Herrero N (2010) Robust key frame extraction for 3D reconstruction from video streams. In: VISAPP (1). pp 231–236

19. Ajmal M, Ashraf MH, Shakir M, Abbas Y, Shah FA (2012) Video summarization: techniques and classification. In: Bolc L, Tadeusiewicz R, Chmielewski LJ, Wojciechowski K (eds). Computer Vision and Graphics: International Conference, ICCVG 2012, Warsaw, Poland, September 24-26, 2012. Proceedings. Springer Berlin Heidelberg, Berlin. pp 1–13. doi:10.1007/978-3-642-33564-8_1. https://doi.org/10.1007/978-3-642-33564-8_1

20. Hu W, Xie N, Li L, Zeng X, Maybank S (2011) A survey on visual content-based video indexing and retrieval. IEEE Trans Syst Man Cybernet Part C Appl Rev 41(6):797-819. doi:10.1109/TSMCC.2011.2109710

21. Gong Y, Lazebnik S, Gordo A, Perronnin F (2013) Iterative quantization: a procrustean approach to learning binary codes for large-scale image retrieval. TPAMI 35(12):2916–2929

22. Norouzi M, Punjani A, Fleet DJ (2012) Fast search in hamming space with multi-index hashing. In: 2012 IEEE Conference on Computer Vision and Pattern Recognition. pp 3108–3115. doi:10.1109/CVPR.2012.6248043

23. Scaramuzza D, Fraundorfer F (2011) Visual odometry [tutorial]. IEEE Robot Automation Mag 18(4):80–92. doi:10.1109/MRA.2011.943233

24. Zheng E, Wang K, Dunn E, Frahm JM (2014) Joint object class sequencing and trajectory triangulation (jost). In: Fleet D, Pajdla T, Schiele B, Tuytelaars T (eds). Computer Vision – ECCV 2014. Lecture Notes in Computer Science, vol. 8695. Springer, New York. pp 599–614

25. Zach C, Gallup D, Frahm JM (2008) Fast gain-adaptive KLT tracking on the GPU. In: 2008 IEEE Computer Society Conference on Computer Vision and Pattern Recognition Workshops. pp 1–7. doi:10.1109/CVPRW.2008.4563089

26. Shi J, Tomasi C (1994) Good features to track. In: 1994 Proceedings of IEEE Conference on Computer Vision and Pattern Recognition. pp 593–600. doi:10.1109/CVPR.1994.323794

27. Kim SJ, Frahm JM, Pollefeys M (2007) Joint feature tracking and radiometric calibration from auto-exposure video. In: 2007 IEEE 11th International Conference on Computer Vision. IEEE. pp 1–8. doi:10.1109/ICCV.2007.4408945

28. Hartley RI, Zisserman A (2004) Multiple view geometry in computer vision, 2nd edn. Cambridge University Press, Cambridge

29. Lowe DG (2004) Distinctive image features from scale-invariant keypoints. IJCV 60(2):91–110

30. Nistér D, Stewenius H (2006) Scalable recognition with a vocabulary tree. In: 2006 IEEE Computer Society Conference on Computer Vision and Pattern Recognition (CVPR'06), vol. 2. pp 2161–2168. doi:10.1109/CVPR.2006.264

31. Lou Y, Snavely N, Gehrke J (2012) MatchMiner: efficient spanning structure mining in large image collections. In: Fitzgibbon A, Lazebnik S, Perona P, Sato Y, Schmid C (eds). Computer Vision – ECCV 2012: 12th European Conference on Computer Vision, Florence, Italy, October 7-13, 2012, Proceedings, Part II. Springer Berlin Heidelberg, Berlin. pp 45–58. doi:10.1007/978-3-642-33709-3_4. https://doi.org/10.1007/978-3-642-33709-3_4

32. Comaniciu D, Meer P (2002) Mean shift: a robust approach toward feature space analysis. IEEE Trans Pattern Anal Mach Intell 24(5):603–619. doi:10.1109/34.1000236

33. Schonberger JL, Frahm JM (2016) Structure-from-motion revisited. In: 2016 IEEE Conference on Computer Vision and Pattern Recognition (CVPR). pp 4104–4113. doi:10.1109/CVPR.2016.445

34. Agarwal S, Mierle K Others: ceres solver. http://ceres-solver.org. Accessed 02 Dec 2017

35. Klingner B, Martin D, Roseborough J (2013) Street view motion-from-structure-from-motion. In: 2013 IEEE International Conference on Computer Vision. pp 953–960. doi:10.1109/ICCV.2013.122

36. Muja M, Lowe DG (2014) Scalable nearest neighbor algorithms for high dimensional data. IEEE Trans Pattern Anal Mach Intell 36(11):2227-2240. doi:10.1109/TPAMI.2014.2321376

37. He K, Zhang X, Ren S, Sun J (2016) Deep residual learning for image recognition. In: 2016 IEEE Conference on Computer Vision and Pattern Recognition (CVPR). pp 770–778. doi:10.1109/CVPR.2016.90

38. Havlena M, Schindler K (2014) Vocmatch: efficient multiview correspondence for structure from motion. In: Fleet D, Pajdla T, Schiele B, Tuytelaars T (eds). Computer Vision – ECCV 2014: 13th European Conference, Zurich, Switzerland, September 6-12, 2014, Proceedings, Part III. Springer International Publishing, Cham. pp 46–60. doi:10.1007/978-3-319-10578-9_4. https://doi.org/10.1007/978-3-319-10578-9_4

39. Schönberger JL, Berg AC, Frahm JM (2015) Paige: pairwise image geometry encoding for improved efficiency in structure-from-motion. In: 2015 IEEE Conference on Computer Vision and Pattern Recognition (CVPR). pp 1009–1018. doi:10.1109/CVPR.2015.7298703

15

A learned sparseness and IGMRF-based regularization framework for dense disparity estimation using unsupervised feature learning

Sonam Nahar[1]* ⓘ and Manjunath V. Joshi[2]

Abstract

In this work, we propose a new approach for dense disparity estimation in a global energy minimization framework. We propose to use a feature matching cost which is defined using the learned hierarchical features of given left and right stereo images and we combine it with the pixel-based intensity matching cost in our energy function. Hierarchical features are learned using the *deep deconvolutional network* which is trained in an unsupervised way using a database consisting of large number of stereo images. In order to perform the regularization, we propose to use the inhomogeneous Gaussian Markov random field (IGMRF) and sparsity priors in our energy function. A *sparse autoencoder*-based approach is proposed for learning and inferring the sparse representation of disparities. The IGMRF prior captures the smoothness as well as preserves sharp discontinuities while the sparsity prior captures the sparseness in the disparity map. Finally, an iterative two-phase algorithm is proposed to estimate the dense disparity map where in phase one, sparse representation of disparities are inferred from the trained sparse autoencoder, and IGMRF parameters are computed, keeping the disparity map fixed and in phase two, the disparity map is refined by minimizing the energy function using graph cuts, with other parameters fixed. Experimental results on the Middlebury stereo benchmarks demonstrate the effectiveness of the proposed approach.

Keywords: Stereo, Disparity, IGMRF, Sparsity, Unsupervised feature learning

1 Introduction

Stereo vision has been an active research area in the field of computer vision for more than three decades. It aims to find the 3D information of a scene by using two or more 2D images captured from different viewpoints. Stereo vision has a wide range of applications, including 3D reconstruction, video coding, view synthesis, object recognition, and safe navigation in spatial environments. The main goal of binocular stereo vision is to find corresponding pixels, i.e., pixels resulting from the projection of the same 3D point onto the two image planes. The displacement between corresponding pixels is called disparity, and obtaining disparity at each pixel location forms a dense disparity map. For simplicity, the stereo images are

rectified so that the corresponding points lie on the same horizontal epipolar line and this reduces the correspondence search to 1D.

In general, disparities are found by comparing pixel intensities or their features in the two images. However, estimation of disparities is an ill-posed problem due to depth discontinuities, photometric variation, lack of texture, occlusions etc., and a variety of approaches have been proposed for the same [1]. A comparison of current dense stereo algorithms is given in the Middlebury website [2]. Dense stereo matching algorithms can be classified into local and global methods. Local approaches aggregate the matching cost within a finite window and find the disparity by selecting the lowest aggregated cost. These methods assume that the disparity is the same over the entire window and hence produces unreliable matches in textureless regions and near depth discontinuities. Use of adaptive windows [3], multiple windows [4], adaptive weights [5],

*Correspondence: sonam@lnmiit.ac.in
[1]The LNM Institute of Information Technology, Jaipur, India
Full list of author information is available at the end of the article

or bilateral filtering [6] in local methods reduce these effects but cannot avoid it completely. Global approaches tackle such problems by incorporating regularization such as explicit smoothness assumption and estimate the dense disparity map by minimizing an energy function. The most prominent stereo algorithms for minimizing the global energy function are based on graph cuts [7] and belief propagation [8] optimization methods. In general, the energy function represents a combination of a data term and a regularization term that restricts the solution space. Global approaches perform well in textured and textureless areas as well as at depth discontinuities. In this paper, we solve the dense disparity estimation problem in a global energy minimization framework.

1.1 Motivation and related work

Global stereo methods mainly focus on minimizing energy functions efficiently to improve performance. However, solutions with lower energy do not always correspond to better performance [9]. Therefore, it is important to define a proper energy function than to search for optimization techniques in order to improve the performance. Hence, in our work, we propose a new and a suitable energy function for estimating the dense disparity map in an energy minimization framework.

In the global stereo methods, the data term is generally defined by using the pixel-based matching cost between the corresponding pixels in the left and right images [1]. A pixel-based cost function determines the matching cost for disparity on the basis of a descriptor that is defined for one single pixel. Pixel-based cost function can be extended to patch (window)-based matching cost by integrating pixel-based costs within a certain neighborhood and such cost are based on census transform, normalized cross correlation, etc. [10]. Most of the pixel-based matching costs are built on the brightness constancy assumption and include absolute differences (AD), squared differences (SD), sampling insensitive absolute differences of Birchfield and Tomasi (BT), or truncated costs [10]. They rely on raw pixel values, and are less robust to illumination changes, view point variation, noise, occlusion, etc. One can represent stereo images in a better way by using a feature space where they are robust, distinct, and transformation invariant [11, 12]. Feature-based stereo methods use the features such as edges, gradients, corners, segments, or hand-crafted features such as scale-invariant feature transform (SIFT) [13, 14]. In order to obtain dense disparities, feature matching has been used in the global stereo framework. In [15] and [16], nonoverlapping segments of stereo images are used as features, and the dense stereo matching problem is cast as an energy minimization in segment domain instead of pixel domain where the disparity plane is assigned to each segment via graph cuts or belief propagation. These approaches assume that the

disparities in a segment vary smoothly which is not true in practice due to the depth discontinuities. Also, the solution here relies on the accuracy of segmentation which is itself a non trivial task. In [17], the sparse correspondences are found by feature points and then the dense correspondences are obtained from these sparse matches using the propagation and seed growing methods. In such approaches, the accuracy depends on the initial support points. In [18], the mutual information (MI)-based feature matching is used in a Markov random field (MRF) framework for estimating the dense disparities. However, matching with basic image features still results in ambiguities in correspondence search, especially for textureless areas and wide baseline stereo. Hence, to reduce these ambiguities, one needs to use more descriptive features. Recently in [19], authors proposed a SIFT flow algorithm for finding the dense correspondences by matching the SIFT descriptors while preserving spatial discontinuities using MRF regularization. In [20], a deformable spatial pyramid model is proposed in a regularization framework for estimating dense disparities using multiple SIFT features. Hand-crafted features of stereo images are designed and then embedded in an MRF model in [21]. The drawback of these approaches is that designing such features is computationally expensive, time consuming, and requires domain knowledge of the data.

In recent years, learning features from unlabeled data using unsupervised feature learning and deep learning approaches have achieved superior performance in solving many computer vision problems [22–25]. Feature learning is attractive as it exploits the availability of large amount of data and avoids the need of feature engineering. It has also attracted the attention of stereo vision researchers in recent years. The method proposed in [26] uses the deep convolutional neural network for learning similarity measure on small image patches, and the training is carried in a supervised manner by constructing a binary classification dataset with examples of similar and dissimilar pair of patches. Based on the learned similarity measure, the disparity map is estimated using state-of-the-art local stereo methods. Here, the learning is done on small size patches instead of entire image, i.e., global contextual constraint is not taken into account while learning the similarity measure. The method does not provide a single framework for dense disparity estimation though it improves the results of state of the art stereo methods. In this work, we focus on the approaches which use feature matching cost in a global energy minimization framework for estimating the dense disparities. In [27], authors proposed unsupervised feature learning for dense stereo matching within a energy minimization framework. They learn the features from a large amount of image patches using K-singular value decomposition (K-SVD) dictionary learning approach. The limitation of their approach is that the features are learned from a set of image patches and do not consider the entire image, i.e., global contextual constraint is not taken into account while learning the features. Also, higher level features are not learned, instead, they are estimated using a simple max pooling operation from the layer beneath. Here, the higher layer correspondence matches are used to initialize the lower layer matching and hence the accuracy depends on the higher layer matches only. Recently, unsupervised feature learning and deep learning methods have shown superior performance in learning efficient representation of images at multiple layers [24, 28–33].

In this paper, we propose to use a feature matching cost which is defined using the learned hierarchical features of stereo image pair. In order to learn these hierarchical features, we propose to use a *deep deconvolutional network* [31], an unsupervised feature learning method. The deep deconvolutional network is trained over a large set of stereo images in an unsupervised way, which in turn results in a diverse set of filters. These learned filters capture image information at a different levels in the form of low-level edges, mid-level edge junctions, and high-level object parts. Features at each layer of deconvolutional network are learned in a hierarchy using the features in the previous layer. The deep deconvolutional network is quite different to the deep convolutional neural networks (CNN). Deep CNN is a bottom-up approach where an input image is subjected to multiple layers of convolutions, nonlinearities, and subsampling whereas deep deconvolutional network is a top-down approach where an input image is generated by a sum over convolutions of the feature maps with learned filters. Unlike deep CNN [33], the deep deconvolutional network does not spatially pool features at successive layers and hence preserves the mid-level cues emerging from the data such as edge intersections, parallelism, and symmetry. They scale well to complete images and hence learn the features for the entire input image instead of small size patches. It makes them to consider global contextual constraint while learning. In order to estimate the dense disparity map, we combine our learning-based multilayer feature matching cost with the pixel-based intensity matching cost and hence our data term has the sum of these costs.

Since the disparity estimation is an ill-posed problem, use of global stereo matching makes it better posed by incorporating a regularization prior in the energy function. Selection of the appropriate prior leads to a better solution. One common feature of the disparities is that they are piecewise smooth, i.e., they vary smoothly except at discontinuities, thus making them inhomogeneous. This spatial correlation among disparities can be captured by MRF-based models. It is well known that MRFs are the most general models used as priors during regularization when solving ill-posed problems [34]. Hence, many of

the current better-performing global stereo methods are based on the MRF formulations as noted in [1]. Homogeneous MRF models tend to oversmooth the disparity map and fail to preserve the discontinuities [35]. Hence, a better model would be one that reconstructs the smooth disparities while preserving the sharp discontinuities. In order to achieve this, variety of discontinuity preserving MRF priors are used in global stereo methods as proposed in [36–40]. Many of these techniques use single or a set of global MRF parameters which are either manually tuned or estimated. These global parameters may not adapt to the local structure of the disparity map and hence fail to better capture the spatial dependence among disparities. We need a prior that considers the spatial variation among disparities locally. This motivates us to use an inhomogeneous Gaussian markov random field (IGMRF) prior in our energy function which was first proposed in [41] for solving the satellite image deblurring problem. IGMRF can handle smooth as well as sharp changes in disparity map because the local variation among disparities is captured using IGMRF parameters at each pixel location. In our approach, the IGMRF parameters are not known and are estimated.

Although IGMRF prior captures the smoothness with discontinuities, it fails to capture additional structure such as sparseness in the disparity map. In general, disparity maps are made up of homogeneous regions with limited number of discontinuities resulting in redundancy. Because of this, one can represent the disparities in a domain in which they are sparse. This transform domain representation can be obtained using the fixed set of basis such as discrete cosine transform (DCT), discrete wavelet transform (DWT), or it can be learned as an overcomplete dictionary using large number of true disparities. In [42], the disparities are reconstructed from few disparity measurements using the concepts of compressive sensing. Here, the sparseness is represented over a fixed wavelet basis and the accuracy of disparity estimation depends on the reliable measurements. Learned sparseness using the overcomplete dictionary has been successfully used as regularization for solving the inverse problems [43, 44]. The advantage of using a learned dictionary is that the representation would be more accurate than obtained with the use of fixed basis and this is done by adapting its atoms to fit a given training data [45]. Recently in [46], authors proposed a two-layer graphical model for inferring the disparity map by including a sparsity prior over learned sparse representation of disparities in an existing MRF-based stereo matching framework. Here, the sparse representation of disparities are inferred by a dictionary which is learned using a sparse coding technique which can cope up with non stationary depth estimation errors. Although it performs better when compared to discontinuity preserving homogeneous MRF prior, the solution can be improved by using inhomogeneous MRF prior. Also, their method is complex and computationally intensive.

A practical problem with dictionary learning techniques is that they are computationally expensive because the dictionaries are learned by iteratively recovering sparse vectors and updating the dictionary atoms [45, 46]. Though these methods perform well in practice, they use a linear structure. Recent research suggests that non-linear, neural networks can achieve superior performance in learning efficient representation of images [22, 24, 28, 29]. One example of these networks is a sparse autoencoder. It encodes the input data with a sparse representation in hidden layer and is trained using a large database of unlabeled images [29]. Sparse autoencoders are very efficient and they can be easily generalized to represent complicated models. In this paper, we propose to use the sparse autoencoder for learning and inferring the sparse representation of disparity map. The sparse autoencoder is trained using a large set of true disparities. We define a sparsity prior using the learned sparseness of disparities and incorporate this prior in addition to IGMRF prior in our energy function. Such sparsity priors capture higher order dependencies in the disparity map and complement the IGMRF prior.

In order to obtain the dense disparity map, we propose an iterative two-phase algorithm. In phase one, sparseness is inferred using the learned weights of the sparse autoencoder, and IGMRF parameters are computed based on the current estimate of disparity map, while in the second phase, the disparity map is refined by minimizing the energy function with other parameters fixed. We use graph cuts [7] as an optimization technique for minimizing our proposed energy function. Our experimental results demonstrate the effectiveness of our learning-based feature matching cost, IGMRF prior, and sparsity prior when used in an energy minimization framework. The experiments indicate that our method generates the state-of-the-art result and can compete the state-of-the-art global stereo methods.

The outline of the paper is as follows. In the "Problem formulation" section, we formulate our problem of dense disparity estimation in an energy minimization framework. In the "Deep deconvolutional network for extracting hierarchical features" section, we present the deep deconvolutional network model for learning the hierarchical features of stereo images and then discuss the formation of our learning-based multilayer feature matching cost. The IGMRF prior model and estimation of IGMRF parameters are addressed in the "IGMRF model for disparity" section. In "Sparse model for disparity" section, we discuss the sparse autoencoder for learning and inferring the sparse representation of disparities and then discuss the formation of sparsity prior. The

formation of final energy function and the proposed algorithm for dense disparity estimation are discussed in the "Dense disparity estimation". The experimental results and the performance of the proposed approach are dealt in the "Experimental results" section, and concluding remarks are drawn in the "Conclusion" section.

2 Problem formulation

In this paper, our main goal is to find the disparity map $d \in \mathbb{R}^{M \times N}$ for a given rectified pair of stereo images, left image $I_L \in \mathbb{R}^{M \times N}$ and right image $I_R \in \mathbb{R}^{M \times N}$. In other words, we wish to compute the disparity $d(x, y)$ at every pixel location (x, y) in the reference image such that pixels in I_L project to their corresponding pixels in the right image I_R when the correct disparity is selected. In the framework of global approach, the dense stereo matching problem is formulated in terms of energy minimization where the objective is to estimate the disparity map d by minimizing the following energy function:

$$E(d) = E_D(d) + E_P(d), \tag{1}$$

where the data term $E_D(d)$ measures how well the d to be estimated agrees with I_L and I_R of a scene. The prior term $E_P(d)$ measures how good it matches with the prior knowledge about the disparity map. For finding the correspondences, we consider search from left to right as well as from right to left and hence relax the traditional ordering constraint used in disparity estimation.

In our work, the data term is defined as a sum of the intensity and feature matching costs i.e.,

$$E_D(d) = E_I(d) + \mu E_F(d), \tag{2}$$

where μ controls the weightage of $E_F(d)$. For a given d, the intensity matching cost $E_I(d)$ measures the dissimilarity between the corresponding pixel intensities of I_L and I_R, while the feature matching cost $E_F(d)$ measures the dissimilarity between the corresponding learned features of I_L and I_R. In order to define $E_I(d)$, we use the robust and sampling insensitive measure proposed by Birchfield and Tomasi (BT) in [47]. At pixel location (x, y) having disparity $d(x, y)$, it is given as minimum absolute intensity difference between $I_L(x, y)$ and $I_R(x + d(x, y), y)$ in the real valued range of disparities along the epipolar line and hence can be written as:

$$E_I(d) = \sum_{(x,y)} \min \left(\left(\min_{d(x,y) \pm \frac{1}{2}} |I_L(x, y) - I_R(x + d(x, y), y)| \right), \tau^I \right), \tag{3}$$

where τ^I is the truncation threshold which is used to make intensity matching cost more robust against outliers. For defining the feature matching cost $E_F(d)$, we extract the features of stereo image pair at multiple layers of deep deconvolutional network and is discussed in the next section.

In order to perform the regularization, we model d using its prior characteristics and form the energy term $E_P(d)$. We define $E_P(d)$ as a sum of IGMRF and sparsity priors, and it is given as:

$$E_P(d) = E_{\text{IGMRF}}(d) + \gamma E_{\text{sparse}}(d), \tag{4}$$

where $E_{\text{IGMRF}}(d)$ and $E_{\text{sparse}}(d)$ represent the IGMRF and sparsity prior terms, respectively. Here, γ controls the weightage of the term $E_{\text{sparse}}(d)$.

3 Deep deconvolutional network for extracting hierarchical features

In this section, we first describe the method of learning the hierarchical features of a given stereo pair and then describe how these features are used to define our feature matching cost $E_F(d)$.

Deconvolutional network [31] is an unsupervised feature learning model that is based on the convolutional decomposition of images under sparsity constraint and generates sparse, overcomplete features. Stacking such network in a hierarchy results in a deep deconvolutional network. Layers of such network learn both the filters and features as done in an image deconvolution problem in which given a degraded image, the task is to estimate both the blur kernel and the restored image. In order to explain how deep deconvolutional network extract hierarchical features, we first consider a deep deconvolutional network consisting of a single layer. To train this network for extracting features, a training set consisting of large number of stereo images $\mathcal{I}=\{I^1, \ldots, I^{m_s}\}$ are used where each image I^i is considered as an input to the network. Here, m_s is the number of images in the training set $\mathcal{I}$, and we consider only left images of different scenes for training the network. Note that one may use right stereo images as well. Let P_1 be the number of $2D$ feature maps in a first layer. Considering the input at layer 0, we can write each image I^i as composed of P_0 channels $\{I_1^i, \ldots, I_{P_0}^i\}$. For example, if we consider a color image, then we have $P_0=3$. Each channel c of input image I^i can be represented as a linear sum of P_1 feature maps s_p^i convolved with filters $f_{p,c}$ i.e.,

$$\sum_{p=1}^{P_1} s_p^i \oplus f_{p,c} = I_c^i, \tag{5}$$

where $\oplus$ represents the 2D convolution operator. Note that in this work, we use gray scale stereo images only and hence $P_0 = 1$. Equation (5) represents an underdetermined system since both the features and filters are unknown and hence to obtain a unique solution, a regularization term is also added that encourages sparsity in the latent feature

maps. This gives us an overall cost function for training a single-layer deconvolutional network as:

$$C_1(\mathcal{I}) = \sum_{i=1}^{m_s} \left[\frac{\alpha}{2} \sum_{c=1}^{P_0} \left\| \sum_{p=1}^{P_1} s_p^i \oplus f_{p,c} - I_c^i \right\|_2^2 + \sum_{p=1}^{P_1} |s_p^i|^1 \right]. \tag{6}$$

Here, $|s_p^i|^1$ is the L_1-norm on the vectorized version of s_p^i. The relative weighting of the reconstruction error of each I^i and sparsity of their feature maps s_p^i is controlled by the parameter α. This network is learned by minimizing $C_1(\mathcal{I})$ with respect to s_p^is and $f_{p,c}$s when the input to network is $\mathcal{I}$. Note that the set of filters $f_{p,c}$ are the parameters of the network, common to all images in the training set while each image has its own set of feature maps s_p^i.

The single-layer network described above can be stacked to form a deep deconvolutional network consisting of multiple layers. Let the deep network is formed by NL number of layers, $(l = 1 \ldots NL)$. This hierarchy is achieved by considering the feature maps of layer $l-1$ as the input to layer l, $l > 0$. Let P_{l-1} and P_l the number of feature maps at layer $l-1$ and l, respectively. The cost function for training the lth layer of a deep deconvolutional network can be written as a generalization of Eq. (6) as:

$$C_l(\mathcal{I}) = \sum_{i=1}^{m_s} \left[\frac{\alpha}{2} \sum_{c=1}^{P_{l-1}} \left\| \sum_{p=1}^{P_l} g_{p,c}^l (s_{p,l}^i \oplus f_{p,c}^l) - s_{c,l-1}^i \right\|_2^2 + \sum_{p=1}^{P_l} |s_{p,l}^i|^1 \right], \tag{7}$$

where $s_{c,l-1}^i$ and $s_{p,l}^i$ are the feature maps of image I^i at layer $l-1$ and l, respectively, and thus, it shows that layer l has as its input coming from P_{l-1} channels. $f_{p,c}^l$ are the filters at layer l and $g_{p,c}^l$ are the elements of a fixed binary matrix that determine the connectivity between the feature maps at successive layers, i.e., whether $s_{p,l}^i$ is connected to $s_{c,l-1}^i$ or not. For $l = 1$, we assume that $g_{p,c}^l$ is always 1, but for $l > 1$, we make this connectivity as sparse. Since $P_l > 1$, the model learns overcomplete sparse, feature feature maps. This structure is illustrated in Fig. 1.

A deep deconvolutional network consisting of NL number of layers is trained upwards in a layer-wise manner starting with the first layer ($l = 1$) where the inputs are the training images $\mathcal{I}$. Each layer l is trained in order to learn a set of filters $f_{p,c}^l$ which is shared across all images in $\mathcal{I}$ and infer the set of feature maps $s_{p,l}^i$ of each image I^i in $\mathcal{I}$. To learn the filters, we alternately minimize $C_l(\mathcal{I})$ w.r.t. the filters and feature maps by keeping one of them constant while minimizing the other. We follow the optimization scheme as proposed in [31].

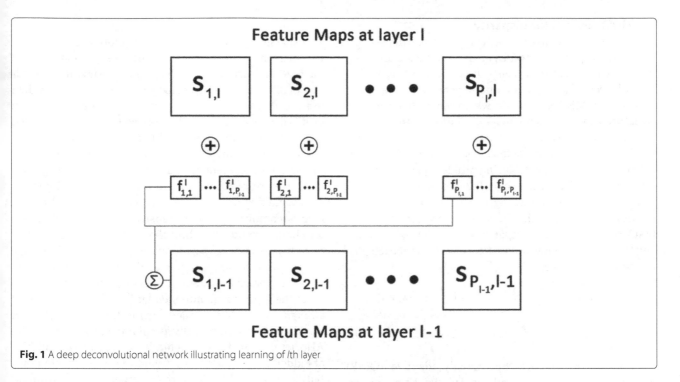

Fig. 1 A deep deconvolutional network illustrating learning of *l*th layer

3.1 Feature encoding

Once the deep deconvolutional network is trained, we can use it to infer the multilayer features of a given left I_L and right I_R stereo images for which we want to estimate the dense disparity map. The network described above is top-down in nature, i.e., given the latent feature maps, one can synthesize an image but there is no direct mechanism for inferring the feature maps of a given image without minimizing the cost function given in Eq. (7). Hence, once the network is learned/trained, we apply given I_L and I_R separately as input image to the trained deep deconvolutional network with the fixed set of learned filters and infer the feature maps $s_{p,l}^{I_L}$ and $s_{p,l}^{I_R}$ of I_L and I_R at layer l, respectively, by minimizing the cost functions $C_l(I_L)$ and $C_l(I_R)$, respectively. Once, they are learned, we create a feature vector at each pixel location in I_L and I_R separately. In order to obtain the features of I_L at a layer l, we stack the P_l number of inferred feature maps $s_{p,l}^{I_L}$ and obtain a single feature map $Z_l^{I_L}$ where at each pixel location (x,y) in $Z_l^{I_L}$, we get a feature vector of dimension $P_l \times 1$. Similarly, using the same process we obtain the features of I_R. Thus, $Z_l^{I_L}$ and $Z_l^{I_R}$ represents the lth layer features of I_L and I_R, respectively.

3.2 Defining $E_F(d)$

Once the multi-layer features of I_L and I_R are obtained, we can define our feature matching cost $E_F(d)$ as:

$$E_F(d) = \sum_{l=1}^{NL} \sum_{(x,y)} \min\left(|Z_l^{I_L}(x,y) - Z_l^{I_R}(x + d(x,y),y)|, \tau^F\right). \quad (8)$$

At each pixel location (x,y) having disparity $d(x,y)$, it measures the absolute distance between the feature vector $Z_l^{I_L}(x,y)$ and corresponding matched feature $Z_l^{I_R}(x + d(x,y),y)$. Here, τ^F is the truncation threshold which is used to make feature matching cost more robust against outliers and NL is the number of layers in the network. These multiple layers feature matching technique highly constrains the solution space and hence results in unambiguous and accurate disparities.

In our energy function, the data term $E_D(d)$ is not constructed using the feature matching cost $E_F(d)$ only because the deep deconvolutional network extracts the sparse (significant) features in stereo images at few locations such as edges, corners, junctions. If one uses feature matching cost as a data term, then at those pixel locations where the features are not significant, it results in ambiguous disparity estimates. One can obtain the disparities only at the pixel locations where significant features have been obtained. However, this results in a sparse disparity map. Our goal here is estimate the dense disparity map, i.e., finding the disparity at every pixel location. Although this can be obtained simply by interpolating the sparse disparity, it leads to inaccurate disparities at occluded regions and disparity discontinuities. Since we use intensity term as well, the intensity values are available at every pixel location, giving us a dense disparity map. Hence, in our work, we define our data term using a combination of intensity and feature matching costs. The combination of intensity and features matching not only produce dense disparities but also better constrains the solution and hence results in accurate disparity map.

4   IGMRF model for disparity

Object distances from the camera, i.e., depths are inversely proportional to disparities and hence are made up of various textures, sharp discontinuities as well as smooth areas making them inhomogeneous. In our work, we use an IGMRF prior model which can adapt to the local structure of the disparity map, i.e., enforces the smoothness in disparities while preserving the discontinuities. IGMRF-based prior model has been successfully used in solving satellite image deblurring problem [41], multiresolution fusion of satellite images [48], and super-resolution of images [49]. For modeling IGMRF, $E_{\text{IGMRF}}(d)$ is chosen as the square of finite difference approximation to the first-order derivative of disparities. Considering the differentiation in horizontal and vertical directions at each pixel location, one can write $E_{\text{IGMRF}}(d)$ as [41]:

$$E_{\text{IGMRF}}(d) = \sum_{(x,y)} b^X_{(x,y)}(d(x-1,y) - d(x,y))^2$$
$$+ b^Y_{(x,y)}(d(x,y-1) - d(x,y))^2. \qquad (9)$$

Here, b^X and b^Y are the spatially adaptive IGMRF parameters in horizontal and vertical directions, respectively. Thus, $\{b^X_{(x,y)}, b^Y_{(x,y)}\}$ forms a 2D parameter vector of IGMRF at each pixel location (x,y) in the disparity map. A low value of b indicates the presence of an edge between two neighboring disparities. These parameters help us to obtain a solution which is less noisy in smooth areas and preserve the depth discontinuities in other areas. The IGMRF parameters at each pixel location (x,y) are estimated using the maximum likelihood estimation (MLE) and are computed as [41]:

$$b^X_{(x,y)} = \frac{1}{\max(4(d(x-1,y) - d(x,y))^2, 4)}. \qquad (10)$$

$$b^Y_{(x,y)} = \frac{1}{\max(4(d(x,y) - d(x,y-1))^2, 4)}. \qquad (11)$$

In order to avoid computational difficulty, we set an upper bound $b = 1/4$ whenever gradient becomes zero, i.e., whenever the neighboring disparities are the same.

In order to estimate IGMRF parameters, we need the true disparity map which is unknown and has to be estimated. Therefore, to start the regularization process, we use an initial estimate of disparity map obtained using a suitable approach and compute these parameters which are then used to estimate the d. In our proposed algorithm, these parameters and d are refined alternatively and iteratively for obtaining the better d.

5   Sparse model for disparity

In order to model the higher order dependencies in the disparity map, we model the disparity map in our energy function by another prior called sparsity prior $E_{\text{sparse}}(d)$. The sparsity prior regularizes the solution by modeling the sparseness in d. In this work, we present a novel method for learning and inferring the sparse representation of disparities using sparse autoencoder, which is then used to define the sparsity prior. An autoencoder is an artificial neural network (ANN) which sets the desired output same as the input and has one hidden layer [29]. It comprises of an encoder that maps an input vector to a hidden representation and a decoder that maps this hidden representation back to a reconstructed input. In reality, finding the sparse representation of a disparity map is computationally expensive, and therefore, a better choice would be to find the sparse representation of disparity patches of small size individually and average the resultant sparse patches at the end in order to get complete sparse representation of disparity map.

Let the input to an autoencoder be a disparity patch of size $\sqrt{n} \times \sqrt{n}$ pixels, extracted at location (x,y) in d and it is ordered lexicographically as column vector $d^{(x,y)} \in \mathbb{R}^n$. Also, let the corresponding hidden representation of $d^{(x,y)}$ at hidden layer be $a^{(x,y)} \in \mathbb{R}^K$ and the reconstructed output be $\tilde{d}^{(x,y)} \in \mathbb{R}^n$. Thus, the number of units at input, hidden, and output layers are n, K, and n, respectively. The autoencoder has weights (W, U, r, s), where $W \in \mathbb{R}^{n \times K}$ is the encoder weight matrix between the input and hidden layers, $U \in \mathbb{R}^{K \times n}$ is the decoder weight matrix between the hidden and output layers, and $r \in \mathbb{R}^K$ and $s \in \mathbb{R}^n$ are the bias weight vectors for hidden and output layers, respectively. For a fixed set of weights (W, U, r, s), the $a^{(x,y)}$ and $\tilde{d}^{(x,y)}$ can be computed as follows:

$$a^{(x,y)} = f\left(W^T d^{(x,y)} + r\right), \qquad (12)$$

$$\tilde{d}^{(x,y)} = f\left(U^T a^{(x,y)} + s\right), \qquad (13)$$

where f is an activation function and we use sigmoid for this. An autoencoder is called as sparse autoencoder when the sparsity constraint is imposed on its hidden layer. Sparse autoencoder learns an overcomplete sparse representation of data in the hidden layer when the number of hidden units K are greater than the number of input units n, i.e., $K > n$. An example of a sparse autoencoder is shown in Fig. 2.

Let $a^{(x,y)}_j$ be the activation of hidden unit j. A sparsity constraint on the activations of hidden units are imposed by forcing them to be inactive most of the time. A unit is active when its activation value is close to one and inactive when it is close to zero. We define ρ as a global sparsity parameter for all hidden units, typically a small value close to zero. Let $\hat{\rho}_j$ be the average activation of hidden unit j (averaged over training set). Then, the sparsity constraint

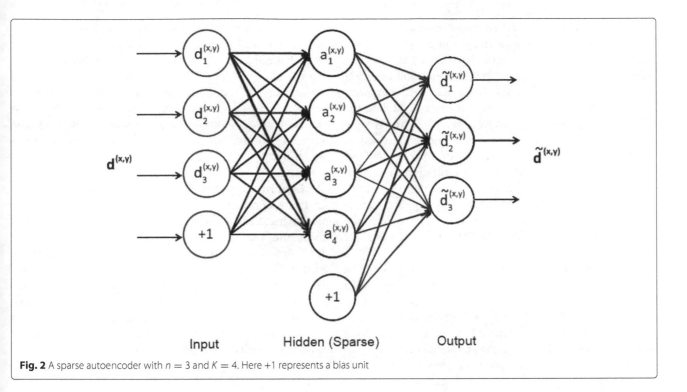

Fig. 2 A sparse autoencoder with $n = 3$ and $K = 4$. Here +1 represents a bias unit

for each jth hidden unit is enforced by a penalty term which penalizes $\hat{\rho}_j$ deviating significantly from ρ as:

$$\sum_{j=1}^{K} KL(\rho||\hat{\rho}_j) = \sum_{j=1}^{K} \rho \log \frac{\rho}{\hat{\rho}_j} + (1-\rho) \log \frac{1-\rho}{1-\hat{\rho}_j}, \quad (14)$$

where $KL(\rho||\hat{\rho}_j)$ is the Kullback-Leilbler (KL) divergence. This term has a value 0, if $\hat{\rho}_j = \rho$; otherwise, it increases monotonically as $\hat{\rho}_j$ diverges from ρ.

Consider a training set consisting of large number of disparity patches $\mathcal{G} = \{d^{(1)}, d^{(2)}, \ldots, d^{(m_d)}\}$, with each patch $d^{(i)} \in \mathbb{R}^n$. One can extract these disparity patches from the available ground truth disparity maps. Using the known disparity patches, we can train the sparse autoencoder to learn the weights (W, U, r, s). To do this, the following objective function is formed using Eqs. (12), (13), and (14) as:

$$\frac{1}{m} \sum_{i=1}^{m_d} \left(\frac{1}{2} \left\| d^{(i)} - f\left(U^T \left(f\left(W^T d^{(i)} + r\right)\right)\right) + s \right\|_2^2 \right.$$

$$+ \frac{\lambda}{2} \left(\sum_{i=1}^{n} \sum_{j=1}^{K} (W_{ij})^2 + \sum_{i=1}^{K} \sum_{j=1}^{n} (U_{ij})^2 \right)$$

$$+ \beta \sum_{j=1}^{K} KL(\rho||\hat{\rho}_j). \quad (15)$$

Here, the first term represents the average reconstruction error over all training inputs. The second term is a

regularization term on the weights to prevent the over-fitting by making them smaller in magnitude, and λ controls the relative importance of this term. β controls the weightage of the third term which corresponds to sparsity penalty term. We minimize this Eq. (15) w.r.t. W, U, r, s using well known back propagation algorithm [50].

Once the autoencoder is trained, d can be modeled by the sparsity prior $E_{\text{sparse}}(d)$ as follows:

$$E_{\text{sparse}}(d) = \sum_{(x,y)} \left\| d^{(x,y)} - f\left(U^T a^{(x,y)} + s\right) \right\|_2^2. \quad (16)$$

$E_{\text{sparse}}(d)$ measures how well each disparity patch at location (x, y) in d agrees with its sparse representations. In our proposed approach, the disparity map and its sparse representation are inferred alternatively.

6 Dense disparity estimation

$$E(d) = \sum_{(x,y)} \min\left(\left(\min_{d(x,y) \pm \frac{1}{2}} \left| I_L(x,y) - I_R(x + d(x,y), y) \right| \right), \tau^I \right)$$

$$+ \mu \sum_{l=1}^{NL} \sum_{(x,y)} \min\left(\left| Z_l^{I_L}(x,y) - Z_l^{I_R}(x + d(x,y), y) \right|, \tau^F \right)$$

$$+ \sum_{(x,y)} \left(b_{(x,y)}^X (d(x-1,y) - d(x,y))^2 + b_{(x,y)}^Y (d(x,y-1) \right.$$

$$\left. - d(x,y))^2 \right) + \gamma \sum_{(x,y)} \left\| d^{(x,y)} - f\left(U^T a^{(x,y)} + s\right) \right\|_2^2.$$

$$(17)$$

Our main goal is to estimate the dense disparity map using a given pair of stereo images in an energy minimization framework. Our data term defined in Eq. (2) is formed by adding intensity and feature matching costs using Eqs. (3) and (8), respectively. Similarly, our prior energy term defined in Eq. (4) is formed by adding the IGMRF and sparsity priors using Eqs. (9) and (16), respectively. Finally, our proposed energy function defined in Eq. (1) can be rewritten as given in Eq. (17) and we minimize it using graph cuts optimization based on α-β swap moves [7]. We do not consider the occlusions explicitly but they are handled by clipping matching costs using thresholds $\tau = \{\tau^I, \tau^F\}$ that prevents the outliers from disturbing the estimation (see Eqs. (3) and (8)).

In order to estimate the dense disparity map, we propose an iterative two-phase algorithm. It proceeds with the use of an initial estimate of disparity map and iterates and alternates between two phases until convergence as given in Algorithm 1. We use a classical local stereo method [1] for obtaining the initial disparity map in which the *absolute intensity differences* (AD) with truncation, aggregated over a fixed window is used as matching cost. In order to reduce computation time, we optimize this cost by graph cuts instead of the classic *winner take all* (WTA) optimization. Postprocessing operations such as left-right consistency check, interpolation, and median filtering [1] are applied in order to obtain a better initial estimate for faster convergence while regularizing. However, any other suitable disparity estimation method can also be used in obtaining the initial estimate.

Algorithm 1: Proposed algorithm

Input: Stereo image pair I_L and I_R, a set of ground truth disparity patches $\mathcal{G}=\{d^{(1)}, d^{(2)}, \ldots, d^{(m_d)}\}$, and a set of stereo images $\mathcal{I}=\{I^1, \ldots, I^{m_s}\}$.

1 Train a sparse autoencoder using $\mathcal{G}$ by minimizing Eq.(15) and obtain weights (W, U, r, s);
2 Train a deep deconvolutional network consisting of NL number of layers, by minimizing Eq.(7) for each layer l and learn a set of filters;
3 Infer the multi-layer features $Z_l^{I_L}$ and $Z_l^{I_R}$ of I_L and I_R, respectively ($l = 1 \ldots NL$);
4 Obtain an initial disparity map d_0;
5 Initialization: $d = d_0$;
6 **repeat**
7 | **Phase 1:** With d being fixed, infer the sparse vector $a^{(x,y)}$ for each disparity patch $d^{(x,y)}$ in d using Eq.(12). Compute IGMRF parameters $b_{(x,y)}^X$ and $b_{(x,y)}^Y$ using Eqs.(10) and (11), at each pixel location;
8 | **Phase 2:** With $\{a^{(x,y)}\}$, $\{b_{(x,y)}^X, b_{(x,y)}^Y\}$ fixed as obtained in phase 1, minimize the Eq.(17) for d using graph cuts;
9 **until** *convergence*;

In general, for nonconvex energy functions, graph cuts result in a local minimum that is within a known factor of global minimum. In order to ensure global minimum, we use an iterative optimization with proper settings of parameters. At every iteration, the IGMRF parameters and sparseness are refined in order to obtain better disparity estimates (converging towards global optima). The number of iterations may vary for different stereo pairs and the choice of initial estimate.

7   Experimental results

In this section, we demonstrate the efficacy of the proposed method by conducting various experiments and evaluating our results on the Middlebury stereo benchmark images [2]. In order to perform the quantitative evaluation, we use the percentage of bad matching pixels ($B\%$) as the error measure with a disparity error tolerance δ. The error measure is computed over the entire image as well as in the nonoccluded regions. For an estimated disparity map d, the $B\%$ is computed with respect to the ground truth disparity map g as follows [1]:

$$B = \frac{1}{M * N} \sum_{(x,y)} |d(x, y) - g(x, y)| > \delta, \qquad (18)$$

In this work, all the experiments were conducted on a computer with Core i7-3632QM, 2.20 GHz processor and 8.00 GB RAM.

7.1   Parameter settings

We first provide the details of various parameters used in training the deep deconvolutional network. A two-layer deep deconvolutional network was trained over m_s=75 left stereo images obtained from the Middlebury 2005 and 2006 datasets and Middlebury 2014 training dataset [2]. Considering $NL = 2$ i.e., for a two-layer deep architecture, we set the number of feature maps as $P_1 = 9$ and $P_2 = 45$, respectively. The feature maps at layer 1 were fully connected to the input having single channel. In order to reduce the computations, each feature map in layer 1 was connected to any nine feature maps in layer 2. In other words, 36 feature maps in layer 2 were connected to a pair of maps in layer 1 and remaining 9 were singly connected. In this way, we obtained 9 and $36 * 2 + 9 = 81$ filters at layers 1 and 2, respectively. The parameter α in Eq. (7) was set as 1 and the filters of size 7×7 were learned. These parameters were manually set as per the experimental settings done in [31] except that we used gray scale stereo images for training, i.e., P_0=1. With these parameter settings, our two-layer network was trained to obtain the set of filters. The learned filters at the first and second layers are shown in Fig. 3 where the first layer learns Gabor like filters, and the filters in the second layer lead to mid-level features such as center-surround corners, T and angle-junctions, and curves.

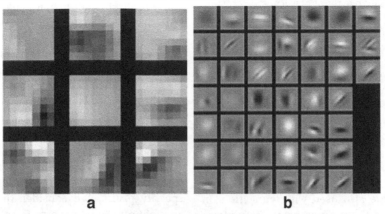

Fig. 3 Filters learned at first and second layers of deep deconvolutional network. **a** Number of filters learned at first layer are 9. **b** Number of filters learned at second layer are 81 where 36 filters in pair are shown in color and remaining 9 filters are shown as *gray* scale

We now provide the parameters used while training the sparse autoencoder. We trained the sparse autoencoder using a set of $m_d = 5 \times 10^5$ true disparity patches of the stereo images used during the training of deep deconvolutional network. The size of each disparity patch was chosen as 8×8, i.e., $n = 64$. In order to achieve the over-completeness in hidden layer, we set $K = 4 * n$, i.e., the number of hidden units were $K = 256$. The parameters in Eq. (15) were empirically chosen as $\lambda = 10^{-4}$, $\beta = 0.1$, and $\rho = 0.01$. With these parameter settings, the sparse autoencoder was trained to obtain the weights (W, U, r, s). The learned weights W between the input and the hidden layers are shown in Fig. 4.

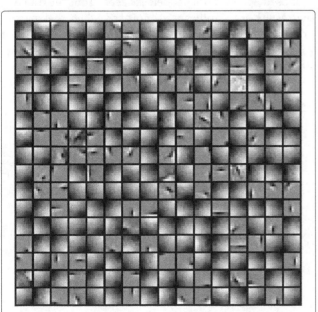

Fig. 4 Learned weights W between the input and the hidden layer in the trained sparse autoencoder. Here, each square block is of size 8×8 which shows the weights between a hidden unit and each input unit. Note that there are 256 hidden and 64 input units

Note that the training of deep deconvolutional network and the autoencoder is an offline operation, and hence, they do not add to the computational complexity. In order to estimate the dense disparity map, we experimented on the *Venus*, *Cones*, and *Teddy* stereo pairs, belonging to Middlebury stereo 2001 and 2003 datasets [2] which were different from the training datasets used earlier. We also performed the experiments using the recently released Middlebury stereo 2014 (version 3) dataset. Our algorithm was initialized with the initial estimate of disparity map and the algorithm converged with in five iterations for all the stereo pairs used in our experiments. While minimizing Eq. (17), the data cost thresholds $\{\tau^I, \tau^F\}$ were set as 0.08 and 0.04, respectively, and the parameter μ was chosen as 1. The parameter γ was initially set to 10^{-4} and exponentially increased at each iteration from 10^{-4} to 10^{-1}. We used the same parameters for all the experiments, and this demonstrates the robustness of our method.

7.2 Performance evaluation using different data terms $E_D(d)$ with IGMRF prior

As discussed earlier, the data term $E_D(d)$ in our energy function is defined using a combination of $E_I(d)$ and $E_F(d)$. In order to demonstrate the effectiveness of our proposed data term, we consider the energy functions consisting of different data terms $E_D(d)$ and IGMRF prior only. Note that we do not consider the sparsity prior here. We then compare the performance using the proposed $E_D(d)$ with $E_D(d)$ made up of traditional pixel based data terms such as AD and BT. We also consider BT+gradient data term for comparison where the BT is combined with gradient-based feature matching. Note that our intensity matching cost $E_I(d)$ is made up of BT. Since, in the proposed method, we use $\{\tau^I, \tau^F\}$ for data cost truncation and hence in order to perform a fair comparison, data terms

Table 1 Performance evaluation in terms of percentage of bad matching pixels computed over the whole image with $\delta = 1$. Here, the optimization of energy function is carried out using different data terms $E_D(d)$ with IGMRF as prior term $E_P(d)$

$E_D(d)$	Venus	Teddy	Cones
AD	1.90	16.49	12.14
BT	0.95	15.67	11.89
BT+gradient	0.89	14.9	11.32
$E_I(d) + E_F(d)$	0.40	11.41	9.98

of the other methods are also used with truncation on their costs. The results of these experiments are summarized in Table 1. The results show that the approach using proposed $E_D(d)$ outperforms those with traditional pixel-based $E_D(d)$. These results show the effectiveness of using the learning-based multilayer feature matching cost $E_F(d)$ in our approach. In other words, when the intensity and the learning-based feature matching are combined, the estimated disparities are more robust and accurate. The results also show that data term defined using the deep-learned features gives better disparities as compared to the one which uses basic gradient features.

We now demonstrate the performance of our approach by varying the number of layers in the feature matching cost $E_F(d)$. Once again, we consider the same energy function consisting of data term $E_D(d)$ and IGMRF prior where $E_D(d)$ is defined using $E_I(d)$ and $E_F(d)$. We first obtained the disparity map when $E_F(d)$ is defined using the learned features of first layer only. Next, the results are obtained when $E_F(d)$ is defined using the learned features of both first and second layers. In other words, we consider NL = 1 and NL = 2 in Eq. (8) for these two cases. Figure 5 shows that the performance improves when we

use two-layer feature matching. We also experimented with the use of three layers but we did not find significant improvement when the number of layers NL is greater than 2 (see Fig. 5). Based on these observations, we used only two-layer deep deconvolutional network in our work. This shows the effectiveness of the use of deep learning with limited number of layers.

7.3 Performance evaluation using different prior terms $E_P(d)$ with proposed $E_D(d)$

As discussed earlier, the prior term $E_P(d)$ in our energy function is defined using the combination of IGMRF and sparsity priors. We consider the energy function consists of proposed data term $E_D(d)$ and $E_P(d)$ and evaluate the performance of our approach using different choices of $E_P(d)$. For doing the same, we first choose $E_P(d)$ as $E_{IGMRF}(d)$ and compare by choosing other discontinuity preserving MRF priors such as truncated quadratic, truncated linear, and Potts models. The results in Table 2 show that the approach using the IGMRF prior combined with proposed $E_D(d)$ performs significantly better when compared to the use of other discontinuity preserving priors. This shows the effectiveness of using IGMRF prior since it better captures the spatial variation among disparities. We then evaluate the performance by choosing $E_P(d)$ as a combination of $E_{IGMRF}(d)$ and $E_{sparse}(d)$. For this, we consider three cases. In the first case, the $E_{sparse}(d)$ is obtained using the fixed DCT bases, in the second case, it is learned using the K-SVD dictionary learning method, and in the last case, we define the $E_{sparse}(d)$ using the proposed sparse autoencoder. As seen from the Table 2, the results are significantly improved when the sparsity prior is combined with the IGMRF prior and the proposed data term. This is expected because IGMRF and sparsity priors together capture the disparity characteristics

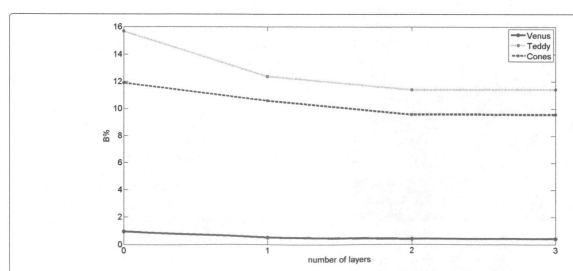

Fig. 5 Results in terms of percentage of bad matching pixels using proposed $E_D(d)$ with IGMRF prior by varying the number of layers NL in $E_F(d)$

Table 2 Performance evaluation using different prior terms $E_P(d)$ with proposed $E_D(d)$. The errors are shown in terms of bad matching pixels and these are computed over the whole image with $\delta=1$

$E_P(d)$	Venus	Teddy	Cones
Truncated quadratic	1.95	15.38	11.62
Truncated linear	0.91	12.86	10.96
Potts	1.11	13.93	11.01
$E_{IGMRF}(d)$	0.40	11.41	9.64
$E_{IGMRF}(d)+E_{sparse}(d)$ using DCT	0.38	11.1	9.36
$E_{IGMRF}(d)+E_{sparse}(d)$ using K-SVD	0.30	10.60	9.12
$E_{IGMRF}(d)+E_{sparse}(d)$ using autoencoder	0.20	9.76	8.46

in different ways and their combination serves as a better regularizer. The results also show that the use of sparsity prior obtained using proposed sparse autoencoder perform better when compared to those obtained using K-SVD or fixed basis. This is because the sparseness is better captured by the learned weights of autoencoder.

7.4 Qualitative and quantitative assessment and comparison with state of the art methods

Here, we first show the qualitative and quantitative performances of our algorithm experimented using Middlebury stereo 2001 and 2003 datasets [2]. Figure 6 shows the estimated disparity maps of the proposed approach using these datasets. One can see that the final disparity maps

are piecewise smooth and visually plausible. We also display the error maps associated with the final disparity maps as shown in the last column of Fig. 6. The error maps show the regions where the estimated disparities differ from the ground truth (black and gray regions correspond to errors in occluded and non occluded regions, respectively and white indicates no error). We can see that the proposed method has higher accuracy in discontinuous as well as nonoccluded regions. This is because the IGMRF prior preserves the discontinuities and the sparsity prior learns the edge-like sparse features in disparity map, and using these two with the proposed data term produces accurate disparities. As can be seen from Fig. 6, our method not only preserves geometrical details near depth discontinuities but performs better in textureless regions as well. We mention here that although we do not consider occlusions in our problem formulation, our method works well in these regions as well. Performance improvement in occluded regions is due to the presence of data term truncation thresholds, i.e., $\tau = \{\tau^I, \tau^F\}$.

The quantitative assessment of our algorithm experimented using Middlebury stereo 2001 and 2003 datasets [2] is shown in Table 3. In order to validate the results of our method, we compare it with state-of-the-art global dense stereo methods in terms of percentage of bad matching pixels ($B\%$). The compared approaches include feature based [16–18] and regularization based such as MRF priors [36–39], Mumford Shah regularization [51], ground control points [52], learned conditional random field (CRF) [53], and sparsity prior [42, 46] methods.

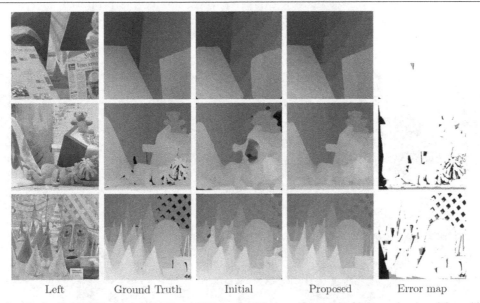

| Left | Ground Truth | Initial | Proposed | Error map |

Fig. 6 Experimental results for the Middlebury stereo 2001 and 2003 datasets [2], *Venus* (*first row*), *Teddy* (*second row*), and *Cones* (*third row*). The left image I_L and the ground truth disparity map are shown in *first and second columns*, respectively. The *third column* shows the initial disparity map used in optimizing the energy function given in Eq. (17). The final disparity and the error maps estimated using the proposed method are shown in the *fifth and the sixth columns*, respectively

Table 3 Quantitative evaluation on Middlebury stereo 2001 and 2003 datasets [2] and comparison with state-of-the-art global dense stereo methods in terms of bad matching pixels over entire image as well as non occluded regions with $\delta = 1$

Method	Venus		Teddy		Cones	
	All	Nonocc	All	Nonocc	All	Nonocc
Initial	3.47	2.00	19.65	5.61	16.43	7.15
Proposed	*0.20*	*0.10*	9.76	*3.44*	8.46	*2.36*
AdaptBP [16]	0.21	0.10	7.06	4.22	7.92	2.48
DoubleBP [38]	0.45	0.13	8.30	3.53	8.78	2.90
GCP [52]	0.53	0.16	11.5	6.44	9.49	3.59
TwoStep [17]	0.45	0.27	12.6	7.42	10.1	4.09
SemiGlob [18]	1.57	1.00	12.2	6.02	9.75	3.06
2OP [39]	0.49	0.24	15.4	10.9	10.8	5.42
CompSens [42]	0.68	0.31	13.30	7.88	9.79	3.97
MultiGC [37]	3.13	2.79	17.6	12.0	11.8	4.89
Mumford [51]	0.76	0.28	14.3	9.34	9.91	4.14
GC [36]	3.44	1.79	25.0	16.5	18.2	7.70
CRF [53]	1.3	–	11.1	–	10.8	–
Sparse [46]	–	–	11.98	–	8.14	–

Here, *en dash* indicates the result not reported. First row shows the results using initial estimate

These results are compared without using any post processing operations. We do not compare our method with global stereo methods based on handcrafted and learned features [19–21, 27] since their results are not available for the Middlebury datasets. As seen from the Table 3, our method performs best among all the other methods in nonoccluded regions. It also gives least bad matching pixels over entire image as well as in nonoccluded regions for the Venus stereo pair. We see that the overall performance of the proposed method is comparable to state-of-the-art global stereo methods. The results also indicate the effectiveness of the proposed energy function in the global energy minimization framework for dense disparity estimation.

Finally, we show the qualitative and quantitative performance of our algorithm experimented on Middlebury stereo 2014 datasets [2] that consists of 15 training and 15 test stereo pairs. Figure 7 shows the estimated disparity maps of the proposed approach using some of these datasets. In order to validate and compare the

Fig. 7 Experimental results for the Middlebury stereo 2014 datasets [2], *Adirondack, Motorcycle, Pipes, Playroom, PlaytableP, Recycle, Shelves, Vintage*. The *left image* I_L, ground truth and disparity map estimated using the proposed method for each stereo pair are shown in the *first, second, and third rows*, respectively

performance of our method with other latest stereo methods listed on [2], we submitted these estimated disparity maps online to the server available on Middlebury website [2] which in turn returned the overall evaluation and comparison chart. Since the test dataset does not have ground truth, evaluation is only done by submitting the estimated disparity maps on this online server. We mention here that one cannot adjust the parameters for test datasets because the submission can be done only once. The qualitative and quantitative results and the comparisons can be seen on Middlebury stereo evaluation page. We achieve a ranking of 43 for training set and ranking of 48 on test set. Our method does not rank among the top methods because the accuracy of our method is sensitive to the parameters of the model. One can enhance the results by carefully choosing the parameters. Experimental results indicate that our method is better than the state-of-the-art regularization-based methods and comparable to other latest stereo methods.

8 Conclusion

We have presented a new approach for dense disparity map estimation based on inhomogeneous MRF and sparsity priors in an energy minimization framework. The data term is defined using the combination of intensity and the learning-based multilayer feature matching costs. The feature matching cost is defined over the deep learned features of given stereo pair, and we have used deep deconvolutional network for learning these hierarchical features. The IGMRF prior captures the smoothness in disparities and preserves the discontinuities in terms of IGMRF parameters. The sparsity prior is defined over the learned sparseness of disparities where the sparse representation of disparities are learned using the sparse autoencoder. We have presented an iterative two-phase algorithm for disparity estimation where in phase one, the disparity map is estimated by minimizing our energy function using graph cuts and in phase two, the IGMRF parameters and sparse representation of disparity maps are obtained. Experiments conducted on various datasets of Middlebury site verify the effectiveness of the proposed data term, IGMRF, and sparsity priors when used in an energy minimization framework. Performance of the proposed method is comparable to many of the better performing and latest dense stereo methods.

Authors' contributions
Both authors have equally contributed to the manuscript. Both authors read and approved the final manuscript.

Authors' information
Sonam Nahar received the B.E. degree in Information Technology from Manikya Lal Verma Textile Enginerring College, Bhilwara, India, in 2008, and M.Tech. degree in Information and Communication Technology from Dhirubhai Ambani Institute of Information and Technology (DA-IICT), Gandhinagar, India, in 2010. She is currently pursuing the Ph.D degree from DA-IICT, Gandhinagar, India, and serving as an Assistant Professor with The LNM Institute of Information Technology (LNMIIT), Jaipur, India, in Computer Science and Engineering Department. Her research interests include computer vision, image processing, and deep learning. Manjunath V. Joshi received the B.E. degree from the University of Mysore, Mysore, India, and the M.Tech. and Ph.D. degrees from the Indian Institute of Technology Bombay (IIT Bombay), Mumbai, India. Currently, he is serving as a Professor with the Dhirubhai Ambani Institute of Information and Communication Technology, Gandhinagar, India. He has been involved in active research in the areas of signal processing, image processing, and computer vision. He has coauthored two books entitled Motion-Free Super Resolution (Springer, New York) and Digital Heritage Reconstruction Using Super resolution and Inpainting (Morgan and Claypool). Dr. Joshi was a recipient of the Outstanding Researcher Award in Engineering Section by the Research Scholars Forum of IIT Bombay. He was also a recipient of the Best Ph.D. Thesis Award by Infineon India and the Dr. Vikram Sarabhai Award in the field of information technology constituted by the Government of Gujarat, India.

Competing interests
The authors declare that they have no competing interests.

Author details
[1]The LNM Institute of Information Technology, Jaipur, India. [2]Dhirubhai Ambani Institute of Information Technology, Gandhinagar, India.

References
1. Scharstein D, Szeliski R, Zabih R (2002) A taxonomy and evaluation of dense two-frame stereo correspondence algorithms. Int J Comput Vis 47(1/2/3):7–42
2. Scharstein D, Szeliski R, Zabih R (1987) Middlebury Stereo. http://vision.middlebury.edu/stereo
3. Kanade T, Okutomi M (1994) A stereo matching algorithm with an adaptive window: theory and experiment. Pattern Anal Mach Intell IEEE Trans 16(9):920–932
4. Fusiello A, Roberto V, Trucco E (1997) Efficient stereo with multiple windowing. In: Proceedings of IEEE Computer Society Conference on Computer Vision and Pattern Recognition. pp 858–863. doi:10.1109/CVPR.1997.609428
5. Yoon KJ, Kweon IS (2006) Adaptive support-weight approach for correspondence search. Pattern Anal Mach Intell IEEE Trans 28(4):650–656
6. Hosni A, Rhemann C, Bleyer M, Rother C, Gelautz M (2013) Fast cost-volume filtering for visual correspondence and beyond. Pattern Anal Mach Intell IEEE Trans 35(2):504–511
7. Kolmogorov V, Zabih R (2004) What energy functions can be minimized via graph cuts? Pattern Anal Mach Intell IEEE Trans 26(2):147–159
8. Sun J, Zheng NN, Shum HY (2003) Stereo matching using belief propagation. Pattern Anal Mach Intell IEEE Trans 25(7):787–800
9. Tappen MF, Freeman WT (2003) Comparison of graph cuts with belief propagation for stereo, using identical MRF parameters, vol.2. In: Proceedings Ninth IEEE International Conference on Computer Vision Vol. 2. pp 900–906. doi:10.1109/ICCV.2003.1238444
10. Hirschmuller H, Scharstein D (2007) Evaluation of cost functions for stereo matching. In: 2007 IEEE Conference on Computer Vision and Pattern Recognition. pp 1–8. doi:10.1109/CVPR.2007.383248
11. Tola E, Lepetit V, Fua P (2010) Daisy: An efficient dense descriptor applied to wide-baseline stereo. Pattern Anal Mach Intell IEEE Trans 32(5):815–830
12. Joglekar J, Gedam SS, Mohan BK (2014) Image matching using sift features and relaxation labeling technique:a constraint initializing method for dense stereo matching. Geosci Remote Sensing, IEEE Trans 52(9):5643–5652
13. Grimson WEL (1985) Computational experiments with a feature based stereo algorithm. Pattern Anal Mach Intell IEEE Trans 7(1):17–34
14. Ayache N, Faverjon B Efficient registration of stereo images by matching graph descriptions of edge segments. International Journal of Computer Vision:107–131
15. Hong L, Chen G (2004) Segment-based stereo matching using graph cuts. In: Proceedings of the 2004 IEEE Computer Society Conference on Computer Vision and Pattern Recognition, 2004. CVPR 2004, Vol.1 I-74-I-81. doi:10.1109/CVPR.2004.1315016

16. Klaus A, Sormann M, Karner K (2006) Segment-based stereo matching using belief propagation and a self-adapting dissimilarity measure, vol.3. In: 18th International Conference on Pattern Recognition (ICPR'06). pp 15–18. doi:10.1109/ICPR.2006.1033

17. L. Wang ZL, Zhang Z (2014) Feature based stereo matching using two-step expansion. Math Probl Eng 14:14

18. Hirschmüller H (2008) Stereo processing by semi-global matching and mutual information. Pattern Anal Mach Intell IEEE Trans 30(2):328–341

19. Liu C, Yuen J, Torralba A (2011) Sift flow: dense correspondence across scenes and its applications. Pattern Anal Mach Intell IEEE Trans 33(5):978–994

20. Kim J, Liu C, Sha F, Grauman K (2013) Deformable spatial pyramid matching for fast dense correspondences. In: 2013 IEEE Conference on Computer Vision and Pattern Recognition. pp 2307–2314. doi:10.1109/CVPR.2013.299

21. Saxena A, Chung SH, Ng AY (2007) 3-D depth reconstruction from a single still image. Int J Comput Vis 76:2007

22. Vincent P, Larochelle H, Lajoie I, Bengio Y, Manzagol P (2010) Stacked denoising autoencoders: learning useful representations in a deep network with a local denoising criterion. J Mach Learn Res 11:3371–3408

23. Krizhevsky A, Sutskever I, Hinton GE (2012) Imagenet classification with deep convolutional neural networks. In: Advances in Neural Information Processing Systems 25. pp 1097–1105

24. Bengio Y (2009) Learning deep architectures for AI. Foundations Trends Mach Learn 2(1):1–127

25. Dong C, Loy CC, He K, Tang X (2015) Image super-resolution using deep convolutional networks. CoRR abs/1501.00092

26. Zbontar J, LeCun Y (2014) Computing the stereo matching cost with a convolutional neural network. CoRR abs/1409.4326

27. Zhang C, Shen C (2015) Unsupervised feature learning for dense correspondences across scenes. CoRR abs/1501.00642

28. Poultney C, Chopra S, Lecun Y (2006) Efficient learning of sparse representations with an energy-based model. In: Advances in Neural Information Processing Systems

29. Lee H, Ekanadham C, Ng AY (2007) Sparse deep belief net model for visual area v2. In: Neural Information Processing Systems. pp 873–880

30. Hinton GE, Osindero S (2006) A fast learning algorithm for deep belief nets. Neural Comput 18:2006

31. Zeiler MD, Krishnan D, Taylor GW, Fergus R (2010) Deconvolutional networks. In: 2010 IEEE Computer Society Conference on Computer Vision and Pattern Recognition. pp 2528–2535. doi:10.1109/CVPR.2010.5539957

32. Zeiler MD, Taylor GW, Fergus R (2011) Adaptive deconvolutional networks for mid and high level feature learning. In: Computer Vision, IEEE International Conference On. pp 2018–2025

33. Jarrett K, Kavukcuoglu K, Ranzato MA, Lecun Y (2009) What is the best multi-stage architecture for object recognition? In: 2009 IEEE 12th International Conference on Computer Vision. pp 2146–2153. doi:10.1109/ICCV.2009.5459469

34. Li SZ (1995) Markov random field modeling in computer vision. Springer, New York

35. Roy S (1999) Stereo without epipolar lines: a maximum-flow formulation. Int J Comput Vis 34(2–3):147–161

36. Boykov Y, Veksler O, Zabih R (2001) Fast approximate energy minimization via graph cuts. Pattern Anal Mach Intell IEEE Trans 23(11):1222–1239

37. Kolmogorov V, Zabih R (2002) Multi-camera scene reconstruction via graph cuts. In: Computer Vision, European Conference On. pp 82–96

38. Yang Q, Wang L, Yang R, Stewenius H, Nister D (2009) Stereo matching with color-weighted correlation, hierarchical belief propagation, and occlusion handling. Pattern Anal Mach Intell IEEE Trans 31(3):492–504

39. Woodford O, Torr P, Reid I, Fitzgibbon A (2008) Global stereo reconstruction under second order smoothness priors. In: Computer Vision and Pattern Recognition, IEEE Conference On. pp 1–8

40. Zhang L, Seitz SM (2005) Parameter estimation for MRF stereo, vol.2. In: 2005 IEEE Computer Society Conference on Computer Vision and Pattern Recognition (CVPR'05), Vol. 2. pp 288–295. doi:10.1109/CVPR.2005.269

41. Jalobeanu A, Blanc-Feraud L, Zerubia J (2004) An adaptive gaussian model for satellite image deblurring. Image Process IEEE Trans 13(4):613–621

42. Hawe S, Kleinsteuber M, Diepold K (2011) Dense disparity maps from sparse disparity measurements. In: 2011 International Conference on Computer Vision. pp 2126–2133. doi:10.1109/ICCV.2011.6126488

43. Elad M, Aharon M (2006) Image denoising via sparse and redundant representations over learned dictionaries. Image Process IEEE Trans 15(12):3736–3745

44. Xie J, Xu L, Chen E (2012) Image denoising and inpainting with deep neural networks. In: Advances in Neural Information Processing Systems 25. pp 350–358

45. Aharon M, Elad M, Bruckstein A (2006) K -SVD: An algorithm for designing overcomplete dictionaries for sparse representation. Signal Process IEEE Trans 54(11):4311–4322

46. Tosic I, Olshausen BA, Culpepper BJ (2011) Learning sparse representations of depth. Selected Topics Signal Process IEEE J 5(5):941–952

47. Birchfield S, Tomasi C (1998) A pixel dissimilarity measure that is insensitive to image sampling. Pattern Anal Mach Intell IEEE Trans 20(4):401–406

48. Joshi M, Jalobeanu A (2010) Map estimation for multiresolution fusion in remotely sensed images using an IGMRF prior model. Geosci Remote Sensing IEEE Trans 48(3):1245–1255

49. Gajjar PP, Joshi MV (2010) New learning based super-resolution: use of DWT and IGMRF prior. Image Process IEEE Trans 19(5):1201–1213

50. Mitchell TM (1997) Machine learning. McGraw-Hill, New York, USA

51. Ben-Ari R, Sochen N (2010) Stereo matching with Mumford-Shah regularization and occlusion handling. Pattern Anal Mach Intell IEEE Trans 32(11):2071–2084

52. Wang L, Yang R (2011) Global stereo matching leveraged by sparse ground control points. In: CVPR 2011. pp 3033–3040. doi:10.1109/CVPR.2011.5995480

53. Scharstein D, Pal C (2007) Learning conditional random fields for stereo. In: Computer Vision and Pattern Recognition, IEEE Conference On. pp 1–8

16

Nuclear detection in 4D microscope images of a developing embryo using an enhanced probability map of top-ranked intensity-ordered descriptors

Xian-Hua Han[1,2*], Yukako Tohsato[3], Koji Kyoda[3], Shuichi Onami[3], Ikuko Nishikawa[2] and Yen-Wei Chen[2]

Abstract

Nuclear detection in embryos is an indispensable process for quantitative analysis of the development of multicellular organisms. Due to the overlap in the distribution of pixel intensity of nuclear and cytoplasmic regions and the large variation of pixel intensity even within the same type of cellular components in different embryos, it is difficult to separate nuclear regions from the surrounding cytoplasmic region in differential interference contrast (DIC) microscope image. This study explores a discriminative representation of a local patch around a fixed pixel, called top-ranked intensity-ordered descriptor (TRIOD), which is prospected to distinguish the smoothed texture in the nucleus from the irregular texture in cytoplasm containing yolk granules. Then, a probability process is employed to model nuclear TRIOD prototypes, and the enhanced nuclear probability map can be constructed with the TRIODs of all pixels in a DIC microscope image. Finally, a distance-regularized level set method, which not only considers the probability change in a nearby pixel but also regularizes the contour smoothness, is applied to refine the initial localization by simply thresholding on the enhanced probability map. Experimental results show that the proposed strategy can give much better performance for segmentation of nuclear regions than the conventional strategies.

Keywords: Top-ranked intensity-ordered descriptor, TRIOD, Enhanced probability map, Nuclear detection, Level set method

1 Introduction

Identification of gene function during animal development is the main task of developmental biology. Genetic perturbation and analysis in animal embryos often clarify the function of the specific gene. Due to the complete genome sequence (roughly 20,000 protein-coding genes [1]) and short lifetime, the nematode *Caenorhabditis elegans* is generally used as a model organism in biology. By observing a perturbed early *C. elegans* embryo using a microscope of Nomarski differential interference contrast (DIC) optics [2], biologists manually analyze early embryonic events and evaluate the roles of a specific gene in the developmental process. Detection of various components

of interests in the embryo is the first indispensable step to extract the quantitative measure of the early embryonic events such as growth of cell number, changes of nuclear position and shape, and timing of cell division.

Since the early embryonic events are closely related to the position, morphological variations, number changes of nuclei, and so on, automated detection of nuclei in DIC microscope images plays an essential role for understanding animal development. This work focuses on detecting nuclei and cytoplasm in 3-dimensional (3D) time-lapse images of a *C. elegans* embryo recorded by DIC microscope [2]. Two images of the 3D DIC microscope images are shown in Fig. 1a, which are obtained from different *C. elegans* embryos. It can be seen that the nuclear region is much smoother than the cytoplasmic region with yolk granules. We take one nuclear and cytoplasmic regions from both images as explored regions (Fig. 1a) denoted by different color frames and compare the statistical

*Correspondence: hanxh1216@gmail.com
[1]The Artificial Intelligence Research Center, Advanced Industrial Science and Technology, Tokyo 135-0064, Japan
Full list of author information is available at the end of the article

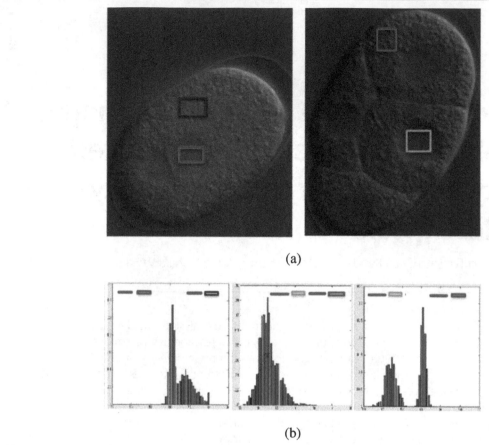

(a)

(b)

Fig. 1 The statistical analysis of intensity distribution from cytoplasmic and nuclear regions. **a** Two DIC microscope images and their explored regions (*red, blue, pink,* and *green frames*). **b** The compared intensity histograms from different explored regions, where the *blue, red, green,* and *pink rectangles* mean the corresponding explored regions framed by *blue, red, green,* and *pink colors* in Fig. 1a. The *blue* and *red histograms* in the *left figure* are for the framed regions by *blue* and *red colors* in Fig. 1a, and those in the *middle figure* are for the framed regions by *green* and *pink colors* in Fig. 1a, respectively, while those in the *right figure* are for the framed regions by *green* and *blue colors*

distributions of (1) different types of explored regions from the same embryo and (2) the same type of explored regions from different embryos shown in Fig. 1b. Figure 1b manifests that the intensities of different cellular components can be completely overlapped (the middle histogram in Fig. 1b). However, the same type of explored regions from different embryos possibly has very different intensity distributions (the right histogram in Fig. 1b). Therefore, it would be impossible to only use the intensity to identify the nuclear and cytoplasmic regions, and thus, exploring a discriminating representation using texture is necessary for distinguishing the cytoplasmic and nuclear regions.

There are several studies that attempt to explore the dynamic information of 3D time-lapse DIC microscope images. Two computer-assisted systems: SIMI BioCell [3] and 3D-DIASemb [4], have been constructed for tracking the changes of the 3D nuclear positions in the 3D time-lapse DIC microscope images. These two systems

identify the positions and sizes of the nuclei via displaying 3D time-lapse DIC microscope images with a graphical user interface. However, the nuclei are still detected manually, and thus, it is a laborious task. In order to efficiently implement the task of analyzing dynamic changes in DIC microscope images, several efforts aimed to automatically identify different types of regions of the *C. elegans* embryo image and especially detect the nuclear regions from the surrounding cytoplasm. Yasuda et al. [5] combined several types of edge features for detecting the nuclear and membrane regions. Because of the large variation in the same type of regions and possibly similar intensity distribution between different types of regions, this method leads to a lot of numbers of false positive and missing detection, which were required to be corrected by laborious hand-tuning. Hamahashi et al. [6] proposed to transform a raw image in 3D time-lapse DIC microscope images into local entropy domain (local entropy image) to enhance the cytoplasmic region (suppress the nuclear region) and then track the nuclei in dynamic image sequence.The method used the statistics (local entropy) of a local patch centered on the focused pixel instead of pixel intensity and can adapt any 3D time-lapse images for enhancing the cytoplasmic region. However, since only one statistic of the local patch based on its distribution is computed, it produced low contrast and blurred boundary between the nuclear and cyto-plasmic regions in a local entropy image. On the other hand, Ning et al. [7] explored a multilayer convolutional neural network with the intensities of local patches as the initial input and attempted to recognize five cate-gories: cell wall, cytoplasm, nucleus membrane, nucleus, and outside medium. This complex framework needs strength effort as post-processing for giving acceptable identification by using an energy-based model and a set of elastic models and thus leads to high computational cost.

This study proposes a simple but efficient framework for automatically recognizing the nuclear regions from the surrounding cytoplasmic region. It is well known that the cytoplasm contains a lot of yolk granules which can appear in any position under irregular frequency on the back-ground with similar intensity, in contrast to the smooth nuclear region. Therefore, it is impossible to distinguish the nuclear pixel from the cytoplasm pixel by only using

pixel intensity, while it is also difficult to recognize using a local patch, which is the feature for representing the cen-tered pixel, due to the irregular appearance of yolk gran-ules. In this study, we explore a discriminated descriptor for a local patch centered in a pixel, called top-ranked intensity-ordered descriptor (TRIOD), which can retain the intensity variation of the yolk granules in cytoplasm local patch without destroying the smooth intensity in nuclear local patch. Due to the small variation of the TRI-ODs for nuclear pixel representation, we collect a set of nuclear TRIODs as prototypes and apply a probability process to model them. With the constructed model, we can transform a raw DIC microscope image into a nuclear-enhanced probability map, which achieves very high con-trast between the nuclear and cytoplasmic regions. Finally, a distance-regularized level set (DRLS) method [8], which not only considers the probability change in a nearby pixel but also regularizes the contour smoothness, is applied to refine the initial localization by simply thresholding on the enhanced probability map. The proposed frame-work for nuclear detection is shown in Fig. 2, where the top figure manifests the construction procedure of prob-ability models for the nuclear TRIOD prototypes and the bottom part gives the computation step of a nuclear-enhanced probability map, and the DRLS-based refine-ment is employed for obtaining final detection results.

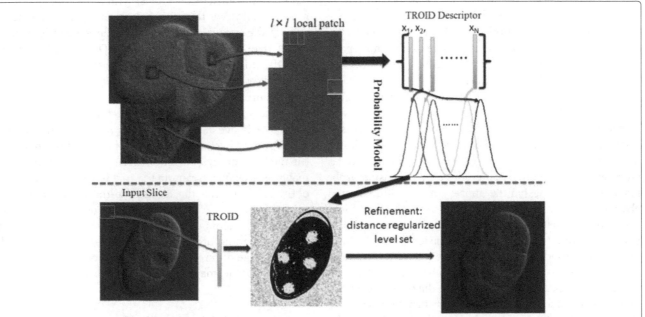

Fig. 2 The proposed nuclear detection framework. The *top figure* denotes the construction procedure of probability models based on TRIODs, and the *bottom part* gives the procedure of nuclear detection. For constructing of probability models, we firstly extract some nuclear regions from several randomly selected embryo images and then obtain the TRIODs from all $l \times l$ local patches centered on the pixels in the nuclear regions, which are used as the input vector for constructing the nuclear models. In the nuclear detection procedure, the TRIODs for all pixels in the input embryo are computed as the input vector to the constructed probability model for obtaining the transformed nuclear-enhancement map, and then, the level set method is used for nuclear detection on the transformed map

We evaluate the effectiveness and performance of our proposed framework for nuclear detection.

This paper is organized as follows. Section 2 describes the discriminated TRIOD for representing the nuclear and cytoplasm pixel and introduces the construction of the probability models for computation of the nuclear-enhanced probability map. A refinement detection via a distance-regularized level set method is investigated in Section 3. Experimental results and conclusions are given in Sections 4 and 5, respectively.

2 Enhanced probability map based on top-ranked intensity-ordered descriptors

This section firstly introduces a discriminative representation for irregular texture, called top-ranked intensity-ordered descriptors. Due to the small variance of the nuclear region (smooth), we propose to model nuclear TRIODs as a multiple Gaussian process and transform the raw DIC microscope image into a nuclear-enhanced probability map for final segmentation. In the following, we evaluate the transformed probability maps under different parameters.

2.1 Top-ranked intensity-ordered descriptors

As statistically analyzed in the above section, the cytoplasmic region includes a lot of yolk granules bulging out from the background, which can be considered as irregular texture variance. For local texture representation, a number of methods have been proposed in the literature for computer vision problems. The most popular strategies are based on histograms such as SIFT (Scale-Invariant Feature Transform) [9], GLOH (Gradient Location-Orientation Histogram), and their recently improved versions [10, 11] for partially dealing with some kinds of variations and distortions in the processed images. However, while the above descriptors have shown promising performance for representing local patches with regular structure in different computer vision problems, they cannot handle more complex illumination change. On the other hand, in order to obtain robust features to illumination change, local binary pattern (LBP) texture operator and its many extensions [12, 13] have been widely used in vision literature and obtained good performance vis-a-vis illumination change. All the local feature representations developed in the computer vision field would encounter difficulty for handling irregular structures like the unorganized yolk granules in the cytoplasmic region of DIC microscope images. Therefore, a local entropy method [6] was introduced to deal with the irregular texture in DIC microscope image, which only considers the frequency of pixel intensity and gives the statistic measure of information capacity

in a local patch. This method can work well despite the large intensity variance in the DIC microscope images of different organisms. However, only one statistic measure (local entropy) for a local patch is extracted, and thus, the representation ability is limited for distinguishing the large variant cytoplasmic and smooth nuclear regions.

This study proposes a discriminative irregular texture representation, which is prospected to give similar descriptors for the cytoplasm texture even with large variance and also a consistent representation of nuclear but different from the cytoplasmic one. Let us represent the ith focused pixel in a DIC microscope image as a small $l \times l$ patch, which can be re-arranged into a vector $\mathbf{s}_i = [s_{i,0}, s_{i,1}, \cdots, s_{i,D-1}]$, and $\mathbf{s}_i \in R^D$ ($D = l \times l - 1$). Since the yolk granules possibly appear at any location in the local patch, they will give a very different vector even for the same cytoplasm type of pixels. Thus, we attempt to sort the un-ordered vector and only take a subset of the top-ranked value as the descriptor. In order to handle the intensity variance in DIC microscope images of different organisms, we firstly subtract the mean value from the vector $\mathbf{s}_i$ and calculate the absolute magnitudes:

$$\bar{s}_{i,j} = |s_{i,j} - \frac{1}{D}\sum_{d=0}^{D-1} s_{i,d}|. \tag{1}$$

Then, we sort the vector $\bar{\mathbf{s}}_i$ in a non-ascending order and obtain the re-ordered vector $\hat{\mathbf{s}}_i$ with $\hat{s}_{i,0} \geq \hat{s}_{i,1} \geq \cdots \geq \hat{s}_{i,D-1}$. Finally, we take the K-large magnitude elements in $\hat{\mathbf{s}}_i$ as the texture representation, named as top-ranked intensity ordered descriptors (TRIODs). For all pixels in the DIC microscope image, the K-dimensional TRIODs can be extracted from the $l \times l$ local patches around the focused pixels. We visualize the first and the second top-three-magnitude elements of all pixels by combining them into color images as shown in Fig. 3b, c, which manifest the proposed TRIODs can obtain high contrast between the nuclear and cytoplasmic regions. The first top-three-magnitude elements denote the first to the third elements of the TRIOD, while the second top-three-magnitude elements denote the fourth to the sixth ones of the TRIOD. Since the elements in the TRIODs have already sorted in a non-ascending order, the near elements in the TRIOD have no large difference, and thus, almost all pixels in the combined color images have gray intensity.

2.2 Nucleus model construction for probability map transformation

As shown in Fig. 3, it can be seen that the variance of the nuclear TRIOD elements are much smaller than those for cytoplasm pixels, and thus, it would be much easier to model the nuclear TRIODs than the cytoplasmic ones.

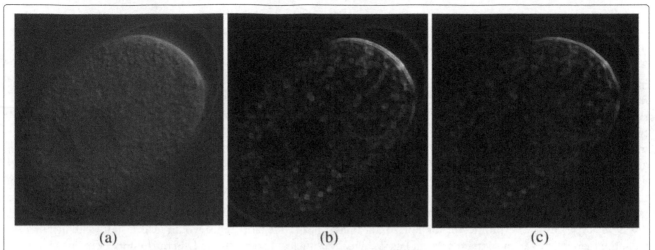

Fig. 3 The visualization of the proposed TRIODs. **a** A raw slice DIC microscope image. The corresponding color image by combining the first top-three elements (**b**) and the second top-three elements (**c**) of the TRIODs

Therefore, this study attempts to construct a probability model of nuclear TRIODs and transform any TRIOD with the constructed model to a nuclear-enhanced probability map. Given some nuclear regions from the DIC microscope image of any organism, a set of nuclear TRIODs $\mathbf{X} = [\mathbf{x}_1, \mathbf{x}_2, \cdots, \mathbf{x}_N]$, called nuclear TRIOD prototypes, can be extracted. The intuitive way to use the N TRIODs for constructing the nuclear model is to directly use M Gaussian models as follows:

$$P(\mathbf{X}) = \sum_{m=1}^{M} w_m N(\mathbf{X}|\mu_m, \Sigma_m), \qquad (2)$$

where $N(\mathbf{X}|\mu_m, \Sigma_m)$ is a Gaussian model. If we set K as the nuclear TRIOD prototype number, the mean vector of the mth Gaussian model is the mth TRIOD, i.e., $\mu_m = \mathbf{x}_m$. Σ_m and w_m are the co-variance matrix and weight parameters of the mth Gaussian model, respectively. Since the M Gaussian models are centered on the $N = M$ TRIODs, respectively, all model weights can be set as $\frac{1}{M}$ which means all the models have the same contribution to the final probability process. For simplicity, we assume Σ_k is a diagonal matrix and its determinant is σ_m^2, which is calculated as the mean of the square distances between the the mean vectors of the Gaussian model and their five nearest neighbors as follows:

$$\sigma_m^2 = \sum_{\mathbf{x}_i \in NN_5(\mu_m)} |\mathbf{x}_i - \mu_m|^2, \qquad (3)$$

where $\mathbf{x}_i \in NN_5(\mu_m)$ denotes the five nearest neighbors in $\mathbf{X}$ to the mean μ_m of the mth Gaussian model.

In the constructed nuclear model, if the Gaussian component number M (such as $M = N$) is large, it needs to calculate the fitting degrees (probability) of a test TRIOD to all constructed Gaussian models, and thus, the computational cost will be increased linearly to the component number. In order to reduce computational time, we simply cluster the N nuclear TRIOD prototypes into M ($M << N$) groups and obtain group centers as the mean $[\mu_1, \mu_2, \cdots, \mu_M]$.

For any test TRIOD $\mathbf{x}_t$, we can calculate its probability belonging to the mth Gaussian model as

$$\gamma(m|\mathbf{x}_t) = \frac{w_m N(\mathbf{x}_t|\mu_m, \sigma_m^2)}{\sum_{m=1}^{M} w_m N(\mathbf{x}_t|\mu_m, \sigma_m^2)}. \qquad (4)$$

Since all the M Gaussian models are for fitting nuclear TRIODs, it is prospected that any test nuclear TRIOD always can be well fitted by several similar models. However, the cytoplasm TRIODs are generally far from the constructed models, and then, the probability to any constructed model will be low. This study uses the J highest probabilities to give the final map magnitude for a TRIOD $\mathbf{x}_t$ as follows:

$$\mathrm{PM}(\mathbf{x}_t) = \frac{1}{J} \sum_{j=1}^{J} \hat{\gamma}(j|\mathbf{x}_t), \qquad (5)$$

where $\hat{\gamma}(j|\mathbf{x}_t)$ is the jth largest probability of the M models.

2.3 Evaluation of the transformed probability maps under different parameters

As shown in the flowchart of our proposed nuclear detection strategy (Fig. 2), we randomly select the slices from the DIC microscope images of three embryos, from which several nuclear regions can be manually given for preparing the nuclear prototypes. In our experiments, about 2000 K ($K = $ int $\left(\frac{l \times l - 1}{2}\right) + 1$, "int" means taking the integer number) nuclear TRIOD prototypes are extracted from $l \times l$ local patches in the given nuclear regions, and thus, the computational cost would be high if all prototypes are used as the mean parameters of the probability models. Therefore, we employ clustering algorithm for grouping them into M representative TRIOD prototypes, which correspond to K Gaussian models. Figure 4 shows the nuclear-enhanced probability maps under different model numbers of TRIODs, which are extracted from 9×9 local patches. The profiles of the horizontal lines from the map images are also manifested in Fig. 4c, which shows the higher contrasts between the cytoplasmic and nuclear regions using larger numbers of probability models. With the probability map using the Gaussian models of all TRIOD prototypes as criterion measure, we calculate the summed squared difference of all pixels between the probability maps, and the summed difference values for four DIC slices from different organisms are given in Fig. 4d. It can be seen that the summed differences after 50 probability models change a little and seem to give the local minimums for all four samples. The computational times (second) are also given in Fig. 4e. In order to balance

the trade-off between computational cost and contrast, we select 50 probability models to fit the nuclear TRIODs in the following experiments.

Next, we validate the effect of the local patch sizes to the probability maps by setting the parameters l of the local patch ($l \times l$) as $3, 5, 7, 9, \cdots$, and the top-ranked intensity-ordered descriptors with $K = $ int $\left(\frac{l \times l - 1}{2}\right) + 1$ elements are extracted for pixel representation. The resulted probability maps with different local patch sizes are shown in Fig. 5, which indicates that the proposed strategy with small local patch sizes can correctly enhance almost all nuclear pixels (true positive) but inaccurately emphasize some cytoplasm pixels (false positive), while using a large size of local patches would lead to miss-enhancement of nuclear pixels especially in the boundary regions but more clear enhanced probability maps.

Finally, the different dimensions of the TRIOD feature are evaluated. We set the dimension (K) of the TRIOD feature as 1, int $\left(\frac{l \times l}{8}\right) + 1$, int $\left(\frac{l \times l - 1}{4}\right) + 1$, int $\left(\frac{(l \times l - 1) \times 3}{8}\right) + 1$, int $\left(\frac{l \times l}{2}\right) + 1$, $\cdots$ with $l = 5, 7$, and 9. Figure 6 shows the transformed probability maps with $K = 1$, int $\left(\frac{l \times l}{4}\right) + 1$, int $\left(\frac{l \times l - 1}{2}\right) + 1$, int $\left(\frac{(l \times l - 1) \times 3}{4}\right) + 1$ under $l = 5, 7, 9$. We also define the discriminated degrees for measuring the distinguish ability of the transformed probability maps

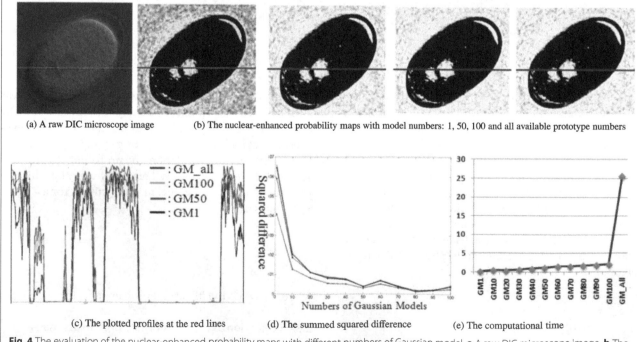

(a) A raw DIC microscope image   (b) The nuclear-enhanced probability maps with model numbers: 1, 50, 100 and all available prototype numbers

(c) The plotted profiles at the red lines   (d) The summed squared difference   (e) The computational time

Fig. 4 The evaluation of the nuclear-enhanced probability maps with different numbers of Gaussian model. **a** A raw DIC microscope image. **b** The nuclear-enhanced probability maps with model numbers: 1, 50, 100, and all available prototype numbers. **c** The plotted profiles at the *red lines*. **d** The summed squared difference. **e** The computational time

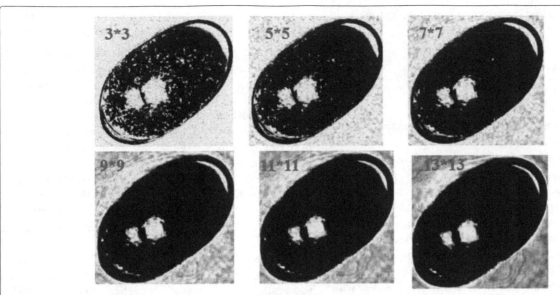

Fig. 5 The evaluation of the nuclear-enhanced probability maps with different local patch sizes

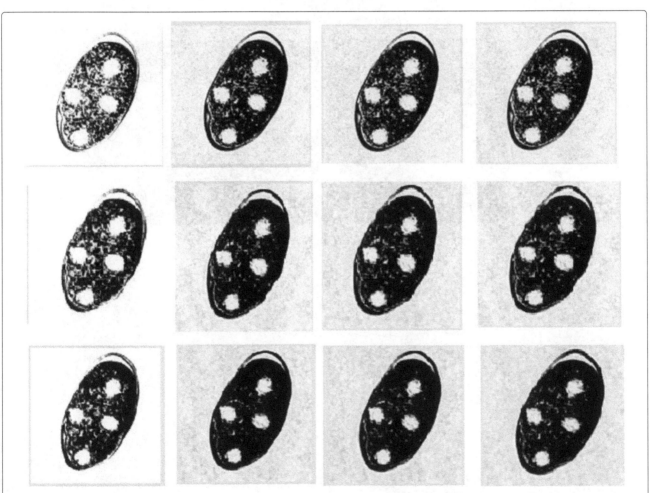

Fig. 6 The transformed probability maps with different dimensions K of the TRIODs, which are extracted from the local patch sizes $l = 5, 7, 9$. The *row images* from the *top* to the *bottom* denote the transformed maps with $l = 5, 7, 9$, and the *column images* from the *left* to the *right* denote those with the TRIOD dimensions $K = 1$, $\text{int}\left(\frac{l \times l}{4}\right) + 1$, $\text{int}\left(\frac{l \times l - 1}{2}\right) + 1$, $\text{int}\left(\frac{(l \times l - 1) \times 3}{4}\right) + 1$, respectively

between the nuclear and the surrounding cytoplasmic regions as follows:

$$DS(\mathbf{p}) = \frac{(m1_p - m2_p)^2}{4 \times (s1_p + s2_p)}, \tag{6}$$

where $\mathbf{p}$ denotes a transformed probability map, $m1_p$ and $m2_p$ are the mean values of the nuclear and cytoplasmic pixels in the transformed map such as the pixel in the regions shown in Fig. 7a, and $s1_p$ and $s2_p$ denote the variances of the nuclear and cytoplasmic pixels in the transformed map, respectively. The larger the DS($\mathbf{p}$) is, the higher the contrast between the nuclear and the surrounding cytoplasmic regions would be. Figure 7b gives the quantitative measurements of the transformed probability maps with different K under $l = 5$ and 9. From Fig. 6b, it can be seen that the discriminated degrees with $K = \mathrm{int}\left(\frac{l \times l}{2}\right) + 1$ manifest acceptable distinguish ability

and cannot be greatly improved even increasing K. Therefore, we set $K = \mathrm{int}\left(\frac{l \times l}{2}\right) + 1$ for the proposed TRIOD features in all the following experiments. Segmentation of the nuclear region with the level set method introduced in the next section will be based on the enhanced probability maps with different patch sizes l and the corresponding TRIOD feature dimension K.

In addition, we will also give compared nuclear detection results with the local entropy method [6], which possibly uses different patch sizes for measuring the local entropy of a pixel. In our experiments, the local entropy method is implemented, and the transformed local entropy images with different patch sizes ($l = 5, 9, 13, 17, 21$) are shown in Fig. 8a. Furthermore, Fig. 8b manifests the discriminated degrees of the transformed local entropy images with different patch sizes calculated by Eq. (6), which denotes the transformed image with patch size $l = 9$ has much highest distinguish ability as being proven in [6]. Therefore, the following nuclear

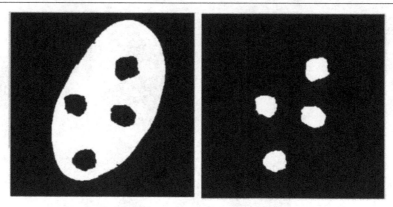

(a)The cytoplasmic and nuclear regions for quantitative evaluation.

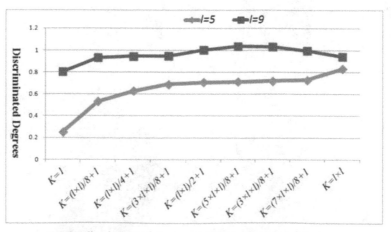

(b)The discriminated degree of different transformed maps.

Fig. 7 The quantitative evaluation for the transformed probability maps with different dimensions K of the TRIODs. **a** The cytoplasmic and nuclear regions for quantitative evaluation. **b** The discriminated degree of different transformed maps

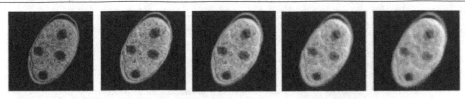

(a)The transformed local entropy images with different local patch sizes

$(l = 5, 9, 13, 17, 21)$

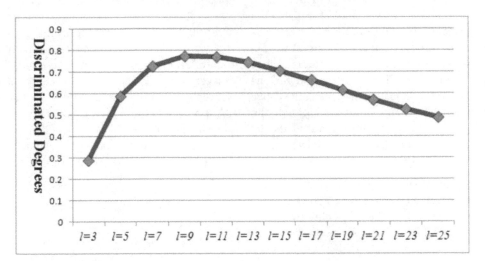

(b)The discriminated degrees of the transformed local entropy images with

different patch sizes calculated by Eq. (6)

Fig. 8 The quantitative evaluation for the local entropy images with local patch sizes. **a** The transformed local entropy images with different local patch sizes. **b** The discriminated degrees of the transformed local entropy images with different patch sizes calculated by Eq. (6)

detection is based on the transformed local entropy image with the same seed points as the proposed framework for fair comparison.

3   Level set-based detection

The basic idea of the level set method is to represent a contour as the zero level set of a function, called a level set function (LSF), and formulate the contour's motion as the evolution of the level set function. For image segmentation, the level set function can be formulated as $\phi(x, y, t)$, on the image coordinate space $[x, y] \in \Omega$ and time direction, which embeds the dynamic contour at the zero level set. Assuming the LSF ϕ takes positive values outside the zero level contour and negative values inside, the inward normal vector of the embedding contour can be expressed as $\aleph = -\nabla\phi/|\nabla\phi|$, where ∇ is the gradient operator. The evolution of the LSF ϕ can be formulated as the following partial differential equation (PDE):

$$\frac{\partial\phi}{\partial t} = F|\nabla\phi|, \tag{7}$$

where F is the speed function that controls evolution of the LSF. The conventional level set method generally results in LSF irregularity [14, 15] in the evolution procedure, and thus, Li et al. proposed a general variational level set formulation with a distance regularization term and an external energy term that controls the evolution of the zero level contour toward the desired locations. The designed objective energy function to be minimized is formulated as

$$E(\phi) = \lambda R_p(\phi) + E_{\text{ext}}(\phi), \tag{8}$$

where $\lambda > 0$ is a constant for controlling the trade-off between two terms and $E_{\text{ext}}(\phi)$ is the external energy on the processed images, which is defined such that it achieves a minimum when the zero level set of LSF ϕ is evolved to an object boundary (refer to detail in formation of [8]). $R_p(\phi)$ is the level set regularization term as defined in [8].

This study attempts to segment the nuclear regions based on the enhanced probability maps using the level set method, which needs initial contour (initial LSF) for evolution. According to the evaluation of the proposed nuclear-enhanced strategy in the above section, we can see that the probability maps with the large local patch size (13 × 13) can achieve a very clear nuclear-enhanced region except some missed pixels in the nuclear boundary, which promises the possibility of well-recognizing the enhanced nuclear pixels from their surround via a simple thresholding procedure. The achieved nuclear regions by thresholding can be used to produce the initial level set, which then is evolved on the enhanced probability map with a small local patch size (such as 3 × 3) for giving the precise nuclear boundary. In addition, the series of available DIC microscope images at a fixed time point is a 3D volume, where the nuclear regions in the middle Z-slice are usually larger than others. Thus, the nuclear regions are firstly segmented in the middle Z-slice using the above strategy and automatically extend the segmentation to the top/down for all slices. The procedure of automatically segmenting the nuclear regions from a 3D DIC volume at a fixed time point is as follows

(1) Implementing the initial segmentation (Fig. 9a) of the middle Z-slice image on the nuclear-enhanced probability map with 13 × 13 local patches by a thresholding procedure and calculating the initial LSF ϕ.

(2) Evolving the LSF ϕ on the nuclear-enhanced probability map with 3 × 3 local patches and achieving the final refinement of the segmentation result for the middle Z-slice image (Fig. 9b).

(3) Top-slice segmentation procedure: (a) eroding the previous segmentation regions (Fig. 9c) using morphological filter for calculating the initial LSF and (b) refining the segmentation results (Fig. 9d) on the probability map with 3 × 3 local patches.

(4) Down-slice segmentation procedure as in step (3).

With the above procedure, the nuclear regions of a 3D DIC volume can be automatically segmented

4 Experimental results
4.1 Material
Our nuclear detection method was implemented on three dimensional (3D) time-lapse microscope images of a *C. elegans* embryo obtained from the Worm Developmental Dynamics Database (WDDD; http://so.qbic.riken.jp/wddd/cdd/index.html) constructed by Kyoda et al. [16]. WDDD provides 3D time-lapse DIC microscope images for 50 wild-type embryos and 136 RNAi embryos in which one embryonic lethal gene was silenced by RNA interference. All sets of time-lapse images were recorded at 40-s intervals during the first three rounds of cell division of an embryo. At each time point, DIC microscope images were recorded with 66 consecutive focal planes spaced at 0.5-μ m intervals and 600 × 600 pixels spaced at 0.1 μ m × 0.1 μ m intervals. We randomly selected three slice images of three wild-type embryos from WDDD for constructing the nuclear models and then implemented our proposed method on the DIC microscope images of five other randomly selected wild-type embryos for evaluation.

4.2 Results
We firstly compare the transformed probability maps of two DIC microscope images from different embryos using our proposed TRIOD and directly using the local patch for pixel representation, respectively, and the local image entropy [6] in Fig. 10. From Fig. 10, we can see that the probability map images with the TRIOD can give a much clearer enhanced nuclear region than those directly using the local patch for pixel representation. On the other hand, the local entropy image can increase the contrast between the cytoplasmic and nuclear regions in some extent; however, the boundary of the transformed entropy images is quite blurred, and the intensity variance in the same regions of cellular components (cytoplasm/nucleus) is also large.

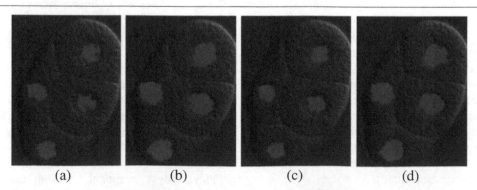

| (a) | (b) | (c) | (d) |

Fig. 9 Comparison of the detected nuclear regions with/without DRLS refinement. **a** The initial segmentation using simple thresholding on the middle Z-slice (initial LSF). **b** The final localization result via DRLS refinement. **c** The initial eroded segmentation from the previous slice (**b**). **d** The final localization of the next slice of **b**

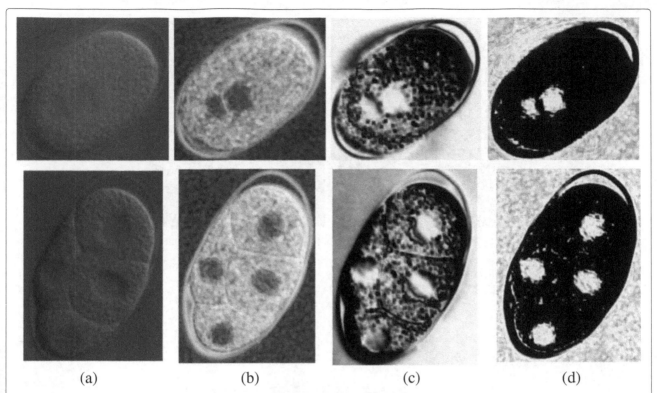

| (a) | (b) | (c) | (d) |

Fig. 10 Comparison of the transformed maps with different methods. **a** Raw DIC microscope images. **b** The local entropy images [6]. **c** The nuclear-enhanced probability maps directly using the local patches for pixel representation (the same modeling process using the local patches instead of TRIODs). **d** The probability maps using TRIODs

Next, the distance-regularized level set method is employed for segmentation from the middle Z-slice to the top/down slices on the transformed maps (local entropy image and the probability map with TRIODs). Three images with segmented results are shown in Fig. 11, where red, green, and blue lines denote the segmented results using local entropy, our proposed probability map, and manual segmentation (ground-truth segmentation), respectively. For segmentation results using local entropy, the initial LSF of the middle Z-slice is given manually, and the initial LSF for the next slice is propagated in the same way as introduced in Section 3. Figure 11

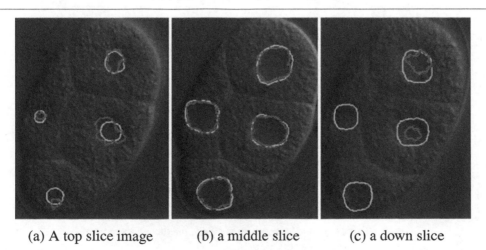

| (a) A top slice image | (b) a middle slice | (c) a down slice |

Fig. 11 The final results of the nuclear regions detected by different methods for three slice images of an embryo, which are refined by DRLS on the transformed local entropy images (*green curve*), and our proposed probability maps (*red curve*), and manually created ground-truth region (*blue curve*). **a** A top slice image. **b** A middle slice. **c** A down slice

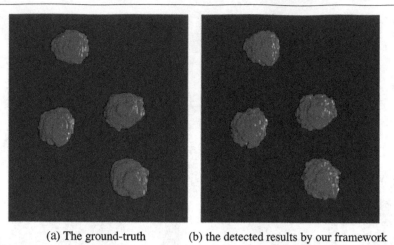

(a) The ground-truth   (b) the detected results by our framework

Fig. 12 The rendered surface of the detected nuclear regions for an embryo. **a** The rendered surface of the ground-truth nuclear regions. **b** The surface of the final nuclear localization results using our proposed strategy

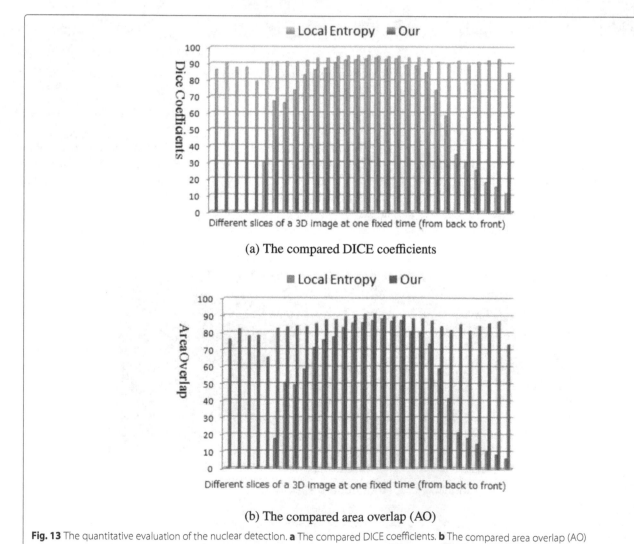

(a) The compared DICE coefficients

(b) The compared area overlap (AO)

Fig. 13 The quantitative evaluation of the nuclear detection. **a** The compared DICE coefficients. **b** The compared area overlap (AO)

manifests that the segmented nuclear regions are easy to be diffused to the cytoplasmic region or be diminished to very small regions especially on the top/down slices. Figure 12a, b shows the 3D visualization of the nuclear regions in ground-truth and by our proposed strategy for an embryo volume, respectively. In order to evaluate the detected nuclear regions qualitatively, we use two metrics: dice coefficient (DICE) and area overlap (AO), which are defined as follows:

$$\text{DICE} = \frac{2|S_{\text{GT}} \cap S_{\text{Seg}}|}{|S_{\text{GT}}| + |S_{\text{Seg}}|}; \text{AO} = \frac{|S_{\text{GT}} \cap S_{\text{Seg}}|}{|S_{\text{GT}} \cup S_{\text{Seg}}|}, \quad (9)$$

where S_{G} and S_{Seg} denote the nuclear regions of ground-truth and using our proposed strategy, respectively. The compared performances are given in Fig. 13a, b on DIC microscope images of one wild-type embryo which shows that our proposed method can give 80 ~ 90 %

dice coefficients and 70 ~ 90 % AO values even for two sides of images while the local entropy-based method failed for two sides of images despite the similar detection performances to our proposed method around the middle Z-slice. The similar detection performances were achieved by our proposed method on DIC microscope images of other wild-type embryos, and some examples of the detected nuclear on our proposed probability map and the local entropy image are shown in Figs. 14 and 15, respectively. Figure 14 gives the transformed probability maps, the local entropy images, and the nuclear detection results of two slice images from one wild-type embryo, where the red and green contours denote the detected nuclear boundary on our probability maps and the local entropy images, respectively. Figure 15 gives the nuclear detection results on four slice images from four wild-type embryos and validates that our proposed strategy (red contours) achieves much better detection performance than the local entropy-based method (green contours).

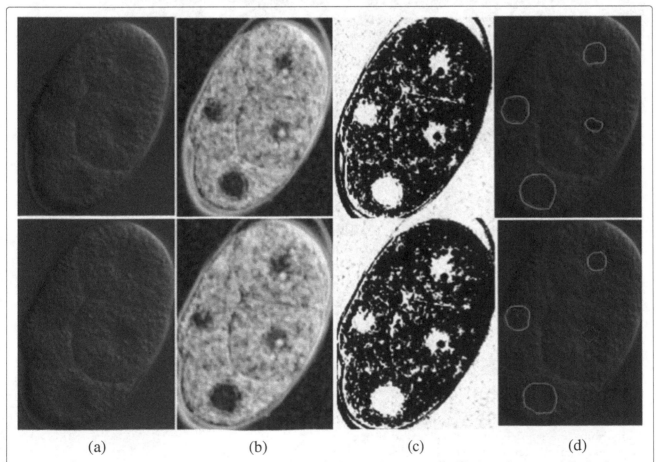

(a)   (b)   (c)   (d)

Fig. 14 The compared results using our proposed probability map- and local entropy-based methods. **a** The input slice images. **b** The local entropy images. **c** The transformed probability. **d** The detected nuclear regions. *Red contour* denotes the detected nuclear boundary by our method, and *green contour* denotes the boundary by the local entropy-based method

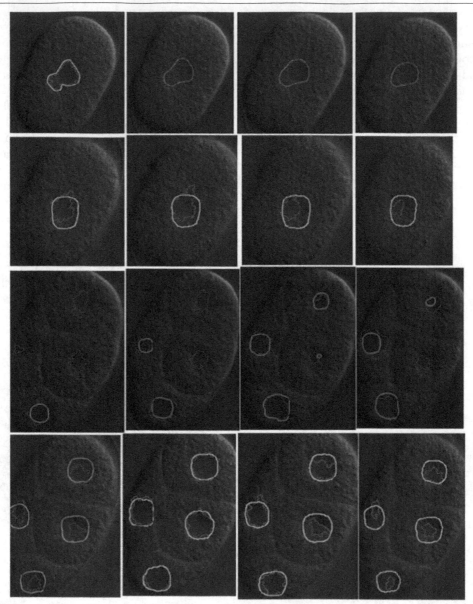

Fig. 15 The compared results using our proposed probability map- and local entropy-based methods. Each *row* shows four slice images from a wild-type embryo. *Red contour* denotes the detected nuclear boundary by our method, and *green contour* denotes the boundary by the local entropy-based method

5   Conclusions

This study presented a nucleus-enhanced probability process with top-ranked intensity-ordered descriptors (TRIOD) and employed the distance-regularized level set method for accurately localizing the nuclear regions. The proposed TRIOD is explored to represent the irregular texture and has promising discriminative property for distinguishing the smooth nuclear region and irregular cytoplasm textures. After the nucleus-enhancing processing by a probability model, the distance-regularized level set method is used for automated detection of nuclear regions from 3D DIC microscope images. Experiments showed that our proposed framework can achieve very promising performance.

Acknowledgements
This work was supported in part by the National Bioscience Database Center (NBDC) of the Japan Science and Technology Agency (JST), the Grant-in-Aid for Scientific Research from the Japanese Ministry for Education, Science, Culture and Sports (MEXT) under the Grant No. 15K00253 and 16H01436 and the New Energy and Industrial Technology Development Organization (NEDO).

Authors' contributions
XHH carried out the nuclear detection studies, conducted the experiments, and drafted the manuscript. YT and KK participated in the acquisition of the data and the analysis and interpretation of the data and drafted the manuscript. SO, IN, and YWC have revised the draft critically for important

intellectual content and given the final approval of the version to be published. All authors read and approved the final manuscript.

Competing interests

The authors declare that they have no competing interests.

About the authors

Xian-Hua Han received a B.E. degree from Chongqing University, Chongqing, China, a M.E. degree from Shandong University, Jinan, China, and a D.E. degree in 2005, from the University of the Ryukyus, Okinawa, Japan. From April 2007 to March 2013, she was a post-doctoral fellow and an associate professor at the College of Information Science and Engineering, Ritsumeikan University, Japan. She is now a senior researcher at the National Institute of Advanced Industrial Science and Technology (AIST), Tokyo, Japan. Her current research interests include image processing and analysis, feature extraction, machine learning, computer vision, and pattern recognition. She is a member of the IEEE, IEICE.

Yukako Tohsato received her M.E. from Kyushu Institute of Technology University in 1997 and her Ph.D. degree from Osaka University in 2002. She worked as a research associate and then as an assistant researcher at Osaka University from 2002 to 2004. She was an assistant professor at Ritsumeikan University from 2004 to 2012. She is currently a research scientist at RIKEN Quantitative Biology Center. Her research interest is in bioinformatics and systems biology.

Koji Kyoda received his Ph.D. from Keio University in 2005. He is now a research scientist at RIKEN Quantitative Biology Center. His research interests include systems biology, bioimage informatics, high-throughput biological data analysis, and biological database integration.

Shuichi Onami received his D.V.M. from The University of Tokyo in 1994 and his Ph.D. from The Graduate School for Advanced Studies in 1998. He was an associate professor at Keio University from 2002 to 2006 and joined RIKEN as a senior scientist at Genomic Sciences Center in 2006. He is now a team leader at RIKEN Quantitative Biology Center. His current research interests include mathematical modeling of animal development and its application to medicine.

Ikuko Nishikawa received the degrees of Bachelor, Master, and Doctor of Science from Kyoto University by the research in physics. She is now a professor at Ritsumeikan University. Her current research interests include bioinformatics, machine learning, and optimization.

Yen-Wei Chen received a B.E. degree in 1985 from Kobe University, Kobe, 584 Japan, a M.E. degree in 1987, and a D.E. degree in 1990, both from Osaka University, Osaka, Japan. From 1991 to 1994, he was a Research Fellow at the Institute of Laser Technology, Osaka. From October 1994 to March 2004, he was an associate professor and a professor with the Department of Electrical and Electronics Engineering, University of the Ryukyus, Okinawa, Japan. He is currently a professor with the College of Information Science and Engineering, Ritsumeikan University, Japan. He is also a chair professor with the college of Computer Science and Technology, China. He was an Overseas Assessor of the Chinese Academy of Science and Technology, an associate Editor of the International Journal of Image and Graphics (IJIG), an Editorial Board member of the International Journal of Knowledge-Based Intelligent Engineering Systems. His research interests include computer vision, pattern recognition and image processing He has published more than 300 research papers in these fields. Dr. Chen is a member of the IEEE, IEICE, Japan.

Author details

[1] The Artificial Intelligence Research Center, Advanced Industrial Science and Technology, Tokyo 135-0064, Japan. [2] Ritsumeikan University, Kusatsu, Shiga 525-8577, Japan. [3] Laboratory for Developmental Dynamics, RIKEN Quantitative Biology Center, Kobe 650-0047, Japan.

References

1. The *C. elegans* Sequencing Consortium (1998) Genome sequence of the nematode *C. elegans*: a platform for investigating biology. Science 282(5396):2012–2018

2. Thomas C, DeVries P, Hardin J, White J (1996) Four-dimensional imaging: computer visualization of 3D movements in living specimens. Science 273(5275):603–607

3. Schnabel R, Hutter H, Moerman D, Schnabel H (1997) Assessing normal embryogenesis in *Caenorhabditis elegans* using a 4D microscope: variability of development and regional specification. Dev Biol 184(2):234–265

4. Heid PJ, Voss E, Soll DR (2002) 3D-DIASemb: a computer-assisted system for reconstructing and motion analyzing in 4D every cell and nucleus in a developing embryo. Dev Biol 245(2):329–347

5. Yasuda T, Bannai H, Onami S, Miyano S, Kitano H (1999) Towards automatic construction of cell-lineage of *C. elegans* from Nomarski DIC microscope images. Genome Inform 10:144–154

6. Hamahashi S, Onami S, Kitano H (2005) Detection of nuclei in 4D Nomarski DIC microscope images of early *Caenorhabditis elegans* embryos using local image entropy and object tracking. BMC Bioinformatics 6:125

7. Ning F, Delhomme D, LeCun Y, Piano F, Bottou L, Barbano PE (2005) Toward automatic phenotyping of developing embryos from videos. IEEE Trans Image Process 14(9):1360–1371

8. Li C, Xu C, Gui C, Fox M (2010) Distance regularized level set evolution and its application to image segmentation. IEEE Trans Image Process 19(12):3243–3254

9. Lowe DG (2004) Distinctive image features from scale-invariant keypoints. Int J Comput Vis 60(2):91–110

10. Mikolajczyk K, Schmid C (2005) A performance evaluation of local descriptors. IEEE Trans Pattern Anal Mach Intell 27(10):1615–1630

11. Tola E, Lepetit V, Fua P (2010) DAISY: an efficient dense descriptor applied to wide-baseline stereo. IEEE Trans Pattern Anal Mach Intell 32(5):815–830

12. Ojala T, Pietikainen M, Maenpaa T (2002) Multiresolution gray-scale and rotation invariant texture classification with local binary patterns. IEEE Trans Pattern Anal Mach Intell 24(7):971–987

13. Gupta R, Patil H, Mittal A (2010) Robust order-based methods for feature description. In: Proceedings of 2010 IEEE Conference on Computer Vision and Pattern Recognition. IEEE, Piscataway. pp 334–341

14. Sethian J (1999) Level set methods and fast marching methods. Cambridge University Press, Cambridge

15. Osher S, Fedkiw R (2002) Level set methods and dynamic implicit surfaces. Springer-Verlag New York, Inc., New York

16. Kyoda K, Adachi E, Masuda E, Nagai Y, Suzuki Y, Oguro T, Urai M, Arai R, Furukawa M, Shimada K, Kuramochi J, Nagai E, Onami S (2013) WDDD: Worm Developmental Dynamics Database. Nucleic Acids Res 41(Database issue):D732–D737

17

Effective elliptic arc selection from connected edge points

Tomonari Masuzaki[*] and Yasuyuki Sugaya

Abstract

Extracting edge points from an image and fitting ellipses to them is a fundamental technique for computer vision applications. However, since the extracted edge points sometimes contain non-elliptic arcs such as line segments, it is a very difficult to extract only elliptic arcs from them. In this paper, we propose a new method for extracting elliptic arcs from a spatially connected point sequence. We first fit an ellipse to an input point sequence and segment the sequence into partial arcs at the intersection points of the fitted ellipse. Next, we compute residuals of the fitted ellipse for all input points and select elliptic arcs among the segmented arcs by checking the curvatures of the residual graph. Then, we fit an ellipse to the selected arcs and repeat the above process until the selected arcs do not change. By using simulated data and real images, we compare the performance of our method with existing methods and show the efficiency of our proposed method.

Keywords: Elliptic arc selection, Ellipse fitting, Outlier detection

1 Introduction

A circular object in a scene is projected onto the image plane as an ellipse, and we can compute its 3-D positions from that ellipse [5]. Therefore, detecting circles and ellipses in images is the first step of many computer vision applications including industrial robotic operations and autonomous navigation. For this purpose, many methods for extracting elliptic arcs from an image and for fitting an ellipse to the extracted elliptic arcs are studied [6, 15, 20].

In order to detect ellipses in images, we usually extract edge points from images and fit or estimate the ellipse parameters from them. We classify ellipse detection problems into two stages. One stage is to estimate ellipse parameters accurately for given points. The other is to select elliptic arcs from the extracted edge points.

For the former problem, many methods have been proposed. The simplest method for fitting an ellipse is *least squares* (*LS*) which minimizes the sum of squares of the ellipse equation. A more accurate method was proposed by Taubin [17]. Moreover, *hyper-LS* [8, 9] and *hyper-renormalization* [10] whose solution has no deviation up to high-order noise terms are also proposed. *Maximum*

likelihood (*ML*) is also a well-known method, which minimizes the *reprojection error*, i.e., the sum of the distances from data points to the fitted ellipse [4]. Many ML-based methods have been proposed [1, 7, 11, 13].

Ellipse-specific methods also have been proposed [3, 12, 16, 18, 19]. It is Fitzgibbon et al. [3] who first proposed a method that only fits an ellipse.

The latter problem of ellipse detection is to select elliptic arcs from the extracted edge points. Since all the above methods do not consider the presence of non-elliptic arcs, which we call "outliers" in this paper, in the input point sequence, the accuracy of those solutions deteriorate if the input point sequence includes outliers. So, it is an important task to separate elliptic arcs from the input point sequence.

Ad hoc and simple methods for detecting non-elliptic arcs are line fitting and curvature-based methods. However, these methods may detect special targets, for example, line-fitting methods detect only line segments, so they cannot always remove all outliers. Random sample consensus (RANSAC) is a well-known framework for dealing with outliers [2]. RANSAC has problems that it needs a lot of iterations and does not work well if the number of outliers are larger than that of inliers. Yu et al. [20] detected an outlier point sequence from fitting residuals and removed it from the input data. By iteratively

---

*Correspondence: masuzaki@iim.cs.tut.ac.jp
Department of Computer Science and Engineering, Toyohashi University of Technology, Toyohashi, Aichi 441-8580, Japan

applying the above procedure, they fitted an ellipse to the remaining inliers. Shao et al. [14] segment an input point sequence into some spatially connected arcs and detect elliptic arcs by fitting ellipses to all the combinations of the segmented arcs.

We propose a new method for extracting elliptic arcs from a spatially connected point sequence. Assuming that input data is a spatially connected sequence of edge points, we segment it into partial arcs by considering the ellipse fitting residuals and detect inliers by computing the curvature of the residual graph of each of the segmented arcs.

Our method has several advantages over existing methods. (1) The proposed method can automatically segment an input point sequence at the intersections of the fitted ellipse and select inlier elliptic arcs by repeating point segmentation and ellipse fitting. (2) Our method involves iterations, but the number of iterations is much less than those of iterative methods like RANSAC and Yu's method. (3) Moreover, in contrast to Yu's method, our method has the possibility of fitting a more accurate ellipse because inliers are selected from all the input data in each iteration step, meaning that the number of data to fit an ellipse does not decrease by iterations. (4) Our method also detect outlier arcs which are smoothly connected to inlier arcs. This type of outliers cannot detect by the curvature-based method.

2 Ellipse fitting

Curves represented by a quadratic equations in x and y in the form

$$Ax^2 + 2Bxy + Cy^2 + 2f_0(Dx + Ey) + f_0^2 F = 0, \quad (1)$$

are called "conics," which include ellipses, parabolas, hyperbolas, and their degeneracies such as two lines [5]. The condition that Eq. (1) represents an ellipse is

$$AC - B^2 > 0. \quad (2)$$

Our task is to compute the coefficients $A, ..., F$ so that the ellipse of Eq. (1) passes through the detected points $(x_\alpha, y_\alpha), \alpha = 1, ..., N$, as closely as possible (Fig. 1). In Eq. (1), f_0 is a constant that has the order of the image size for stabilizing finite length numerical computation.[1] For a point sequence $(x_\alpha, y_\alpha), \alpha = 1, ..., N$, we define 6-D vectors

$$\xi_\alpha = (x_\alpha^2, 2x_\alpha y_\alpha, y_\alpha^2, 2f_0 x_\alpha, 2f_0 y_\alpha, f_0^2)^\top,$$
$$\theta = (A, B, C, D, E, F)^\top. \quad (3)$$

The condition that (x_α, y_α) satisfies Eq. (1) is written as

$$(\xi_\alpha, \theta) = 0, \quad (4)$$

where (a, b) denotes the inner product of vectors a and b. Since vector θ has scale indeterminacy, we normalize it to unit norm: $||\theta|| = 1$.

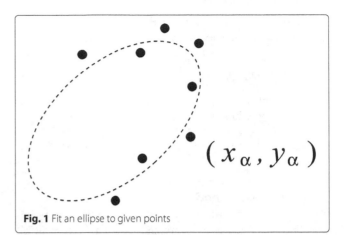

Fig. 1 Fit an ellipse to given points

Since Eq. (4) is not exactly satisfied in the presence of noise, we compute a θ such that $(\xi_\alpha, \theta) \approx 0, \alpha = 1, ..., N$. For computing a θ that is close to its true value, we need to consider the statistical properties of noise. The standard model is to regard the noise in (x_α, y_α) as an independent Gaussian random variable of mean 0 and standard deviation σ. Then, the covariance matrix of the vector ξ_α has the form $\sigma^2 V_0[\xi_\alpha]$, where

$$V_0[\xi_\alpha] = 4 \begin{pmatrix} x_\alpha^2 & x_\alpha y_\alpha & 0 & f_0 x_\alpha & 0 & 0 \\ x_\alpha y_\alpha & x_\alpha^2 + y_\alpha^2 & x_\alpha y_\alpha & f_0 y_\alpha & f_0 x_\alpha & 0 \\ 0 & x_\alpha y_\alpha & y_\alpha^2 & 0 & f_0 y_\alpha & 0 \\ f_0 x_\alpha & f_0 y_\alpha & 0 & f_0^2 & 0 & 0 \\ 0 & f_0 x_\alpha & f_0 y_\alpha & 0 & f_0^2 & 0 \\ 0 & 0 & 0 & 0 & 0 & 0 \end{pmatrix}, \quad (5)$$

which we call the "normalized covariance matrix" [7]. We use the normalized covariance matrix to compute residuals of ellipse fitting.

3 Fitzgibbon's method

In order to segment an input point sequence at intersection points of a fitted ellipse, we fit an ellipse by Fitzgibbon's method. For fitting only an ellipse, Fitzgibbon et al. [3] proposed to minimize the *algebraic distance*

$$J_{LS} = \sum_{\alpha=1}^{N} (\xi_\alpha, \theta)^2, \quad (6)$$

subject to $AC - B^2 = 1$. This constraint is written as

$$(\theta, N_F \theta) = 1, \quad N_F \equiv \begin{pmatrix} 0 & 0 & 1 & 0 & 0 & 0 \\ 0 & -2 & 0 & 0 & 0 & 0 \\ 1 & 0 & 0 & 0 & 0 & 0 \\ 0 & 0 & 0 & 0 & 0 & 0 \\ 0 & 0 & 0 & 0 & 0 & 0 \\ 0 & 0 & 0 & 0 & 0 & 0 \end{pmatrix}. \quad (7)$$

The solution that minimizes Eq. (6) subject to this constraint is obtained by solving a generalized eigenvalue problem

$$N_{\mathrm{F}}\theta = \mu M_{\mathrm{LS}}\theta, \tag{8}$$

and computing the unit eigenvector θ for the largest eigenvalue μ, where the matrix M_{LS} is defined by

$$M_{\mathrm{LS}} = \frac{1}{N}\sum_{\alpha=1}^{N}\xi_{\alpha}\xi_{\alpha}^{\top}. \tag{9}$$

4 Proposed method

We assume that input data is spatially connected points and that the fitted ellipse intersects the curve at multiple points (Fig. 2a). We automatically segment the input curve into partial arcs at these intersection points. We compute the variation of the tangent angle to the graph of the fitting residual, which we simply call "error curvature" in this paper, and judge if each arc is an inlier or an outlier based on this "error curvature."

The principle of our inlier arc selection is nearly equivalent to the curvature-based method. However, our method is more efficient, because our method computes the curvature of the residual graph at only one point where the residual takes a maximum in each segmented arc.

In Fig. 2, the input point sequence is divided into five partial arcs by the fitted ellipse. The residual value of the arc PQ, which consists only of an elliptic arc, smoothly changes around the peak value. On the other hand, we can see that the residual graph has a peaky shape over the arcs consisting of non-elliptic arcs.

Moreover, we can see that the arcs PP' and QQ', which are connected to the elliptic arc PQ, are also elliptic arcs. The points P' and Q' are the peak points of the partial arcs adjacent to the elliptic arc PQ. Therefore, if we use

not only the detected inlier arc but also the adjacent arcs like the arcs PP' and QQ' for ellipse fitting, we can effectively fit a correct ellipse. The algorithm of our method is summarized as follows:

1. Fit an ellipse to a point sequence by Fitzgibbon's method [3].
2. Compute the sign of the left-hand side of Eq. (4) for all the points and segment the point sequence into partial arcs at the points across which the computed sign changes.
3. For each segmented arc, detect the point where the residual value takes a maximum and compute its error curvature ϕ at this point.
4. Go to step (a) if it is the first inlier selection, else go to step (b).

    (a) Select an inlier arc which has the smallest value ϕ among those arcs whose arc lengths are longer than a threshold[2] and extend it to each peak point of adjacent arcs. Then, we fit an ellipse to the selected arc.

    (b) Select the arcs whose error curvature ϕs are smaller than a threshold $\hat{\phi}$[3] and fit an ellipse to them.

5. Repeat the procedures from step 2 to step 4 until the number of inliers does not change.

As discussed before, if a selected arc is an elliptic arc, the adjacent arcs are also elliptic arcs. Therefore, we can effectively fit a correct ellipse if we use those arcs. However, if we select a non-elliptic arc as an inlier and add adjacent outlier arcs to fit an ellipse, we cannot fit a correct ellipse.

For this reason, in the first iteration of our algorithm, we select among the arcs that are sufficiently long the one

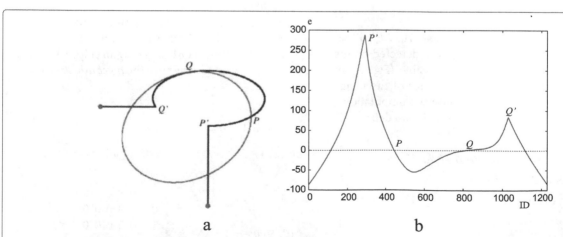

Fig. 2 a An ellipse fitted to a point sequence which includes non-elliptic arcs. A *black line* is an input point sequence. **b** Fitting residual graph. The *horizontal axis* shows the index of the points, which starts from the *blue point* to the *red point* shown in (**a**). The *vertical axis* shows the signed fitting residual whose sign is computed by the left-hand side of Eq. (4)

whose error curvature ϕ at its peak point is the smallest. We regard it as a reliable inlier and extend it to the adjacent partial arcs. After the first iteration, we select all arcs whose error curvature ϕs are smaller than a threshold $\hat{\phi}$. We do not extend those arcs, because the adjacent arcs are non-elliptic arcs if the selected inlier arcs approximately belong to the correct ellipse.

In the following sections, we describe the details of our method.

5   Segmentation of the point sequence

The left-hand side of Eq. (4) at the point p_α has a different sign outside and inside the ellipse θ. Using this fact, we can segment the input point sequence $\{p_\alpha\}$ into partial arcs at those p_α points which have different signs from their neighboring points.

However, the value (ξ_α, θ) may not be exactly zero even if the point p_α lies on the fitted ellipse θ; the points lying on the fitted ellipse may irregularly change their signs, so these points may be segmented in very short arcs. To avoid this, we regard those partial arcs whose fitting residual values are close to zero as elliptic arcs and judge that they are inlier arcs without computing their curvatures. We call such arcs "tangent arcs."

For fitted ellipse θ, we first compute a fitting residual e_α of a point p_α, $\alpha = 1, ..., N$ by Eq. (10), which is a first approximation of the distance between the fitted ellipse and the point p_α. We also compute a sign of the residual by the value of the left-hand side of Eq. (4).

$$e_\alpha = \sqrt{\frac{(\xi_\alpha, \theta)^2}{(\theta, V_0[\xi_\alpha]\theta)}}. \tag{10}$$

Next, we segment the input point sequence into partial arcs at those p_α points which have different signs from their neighboring points. If the maximum residual in the segmented arc is smaller than a threshold $E_{\min}$[4], we regard the arc R_κ as a *tangent arc*.

6   Inlier arc selection

After segmenting the point sequence, we detect the point α^* where the fitting residual takes its maximum and compute its *error curvature* at this point by using its neighboring points β and γ (Fig. 3). If the computed curvature is larger than a threshold, we regard this arc as an outlier. Since the horizontal axis of the residual graph $\bar{Q}_\alpha = (\alpha, e_\alpha)^\top$ is an index of the input point sequence, the computed error curvature depends on the scale of the horizontal axis of the residual graph. For example, if two point sequences have the same shape and different scales, the curvatures of their sequences have different values.

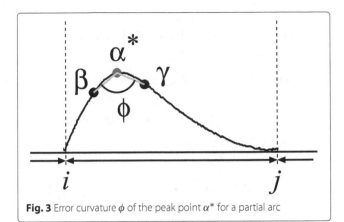

Fig. 3 Error curvature ϕ of the peak point α^* for a partial arc

Therefore, we normalize the scale of the horizontal axis of the residual graph in the form

$$Q_\alpha = \left(\frac{\lambda e_{\max}\alpha}{N}, e_\alpha\right)^\top, \tag{11}$$

where $e_{\max}$ is the maximum value of all ellipse-fitting residuals[5] and λ is a constant for normalization.[5] If $e_{\max}$ is extremely large, the normalization of Eq. (11) may not work well. So, if $e_{\max}$ is larger than a threshold $E_{\max}$[6], we replacing the value $e_{\max}$ with the threshold $E_{\max}$ in the normalization computation.

In order to compute the error curvature, we need to select neighboring points Q_β and Q_γ. We first select indices β and γ such that $\beta = \alpha^* - d$ and $\gamma = \alpha^* + d$. Here, d is a constant for determining the distance from the point Q_{α^*}. If both of the points Q_β and Q_γ are not included in R_κ, we decrease d until either of them is included in R_κ. If Q_{α^*} is located near the start or the end point of the arc R_κ, we cannot select both of the neighboring points properly. In this case, we select at least one neighboring point and compute its symmetric point to α^*. More details are described in the following algorithm.

For M-segmented arcs $R_\kappa(i, j) = \{Q_\delta | \delta = i, ..., j\}, \kappa = 1, ..., M$, we compute error curvatures for selecting inlier arcs by the following algorithm.

1. Let α^* be the index of the point whose residual takes its maximum in the arc R_κ. Here, if a target arc is a tangent arc, finish this procedure.
2. Select two points whose indices β and γ are such that

$$\beta = \alpha^* - d, \gamma = \alpha^* + d, d = (j - i)/r, \tag{12}$$

where r[7] is a constant for determining the distance between the point α^* and its neighboring points β and γ. If both β and γ are out of R_κ, we update d to $d \leftarrow d - 1$ until either of the two points are in the arc R_κ.

3. Compute two vectors $x^{(1)}$ and $x^{(2)}$ according to the following three rules. Here, $x_b^{(a)}$ denotes the b-th component of the vector $x^{(a)}$.

case a: Points Q_β and Q_γ are both in the arc R_κ.

$$x^{(1)} = Q_{\alpha*} - Q_\beta, \ x^{(2)} = Q_{\alpha*} - Q_\gamma. \quad (13)$$

case b: Point Q_β is in the arc R_κ.

$$x^{(1)} = Q_{\alpha*} - Q_\beta, \ x^{(2)} = \left(-x_1^{(1)}, x_2^{(1)}\right)^\top. \quad (14)$$

case c: Point Q_γ is in the arc R_κ.

$$x^{(2)} = Q_{\alpha*} - Q_\gamma, \ x^{(1)} = \left(-x_1^{(2)}, x_2^{(2)}\right)^\top. \quad (15)$$

4. Compute the error curvature ϕ by

$$\phi = \pi - \cos^{-1}\left(\frac{(x^{(1)}, x^{(2)})}{||x^{(1)}||\,||x^{(2)}||}\right). \quad (16)$$

5. Regard the arc R_κ as an inlier arc if ϕ is smaller than the threshold $\hat{\phi}$.

If it is the first iteration of an inlier selection, we extend the selected inlier arc to each peak point of its adjacent arcs. If the adjacent arc is a *tangent arc*, we check the next adjacent arc and add the partial non-*tangent arc* as an inlier.

7 Experiment
7.1 Inlier selection process
In order to confirm how our proposed method selected inlier arcs, we checked the residual graph and the selected inlier arcs and fitted the ellipse step by step for Fig. 4(1)-(a) and Fig. 5(1)-(a).

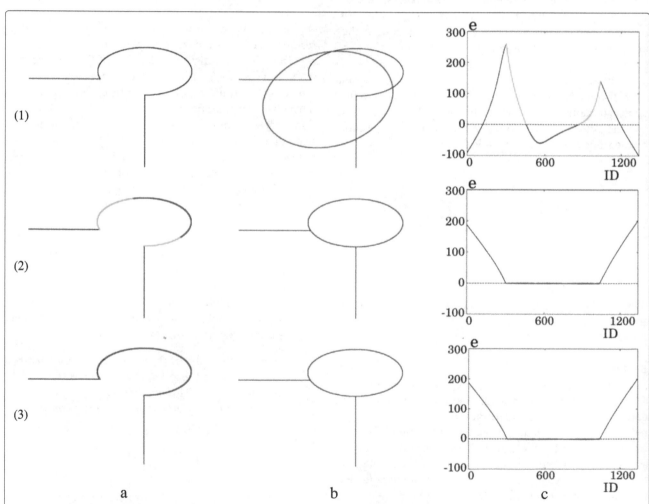

Fig. 4 Inlier arc selection process of our method. **a** Used points to fit the ellipse in (**b**). The *blue arc* is the selected inlier arc. The *green arcs* are the extended arcs from the selected inlier arc. **b** Fitted ellipse. **c** Signed fitting residual graph. The *horizontal axis* shows the index of the points. The *vertical axis* shows the signed fitting residual. The *blue and green arcs* correspond to the arcs in (**a**) in the next row

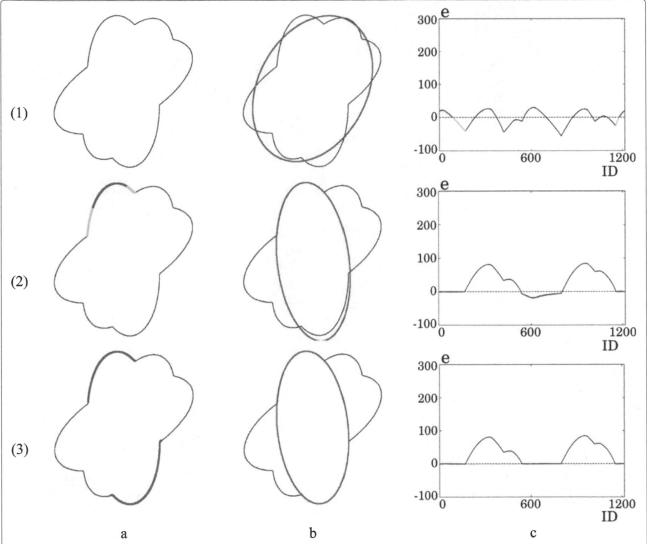

Fig. 5 Inlier arc selection process of our method. **a** Used points to fit the ellipse in (**b**). The *blue arc* is the selected inlier arc. The *green arcs* are the extended arcs from the selected inlier arc. **b** Fitted ellipse. **c** Signed fitting residual graph. The *horizontal axis* shows the index of the points. The *vertical axis* shows the signed fitting residual. The *blue and green arcs* correspond to the arcs in (**a**) in the next row

Figure 4(1)-(b) shows the fitted ellipse to all the input data by Fitzgibbon's method, and Fig. 4(1)-(c) is its signed residual graph. The horizontal and vertical axis of the graph indicate the index of the input points and a signed fitting residual, respectively.

In our first inlier selection, the blue arc was selected as an inlier arc and the green adjacent partial arcs were extended as inliers. These arcs correspond to the blue and green arcs in Fig. 4(2)-(a). In the second step, we fitted an ellipse to the selected inlier arcs (Fig. 4(2)-(a)). The fitted ellipse was shown in Fig. 4(2)-(b). As we can see, the segmented arcs could be obviously separated to inlier arcs (*tangent arcs*) and outlier arcs in Fig. 4(2)-(c). Our method stopped in the third step because the number of inlier points did not change and could fit a correct ellipse to all the inlier points.

The input data of Fig. 5(1)-(a) consists of three different elliptic arcs. Figure 5(1)-(b), (1)-(c) are the fitted ellipse to all the input data and its signed residual graph, respectively. This input point sequence is closed, so we consider that the start and the end points are connected in the residual graph. The blue arc is the selected inlier arc, and the green adjacent arcs are extended arcs as inliers. These arcs correspond to the blue and green arcs in Fig. 5(2)-(a). By checking the selected inlier arcs in Fig. 5(2)-(a), we can confirm that the selected arcs belong to one ellipse. Figure 5(2)-(b) shows the fitted ellipse to them. Since the selected arcs are short for the entire ellipse, the accuracy of the fitted ellipse is not good. However, our method selects the remaining elliptic arcs as inliers from the residual graph of Fig. 5(2)-(c) and fits a correct ellipse in the third step.

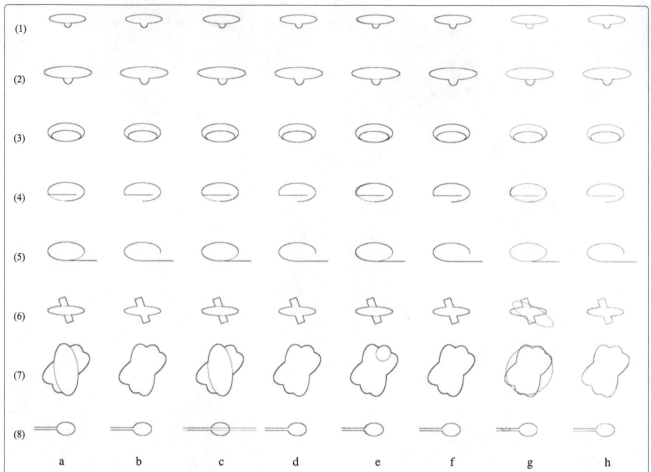

Fig. 6 Comparison of inlier selection. **a**, **c**, **e**, **g** The *red curves* are the fitted ellipses by our method, RANSAC, Yu's method, and Shao's method, respectively. **b**, **d**, **h** The *blue points* are the selected inlier points by our method and RANSAC. **f** The *blue points* are used points to fit the resulting ellipse by Yu's method

From these results, we could confirm that our method could select inlier arcs by repeating inlier selection based on an *error curvature* and ellipse fitting.

7.2   Simulations
In order to confirm the effectiveness of the our proposed method, we compared our method with RANSAC, Yu's method, and Shao's method for many simulation data. Figure 6 shows some of the resulting ellipses. Figure 6(a), (c), (e), (g) are the fitted ellipses by our method, RANSAC, Yu's method, and Shao's method, respectively. The blue points in Fig. 6(b), (d), (h) are the selected inlier points

Table 1 Inlier selection ratios/outlier selection ratios

	Our method	RANSAC	Yu's method	Shao's method
(1)	0.99/0.00	0.99/0.00	0.49/0.01	0.80/0.00
(2)	0.99/0.00	1.00/0.01	0.49/0.02	0.81/0.00
(3)	0.99/0.04	1.00/0.07	0.40/0.04	0.93/0.09
(4)	1.00/0.00	1.00/0.01	0.36/0.00	0.90/0.05
(5)	0.99/0.00	1.00/0.04	0.47/0.00	0.93/0.04
(6)	0.99/0.00	1.00/0.01	0.48/0.01	0.61/0.45
(7)	0.90/0.00	1.00/0.02	0.45/0.06	0.54/0.68
(8)	0.50/0.00	0.02/0.98	1.00/0.10	0.51/0.63

Table 2 Comparison of computation time and number of iterations: computation time in milliseconds (number of iterations)

	Our method	RANSAC	Yu's method
(1)	4 (5)	41 (111)	80 (20)
(2)	8 (5)	61 (113)	148 (48)
(3)	12 (7)	79 (137)	208 (17)
(4)	4 (3)	49 (152)	288 (106)
(5)	8 (9)	42 (148)	600 (178)
(6)	4 (4)	59 (218)	216 (72)
(7)	8 (8)	68 (134)	48 (10)
(8)	4 (3)	64 (143)	424 (157)

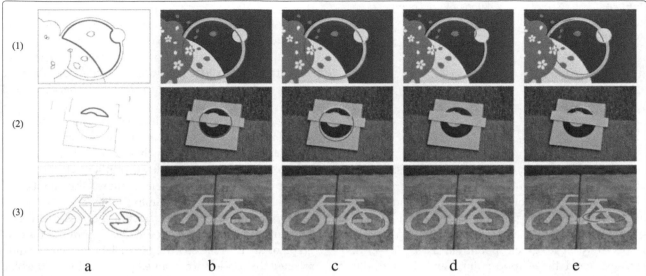

Fig. 7 Real-image experiment. **a** Extracted edge points. We selected *red connected points* as input data. **b–e** Resulting ellipses by our method, RANSAC, Yu's method, and Shao's method, respectively

by our method, RANSAC, and Shao's method, respectively. The blue points in Fig. 6(f) are used points to fit the resulting ellipse by Yu's method.

Input data of Fig. 6(1), (2) have the same shape, but their scales are different. For these data, all the methods fitted a correct ellipse. In Fig. 6(3), two ellipses are tangent to each other. Our proposed method, RANSAC, and Shao's method fitted an ellipse to the outer arc; however, Yu's method fitted an ellipse to the inner arc.

Figure 6(4) is an example which includes a line segment as outlier points. All methods fitted an almost correct ellipse. In Fig. 6(4), since Yu's method fitted an ellipse to a short arc, the accuracy of the resulting ellipse is not good compared with the other methods. Figure 6(5) is an example where an outlier arc is smoothly connected to an inlier arc. For such input data, outlier detection based on the curvature of a point sequence may not work well. However, our method can correctly detect inlier and outlier arcs because it iteratively selects inlier arcs and fits an ellipse. In Fig. 6(6), (7), input point sequences consist of elliptic arcs and contours of other shapes. Our method and RANSAC fitted a correct ellipse for each data. However, Yu's method fitted a small ellipse to a short arc for Fig. 6(7). Shao's method detected many outlier points. The inlier selection process of our method for Fig. 6(7) is shown in Fig. 5. The input data of Fig 6(8) includes many outlier points. Our method and Yu's method output an almost correct ellipse. Since the ratio of outliers was large, RANSAC did not work well.

Table 1 shows the inlier selection ratios for the simulation data shown in Fig. 6. We manually counted the number of inlier and outlier points in the input point sequences and computed inlier and outlier selection ratios. From these results, the capabilities of the inlier arc selection of our method and RANSAC are almost the same, but our method is superior to RANSAC if an input point sequence includes many outlier points. In many cases, Yu's method detects small number of inliers. In Figs. 6(3), (7), since Yu's method detected elliptic arcs from the different ellipse from that of the other methods, we computed the inlier and outlier selection ratios for the corresponding ellipse.

Table 2 shows the number of iterations and computation times for the three methods. We used Intel Core 2 Duo 3.00 GHz ×2 for the CPU with main memory 4 GB and Ubuntu 12.04 for the OS. For RANSAC, we stopped if the solution did not change after 50 consecutive iterations and counted the mean total number of iterations over 10 trials. Since our method, RANSAC, and Yu's method were implemented in C++, but Shao's method was implemented in Matlab, we did not show the computation time of Shao's method. From this result, the number of iterations and the computation time of our method is superior to RANSAC and Yu's method.

7.3 Real image experiment

Figure 7 shows real-image experiments. Figure 7(a) is the extracted edge points by canny operator. We removed

Table 3 Inlier selection ratios/outlier selection ratios

	Our method	RANSAC	Yu's method	Shao's method
(1)	1.00/0.00	1.00/0.02	0.49/0.08	0.95/0.23
(2)	1.00/0.00	1.00/0.02	0.00/1.00	0.71/0.46
(3)	0.83/0.02	0.83/0.05	0.27/0.00	0.36/0.48

Table 4 Comparison of computation time and number of iterations: computation time in milliseconds (number of iterations)

	Our method	RANSAC	Yu's method
(1)	3 (4)	70 (157)	228 (65)
(2)	1 (6)	16 (141)	3 (5)
(3)	4 (10)	49 (208)	56 (35)

successive edge points whose lengths were shorter than 50 pixels. The red points shown in Fig. 7(a) are manually selected edge points to fit an ellipse. Figures 7(b–e) are extracted elliptic points and the fitted ellipses by our method, RANSAC, Yu's method, and Shao's method, respectively. The green points in Figs. 7(b–e) indicate extracted the elliptic points, and the red ellipses are the fitted ellipses to those extracted points. Our method and RANSAC fitted almost correct ellipses. Yu's method fitted small ellipses for three data. We discuss

the reason that Yu's method tends to fit a small ellipse later. Shao's method extracted many outlier points in all data. This is because Shao's method could not separate inlier and outlier arcs in their point sequence segmentation step since they only consider the distance between adjacent points and the length of the segmented arcs.

Table 3 shows the inlier selection ratios for real images shown in Fig. 7. As we can see, our method and RANSAC have almost the same performance of inlier selection. However, our method has lower outlier selection ratio than that of RANSAC. Table 4 shows the number of iterations and computation times for Fig. 7.

Figure 8 shows the inlier selection process and corresponding residual graphs for Fig. 7(1). From the residual graph of the first ellipse fitting (Fig. 8(1)-(c)), our method selected the top-left arc of an ellipse as an inlier (the blue points in Fig. 8(2)-(a)) and extended the adjacent partial arcs as inliers (the green points in Fig. 8(2)-(a)). Since a correct ellipse was fitted to the selected arcs, our method

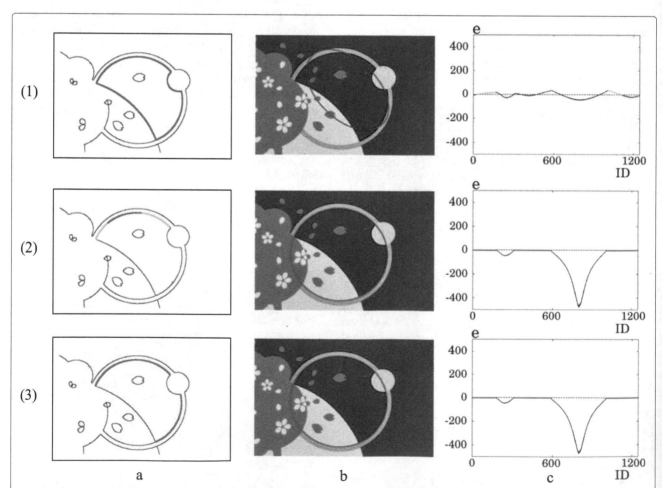

Fig. 8 Inlier arc selection process of our method. **a** Used points to fit the ellipse in (**b**). The *blue arc* is the selected inlier arc. The *green arcs* are the extended arcs from the selected inlier arc. **b** Fitted ellipse. **c** Signed fitting residual graph. The *horizontal axis* shows the index of the points. The *vertical axis* shows the signed fitting residual. The *blue and green arcs* correspond to the arcs in (**a**) in the next row

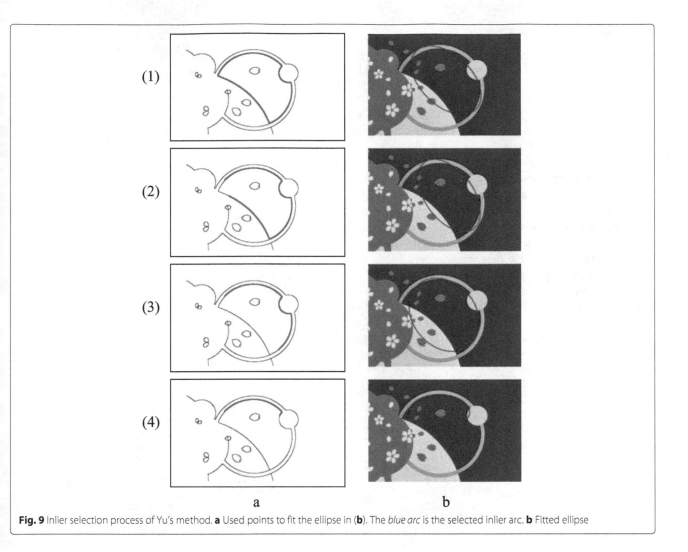

Fig. 9 Inlier selection process of Yu's method. **a** Used points to fit the ellipse in (**b**). The *blue arc* is the selected inlier arc. **b** Fitted ellipse

also selected a right-bottom arc of the correct ellipse and converged in the next step.

We show the inlier selection process of Yu's method in Fig. 9. Figure 9(a) shows the remaining input points in each iteration step. Yu's method fits an ellipse to the input points and removes the points whose fitted residuals are larger than a threshold. So, the number of the input points gradually decreases in the course of the ellipse-fitting step.

For this reason, the number of the remaining inlier points becomes small and the resulting ellipse tends to be small compared with the correct shape.

Figure 10 shows a result where our method selects wrong point sequences. Our method cannot select point sequences on an ellipse if the rate of input points on the correct ellipse is low; hence, our method selects the wrong point sequence at the first iteration.

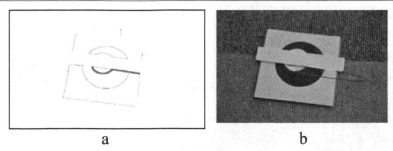

Fig. 10 Wrong selection of our method. **a** Extracted edge points. We selected the *red connected points* as the input data. **b** Fitted ellipse

8 Concluding remarks

We proposed a new method for extracting elliptic arcs from a spatially connected point sequence. Assuming that input points are a spatially connected sequence of edge points, we fit an ellipse to it and automatically segment it into partial arcs at the intersection points of the fitted ellipse. Then, we compute residuals of the fitted ellipse for all input points and select elliptic arcs among the segmented arcs by checking curvatures of the residual graph.

Our proposed method involves iterations, but the number of iterations is much less than those of RANSAC and Yu's method. Moreover, in contrast to Yu's method, our method has the possibility of fitting a more accurate ellipse because inliers are selected from all the input data in each iteration, meaning that the number of data to fit an ellipse does not decrease by iterations.

By using simulated data and real images, we compared the performance of our method with existing methods and showed that the performance of the inlier selection and computation time of the proposed method were superior to existing methods.

Endnotes

[1] We set $f_0 = 600$.

[2] We set the threshold to be 5 % of the number of input edge points.

[3] We set $\hat{\phi} = 80°$.

[4] We set $E_{min} = 1.5$.

[5] We set $\lambda = 2.0$.

[6] We set E_{max} to be (maximum image coordinates of the input points)/3.

[7] We set $r = 8$.

Acknowledgements

The authors thank Kenich Kanatani of Okayama University, Japan, for helpful discussions. The authors also thank Yoshihisa Iriji of OMRON Corporation, Japan, for allowing us to use the source code. This work was supported in part by JSPS Grant-in-Aid for Scientific Research(C) (26330192).

Authors' contributions

YS proposed a method to automatically segment a consecutive edge points and inlier arc selection method. TM tested the proposed method by using simulated and real data, and wrote the manuscript. YS also revised the manuscript written by TM. Both authors read and approved the final manuscript.

Competing interests

The authors declare that they have no competing interests.

References

1. Chojnacki W, Brooks MJ, van den Hengel A, Gawley D (2000) On the fitting of surfaces to data with covariances. IEEE Trans Patt Anal Mach Intell 22(11):1294–1303
2. Fischler MA, Bolles RC (1981) Random sample consensus: a paradigm for model fitting with applications to image analysis and automated cartography. Comm ACM 24(6):381–395
3. Fitzgibbon A, Pilu M, Fisher RB (1999) Direct least squares fitting of ellipses. IEEE Trans Patt Anal Mach Intell 21(5):476–480
4. Hartley R, Zisserman A (2004) Multiple view geometry in computer vision. 2nd ed.. Cambridge University Press, Cambridge, U.K
5. Kanatani K (1993) Geometric computation for machine vision. Oxford University Press, Oxford, U.K
6. Kanatani K, Ohta N (2004) Automatic detection of circular objects by ellipse growing. Int J Image Graphics 4(1):35–50
7. Kanatani K, Sugaya Y (2007) Performance evaluation of iterative geometric fitting algorithms. Comput Stat Data Anal 52(2):1208–1222
8. Kanatani K, Rangarajan P (2011) Hyper least squares fitting of circles and ellipses. Comput Stat Data Anal 55(6):2197–2208
9. Kanatani K, Rangarajan P, Sugaya Y, Niitsuma H (2011) HyperLS and its applications. IPSJ Trans Comput Vis Appl 3:80–94
10. Kanatani K, Al-Sharadqah A, Chernov N, Sugaya Y (2012) Renormalization returns: hyper-renormalization and its applications. Proc 12th Euro Conf Comput Vis 3:385–398
11. Leedan Y, Meer P (2000) Heteroscedastic regression in computer vision: problems with bilinear constraint. Int J Comput Vision 37(2):127–150
12. Masuzaki T, Sugaya Y, Kanatani K (2013) High accuracy ellipse-specific fitting. 6th Pacific-Rim Symposium on Image and Video Technology. Guanajuato, Mexico, p 314–324
13. Matei J, Meer P (2006) Estimation of nonlinear errors-in-variables models for computer vision applications. IEEE Trans Patt Anal Mach Intell 28(10):1537–1552
14. Shao M, Ijiri Y, Hattori K (2015) Grouped outlier removal for robust ellipse fitting. 14th IAPR International Conference on Machine Vision Applications. Tokyo, Japan, p 138–141
15. Sugaya Y (2010) Ellipse detection by combining division and model selection based integration of edge points. 4th Pacific-Rim Symposium on Image and Video Technology, Siggapore, p 64–69
16. Szpak ZL, Chojnacki W, van den Hengel A (2012) Guaranteed ellipse fitting with Sampson distance. Proc 12th Euro Conf Comput Vis 5:87–100
17. Taubin G (1991) Estimation of planar curves, surfaces, and non-planar space curves defined by implicit equations with applications to edge and range image segmentation. IEEE Trans Patt Anal Mach Intell 13(11):1115–1138
18. Waibel P, Matthes J, Gröll L (2015) Constrained ellipse fitting with center on a line. J Math Imaging Vis 53(3):364–382
19. Yu J, Kulkarni SR, Poor HV (2012) Robust ellipse and spheroid fitting. Pattern Recognit Lett 33(5):492–499
20. Yu Q, Ong SH (2007) Arc-based evaluation and detection of ellipses. J Pattern Recognit 40(7):1990–2003

Permissions

The contributors of this book come from diverse backgrounds, making this book a truly international effort. This book will bring forth new frontiers with its revolutionizing research information and detailed analysis of the nascent developments around the world.

We would like to thank all the contributing authors for lending their expertise to make the book truly unique. They have played a crucial role in the development of this book. Without their invaluable contributions this book wouldn't have been possible. They have made vital efforts to compile up to date information on the varied aspects of this subject to make this book a valuable addition to the collection of many professionals and students.

This book was conceptualized with the vision of imparting up-to-date information and advanced data in this field. To ensure the same, a matchless editorial board was set up. Every individual on the board went through rigorous rounds of assessment to prove their worth. After which they invested a large part of their time researching and compiling the most relevant data for our readers.

The editorial board has been involved in producing this book since its inception. They have spent rigorous hours researching and exploring the diverse topics which have resulted in the successful publishing of this book. They have passed on their knowledge of decades through this book. To expedite this challenging task, the publisher supported the team at every step. A small team of assistant editors was also appointed to further simplify the editing procedure and attain best results for the readers.

Apart from the editorial board, the designing team has also invested a significant amount of their time in understanding the subject and creating the most relevant covers. They scrutinized every image to scout for the most suitable representation of the subject and create an appropriate cover for the book.

The publishing team has been an ardent support to the editorial, designing and production team. Their endless efforts to recruit the best for this project, has resulted in the accomplishment of this book. They are a veteran in the field of academics and their pool of knowledge is as vast as their experience in printing. Their expertise and guidance has proved useful at every step. Their uncompromising quality standards have made this book an exceptional effort. Their encouragement from time to time has been an inspiration for everyone.

The publisher and the editorial board hope that this book will prove to be a valuable piece of knowledge for researchers, students, practitioners and scholars across the globe.

List of Contributors

Yutaro Sako and Yasuyuki Sugaya
Toyohashi University of Technology, 1-1-1, Tempakucho, Hibarigaoka, Toyohashi, Aichi 441-8580, Japan

Carlos Morales and Takeshi Oishi
The University of Tokyo, Tokyo, Japan

Katsushi Ikeuchi
Microsoft Research Asia, Beijing, China

Akito Takeki, Tu Tuan Trinh, Ryota Yoshihashi, Rei Kawakami, Makoto Iida and Takeshi Naemura
The University of Tokyo, 7-3-1 Hongo, Bunkyo-ku, Tokyo 113-8656, Japan

Takahito Aoto, Tomokazu Sato, Yasuhiro Mukaigawa and Naokazu Yokoya
Nara Institute of Science and Technology, Takayamacho 8916-5, Ikoma, Japan

Daichi Kusanagi, Shoichiro Aoyama, Koichi Ito and Takafumi Aoki
Graduate School of Information Sciences, Tohoku University, 6-6-05, Aramaki Aza Aoba, Sendai, Japan

Xian-Hua Han
Graduate School of Science and Technology for Innovation, Yamaguchi University, Yamaguchi 753-8511, Japan

Yen-Wei Chen and Gang Xu
Ritsumeikan University, Kusatsu, Shiga 525–8577, Japan

Takaharu Kato and Ikuko Shimizu
Tokyo University of Agriculture and Technology, Tokyo, Japan.

Tomas Pajdla
CTU in Prague, FEE, Prague, Czech Republic

Daniel Soukup and Reinhold Huber-Mörk
AIT Austrian Institute of Technology GmbH, Donau-City-Straße 1, 1220 Vienna, Austria

Linh Tao
Department of Functional Control System, Shibaura Institute of Technology, 307 Fukasaku, Minuma-ku, Saitama City, Saitama, 337-8570, Japan

Tam Bui
School of Mechanical Engineering, Hanoi University of Science and Technology, 1 Dai Co Viet Road, Ha Noi, Viet Nam

Hiroshi Hasegawa
Department of Machinery and Control System, Shibaura Institute of Technology, 307 Fukasaku, Minuma-ku, Saitama City, Saitama, 337-8570, Japan

Takafumi Taketomi
Nara Institute of Science and Technology, 8916-5 Takayama, Ikoma, 630-0192 Nara, Japan

Hideaki Uchiyama
Kyushu University, 744 Motooka, Nishi-ku, 819-0395 Fukuoka, Japan

Sei Ikeda
Ritsumeikan University, 1-1-1 Nojihigashi, Kusatsu, 525-8577 Shiga, Japan

Olasimbo Ayodeji Arigbabu and Iman Yi Liao
School of Computer Science, University of Nottingham Malaysia Campus, Semenyih, Malaysia

Nurliza Abdullah
Department of Forensic Medicine, Hospital Kuala Lumpur, Kuala Lumpur, Malaysia

Mohamad Helmee Mohamad Noor
Radiology Department, Hospital Kuala Lumpur, Kuala Lumpur, Malaysia.

Andreas Maier and Christian Riess
Pattern Recognition Lab, University of Erlangen - Nuremberg, Martensstrasse 3, Erlangen, Germany.

Peter Fuersattel
Pattern Recognition Lab, University of Erlangen - Nuremberg, Martensstrasse 3, Erlangen, Germany. Metrilus GmbH, Henkestrasse 91, Erlangen, Germany

Claus Plank
Ostbayerische Technische Hochschule Regensburg, Pruefeninger Strasse 58, Regensburg, Germany

Berkan Solmaz, Erhan Gundogdu, Veysel Yucesoy and Aykut Koc
Aselsan Research Center, Ankara, Turkey

Ke Wang and Jan-Michael Frahm
Department of Computer Science, UNC Chapel Hill, 201 S Columbia Street, Chapel Hill 27599, USA

Enrique Dunn
Department of Computer Science, Stevens Institute of Technology, 1 Castle Point Terrace, Hoboken 07030, USA

Mikel Rodriguez
MITRE Corporation, 202 Burlington Rd, Bedford 01730, USA

Sonam Nahar
The LNM Institute of Information Technology, Jaipur, India

Manjunath V. Joshi
Dhirubhai Ambani Institute of Information Technology, Gandhinagar, India

Xian-Hua Han
The Artificial Intelligence Research Center, Advanced Industrial Science and Technology, Tokyo 135-0064, Japan

Ikuko Nishikawa and Yen-Wei Chen
Ritsumeikan University, Kusatsu, Shiga 525-8577, Japan

Yukako Tohsato, Koji Kyoda and Shuichi Onami
Laboratory for Developmental Dynamics, RIKEN Quantitative Biology Center, Kobe 650-0047, Japan

Tomonari Masuzaki and Yasuyuki Sugaya
Department of Computer Science and Engineering, Toyohashi University of Technology, Toyohashi, Aichi 441-8580, Japan

Index